Luke and the Last Things

a perspective for the understanding of Lukan thought

by
A. J. Mattill, Jr.

Western North Carolina Press
P. O. Box 29 Dillsboro, NC 28725

Copyright © 1979 by Western North Carolina Press

International copyright secured. All rights reserved

Printed in the United States of America

for

Western North Carolina Press P.O. Box 29 Dillsboro, NC 28725

ISBN 0-915948-03-6
Library of Congress No. 78-72980
Cover Design by Breck Smith
First Printed 1979

PREFACE

As may be seen by a perusal of the bibliography at the close of this study, a vigorous international discussion of Luke's eschatology has been under way for the last quarter of a century. This lively debate has more and more led to the recognition that the question of Luke's view of "the last things" is not just one question among many in respect to Lukan thought but is the central question. If we can achieve a correct understanding of Luke's eschatology we shall have developed a rewarding perspective for viewing every aspect of Luke-Acts, whether it be burning of books, breaking of bread, prayer, "poverty piety," ministering women, or the world mission.

Yet in spite of the centrality of Luke's eschatology there has been to my knowledge no comprehensive, thorough-going, exegetical monograph on this subject. This present work is an attempt to meet this need, and to do so in a way which will be useful not only to scholars but also to clerics and interested laymen. Care has been taken to set forth the relevant data upon which solutions must be based: the concepts which were current in Luke's universe of discourse; the appropriate texts from canonical and non-canonical sources; and the key words which Luke uses to convey his thought. I also seek to present fairly and to evaluate critically the theories which students of the Bible, not only in the last two or three decades but even back to the patristic age, have developed upon the basis of these data. Occasionally I offer what may be new solutions to old problems. But if my suggestions should prove to be inadequate, the reader will still have the data and theories ready at hand for working out his own solutions.

Gratitude is due the librarians of the Gordo Public Library, the University of the South, Vanderbilt Divinity School, and the Princeton Theological Seminary for making available through interlibrary loan and photocopy service the many books and articles necessary to such a research project. Dr. Donald J. Selby, professor of religion and philosophy at Catawba College, has carefully read and criticized the manuscript chapter by chapter, offering many suggestions for its improvement in form and content, plus, what may have been of even greater value, the encouragement to persevere in a lengthy task. I of course remain responsible for any errors and misconceptions. I am also deeply indebted to my wife, with whom I have frequently discussed key points, and who has assumed numerous duties on the place in order to allow me the leisure to pursue the time-consuming labors involved in a work of this magnitude.

Unless otherwise noted, scriptural quotations are from the American Standard Version, that "rock of biblical honesty."

A. J. Mattill, Jr.
Route 2, Box 49
Gordo, Alabama, 35466

Table of Contents

Preface iii
Table of Contents iv
Abbreviations x
Chapter

   I. "Terrors and Great Signs" (Luke 21:11): The Apocalyptic Nature of Luke-Acts.. 1

      A. The Apocalyptic Hope 1
      B. The Component Parts of the Apocalyptic Hope in Luke-Acts 2
         1. "The Last Things" 2
         2. Dualism 3
         3. War to the Finish 4
         4. The Messianic Woes 4
         5. "Soon" 5
         6. Determinism 5
         7. Resurrection 5
         8. "The Restoration of All Things" 5
      C. The Lukan Apocalypses 6
         1. The River of Fire Apocalypse (Luke 3:3-18) 6
         2. The Falling Fire Apocalypse (Luke 10:1-24) 7
         3. The Fire upon the Earth Apocalypse (Luke 12:1-13:35) 7
         4. The Fire of Agony Apocalypse (Luke 16:16-31) 8
         5. The Fire and Brimstone Apocalypse (Luke 17:20-18:8) 8
         6. The Signs in the Stars Apocalypse (Luke 21:5-36) 8
         7. The Judgment by Fire Apocalypse (Luke 23:27-31) 8
      D. Luke's Longing for the Coming of the Kingdom 9
      E. Luke's Magnificent Obsession for Proclaiming the Kingdom 9
      F. The Kerygma 10

   II. "Until John" (Luke 16:16): The De-Apocalypticizing of Luke-Acts ... 13

      A. Anti-Apocalyptic Texts 13
      B. Luke's Displacement of Apocalyptic by Periodized History 13
      C. John the Baptist as a Non-Apocalyptic Preacher of Repentance . 14
      D. John the Baptist as the Elijah-like Forerunner of Jesus 15
         1. Luke's Non-Inclusions 15

  2. John the Forerunner 17
  3. "After Me" 18
  4. The John-Jesus Parallels..................................... 19
 E. John the Baptist as a Preacher of the Kingdom 19
 F. John the Baptist within the Era of Fulfilment (Luke 16:16) 21
 G. Additional Objections to the Threefold Division of Salvation
   History 23
 H. Luke's Program 24

III. "The Happy Side of Hades" (Luke 16:19-31): The
  Platonizing of Luke-Acts...................................... 26

 A. The Immortality of the Soul 26
 B. Dives in Hades (Luke 16:19-31) 27
  1. Luke 16:19-31 and I Enoch 27
  2. "Hades" in the New Testament 31
 C. The Thief in Paradise (Luke 23:43)........................... 33
 D. Cast into Gehenna (Luke 12:4-5) 34
 E. The Rich Fool (Luke 12:13-21)................................ 35
 F. The Dishonest Manager (Luke 16:1-9) 37
 G. A Lukan Inconsistency? 39
 H. Conclusion 40

IV. "Before Long" (Acts 17:31): The Imminent Expectation In Acts..... 41

 A. Introductory Considerations 41
 B. "Judge of the Living and the Dead" (Acts 10:42)............... 41
 C. The Imminent Hope in Acts 17:31; 24:15; 24:25: General
   Considerations 43
  1. Weymouth's Translation of *Mellō* in 17:31; 24:15,25.......... 43
  2. The Root Meaning of *Mellō* 43
  3. *Mellō* in Acts.. 44
  4. An Authentic Pauline Ring 44
  5. *Mellō* in the New Testament 45
 D. *Mellō*, the Son of Man, and the Day of the Lord (Acts 17:31) 45
 E. Resurrection before Long (Acts 24:15)........................ 47
 F. The Judgment Soon to Come (Acts 24:25) 48
 G. The Imminent Expectation in the Rest of Acts 49

V. "On the Tiptoe of Expectation" (Luke 3:15): The Imminent
  Expectation in The Gospel of Luke 55

 A. An Overview of the Chief Passages 55
 B. The Approaching Wrath (Luke 3:7,9) 56
 C. Seeing the Kingdom (Luke 9:26-27) 58
  1. Luke 9:26-27 and Parallels 58

    2. The Transfiguration (Luke 9:28-36) 59
    3. The Resurrection of Jesus (Luke 24:1-49) 59
    4. The Coming of the Holy Spirit at Pentecost (Acts 2:1-4)......60
    5. The Beginning of the Church at Pentecost (Acts 2:40-42) 61
    6. The Spread of Christianity (Acts) 62
    7. The Destruction of Jerusalem, A.D. 70 (Luke 21:20-24) 63
    8. Perception of the Nature of the Kingdom 64
    9. The Coming of the Kingdom of God at the End of the World..67
  D. The Kingdom Is at Your Door (Luke 10:9,11) 70
    1. Near or Here? 70
    2. The Meaning of *Engidzō* (Luke 10:9,11) 71
    3. The Meaning of "Upon You" (Luke 10:9) 76
    4. An Urgent Mission (Luke 10:1-16) 77
    5. The Historical Setting of the Mission 79
  E. A Sign for the People of His Day (Luke 11:30) 79
    1. Literary Analysis (Luke 11:14-36).............................79
    2. Jesus' Preaching as the Sign 82
    3. Jesus' Resurrection as the Sign 82
    4. Jesus' Parousia as the Sign 83
  F. Not a Lost Cause: Parables of Watchfulness (Luke 12:35-48)....85
    1. Parousia Parables? 85
    2. An Imminent Parousia? 86
    3. Setting within the Fire upon the Earth Apocalypse
       (Luke 12:1-13:35)..87
    4. "Watch!" 88
  G. Justice without Delay (Luke 18:1-8) 89
    1. Lukan Touches 89
    2. The Eschatological Nature of the Parable 90
    3. "Suddenly" or "Soon"? 91
    4. The Existential Situation 94
  H. The Accomplishment of All Things (Luke 21:32) 96
    1. The Meaning of *Genea* 96
    2. Other Evasions of the Imminent Expectation in Luke 21:32..100
  I. "That Great and Terrible Day of the Lord" (Luke 21:34-36) 104
    1. Lukan Features 104
    2. Accentuating the Ethical 104
    3. The Pressing Nature of the Times 104
    4. Impressive Parallels 105
  J. Jesus' Vow of Abstinence (Luke 22:18) 109
  K. The Eschatological Urgency of Luke-Acts: Summary 111

VI. "Day By Day" (Luke 11:3): Speedily But Not Immediately.........113

  A. "Changing Ideas in New Testament Eschatology"..............113

B. Heroic Living (Luke 9:23) 114
C. Eating Bread in the Kingdom of God (Luke 11:3)..............115
   1. The Apocalyptic Interpretation of the Lord's Prayer
     (Matt 6:9-13) 115
   2. Lukan Variations in the Third Petition
     (Luke 11:3//Matt 6:11) 117
   3. Luke's Understanding of Bread 118
D. Good Servants and Rebellious Citizens (Luke 19:11-27) 121
   1. Literary Analysis 121
   2. "Be Ready to Wait" 122
   3. No Instant Eschatology 123
   4. Jesus' Resurrection as Parousia 124
   5. Jesus' Ascension as Parousia 125
   6. Conclusion 130
E. "Not Immediately the End" (Luke 21:7-13) 130
   1. Literary Analysis 130
   2. The Parousia Indefinitely Delayed 132
   3. "Not Immediately the End" 133
F. "The Times of the Gentiles" (Luke 21:24) 133
   1. Literary Analysis 133
   2. A Non-Eschatological Period 133
   3. Gentile Lordship over Jerusalem 134
   4. Salvation for the Gentiles 135
   5. The Restoration of Israel 136
G. "At the Right Hand of God" (Luke 22:69) 145
   1. Literary Analysis 145
   2. An Irrefutable Prophecy 146
   3. Alternative Explanations 147
   4. Luke's Scheme of Messianic Progress 148
H. "To the Ends of the Earth" (Acts 1:6-8) 150
   1. Mission or Imminence? 150
   2. The Eschatological World Mission 151
I. Conclusion 154

VII. "In the Midst of You" (Luke 17:21): The Kingdom A Present
    Reality?...158

A. The Relevant Texts...158
B. Greater in the Kingdom (Luke 7:28) 159
   1. The Kingdom of God as Present 159
   2. The Kingdom of God as Future 160
C. "Like a Lightning-Flash" (Luke 10:18) 164
   1. The Beginning of the New Age........................164
   2. The Beginning of the End for Satan.................164

    D. "By the Finger of God" (Luke 11:20) 168
        1. The Kingdom of God as Dynamic Presence 168
        2. The Meaning of *Phthanō* 168
        3. The Lukan Context 176
    E. "Blessed Assurance": Twin Parables of the Kingdom
       (Luke 13:18-21) 177
        1. Literary Analysis 177
        2. Parables of Growth? 178
        3. Parables of Contrast? 179
        4. Parables of Miraculous Results? 180
    F. Storming into the Kingdom (Luke 16:16c) 182
        1. Literary Analysis 182
        2. The Kingdom as a Present Realm 184
        3. A Fourth-Century Solution 185
        4. The Pharisees Speak 185
        5. Pressed by Persuasive Preaching 186
        6. Agonizing into the Kingdom 187
        7. Conclusion 189
    G "Look, Here It Is!" (Luke 17:20-21) 190
        1. Introduction 190
        2. The Text 190
        3. "With Observation" 191
        4. "Is" 192
        5. "Within" 193
        6. "Within You" 193
        7. "In Your Midst" Now 196
        8. "In Your Midst" in the Future 198
        9. "Within Your Power" 201
        10. The Kingdom Group 201
        11. Conclusion 203

    Appendix A: The Meaning of *Entos* 203
        1. The Occurrences of *Entos* 203
        2. The Meanings of *Entos* 204
        3. Conclusions 207

VIII. "Fire Upon The Earth" (Luke 12:49): A Holy War? 208

    A. Literary Analysis of Luke 12:49-56 208
    B. Attempts at De-Apocalypticizing Luke 12:49-56 209
    C. Spiritualizing Interpretations of Luke 12:49 210
    D. Sociological Interpretations of Luke 12:49 211
    E. Literal Interpretations: End-Time Fires 212

1. Jesus' Baptism (Luke 12:50) 212
2. A Fiery Parousia (Luke 12:49) 213
3. Family Strife (Luke 12:51-53) 214
4. The Face of the Earth (Luke 12:54-56) 215
5. Confirmation of a Fiery Parousia by Other Passages in
   Luke-Acts 216
6. The Cosmic Conflagration (Luke 12:49) 217
7. The Flaming Flame (Luke 23:31) 220
8. Luke's Holy War of the Last Days 222
9. "Greet No One on the Way" (Luke 10:4b) 225
10. Luke's Switch to Action 226
11. Luke's Ultimate Weapon 232

Bibliography 236

ABBREVIATIONS

AJT	*American Journal of Theology*
American	*The Bible: An American Translation* ("The Chicago Bible")
ANT	*Apocryphal New Testament*, tr. M. R. James
APOT	*Apocrypha and Pseudepigrapha of the Old Testament*, ed. R. H. Charles
ARW	*Archiv für Religionswissenschaft*
ASV	American Standard Version
ATR	*Anglican Theological Review*
BAG	Bauer, W.; Arndt, W. F.; Gingrich, F. W., *Greek-English Lexicon of the New Testament*
BDF	Blass, F.; Debrunner, A.; Funk, R. W., *A Greek Grammar of the New Testament*
BS	*Bibliotheca Sacra*
BZ	*Biblische Zeitschrift*
CBQ	*Catholic Biblical Quarterly*
CSEL	*Corpus scriptorum ecclesiasticorum latinorum*
CTM	*Concordia Theological Monthly*
DSS	*Dead Sea Scriptures*, tr. T.H. Gaster
ET	*Expository Times*
E.T.	English translation
GKR	*Gegenwart und kommendes Reich: Schülergabe Anton Vögtle*, ed. P. Fiedler und D. Zeller. Stuttgart: Verlag Katholisches Bibelwerk, 1975
HTR	*Harvard Theological Review*
IB	*Interpreter's Bible*, ed. G. A. Buttrick et al.
Int	*Interpretation*
JAAR	*Journal of the American Academy of Religion*
JAC	*Jahrbuch für Antike und Christentum*
JBL	*Journal of Biblical Literature*
JTS	*Journal of Theological Studies*
KJV	King James Version
LXX	Septuagint
NRT	*Nouvelle revue théologique*

NovT	*Novum Testamentum*
NTA	*New Testament Abstracts*
NTS	*New Testament Studies*
NWT	New World Translation
PG	*Patrologia graeca*
1QH	Qumran Cave 1, *Thanksgiving Hymns*
1QpHab	Qumran Cave 1, *Commentary on Habakkuk*
1QM	Qumran Cave 1, *War Scroll*
1QS	Qumran Cave 1, *Manual of Discipline*
RB	*Revue biblique*
RevExp	*Review and Expositor*
RHPR	*Revue d'histoire et de philosophie religieuses*
RQ	*Restoration Quarterly*
RSV	Revised Standard Version
RTL	*Revue théologique de Louvain*
Scr	*Scripture*
Sir	Ecclesiasticus, or the Wisdom of Jesus the Son of Sirach
SJT	*Scottish Journal of Theology*
ST	*Studia theologica*
Str-B	Strack, H. L.; Billerbeck, P., *Kommentar zum Neuen Testament*
TDNT	*Theological Dictionary of the New Testament*, ed. G. Kittell and G. Friedrich; E.T., G. Bromiley
TEV	Today's English Version
TSK	*Theologische Studien und Kritiken*
TZ	*Theologische Zeitschrift*
WA	Weimar Ausgabe
ZNW	*Zeitschrift für die neutestamentliche Wissenschaft*
ZTK	*Zeitschrift für Theologie und Kirche*

Chapter I
"Terrors and Great Signs" (Luke 21:11): The Apocalyptic Nature of Luke-Acts

A. The Apocalyptic Hope

For centuries man has tried to chart the course of history. According to ancient Greek philosophers, the direction of history may be diagrammed by a circle: history begins with a glorious golden age of simplicity and happiness which continues through the first half of the cycle. The latter half is characterized by decay and dissolution, ending in a great destructive conflagration. Then the process begins again, repeating itself every 3,000 years, or 72,000 years according to others. "What has been is, passes, and will be" (Frank Manuel).[1]

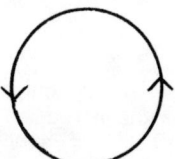

The OT prophets developed a linear philosophy of history, according to which history is divided into two ages, this evil age, which is rather static, neither markedly improving nor declining, and the new age, inaugurated by the day of the Lord (Amos 5:18-20). The new age, which may be introduced by God's anointed one or Messiah (Isa 11:1-9), will be a time of peace, prosperity, security and fertility (Isa 2:1-4; Amos 9:13-15).

```
                  Day of the Lord
                         |
      This Age           |           New Age
  _____  |  _____
                         |
                         |
```

---

[1] On the philosophy of history see such works as Baillie, *Progress*, and Shinn, *History*.

There was no hope for progressive betterment in either the cyclical or prophetic understandings of history. But since the sixteenth century after Christ men began to think in terms of progress because of scientific inventions, mastery over nature, world-wide exploration and communication, growth of democracy, and the theory of evolution. The euphoria generated by these developments led many to regard history as a linear progress from primitive beginnings to a scientific Utopia on this earth. This optimistic philosophy of history reached its peak in the nineteenth century, but cracked like a melon on the rock of the first World War. As a result of the ensuing gloom, a pessimistic view of history gained favor in many circles: history is a dreary drift toward doom and destruction, when the earth will be destroyed by the death of the sun or other cosmic catastrophe and all of men's hopes will set in a sea of disappointment.

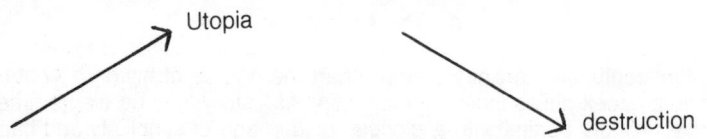

The period between 200 B.C. and A.D. 100 was the Golden Age of yet another philosophy of history known as "apocalypticism." The word "apocalypse" means "revelation," that is, a disclosure of what is hidden from common men, a momentary lifting of the curtain between this world and the world to come. The Apocalypse of John, which is our finest apocalyptic book, was written to make known "what must soon take place" (1:1), and the little apocalypse of Luke 21 describes what will happen "in the days to come"(21:6).

More precisely, we may define apocalypticism as the eschatological expectation that this present evil and increasingly corrupt world, now under the control of Satan, but originally in a state of Edenic perfection, will soon be ended and destroyed, at the predestined time, along with Satan and his demonic and human agents, by the sudden, direct intervention of God, who thereupon will establish a new and perfect age and world under his immediate control, in which the unrighteous will receive their just and everlasting punishment, and in which the righteous from among the living and resurrected dead will enjoy a blessed existence without end.[2]

B. The Component Parts of the Apocalyptic Hope in Luke-Acts

We shall now break this definition down into its component parts and illustrate each part from apocalyptic literature and from Luke-Acts, since the latter is to become our focus of attention.

1. "The Last Things"

Apocalypticism, such as is found in Daniel and Revelation, is eschatological in nature, that is, it is concerned with "last things" (*eschata*). By "last things" is

---

[2] Adapted from Rist, *Daniel and Revelation,* p. 3. On apocalypticism see also Rist, *Revelation,* pp. 347-351; Ladd, *Presence,* pp. 76-101; Charles, *Eschatology;* and the special numbers of *Rev Exp* (April 1960) and *CBQ* (July 1977).

meant such ultimate matters as death (Rev 1:18; Luke 16:22), resurrection (Rev 20:5; Acts 17:32), judgment (Rev 20:11-15; Acts 24:25), eternal life (Rev 2:7; Luke 10:25), and the kingdom of God (Rev 11:15; Luke 23:51). The teaching (*logy*) which deals with "last things" (*eschata*) is "eschatology."

Not all eschatology, however, is apocalyptic. Eschatology is a more general term; apocalypticism is a special type of eschatology. For example, the view that humanity will end when the world freezes over in 10,000,000,000 years is a type of eschatology, for it deals with "last things." But it is not apocalyptic, for it does not have the special characteristics of apocalyptic belief mentioned in the above definition. In other words, all apocalyptic is eschatological but not all eschatology is apocalyptic.

2. Dualism

Apocalypticism is dualistic (*dualis*, two) in nature, and that in several respects:

a) Metaphysical dualism.--There are two opposing supernatural forces, both personal and cosmic or universal in character, the one force being good (God), and the other evil (Satan). John describes the angels' casting down to earth from heaven "the old serpent, he that is called the Devil and Satan" (Rev 12:7-9), and Jesus beholds "satan fallen as lightning from heaven" (Luke 10:18). This God-Satan dualism is not an absolute dualism with two co-equal, co-eternal powers, for in the NT Satan is a creature limited in power to this age.

b) Temporal dualism.--There are two eons, ages, or worlds, this present evil age or world and the future golden age, world to come, or kingdom of God. "The Most High hath made not one age but two" (4 Ezra 7:50). John "saw a new heaven and a new earth: for the first heaven and the first earth are passed away" (Rev 21:1), and the "kingdom of this world is become the kingdom of our Lord" (11:15). Jesus speaks of "the sons of this world (age)" and those "accounted worthy to attain to that world (age)" (Luke 16:8; 20:34-35). It is difficult for those who have riches "to enter into the kingdom of God" (18:25), but those who forsake all "for the kingdom of God's sake" will "receive manifold more in this time, and in the world (age) to come eternal life" (18:29-30). For Jesus, as for John, "heaven and earth shall pass away" (21:33).

This present evil age is under the control of Satan, "the god of this world" (2 Cor 4:4), "the evil one" in whom "the whole world lieth" (1 John 5:19; cf. Rev 12:12), who has authority over "all the kingdoms of the world" (Luke 4:5-6). Luke has the devil say, "It [the power and glory of the kingdoms of the world] hath been delivered unto me [by God]and to whomsoever I will give it" (Luke 4:6). This age becomes more and more evil until the end, when it reaches the lowest possible depths of degradation. 4 Ezra 14:16-18 reads: "For evils worse than those which you have now seen happen shall be done hereafter. For the weaker the world becomes through old age, the more shall evils be multiplied among its inhabitants. For truth shall go further away, and falsehood shall come near." For Luke also the last generation was to be worst of all, "so the people of this time will be punished for the murder of all the prophets killed since the creation of the world" (Luke 11:50)(TEV).

By way of complete contrast, the future perfect age will be under God's direct control, when God will dwell with his people (Rev 21:3) and reign forever and ever

(11:15). "He shall reign over the house of Jacob for ever; and of his kingdom there shall be no end" (Luke 1:33).

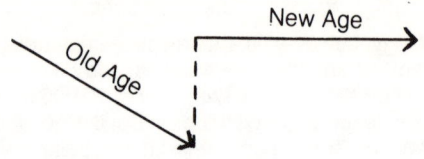

c) Moral dualism.--All mankind is divided into two classes, the righteous and unrighteous. John refers to the obduracy of the unrighteous and the perseverance of the righteous: "He that is unrighteous, let him do unrighteousness still" and "he that is righteous, let him do righteousness still" (Rev 22:11). Paul, according to Luke, looks forward to the resurrection of "the righteous and the unrighteous" (Acts 24:15).

d) Soteriological dualism.--All men are or will be either saved or unsaved. Any "not found written in the book of life" are "cast into the lake of fire" (Rev 20:15). "The Son of man came to seek and to save that which was lost" (Luke 19:10).

3. War to the Finish

At the end of history there will be a final cosmic conflict between the irreconcilable forces of God and of Satan. Between God and Satan can be no peaceful co-existence. There will be war to the finish, but God as the superior power is assured of ultimate victory. Nothing short of a cataclysm on a cosmic scale could hope to unseat the vicious hold of Satan on this present world. The basic feature of apocalyptic belief, then, is this: God will intervene soon, suddenly, swiftly, spectacularly, and surprisingly to close and complete this age through a cosmic conflict and conflagration which will bring a cataclysmic, catastrophic consummation to the cosmos. According to the apocalypse in 2 Peter 3 "the day of the Lord will come as a thief; in which the heavens shall pass away with great noise, and the elements shall be dissolved with fervent heat, and the earth and the works that are therein shall be burned up" (3:10). Likewise Jesus "came to cast fire upon the earth" and he would "that it were already kindled!" (Luke 12:49). Then "the powers of the heavens shall be shaken. And... they shall see the Son of man coming with power and great glory" (21:26-27). Moreover, "if the master of the house had known in what hour the thief was coming, he would have watched, and not have left his house to be broken through. Be ye also ready: for in an hour that ye think not the Son of man cometh" (12:39-40).

4. The Messianic Woes

This catacylismic end (*eschaton*) will be accompanied by "messianic woes." As a woman gives birth to a child out of pain, so too the new age will be born out of suffering and tribulation, including social woes (wars, starvation, family feuds), cosmic woes (stars falling, earthquakes, rivers made bitter), and demonic woes (sufferings caused by Satan and his demons):

There was a great earthquake; and the sun became black as sackcloth of hair, and the whole moon became as blood; and the stars of the heaven fell unto the earth (Rev 6:12-13). Woe unto them that are with child and to them that give suck in those days! for there shall be great distress upon the land (Luke 21:23). Nation shall rise against nation, and kingdom against kingdom; and there shall be great earthquakes, and in divers places famines and pestilences; and there shall be terrors and great signs from heaven (21:10-11). Think ye that I am come to give peace in the earth? I tell you, Nay; but rather division: for there shall be from henceforth five in one house divided, three against two, and two against three (12:51-53).

5. "Soon"

In apocalyptic thought the end is to come soon. Apocalypses were written when the righteous were in trouble to assure them that God would come to their rescue in the very near future, even momentarily. Thus John writes of "the things which must shortly come to pass" (Rev. 1:1), and Jesus tells a parable about an unrighteous judge to show that God will vindicate his elect speedily (Luke 18:8). The early Christians thought of themselves as living in the last century, not in the first, for the hammer of the cosmic clock had risen to strike the last hour.

6. Determinism

The entire history of the world, including the time of the end, and those who are to be saved and lost, is predestined from all eternity by God. The names of the righteous and unrighteous have been written from the foundation of the world in the book of life (Rev 13:8; 21:27; cf. Luke 10:20). All is done according to "the determinate counsel and foreknowledge of God" (Acts 2:23), at "this very hour of this very day of this very month and year" (Rev 9:15) (TEV).

7. Resurrection

At the end of this age comes the resurrection of the dead, a concept which may be the most important contribution made by apocalyptic thought to doctrine: "In the one word 'resurrection' lies the whole of Christianity" (Karl Barth). Belief in the resurrection is expressed in Dan 12:2,3,13; Rev 20: 4-15; and so often by Luke that Luke-Acts may be called "the Good News of the Resurrection" (Luke 14:14; 20:27-40; Acts 4:2; 17:18,32; 23:6-8; 24:15,21; 26:8; plus frequent references to Jesus' resurrection).

8. "The Restoration of All Things"

Eschatology (teaching about last things) and protology (teaching about first things) belong together. If the first book of the Bible,Genesis, deals with protology (creation, Eden), the last book, Revelation, deals with eschatology (new creation, new Eden). The golden age at the end of time is pictured by means of the same symbols of perfection as the golden age at the beginning of time. In the Epistle of Barnabas, a pseudepigraphical writing of about A. D. 130, we read: "The Lord says, Behold, I will make the last things like the first " (6:13). The new Eden will be like the old Eden with a river, tree of life, and fruits (Rev 22:1-2,14). All animals and nature will be transformed so as to be peaceful and harmonious as at the beginning when animals were vegetarians (Gen 1:29-30; Isa 11:6-9; 65:25; Rom 8:18-23). As the German expression has it, "Endzeit gleich Urzeit" (end-time like original-time), or the Greek, *ta eschata hōs ta prōta* (the last things like the first things). Possibly the most striking illustration of this principle is found in the pseudepigraphical book of 1 Enoch 90, where the members of the kingdom of

God are transformed into white bulls like Adam in Eden! In this vein Acts 3:21 speaks of the restoration of all things to their original status.

Apocalyptic at this point may sound like a return to the beginning which could wrongly be confused with the cyclical view of history. But for apocalyptic, history is not moving in cycles, repeating itself over and over. On the contrary, events remain unique and non-repeatable as history moves along a line toward the goal, the new age (see the apocalyptic chart). This new Eden is to be like the first Eden in terms of perfection, and may be described with the same symbols of perfection. But the new Eden is not the old Eden all over again. It is truly a *new* Eden, a new creation, a state which never existed before but will exist forever as the kingdom of God.

C. The Lukan Apocalypses

The above analysis of the definition of apocalypticism into eight component parts showing the presence of these parts in Luke-Acts suggests that Luke-Acts is indeed apocalyptic in nature. It has been stated that "Luke has more eschatological passages than any other Gospel (chapters 12, 17 and 21)" and that more than the other evangelists Luke stresses the eschatological proclamation in the sayings of Jesus, giving three apocalyptic discourses (Luke 12:13-13:9; 17:20-18:8; 21:5-38).[3] All in all, Luke contains seven "miniapocalypses," which constitute some 212 of the 1151 verses of the Third Gospel or about twenty percent of it. Other passages, such as Luke 9:23-27; 11:14-36; 11:49-51; 20:27-40; Acts 1:6-11; and 2:16-21, could also be included here. The Gospel of Luke is probably the most apocalyptic of all four gospels. We shall now summarize these seven little apocalypses.

1. The River of Fire Apocalypse (Luke 3:3-18)

John proclaims "in crackling terms the imminent coming of the heavenly Messiah-Judge."[4] Just as snakes wriggle away from a burning field, so too the people like a brood of vipers (=sons of Satan) must flee from the Messiah's wrath (3:7) which "draws near" (R. Knox); "is on its way" (Rieu); "is at hand" (Alford). These translators, Knox, Rieu, and Alford, bring out the imminent sense of the verb *mellō*, a verb which we shall investigate in Chap. IV. Already, says John, the ax of judgment is sharpened and ready for the woodman to take up to go to work: "And even now the axe also lieth at the root of the trees: every tree therefore that bringeth not forth good fruit is hewn down, and cast into the fire" (3:9). The present tenses "lieth" and "is hewn down" vividly express the nearness of the inevitable event.

The image is that of an orchard full of fruit trees.
An invisible axe is laid at the trunk of every tree.
This figure is connected with that of the fruits (ver. 8).
At the first signal the axe will bury itself in the trunks
of the barren trees; it will cut them down to the very roots.[5]

John then changes the metaphor. The coming Messiah and judge is holding his winnowing-shovel in his hand, "thoroughly to cleanse his threshing-floor, and to

---

[3]Bartsch, "Eschatology," p. 392; *Wachet*, pp. 46, 106, 111.
[4]Grobel, "He That Cometh after Me," p. 399.
[5]Godet, *Luke*, I, 177.

gather the wheat into his garner; but the chaff he will burn up with unquenchable fire" (3:17). Therefore men must repent quickly to escape imminent destruction in the apocalyptic river of fire (3:16), through which all men must pass, either to be purified or destroyed.[6] John's ethical teaching is motivated by the threat of this imminent messianic judgment (3:10-14), and his preaching of good news has strong overtones of eschatological proclamation (Chaps. II.E; V.B).

2. The Falling Fire Apocalypse (Luke 10:1-24)

The Lord (10:1) sends out the seventy as "laborers into his harvest" (10:2) to proclaim the nearness of the kingdom (10:9, 11). He pronounces damning judgment upon unreceptive Galilean cities (10:13-16). When the seventy return he reports his apocalyptic vision of Satan's fall like lightning from heaven and gives the seventy charismatic charm against injuries by demonic creatures (10:17-20). In spiritual ecstasy Jesus continues to rejoice, not only because his disciples' understanding surpasses that of the professional religionists (10:21-22), but also because the disciples are privileged to see the prophecies concerning Jesus' works and words being fulfilled (10:23-24).

3. The Fire upon the Earth Apocalypse (Luke 12:1-13:35)

The disciples must beware of hypocrisy (12:1), for in the last judgment the truth will come to light (12:2-3). In the midst of tribulation the disciples are not to be fearful (12:4,32) or anxious (12:11,22,29), for the Father will give *them* the kingdom (12:32). Unlike Moses, who was a judge of Israel here and now (Exod 2:14), Jesus refuses to arbitrate in earthly matters because of the impending catastrophe and warns against entanglement in the things of this age (12:13-21). Because of the urgency of the times, disciples are to have an apocalyptic indifference to earthly possessions while they seek the kingdom with its imperishable wealth (12:22-34). "The motive for hoarding is gone, if that is at hand which will demonitise all existing wealth."[7]

The approaching end has produced a time of crisis for the disciples, who are to be on the alert for the return of their master from the marriage feast, especially since delay has already occurred (12:35-38). The Son of Man comes unexpectedly like a thief (12:39-40), and stewards are forbidden to think the master is delayed (12:41-46), because punishment, severe but just, is coming (12:46-48).

It is a time of crisis also for Jesus, who came to usher in the fiery end-time woes, when, after his death, he casts fire upon the earth (12:49-50). These woes include the eschatological division of families (12:51-53). It too is a time of crisis for the multitudes, who should be as skilled in interpreting the present time as they are in interpreting the clouds and the winds (12:54-56). Because of impending judgment one must agree quickly with his accuser before he comes to trial before the judge, lest he be cast into prison, never to be released (12:57-59).

Unless that generation repents it will perish in the judgment (13:1-9). The people rejoice over Jesus' healing of a woman with an infirmity because it is one more sign of the nearness of the kingdom (13:10-17). This mighty act leads

---

[6]See Brownlee, "John the Baptist," p. 42. On Luke's understanding of 3:16 see Chap. VIII. E.5.

[7]Manson, *Sayings of Jesus*, p. 406.

Jesus to describe the power of the approaching kingdom, which will be large, comparable to a fully grown tree or to a fully leavened loaf (13:18-21). But great as the kingdom will be, many at the last judgment will be refused admittance through the narrow door to the hall of the messianic banquet (13:22-30).

This apocalypse concludes with sayings on the fate of Jesus and of Jerusalem (13:31-35), with a possible reference to the parousia: "Ye shall not see me, until ye shall say, Blessed is he that cometh in the name of the Lord" (13:35).

4. The Fire of Agony Apocalypse (Luke 16:16-31)

Now that the kingdom of God is being proclaimed as good news everyone is entering it violently (16:16). Yet the kingdom is not opposed to the law, for the law remains valid during this age until heaven and earth pass away (16:17). The kingdom rather heightens the demands of the law (16:18). That Moses and the prophets are sure guides to salvation is accentuated by the fate of Lazarus, the beggar, who dies and is carried away by angels to Abraham's bosom, whereas Dives, the rich man, after death suffers agony in the flame of Hades (16:19-31).

5. The Fire and Brimstone Apocalypse (Luke 17:20-18:8)

Jesus, in response to a question as to when the kingdom is coming, proclaims that men shall not say "Lo, here!" or "There!" for the kingdom is in the midst of you (17:20-21). Yet when the disciples long to see one of the days of the Son of Man some will say, "Lo, there!" or "Lo, here!" But they are false teachers, for the parousia of the Son of Man will be everywhere visible, like the lightning which brightens the sky from one side to the other (17:22-24). The day when the Son of Man is revealed will be like the day when fire and brimstone rained down out of heaven upon Sodom (17:26-30), and it will be too late to rescue earthly possessions (17:31-33). Some will be delivered from destruction, but others will be left to perish with the world (17:34-35). The judgment by the Son of Man will not be "Here!" or "There!" but will be visible far and wide, like buzzards soaring above a carcass (17:37). This day is not far off, for God will vindicate his elect speedily (18:1-8a). "Nevertheless, when the Son of man cometh, shall he find faith on the earth?" (18:8b).

6. The Signs in the Stars Apocalypse (Luke 21:5-36)

When Jesus is asked when "these things" will be (21:7), he advises that the Son of Man will not come immediately (21:8-9) but only after persecution (21:12-19), the fall of Jerusalem (21:20-24), and cosmic woes (21:25-26): "And there shall be signs in the sun and moon and stars" (21:25). When they see all these things taking place they are to take courage because their redemption by the parousia of the Son of Man is drawing near (21:27-28). Then they will know that the kingdom of God is near (21:29-31). All of these end-time events, including the passing of heaven and earth, will take place before this generation passes away (21:32-33).

7. The Judgment by Fire Apocalypse (Luke 23:27-31)

As in the tribulation when men hide themselves in caves and say to the mountains, "Fall on us" (Rev 6:16), so too in the coming days the women of Jerusalem will say to the mountains, "Fall on us" (Luke 23:30). For if the burning of the green wood (Jerusalem) is terrible, how much more so will be the burning of the dry wood (the world)(23:31)?

D. Luke's Longing for the Coming of the Kingdom

It is not that Luke as a disinterested editor hands down to us seven apocalypses which he found in his sources. He does so with feeling and emotion, for from first to last in his two volumes he gives expression to a passionate longing for the consummation. Luke-Acts is "colored by ecstatic joy that the kingdom of God will come."[8]

Simeon is looking for the consolation of Israel (Luke 2:25). The poor anticipate their reward in the kingdom (6:20), where even the lesser ones will be greater than John (7:28), and some of whom will not die before they see the kingdom (9:27). Disciples are to pray first and foremost for the speedy coming of the kingdom (11:2). Jesus urges men to seek the kingdom (12:31), which will be given them by the Father (12:32). Men long to join patriarchs and prophets in the kingdom (13:28), to sit at table in the kingdom (13:29), and to eat bread in the kingdom(14:15). Jesus promises to fulfil this longing of his apostles by appointing for them a kingdom (22:29), so that they may eat and drink at his table in his kingdom (22:30). He himself will not eat the passover again until it is fulfilled in the kingdom (22:16), nor will he drink of the fruit of the vine until the kingdom comes (22:18).

Pharisees want to know when the kingdom is coming (17:20), but Jesus replies that it is not coming with observable signs (17:20), for it is in their midst (17:21). Jesus' exorcisms prove that the kingdom is come upon them (11:20). He declares that the days are coming when they will desire to see one of the days of the Son of Man (17:22). God's elect are crying to him night and day for eschatological deliverance (18:7). Although some men covet riches more than the kingdom (18:24-25), there are those who have been willing to forsake houses and families for the sake of the kingdom (18:29).

Disciples are so overly-anxious for the kingdom that they think it is about to appear immediately (19:11), but Jesus informs them that when they see certain things taking place they will know that the kingdom is near (21:31). The penitent thief begs Jesus to remember him when he comes in his kingdom (23:42). Joseph of Arimathea is looking for the kingdom of God (23:51). The two disciples on the road to Emmaus had hoped that Jesus was the one who would redeem Israel (24:21), while he was still alive. The eleven want the kingdom to be restored at once to Israel (Acts 1:6), and the disciples so yearn for the kingdom that they are willing to endure much tribulation to enter it (14:22). The twelve tribes earnestly serve God day and night, hoping to attain the promises of final redemption (26:7). In short, Luke advises men "to pray endlessly for the End" (18:1).[9]

E. Luke's Magnificent Obsession for Proclaiming the Kingdom

Luke's eschatological zeal is also exhibited by his obsession with proclaiming the kingdom of God. It is possible that Luke was "the brother who is highly respected in all the churches for his work in preaching the gospel" (2 Cor 8:18) (TEV). "Certainly the man who could write the Gospel of Luke and the book of Acts must have been an eloquent preacher."[10] But whether or not Luke was this

---

[8] Reicke, *Luke*, p. 76.

[9] Bundy, *Gospels*, p. 391.

[10] Goodspeed, *Paul*, p. 55. Cf. Acts 16:10, "God had called *us* to preach the gospel."

particular brother, this interest in preaching the kingdom is reflected repeatedly in his writings.

Gabriel announces the kingdom which will have no end (1:33). Jesus must preach the good news of the kingdom, for he was sent for this purpose (4:43). He went through cities and villages, preaching the good news of the kingdom (8:1), and telling his disciples the mysteries of the kingdom (8:10), explaining that it is like a mustard seed (13:18-19) or leaven (13:20-21), a realm which belongs to the childlike (18:16-17). Jesus sent out the twelve to preach the kingdom of God (9:2) and himself spoke of the kingdom (9:11). Jesus instructs a would-be disciple to let the dead bury their own dead (Luke 9:60//Matt 8:22), but he is to go proclaim the kingdom (9:60). Jesus warns that he who keeps looking back toward old interests and ways is of no use for the kingdom (Luke 9:62). The seventy are to warn that the kingdom of God is at hand (10:9,11). From John the Baptist on the good news of the kingdom is preached (16:16). The Risen Lord speaks for forty days the things concerning the kingdom (Acts 1:3). Philip preaches good tidings concerning the kingdom (8:12), as does Paul (19:8; 20:25; 28:23; 28:31).

All in all, there are some thirty-nine explicit references to the kingdom of God in Luke and eight in Acts, most of them peculiar to Luke-Acts, and all of which have been referred to in Sections D and E. We thus see how Luke brings the concept of the kingdom to the foreground, so much so that the kingdom becomes Luke's key theological concept,[11] "the leading category" of Luke's gospel, a term which "retains its primary meaning of 'the reign of God' which is to close and supersede the present world order."[12] Likewise in Acts the kingdom of God is not less apocalyptic than in the synoptics.[13]

F. The Kerygma

But what does Luke mean by preaching the kingdom? The answer is found in the speeches of Peter (Acts 2:14-39; 3:12-26; 4:8-12; 5:30-32; 10:34-43) and of Paul (13:17-41). This "kerygma" or proclamation of the kingdom consists of six component parts as follows:[14]

1. The messianic promises are being fulfilled (2:16; 3:18-26; 13:23,32-33).

2. This fulfilment began to take place through the ministry, death, and resurrection of Jesus according to the "determinate counsel and foreknowledge of God" (2:22-31; 3:13-15; 4:10; 13:23,27-37).

3. By virtue of his resurrection Jesus has been exalted at the right hand of God as messianic head of the new Israel (2:33-36; 3:13; 4:11; 5:31).

4. The Holy Spirit in the church is the sign of Christ's present power and glory (2:17-21,33; 5:32).

5. The new age will soon come with the return of Christ (3:20-21; 10:42).

---

[11]Völkel, "Reich Gottes," p. 61.

[12]Creed, *Luke*, p. lxxii.

[13]Smith, "History and Eschatology," p. 900; similarly, Cadbury, "Acts and Eschatology," p. 311; Cadbury, *MLA*, p. 284: "That the third evangelist shared in general the apocalyptic outlook of his age cannot be gainsaid."

[14]Adapted from Dodd, *Apostolic Preaching*, pp. 19-24.

6. Appeal for repentance, offer of forgiveness and of the Holy Spirit, and the promise of salvation (life of the new age) to those who enter the elect community (2:38-39; 3:19,25-26; 4:12; 5:31; 10:43; 13:38-39).

According to Luke, this is the way the early church preached the good news of the kingdom of God.

In this introductory chapter we have seen the remarkable correspondence between the Lukan materials and the apocalyptic pattern. We have summarized his little apocalypses and have tried to feel something of his impassioned longing for the consummation and his obsession with proclaiming the joyful news of the coming kingdom. In view of all these considerations the apocalyptic character of Luke-Acts would seem to be firmly established. Luke has even been accused of being on an "apocalyptic jag."

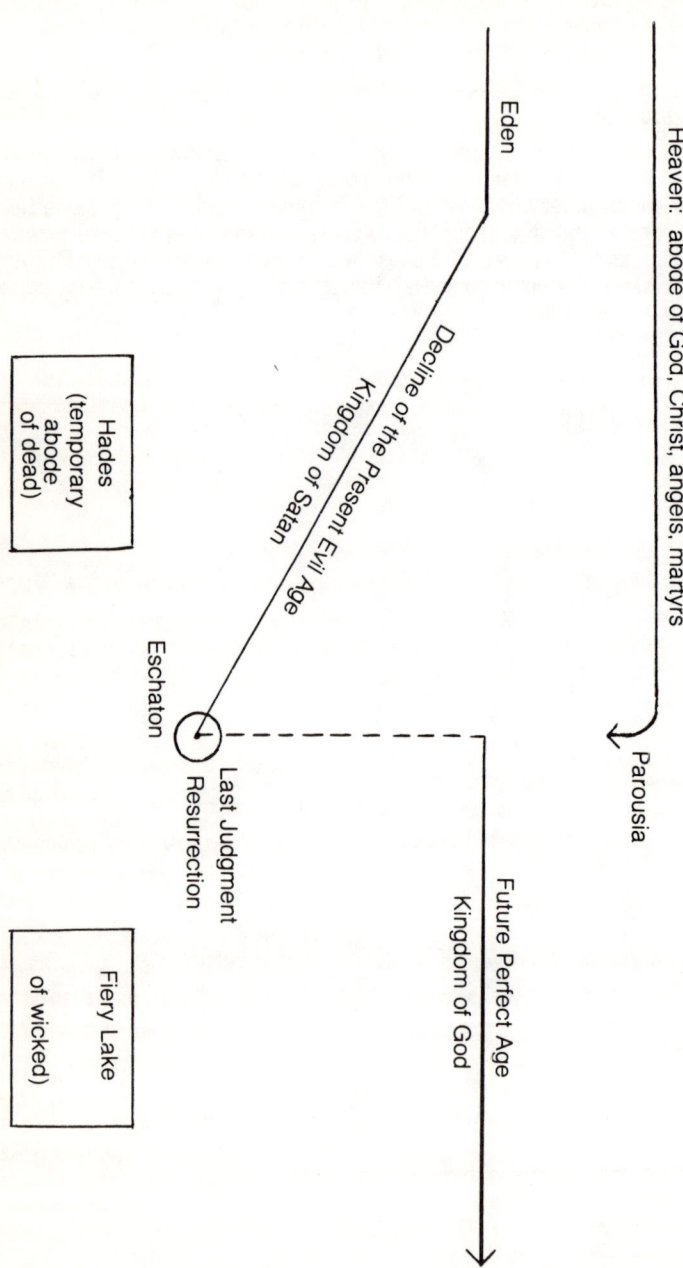

Adapted from Rist, *Daniel and Revelation*, pp. 16, 33.

Chapter II
"Until John" (Luke 16:16):
The De-Apocalypticizing of Luke-Acts

A. Anti-Apocalyptic Texts

In spite of the weighty considerations set forth in Chap. I, the apocalytic nature of Luke-Acts is being questioned by a large segment of modern scholarship, chiefly upon the basis of three texts:

> The law and the prophets were until John: from that time the gospel of the kingdom of God is preached, and every man entereth violently into it (Luke 16:16).

> The Parable of Dives and Lazarus (Luke 16:19-31).

> Verily I say unto thee, Today shalt thou be with me in Paradise (Luke 23:43).

These passages lead some to claim that Luke's "struggle is essentially an anti-apocalyptic one."[1] We shall first consider those objections to the apocalyptic character of Luke-Acts which cluster around Luke 16:16 and then in the next chapter turn to the other two texts.

B. Luke's Displacement of Apocalyptic by Periodized History

The dominant trend in Lukan studies today denies our seemingly obvious and well-supported observations about the apocalyptic framework of Lukan thought and maintains that Luke, confronted by the basic problem of the delay of the parousia, has abandoned the two-age apocalyptic pattern with its imminent end in favor of a timeless conception of the kingdom, the postponement of the parousia to the far-distant future, and a three-fold division of salvation history which stretches from creation to consummation:

1. The Period of Israel (law, prophets, John the Baptist);

2. The Period of Jesus' Ministry ("The Center of Time") (Luke 4:16-30; Acts 10:37-43);

3. The Period of the Church (between ascension and parousia).

The pre-Lukan church, it is held, was an eschatological community eagerly awaiting the return of its Lord: "Remember this! There are some here who will not die until they have seen the Kingdom of God come with power" (Mark 9:1)(TEV). "Remember this! All these things will happen before the people now living have all died" (Mark 13:30)(TEV). But as the years rolled on and even Jerusalem fell without the coming of the end, Luke saw that the primitive eschatology of Mark

---

[1] Conzelmann, *Theology*, p. 123.

and others must be recast. Luke would not be satisfied with a mere patching up but would find a permanent solution which would not be jeopardized again by a further delay of the parousia and kingdom. He would not do as others were wont to do--push the time of the end a little farther away. Rather he would eliminate the imminent expectation altogether. Luke therefore replaced the idea of the imminent coming of the kingdom by a metaphysical conception of the kingdom, with the end endlessly remote, thereby making the kingdom independent of any definite time. Luke insisted that the church, rather than waiting on tiptoe for the parousia to occur at any moment, should concentrate on its own continuing life in this world in the midst of godless surroundings and in the midst of persecution, for there would be a long interval before the end. But this interval, the epoch of the church, would be one stage in God's redemptive program.

This non-apocalyptic interpretation of Luke-Acts apparently began in 1926 with H. von Baer's book on the Holy Spirit in Luke-Acts, was further developed by Rudolf Bultmann, and received its classic expression in Hans Conzelmann's "The Center of Time."[2]

In Chaps. IV-VII we shall take up the problems of the nature of the kingdom and the imminent expectation (German: *Naherwartung*) in Luke-Acts. Now, however, we want to examine the widespread view that Luke thinks in terms of a three-fold periodization of salvation history. This view is based mainly upon Luke 16:16, but it also claims support from Luke's treatment of John the Baptist and from the fact of the existence of the Book of Acts, which describes the period of the church.

C. John the Baptist as a Non-Apocalyptic Preacher of Repentance

Let us begin with Luke's recasting of the traditional picture of John the Baptist, as understood by these anti-apocalyptic interpreters. In the gospel tradition John was Elijah, the eschatological forerunner of Jesus the Messiah:

> Behold, I send my messenger before thy face, Who shall prepare thy way; The voice of one crying in the wilderness, Make ye ready the way of the Lord....John came, who baptized in the wilderness and preached the baptism of repentance unto remission of sins....And John [like Elijah] was clothed with camel's hair, and had a leathern girdle about his loins, and did eat locusts and wild honey. And he preached, saying, There cometh after me he that is mightier than I, the latchet of whose shoes I am not worthy to stoop down and unloose. I baptized you in water; but he shall baptize you in the Holy Spirit. And....Jesus came from Nazareth of Galilee, and was baptized of John in the Jordan (Mark 1:1-11).

Matthew explicitly identifies John with Elijah:

And if ye are willing to receive it, this is Elijah, that is to come (11:14).

And his [Jesus'] disciples asked him, saying, Why then say the scribes that Elijah must first come? And he answered and said, Elijah indeed cometh, and

---

[2]H. von Baer, *Der heilige Geist*; Bultmann, *Theology*, II, 116-118; *Existence and Faith*, pp. 124, 196 ff., 238, 255 ff.; Conzelmann, *Theology*, pp. 16-27. For a clear presentation of these and other aspects of Conzelmann's position see John Reumann's introduction to Ellis, *Eschatology*, pp. i-xvi. A critique of Conzelmann is found in such works as Robinson, *Weg* and Moore, *Parousia*, pp. 80-91.

shall restore all things: but I say unto you, that Elijah is come already, and they knew him not, but did unto him whatsoever they would.... Then understood the disciples that he spake unto them of John the Baptist (17:10-13).

Traditionally, John was also a fiery preacher of the imminent coming of the kingdom of God: "Repent ye; for the kingdom of heaven is at hand" (Matt 3:2). For Luke, however, John is neither the Elijah-like eschatological forerunner nor a proclaimer of the kingdom. Luke, by omitting, altering, and re-arranging the traditional material about John separates John's ministry from that of Jesus and transforms John into a non-apocalyptic preacher of repentance, the last of the prophets, who issues a timeless ethical exhortation:

He that hath two coats, let him impart to him that hath none; and he that hath food, let him do likewise.... Extort no more than that which is appointed you [tax collectors].... Extort from no man by violence, neither accuse any one wrongfully; and be content with your wages (Luke 3:10-14).

Luke omits John's preaching of the kingdom (Matt 3:2) and eradicates any suggestion of a connection between Elijah and John by deleting the references to John's Elijah-like attire (Mark 1:6) and the identifications of John with Elijah found in Matt 11:14 and 17:13.

Whereas Matthew and Mark report John's imprisonment later in their gospels (Matt 14:3-4; Mark 6:17-18), Luke tells of John's imprisonment (3:19-20) before the baptism of Jesus (3:21-22) and nowhere mentions John as the one who baptized Jesus. Luke changes the tradition in these respects to make it clear that the ministries of John and Jesus are separated and belong to two different epochs. This separation is further suggested by Luke's omission of "after me" at 3:16, where John simply says that a mightier one is coming, but fails to say, as he does in Matt 3:11 and Mark 1:17, that this one is coming after him. Luke's John thus does not claim to be the Forerunner but implies that in a new epoch, "the center of time," the Messiah is coming.

It is said, in short, that Luke eliminates the traditional eschatological features associated with the Baptist in order to avoid the impression that John introduces the new age, an impression which would contradict Luke's substitution of three epochs of salvation history for the two ages of apocalyptic.

D. John the Baptist as the Elijah-like Forerunner of Jesus
1. Luke's Non-Inclusions

What are we to make of this anti-apocalyptic interpretation of John the Baptist? Let us look first at Luke's omissions or non-inclusions.

Luke's lack of reference to John's desert garb may have been occasioned by his desire to proceed directly from the prophecy of Isa 40:3-5 (Luke 3:4-6) to John's preaching (3:7-18). As we shall see in Section G Luke's "therefore" in 3:7 makes an important connection between the Isaianic prophecy and John's preaching, a connection which would be broken by a reference to John's attire.

Luke too may have thought of any reference to John's clothing as superfluous, for he twice already had connected John with the wilderness. The child "was in the deserts till the day of his showing unto Israel" (1:80), and John's was "the voice of one crying in the wilderness" (3:3). It is also possible that Luke omitted the description of John's attire in Mark 1:6 precisely because such a description would place "the Baptist firmly within the epoch of the prophets."³ Another suggestion is that Luke made this omission out of his desire to portray John and Jesus as parallel to each other (see D.4).⁴

Luke's avoidance of John's name in connection with Jesus' baptism is not for the purpose of putting John and Jesus in different epochs but for avoiding the embarrassment John's baptism of Jesus was causing Christians, as reflected in Matt 3:13-15, where John objects to baptizing Jesus, and in Acts 18:24-19:7, where Luke shows the inadequacy of John's baptism.

Moreover, it is not certain that Luke does omit all reference to John's baptism of Jesus. Acts 1:21-22 refers to "all the time that the Lord Jesus went in and out among us, beginning from the baptism of John, until the day that he was received up from us." This passage likely has in mind the time from Jesus' baptism to his ascension and thus means "from the baptism [of Jesus] by John."⁵

But why does Luke tell of John's imprisonment (3:19-20) before Jesus' baptism (3:21-22), if not to place John and Jesus in two different epochs? We should observe that Matt 4:12//Mark 1:14 also separates John's ministry from that of Jesus: "Now after John was delivered up, Jesus came into Galilee, preaching the gospel" (Mark 1:14). This fact would suggest that Luke's interest was less in separating the ministries of John and Jesus than in avoiding the questions raised by John's baptism of Jesus.

Moreover, Luke may have mentioned John's imprisonment before Jesus' baptism simply because of his desire to round off one narrative before beginning another. For example, in Acts 11:28 Agabus prophesies a famine which takes place a year or two later, but Luke reports in the same verse that "it came to pass in the days of Claudius."⁶ But whatever theological or literary reasons lie behind Luke's arrangement of Luke 3:19-22, he does not seem concerned elsewhere to separate John from Jesus (cf. 3:1-2, a dating which Luke probably intends to include the appearances of both Jesus and John;⁶ᵃ 7:29-30; 20:1-8; Acts 13:23-25).

The significance of Luke's not reporting the statements of Matt 11:14 and 17:13 which identify John with Elijah is lessened by the fact that Luke may not have known of these verses, since they possibly were not in Q, and are not found in Mark.

Luke's non-inclusion of Elijah's role as the restorer of all things (Matt 17:11; Mark 9:12) may not have been due to Luke's desire to eliminate John's eschatological features but to avoid placing the restoration in the past rather than in the future (Acts 3:21).⁷

---

³Moore, *Parousia*, p. 85.

⁴Bartsch, *Wachet*, p. 45.

⁵Lake and Cadbury, *Acts*, p. 14.

⁶Cf. Wilson, "Lukan Eschatology," pp. 331-332.

⁶ᵃ As is inconsistently admitted by Conzelmann in *Religion in Geschichte und Gegenwart*, 3d ed., III, col 624, as quoted by Flender, *Luke*, p. 122.

⁷Robinson, *Weg*, p. 18. On Acts 3:19-21 see Chap. VI.F.5.1.

2. John the Forerunner

The attempt to depict Luke's John the Baptist as non-eschatological collides with passages which do picture John as the Elijah-like eschatological forerunner of Jesus. From birth John is to be filled with the Holy Spirit, which is an eschatological reality (Chap. IV.G.2). This prophecy (Luke 1:15) is fulfilled in 1:41,44, where the babe John leaps in the womb of his mother, who is filled with the Holy Spirit. This reaction is one of messianic joy, indicating that John is the precursor of the Messiah. As Rebekah's children leaped in her womb (*skirtaō*, the same verb as used in Luke 1:41,44) before the birth of Israel (Jacob), so John leaps to announce the birth of the New Israel.[8]

Luke 1:17 predicts that John will "go before his [Messiah's] face in the spirit and power of Elijah, to turn the hearts of the fathers to the children, and the disobedient to walk in the wisdom of the just; to make ready for the Lord [Jesus] a people prepared for him." Here Luke describes John in language from the prophecy concerning Elijah's eschatological return in Mal 4:6 and Sir 48:10. Again, John will be called "the prophet of the Most High," for he will "go before the face of the Lord (Jesus) to make ready his ways" (Luke 1:76, from Mal 3:1). If it be an overstatement that nowhere is the title Elijah "more firmly attached" to John than in the Lukan infancy narratives,[9] that statement comes closer to the truth than does the overlooking of such verses as these. Yet Conzelmann, in reconstructing Luke's eschatology, omits Luke 1-2 from consideration. It is only by thus "ignoring the birth narratives that Conzelmann can appear to establish his thesis that Luke visualized the story of salvation as emerging in three quite different stages."[10] Conzelmann by-passes Luke 1-2 on the grounds that these two chapters preserve a theology different from the rest of Luke-Acts, especially on the John-the-Baptist question. But this procedure is indefensible, for if Luke's conception of John and the three epochs is as central to Luke's theology as Conzelmann claims, Luke would not have begun his work with two chapters which contradict Luke's main thesis. The very fact that Luke 1-2 is

> only one example among many [examples of Luke's supplementation of other writings about Christian beginnings], including most obviously the entire book of Acts, suggests that Luke 1-2 should be interpreted from the perspective of the Lukan writings as a whole [Luke-Acts] and not from the point of view that Luke 1-2 is a self contained unit of tradition that Luke added to a Markan framework.... Luke's presentation of the origins of Jesus introduces themes and foreshadows developments that will unfold in the entire complex of Luke-Acts. Luke 1-2 is thus quite similar to the Prologue of the Gospel of John and should be considered as a carefully constructed introduction to the Gospel of Luke in particular and his entire work in general.[11]

Even within the body of the Gospel Jesus praises John as "more than a prophet" (7:26), that is, as the forerunner of the Messiah, and then applies to John the classical Elijah passage from Mal 3:1: "This is he of whom it is written, Behold

---

[8]Oliver, "Birth Stories," p. 217.

[9]Oliver, "Birth Stories," p. 218.

[10]See Minear, "Birth Stories," p. 121. Minear's statement is also cited with approval by Michel, "Lukas," p. 107.

[11]Songer, "Origins of Jesus," pp. 453, 463.

I send my messenger before thy face, Who shall prepare thy way before thee" (Luke 7:27). Luke omitted this adaptation of Mal 3:1 at Luke 3:4 (as does Matthew at Matt 3:3) because he would use it later at Luke 7:27 (as does Matthew at Matt 11:10), and because he wanted to avoid Mark's error of attributing it to Isaiah (Mark 1:2). Thus this omission by Luke at Luke 3:4 has nothing to do with Luke's alleged desire to put John and Jesus into two different periods. As a matter of fact, John as a prophet and more than a prophet (1:76; 7:26) is an eschatological figure of the last days, for not only the office of forerunner but also prophecy belong to the end-times, for prophecy is a gift of the Spirit and the Spirit is a sign of the last days and new age (Chap. IV.G.2). The very fact that John is filled with the Spirit does not fit the period of Israel, for prophecy had ceased in Israel.

In Acts 13:23-24 God brought unto Israel a Savior, Jesus, "when John had first preached before his coming the baptism of repentance to all the people of Israel." The intimate preparatory role of John for Jesus could not be more clearly stated than in this passage. Acts 13:24-25 is the fullest account of John in the NT outside the Gospels. Luke would hardly have retained this unit if he had wished to sunder John from Jesus. In 13:25 Luke goes on to quote John as saying "after me": "There cometh one after me ... " So also in 19:4: "They should believe on him that should come after him, that is, on Jesus." And to indicate the close connection between John and Jesus, Luke 3:17 implies that the coming Messiah is already holding his fan in his hand, a meaning explicitly brought out by a recent ecumenical translation, the *Einheitsbibel*: "Already (*schon*) he holds his shovel in his hand." Similarly the TEV: "He has his winnowing-shovel with him."

3. "After Me"

Let us turn now to an approach other than Conzelmann's to the data on John. K. Grobel argues convincingly that Mark 1:7//Matt 3:11 in its pre-synoptic setting meant, "There is a follower (disciple=one who literally walks behind his teacher, according to rabbinic custom) of mine who is more capable than I."[12] Luke, says Grobel, was well aware of this technical meaning of "coming after" (*opisō erchesthai*) a teacher and therefore never uses this expression in connection with the relationship between John and Jesus, for such an expression "had the polemic weakness that it could also be understood as admitting that Jesus had been a disciple of the Baptist." Thus Luke omits "after me" (*opisō mou*) at 3:7. In Acts 13:25 and 19:4 Luke substitutes another word for "after" (*opisō*), namely, *meta*, the latter meaning "following in time," thereby excluding "that following-in-space (*opisō*) which to a Jew was the very badge of discipleship."

Moreover, continues Grobel, "it seems to be one of Luke's obsessions to prove that John was the *temporal* predecessor of Jesus": Luke alone dates John's birth before Jesus; Luke alone antedates John's imprisonment so that the precursor's work will fittingly terminate with the beginning of Jesus' work.[13] In Acts 13:25 John "was finishing his race, ..."

In this way Grobel explains the data adequately in terms of the anti-Baptist polemic: Luke wants to avoid giving the impression that Jesus was John's

---

[12]Grobel, "He That Cometh after Me," pp. 397-401.

[13]One should, however, compare Matt 4:12//Mark 1:14, which also separate the ministries of John and Jesus (see Chap. II.D.1).

disciple. Grobel's explanation appears to fit the facts of the case better than does Conzelmann's attempt to show Luke has eliminated John's role as forerunner. What Luke has eliminated is Jesus' role as John's disciple, but not John's role as Jesus' forerunner. Luke eliminated the spatial relationship involved in Jesus' walking behind John as John's disciple, but he has not eliminated but rather stressed the temporal relationship, which shows John preceding Jesus as his forerunner.

4. The John-Jesus Parallels

In summary of our position we may say that if Luke in chap. 3 seems to have blurred the identification of John with Elijah and seems to have separated John from Jesus during their ministries it is because elsewhere in Luke-Acts, and especially in the infancy narratives of Luke 1-2, he has joined them closely together.[14] Luke expresses this closeness by means of the parallelism which he draws between the infants John and Jesus:

> The babes are relatives born within six months of one another; both have devout parents; the angel Gabriel appears to a parent of each, causing a reaction of distress and promising a supernatural conception in each instance; both annunciations have introductions mentioning the husband, wife, and tribal origin; Gabriel addresses each visionary by name and urges, "Do not be afraid"; both mothers "will bear a son" and "shall call his" name John or Jesus (1:13,31); 1:13 and 1:31 are each followed by a poem predicting that each child "will be great"; this poem in each instance evokes the question "How?"; this question is followed by an indication from the angel of a sign of God's power; there is a journey after each vision; miraculous births occur; the babes are given divinely chosen names; outbursts of prophecy interpret the events as divine acts; both babes are circumcised on the eighth day; and the infants grow to spiritual maturity.

This parallelism continues into their ministries. As the word of God came (*ginomai*) unto John (Luke 3:2), so a voice came (*ginomai*) out of heaven to Jesus (3:22). Each is thought to be Messiah (Luke 3:15; 24:21). Both preach the good news (*euangelidzō*) (John: 3:18; Jesus: 4:18,43; 8:1; 20:1). Each teaches his disciples a model prayer (Luke 11:1-4). Both are rejected by their people (7:33-34). Such parallelism speaks against separating John and Jesus into different periods of salvation history and thereby stripping John of his eschatological role as forerunner.

E. John the Baptist as a Preacher of the Kingdom

Although there is no unambiguous statement in Luke-Acts that John preached the kingdom (cf. Matt 3:2), there are indications that Luke did regard the kingdom of God as part of John's message.[15] Luke sums up John's apocalyptic preaching by saying that John preached good tidings unto the people (*euangelidzō*) (3:18). For Luke John is the first human preacher of good news, preceded only by angels (1:19; 2:10).

Euangelidzó (preach good tidings) is an eschatological word for Luke which he uses twenty-five times.[16] *Euangelidzō* is "the technical term by which the

---

[14]Cf. Oliver, "Birth Stories," p. 218.

[15]For John as a proclaimer of imminent judgment see Chap. V.B.

[16]Luke 1:19; 2:10; 3:18; 4:18,43; 7:22; 8:1; 9:6; 16:16; 20:1; Acts 5:42; 8:4,12,25,35,40; 10:36; 11:20; 13:32; 14:7,15,21; 15:35; 16:10; 17:18.

whole Christian message was designated,"[17] a term which thus would be expected to include the kingdom. "As object of several verbs of speaking, it ["kingdom of God"] constitutes a formula apparently parallel to the writer's more singular verb 'evangelize.'"[18] *Euangelidzō* therefore is a word which Luke would not have used had he wanted to de-eschatologize John. The good news that John brings in connection with his message of doom and destruction (3:18) is surely that of the imminent kingdom, even as Jesus (4:43; 8:1) and Philip (Acts 8:12) bring good news of the kingdom (*euangelidzō*). Likewise the twelve preach good tidings (*euangelidzō*), which are good tidings of the kingdom: "And he sent forth to preach (*euangelidzō*) the kingdom of God" (Luke 9:2; cf. 10:9,11). And if our exegesis of Luke 16:16 in Section F is correct, then Luke explicitly says there that John preaches the kingdom as good news (*euangelidzō*).

That John's preaching of good tidings (3:18) means preaching the kingdom is further indicated by his function of turning many of the children of Israel to the Lord their God to make ready for the Lord a people prepared for him (1:16-17). That this prepared people is the people of the coming kingdom is made clear by 1:33, where Gabriel prophesies that Jesus "shall reign over the house of Jacob for ever; and of his kingdom there shall be no end."

John's preaching of the kingdom is also implied in his giving "the knowledge of salvation unto his people in the remission of their sins" (1:77), for this salvation is that of the kingdom. And John's cry in the wilderness can be about nothing other than the coming of the kingdom when "every valley shall be filled... and all flesh shall see the salvation of God" (3:4-6) (this reference to salvation is peculiar to Luke). A portion of John's message of good tidings is the hope that the messianic judge will "gather the wheat into his granary" (3:17), that is, into his kingdom.

Furthermore, the probability that John preached the kingdom is increased by the possibility that Jesus taught his disciples the same prayer that John taught his followers (Luke 11:1-4), with its petition for the coming of the kingdom.

It is strange that Jesus in Luke 11:1-4 is prompted to teach his disciples the Paternoster only because of their demand that he follow John's example.... What the disciples ask for at Luke 11:1 are not instructions how to pray, but *what* to pray.... What is taught in Luke 11 is a definite set prayer, ... a typical Hebrew prayer such as any rabbi might have taught. But why is the name of John the Baptist associated with this set prayer? It must be that this was a prayer which John himself used. ... Jesus at one stage of his ministry obviously identified himself with the Baptist's movement, and borrowed much of his teaching from John (cf. Matth. 3:7 with 12:34 and 23:33, Matth. 3:10 with 7:19 and Matth. 3:2 with 4:17). It is conceivable that the Paternoster was included in this borrowed material.[19]

The probability that Jesus had been a follower of John is supported by the likelihood that two of Jesus' disciples came from the ranks of John's followers (John 1:35) as well as by Grobel's arguments given above (Chap. II.D.3). Jesus

---

[17] Wink, *John the Baptist*, p. 52.
[18] Cadbury, "Acts and Eschatology," p. 311.
[19] Elliott, "Lord's Prayer," p. 215.

as a disciple of John's would have learned John's prayer and in turn taught it to his disciples when they asked for a set prayer.

But why, then, is Luke the only writer to indicate that Jesus taught his disciples a set prayer as John had done? This curiosity would be explained if, as we shall discuss below (Chap. II.F), Luke also was a former disciple of John's or very close to John's circles and therefore had first-hand knowledge of John's teachings. But even if the Lord's prayer were original with Jesus, Luke in no wise hints that its petition for the coming of the kingdom would have been foreign to John.

All of these considerations forbid us from building too much of a superstructure on the fact that Luke has no parallel to Matt 3:2, according to which John proclaims the kingdom. After all, we have no way of ascertaining that Luke deliberately omitted Matt 3:2, for this verse may have been peculiar to Matthew and not in Q at all. Nor does Luke record the parallel verse about Jesus' preaching the kingdom (Matt 4:17//Mark 1:15). Yet for Luke Jesus is a preacher of the kingdom (Luke 4:43; 8:1; 9:11; Acts 1:3).

F. John the Baptist within the Era of Fulfilment (Luke 16:16)

Turning now to Luke 16:16, which Conzelmann calls "the key to the topography of redemptive history,"[20] we find the exegetical situation well summed up in these words: "Rarely has a scholar [Conzelmann] placed so much weight on so dubious an interpretation of so difficult a logion."[21] And without any proof!

Certainly 16:16 divides salvation history not into three but into two epochs: that of the law and prophets (era of promise and preparation) and that of the proclamation of the kingdom of God (era of fulfilment),[22] the latter continuing until the parousia.[23] Nor does 16:16 give support to the idea that Luke has abandoned the two-age apocalyptic framework in favor of the three epochs of salvation history. The next verse, 16:17, and also 21:33 refer to the passing of the old heaven and the old earth before the coming of the new age of the kingdom. And as we have already seen in Chap. I.C.4, 16:16 begins the fire of agony apocalypse (16:16-31), with its two-age framework. That Luke has not replaced the apocalyptic two-age structure with a non-apocalyptic three-period structure is also shown by Luke's temporal dualism, whereby he brings out the contrast between this age and the age to come (16:8; 18:25,29-30; 20:34-35; 21:33) (Chap. I.B.2.b).

But does John belong to the period of the law and prophets or to the period when the kingdom is being proclaimed as good news? The language of 16:16 is not unambiguous at this point. That "until (*mechri*) John" (16:16a) means up to but not including John is suggested, however, by the only other use in the NT of *mechri* with a person, Rom 5:14: "Death reigned from Adam until Moses." Here Paul refers to the pre-Mosaic period, that is, from Adam up to the time of, but not including, Moses. Nor is 16:16b clear: "from that time the gospel of the kingdom of God is preached." So far as the Greek is concerned, "from that time" (*apo tote*)

---

[20]Conzelmann, *Theology*, p. 23.

[21]Minear, "Birth Stories," p. 122.

[22]After T. W. Manson, *Sayings of Jesus*, p. 426.

[23]Kümmel, *Introduction*, p. 102.

could be either inclusive or exclusive of John. There are, nevertheless, a number of considerations which strongly suggest that Luke intended John to be included in the era of fulfilment when the kingdom is being heralded as good news:

This inclusive sense finds support in John's apocalyptic message of imminent fulfilment in the kingdom of God (Section E) and in his close connection to Jesus as forerunner (Section D). This sense of 16:16 is unambiguously brought out by TEV: "The Law of Moses and the writings of the prophets were in effect up to the time of John the Baptist; since then the Good News about the Kingdom of God is being told, and everyone forces his way in."

According to Luke 1 John belongs to the era of fulfilment because he fulfils the promises:

And behold, thou [Zacharias] shalt be silent and not able to speak, until the day that these things shall come to pass, because thou believedst not my words, which shall be fulfilled in their season (1:20).... And he hath raised up a horn of salvation for us . . . as he spake by the mouth of his holy prophets that have been from of old (1:69-70).

At Luke 3:1-2 Luke not only dates the era of fulfilment from "the Big Seven" of his day but also from John, whom Luke presents as the inaugurator of the era of fulfilment, as it stands written in Isaiah (Luke 3:4). Since 3:1-2 is from Luke's hand, we have here Luke's own view.

Luke at 3:2-7 places the statement about John's preaching a baptism of repentance (Luke 3:3//Mark 1:4) before the quotation from Isa 40:3-5 (Luke 3:4-6), which is the reverse of Mark's order. By means of this inversion Luke accentuates John's fulfilment of Isaiah. Then to underline the point Luke introduces the word "therefore" into 3:7, thereby indicating that John preaches because he is the forerunner of the Lord prophesied by Isaiah.[24]

The inclusive sense of 16:16 is also undergirded by Luke 3:15: "The people were in expectation, and all men reasoned in their hearts concerning John, whether haply he were the Christ." In the Synoptics only this verse informs us that some were reasoning whether John were the Messiah. Surely Luke would have suppressed this statement had he desired to locate John and Jesus in two separate periods.

The key to this crucial verse 3:15 is found when we reflect upon the very large if not disproportionate space which Luke gives to John in his infancy narratives and in Luke-Acts as a whole.[25] This emphasis suggests that Luke must originally have been very close to John's disciples, possibly a disciple himself, who had access to Baptist sources and information.[26] This possibility would be increased

---

[24]This material on Luke 3:1-2, 2-7, was adapted from Wink, *John the Baptist*, p. 51-52, who is followed by Kümmel, "Luke 16:16," p. 412. Wlson, "Lukan Eschatology," p. 336, also includes John within the period of fulfilment. Wink advances beyond Conzelmann by interpreting 16:16 in the inclusive sense (pp. 51-55) and by regarding John as the forerunner (pp. 54, 57, 79). Yet Wink remains too much under Conzelmann's sway: Luke has removed the kingdom to the distant future (pp. 53, 54, 58); Luke has divided redemptive history into three stages (p. 55); John does not preach the kingdom (p. 53)--even though John is within the era when the kingdom is being preached and even though *euangelidzō* is a technical term for the whole Christian message (p. 52).

[25]Luke 1:5-25; 39-45, 57-80; 3:2-22; 5:33; 7:18-35; 9:7-9; 11:1; 16:16; 20:4-6; Acts 1:5,22; 10:37; 11:16; 13:24-25; 18:25; 19:4.

[26]Harnack, *Date of Acts*, p. 154.

if Luke were of Jewish origin, as is sometimes held in order to account for his interest in Jewish matters.[27] But whether or not Luke was Jewish, in Luke 3:15 we see Luke sharing his own puzzlement over the real possibility that John was Messiah. Luke did go so far as to call the twelve Johannines of Ephesus "disciples" (19:1), a term which "must mean Christians," both from its use in Acts and from the context here.[27a] Luke also regarded Apollos as Christian, though Apollos knew only the baptism of John (18:25). Thus we can see that Luke, who himself was on the verge of identifying John as Messiah, and who regarded fringe baptist groups as Christian, would be the last to de-eschatologize John, remove his office as forerunner, and transform him into an ethical teacher belonging to the bygone era of the law and prophets. Rather, Luke, with his high regard for John, **solved the problem of John's identity and relationship to Jesus by** connecting the two eschatological figures closely together as forerunner and Messiah, both "great" (1:15,32), but John, "the prophet of the Most High" (1:76), great *before* Jesus, "the Son of the Most High" (1:32).[28]

G. Additional Objections to the Threefold Division of Salvation History

If John and Jesus belong in the era of fulfilment when the kingdom is being proclaimed, so does the church. We have seen in Chap. I. D-F that Luke's obsession with preaching the kingdom of God and his longing for the coming of the kingdom are found in Luke-Acts from first to last. This fact alone stands in the way of separating sharply the period of Jesus from the period of the church, for whatever differences there may be between these alleged periods they are basically one as the time of kingdom proclamation. For Luke, John, Jesus, and the church belong, not to three separate eras, but to the era of fulfilment when the kingdom is being preached.[29] Preaching of repentance unto forgiveness of sins and works worthy of repentance also shows unity of purpose between John (Luke 3:3,8), Jesus (5:32; 24:47); Peter (Acts 2:38; 5:31), and Paul (20:21; 26:20).

Separation of three epochs is also excluded by Luke's stress on the activity of the Holy Spirit from Luke 1:15 through Acts 28:25, this major Lukan theme being a connective thread running through Luke-Acts, overlapping all three alleged epochs.[30] Zacharias (Luke 1:67), Elisabeth (1:41), John the Baptist (1:15), Jesus (4:1), various disciples (Acts 2:4; 4:31; 6:3; 13:52), Peter (4:8), Stephen (6:5; 7:55), Barnabas (11:24), and Paul (9:17; 13:9) are full of the Holy Spirit. The Holy Spirit comes upon Mary (Luke 1:35), Simeon (2:25), Jesus (3:22; 4:18), the apostles (Acts 1:8), and all flesh (2:17), including the twelve Johannines (19:6). Simeon (Luke 2:27), Jesus (4:1,14; 10:21), and the church (Acts 9:31) are in the

---

[27]Reicke, *Luke*, pp. 21-24; Albright, *Matthew*, pp. 264-267. Franklin, *Christ the Lord*, pp. 177-179, prefers to think of Luke as a proselyte to Judaism or perhaps a Gentile "God-fearer" like Cornelius (Acts 10:2).

[27a] Lake and Cadbury, *Acts*, p. 237.

[28]On Luke's relationship to John see also Chap. II.E. on Luke 11:1-4.

[29]Wilson, "Lukan Eschatology," p. 335, likewise finds that preaching of the kingdom by John, Jesus, and the church suggests that "a three-epoched notion" is "unnatural for Luke."

[30]For an instructive but abortive attempt to force the activity of the Spirit into the three epochs see Tatum, "Epoch of Israel," pp. 184-195. Conzelmann, *Theology*, p. 103, follows von Baer in stressing that "in the period of Jesus' life the Spirit is restricted exclusively to Jesus." But this fact is true of all four Gospels.

Spirit. The Spirit directs the movements of Simeon (Luke 2:27), Jesus (4:1), Philip (Acts 8:29,39), Peter (10:19-20; 11:12), Barnabas and Saul (13:2), Paul and Silas (19:6-7), and Paul (19:21; 20:22; 21:4). The Spirit moves persons to prophesy: Elisabeth (Luke 1:41-45), Zacharias (1:67), Simeon (2:25-32), Jesus (4:16-30; 10:21-24), disciples (Acts 4:31), Peter (4:8-12), Stephen (6:10), Agabus (11:28; 21:11), Paul (13:9-11), the twelve Johannines (19:6), and the disciples at Tyre (21:4). The Spirit reveals information to Simon (Luke 2:26), to the disciples (12:12), and to Paul (Acts 20:23).

For Luke, then, the Spirit long ago had spoken through David (Acts 1:16; 4:25) and Isaiah (28:25). Luke would probably agree with Jewish tradition that since Malachi the Spirit was inactive in Israel. But as the era of the law and prophets draws to a close and the era of fulfilment dawns the Spirit again encounters a select few persons in anticipation of the new age in all its fullness: Zacharias, Elisabeth, Mary, John the Baptist, Simeon, and Jesus. Then at Pentecost the Spirit is poured out upon all flesh: apostles, many disciples, and especially Peter, Stephen, Philip, Paul, Barnabas, and Agabus.

The artificiality of the three-epoch division of Luke-Acts is also suggested by Acts 1:1, for Luke's Gospel contains the beginning and Acts the continuation of Jesus' actions and teachings. Luke thus links the history of the church to Jesus' earthly ministry and thereby precludes any allocation of Jesus and the church to separate epochs. John belongs to Jesus and Jesus to the church, the three standing united at the dawning of the era of fulfilment by their preaching of the kingdom and by their being filled with and controlled by the Spirit.

Israel's hope of redemption is a theme from beginning to ending of Luke-Acts (Chap. VI.F.5), another hindrance to a triple periodization.[31] The contrived nature of these three epochs could be further demonstrated by tracing other Lukan themes through Luke-Acts.[32] Suffice it to say: "Conzelmann's attempt to straitjacket Luke into a strict threefold pattern has failed. This is not the key to Luke's eschatology. Luke was not concerned to draw hard and fast lines between John, Jesus and the Church."[33]

H. Luke's Program

Luke's eschatological program may be illustrated by a divided line representing the old age (law and prophets; era of preparation and promise) and the new age (kingdom of God). The era of fulfilment begins with the appearance of the Baptist, the first advent of the Christ, the proclamation of the kingdom, and the gift of the Spirit to a select few. With the outpouring of the Spirit upon all flesh at Pentecost and afterward, the eschatological drama moves closer to completion at the parousia, when the old heaven and earth will pass away (Luke 16:17; 21:33). In the meantime the church is living in the "last days" (Acts 2:17), promoting the world mission, and enjoying the fulfilment of the promises from of old (Acts 3:18-26).

---

[31] Luke 1:32-33,68-79; 2:25,38; 4:18,19; 17:22-37; 24:21; Acts 1:6; 3:19-21; 15:15-18; 26:6; 28:20.

[32] Cf. my "Evans Reconsidered," pp. 15-46.

[33] Wilson, "Lukan Eschatology," p. 335.

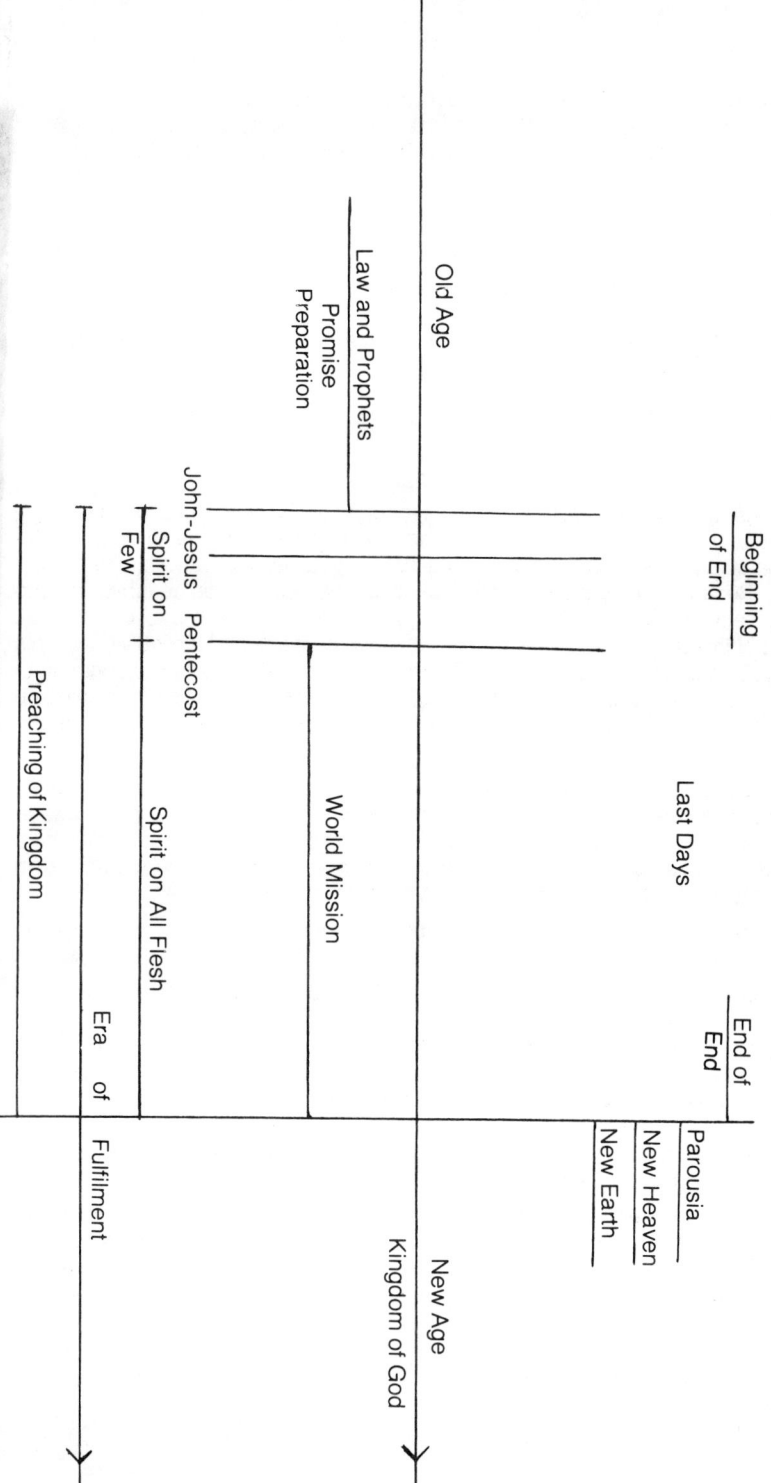

Chapter III
"The Happy Side of Hades" (Luke 16:19-31): The Platonizing of Luke-Acts

A. The Immortality of the Soul

The apocalyptic nature of Luke's eschatology has been questioned not only on the grounds of its alleged abandonment of the two-age division of the apocalyptic philosophy of history for a three-age division of salvation history but also because of its supposed rejection of the apocalyptic teaching on the resurrection of the body at the resurrection at the end of time in favor of the Greek idea of the immortality of the soul at the moment of death of the individual. This Grecizing position involves a displacement of the present-future dichotomy of two ages by a vertical tension between heaven and earth and between time and eternity. It also emphasizes the fate of each individual at death rather than the destiny of mankind as a whole at the last judgment.

According to Plato and many Greek thinkers man is composed of an evil body and a good, eternal, indestructible soul. The body is the prison house of the soul. At death, the soul sloughs off the body, flying from the body as a butterfly flies from a cocoon. The normal state of the soul is life without the body; the soul's sojourn in the body is a severe illness. The body (*sōma*) is a tomb (*sēma*).

This Greek conception of the immortality of the soul comes to expression in the Wisdom of Solomon, an apocryphal book of the first century B.C.:

> But the souls of the righteous are in the hand of God, and no torment will ever touch them. 2 In the eyes of the foolish they seem to have died, and their departure was thought to be an affliction, 3 and their going from us to be their destruction; but they are at peace. 4 For though in the sight of men they were punished, their hope is full of immortality. 5 Having been disciplined a little, they will receive great good, because God tested them and found them worthy of himself; 6 like gold in the furnace he tried them, and like a sacrificial burnt offering he accepted them (3:1-6).

Some commentators find similar ideas in Luke, particularly in the parable of the rich man (*Dives*=Latin, rich) and Lazarus (Luke 16:19-31) and in the words of the dying Jesus, "Today thou shalt be with me in Paradise" (23:43). The Greek word "Hades" (Hebrew: "Sheol") in 16:23 is said to be equivalent to Gehenna (hell) in apocalyptic thought, that is, the final state of the wicked.[1] Abraham is in

---

[1] Wellhausen, *Lucas*, pp. 90-91 (16:23 only); Bruce, *Gospels*, p. 589; Leaney, *Luke*, p. 226.

Paradise or heaven and close by him is Lazarus. Luke here follows a Grecized view of the hereafter, according to which "instead of waiting, all alike, in Hades or Sheol, till the Resurrection and the last Judgment, the good and bad are judged at once. Straightway after death, the good go to heaven, the bad to hell."[2] This parable "exemplifies the timeless, ethical application of the view of the hereafter which fits in well with Luke's idea."[3] Similarly, Jesus promises the dying thief that "he shall not merely 'rise' and take part in the Kingdom, but he shall pass at once after death into paradise. Paradise must mean heaven, the heavenly paradise."[4]

B. Dives in Hades (Luke 16:19-31)

1. Luke 16:19-31 and 1 Enoch

When we read today of Lazarus' bliss and Dives' torment we naturally think of a final state of reward and punishment in heaven and hell. But such a picture of immediate judgment and reward at death would run counter to the NT as a whole and to what we have already seen of the eschatology of Luke-Acts. Hence some interpreters would understand these aspects of the parable simply as part of the setting of the story.[5] Such a solution, however, seems to treat too lightly these important elements of the narrative. Thus we would do well to seek another solution which will be more in harmony with the eschatology of Luke-Acts and which takes seriously the eschatological implications of the parable. The answer may well be found in the pre-Christian book of 1 Enoch 22, where we are given a description of the intermediate state which very much resembles that in Luke 16:19-31, and which was probably the popular view in Jesus' day.

1 Enoch 22

1 And thence I went to another place, and he showed me in the west another great and high mountain and of hard rock. 2 And there were four (three) hollow places in it, deep and very smooth: three (two) of them were dark and one bright; and there was a fountain of water in its midst. And I said: "How smooth are these hollow places, and deep and dark to view." 3 Then Raphael answered, one of the holy angels who was with me, and said unto me: "These hollow places have been created for this very purpose, that the spirits of the souls of the dead should assemble therein, yea that all the souls of the children of men should assemble here. 4 And these places have been made to receive them till the day of their judgement and till their appointed period, till the great judgement (comes) upon them."

5 I saw (the spirit of) a dead man making suit, and his voice went forth to heaven and made suit. 6 And I asked Raphael the angel who was with me, and I said unto him: "This spirit which maketh suit, whose is it, whose voice

---

[2]Montefiore, Gospels, II, 538. Similarly, Wellhausen, Lucas, p. 91; Creed, Luke, pp. 212-213; Dupont, "Mort," pp. 15-17, 20; Michel, "Lukas," p. 111.

[3]Conzelmann, Theology, p. 112.

[4]Montefiore, Gospels, II, 627. Also Gilmour, Luke, pp. 290, 411; Bundy, Gospels, p. 542; Hiers, Kingdom of God, p. 88; Historical Jesus, p. 104; Dupont, "Mort," pp. 19-20; Michel, "Lukas," p. 111; Schneider, Parusiegleichnisse, pp. 83-84.

[5]Ellis, Luke, p. 206.

goeth forth and maketh suit to heaven?" 7 And he answered me saying: "This is the spirit which went forth from Abel, whom his brother Cain slew, and he makes his suit against him till his seed is destroyed from the face of the earth, and his seed is annihilated from amongst the seed of men."

8 Then I asked regarding all the hollow places: "Why is one separated from the other?" 9 And he answered me saying: "These three have been made that the spirits of the dead might be separated. And this division has been made for the spirits of the righteous, in which there is the bright spring of water.

10 And this has been made for sinners when they die and are buried in the earth and judgement has not been executed upon them in their lifetime. 11 Here their spirits shall be set apart in this great pain, till the great day of judgement, scourgings, and torments of the accursed for ever so that (there may be) retribution for their spirits. There He shall bind them for ever.

12 And this division has been made for the spirits of those who make their suit, who make disclosures concerning their destruction, when they were slain in the days of the sinners. 13 And this has been made for the spirits of men who shall not be righteous but sinners, who are godless, and of the lawless they shall be companions: but their spirits shall not be punished in the day of judgement nor shall they be raised from thence."

14 Then I blessed the Lord of Glory and said: "Blessed art Thou, Lord of righteousness, who rulest over the world."

According to 1 Enoch 22, this intermediate state is for the souls of the dead until the day of judgment (22:3-4). This abode of the dead is divided into three "hollow places," which are staging areas appointed for waiting until the last judgment:

1) a division for the spirits of the righteous, "in which there is a bright spring of water" (22:9);

2) a division for prosperous sinners who have escaped punishment in this life; here they are "set apart in this great pain" until they arise to even severer punishments (22:10-11);

3) and a division for those sinners who suffered in this life and who therefore receive less punishment after death (22:12).

The resemblances between Luke 16:19-31 and 1 Enoch 22 are striking:[6]

As in 1 Enoch 22 the souls of the dead are in an intermediate state awaiting the judgment, so too in Luke the scene depicted is one taking place in this age before the end, the resurrection, and the last judgment, for the five brothers are living on this earth and have not yet died or experienced the end-time events such as those described in Luke 20:27-40; 21:5-36, and in other Lukan apocalypses. Of course, if the souls of Dives and Lazarus have gone directly to their final reward in heaven and hell, the brothers would also be living on earth. But in view of Luke's apocalyptic emphasis elsewhere, it is more natural to suppose that he is here thinking of conditions in the nether world preceding the

---

[6]Dupont, "Mort," p. 21, finds the closest parallels to Luke's "individual eschatology" in 1 Enoch, yet he makes no use of Enoch, not even in his discussion of Luke 16:19-31.

end and all of the realistic events connected therewith.

The Hades of 1 Enoch 22 is divided so as to separate the righteous from the unrighteous. Likewise the Hades of Luke 16 is divided, with a "great gulf fixed" (16:26) between Dives in one division and Lazarus, we may suppose, in the other, in the place of honor at a feast, at the table reclining in Abraham's bosom (cf. John 13:23). The phrase "great gulf" (*chasma mega*) is found in the NT only in Luke 16:26, but it also occurs in 1 Enoch 18:11, where it is used of a deep abyss, a place of punishment, beyond which Enoch sees another place of punishment, a horrible place without water (18:12).[7]

Enoch's division for the righteous has a "fountain of water in its midst" (22:2), a "bright spring of water" (22:9). This feature makes sense of Dives' request: "Father Abraham, . . . send Lazarus to dip the end of his finger in water and cool my tongue" (Luke 16:24). In the light of 1 Enoch we can see that Dives is alluding to the spring of water flowing through the abode of the righteous in Sheol. This abode may contain, in addition to the spring, Abraham's bosom. Moreover, the water of 1 Enoch 22:2,9 may be the magical water of life mentioned in 1 Enoch 17:4. If so, then we can understand how a mere drop of the water could completely quench Dives' thirst (Luke 16:24).[8]

The second division of Enoch's Hades (22:10-11) is made to order for Dives: In Jesus' parable, Dives "feasted sumptuously every day" (Luke 16:19) and received his "good things" in his "lifetime" (*zōē*), and thus suffers the fate of Enoch's prosperous sinners upon whom judgment has not been executed in their "lifetime" (*zōē*) (1 Enoch 22:10). Both 1 Enoch 22:10 and Luke 16:25 use *zōē* for "lifetime." "This parallel is very striking, since the use of *zōē* in this sense of 'lifetime' is almost if not quite unique in the New Testament. 1 Cor 15:19 and, less clearly 1 Ti 4:8, are the only passages which show any resemblance to this usage."[9] The same phrase "in their lifetime" (*zōē*) also appears twice in 1 Enoch 103:5-6, in a passage also dealing with the fate of the unrighteous in Sheol, a passage which fits Dives' sumptuous life quite well: "Blessed were the sinners all their days that they saw in their lifetime, And they have died in glory, and there was no judgment in their lifetime."[10]

Dives died and was buried honorably (Luke 16:22) like the sinners of Enoch's second division "made for sinners when they die and are buried in the earth" (1 Enoch 22:10). These intentional references to burial are not superfluous, for lack of burial was regarded as punishment with atoning power, whereas proper burial indicated that the person had escaped earthly punishment and therefore would receive the full measure of his punishment after death.

As Dives is in anguish and torment (Luke 16:23,24,25,28), so Enoch's sinners who escaped punishment in this life are "set apart in this great pain," with scourgings and torments till the final judgment (1 Enoch 22:11). The phrase "in torments" (*en basanois*) appears in 1 Enoch 22:11 and Luke 16:23. Luke 16:28 refers to "this place of torment," using the same word again (*basanos*), but with

---

[7]Grensted, "Enoch," p. 334.

[8]Grensted, "Enoch," p. 334, who credits W. H. Bennett with this suggestion. Standen, "Enoch 22," p. 523, also finds echoes of 1 Enoch 22 in Luke 16:19-31.

[9]Grensted, "Enoch," p. 334.

[10]From Aalen, "Enoch," p. 5.

the definite article suggesting "the influence of some well-known account of the next world."[11] *Basanos* occurs in the NT only in this parable and in Matt 4:24, where it refers to diseases.

Similarly in 1 Enoch 103:5-8, prosperous sinners who die in their wealth without beng punished in this life descend into the intermediate state of Hades, into "darkness and chains and a burning flame" (*en phlogi kaiomenē*) (103:8), a condition which recalls Dives' "anguish in this flame" (*en tē phlogi tautē*).

It is commonly held that in 1 Enoch 103:5-8 "Sheol" means, not the place of preliminary punishment lasting until the last judgment, but "hell," the final place of eternal punishment.[12] But since the publication of the Greek text in 1937 the situation has changed. The Greek version of 103:7-8 reads: "You yourselves know that they will take your souls down to Hades, and there they shall be in great anguish 8 and in darkness and in toils and in burning flame. And your souls shall come into a great judgement in all the generations of the age (or: eternity)."[13] On this text Aalen comments: "It seems clear that the Greek text speaks of two stages in the lot of the impious: the punishment in Hades (with 'burning flame') and the Great Judgement. From 98.10; 99.15; 100.4; 104.5 it is evident that the 'Great Judgement' refers to the eschatological judgement."[14] Thus the description of Hades in 1 Enoch 103:7-8 as the intermediate state increases the likelihood that the Hades of Luke 16:19-31 is also the intermediate state.

Returning to 1 Enoch 22, we find that the righteous and wicked in Hades see each other as in the Hades of Luke 16, even as they do in the intermediate state of 4 Ezra 7:85-86,93, though this phenomenon is also true of the final state (Luke 13:28).

As Dives has full consciousness of both his present condition and earthly life, including remembrance of his brothers and their danger of torment in Hades, so too Abel is also fully conscious and recalls his brother, who also stands under judgment (1 Enoch 22:5-7). Finally, the phrase "retribution for their spirits" (1 Enoch 22:11) "suggests the very moral of the parable" (Luke 16:19-31).[15]

What, then, are we to make of these marked similarities between Luke 16:19-31 and 1 Enoch 22? Here are the conclusions of the three authors whose works we have used in this unit:

> Clearly these resemblances postulate Jesus' use of the visions of Enoch, at all events, in the teaching of this parable.[16]

> It seems difficult to believe that these are accidental coincidences, especially in the case of the words *chasma* (gulf), *zōē* (lifetime), and *basanos* (torment). But if not we must conclude that the whole parable is based on Enoch, and, in particular, the problem whether Lazarus was also "in Hades" has found its

---

[11] Grensted, "Enoch," p. 334.
[12] *APOT*, II, 275; Charles, *Eschatology*, pp. 251-252; contrariwise, Str-B, 4.2.1017-1018.
[13] From Aalen, "Enoch," p. 9; the Greek translation probably dates before A.D. 70 (p. 10).
[14] Aalen, "Enoch," p. 9.
[15] Grensted, "Enoch," p. 334.
[16] Standen, "Enoch 22," p. 523.

solution.[17]

Confronted with such affinities one is tempted to ask: Was the relationship in question more than a literary one? Was Luke personally acquainted with the man who translated 1 Enoch? Or was he perhaps himself this man?[18]

But whatever the precise relationship between Luke 16:19-31 and 1 Enoch, it seems quite probable that Luke has handed down to us Enoch's popular conception of Hades as a divided intermediate state, with Lazarus in the happy side, which includes Abraham's bosom and the fountain of magical, living water, and Dives in the unhappy side, separated by a great chasm. Here Dives and Lazarus experience preliminary blessing and punishment and await the resurrection, when the souls in Hades will be united with their bodies to stand in the last judgment. This was the view held in the church until about A.D. 200.[19]

2. "Hades" in the New Testament

These results are confirmed by a study of the word "Hades" in the NT. "Hades" appears only ten times in the entire NT: twice in Matthew (11:23; 16:18); four times in Luke-Acts (Luke 10:15; 16:23; Acts 2:27,31); and four times in Revelation (1:18; 6:8; 20:13; 20:14).

In the Apocalypse of John, Hades is clearly the temporary abode of all the dead, both good and evil, with the exception of Moses and Elijah (11:3-12), who according to tradition ascended to heaven, and the martyrs (6:9), whose souls as a special reward for martyrdom have gone directly to heaven to await there the resurrection. Christ is pictured as having "the keys of death and of Hades" (1:18), Hades being the abode of the dead. Hades is personified as sickness and death from war and famine and as such follows the angel of death riding upon the pale horse (6:8). Before the last judgment, Hades as the intermediate abode of the dead gives up the dead in it (20:13), and since its function is over, Hades is once and for all disposed of in the fiery lake (20:14).

In Matt 11:23//Luke 10:15 Jesus warns that Capernaum will be brought down unto Hades. Here Hades may well be the temporary abode of the dead, for in this same pericope Jesus refers to the last judgment (Matt 11:22,24; Luke 10:13), which Capernaum would await in Hades. According to Matt 16:18 "the gates of Hades shall not prevail' against the church. This is probably an allusion to the powers of darkness issuing from the intermediate dwelling-place of the dead.

In Acts 2:27 Luke quotes from Ps 16:10: "Because thou wilt not leave my soul unto Hades, Neither wilt thou give thy Holy One to see corruption." In the OT, Hades (Hebrew: *Sheol*) is a dark, deep, dreary, depressing den of the deceased, a scene of silence, shadows, shades, sameness, and separation from living men and the living God. According to the OT, Hades was not a state of utter non-existence nor of total extinction, but a weakened, undesirable kind of

---

[17]Grensted, "Enoch," p. 334.

[18]Aalen, "Enoch," p. 13.

[19]Irenaeus, *Adversus Haereses* 5.31.2; Tertullian, *Contra Marcion* 4.34, though apparently there are no parallels in Jewish literature which refer to the happy side of Sheol as Abraham's bosom (Str-B 2.226-227). Godet, *Luke*, II, 179, 335, locates Paradise and Gehenna in Hades, as does Plummer, *Luke*, p. 393, but Plummer goes on to say that in this parable "there is nothing to show whether Hades is intermediate or final" (p. 398).

existence to which all must eventually come, but which was to be avoided so long as possible.[20]

For Luke, however, Hades is only a temporary abode, as indicated by the explanation of Ps 16:10 given in Acts 2:31: "He [David] foreseeing this [the establishment of the throne of David's kingdom forever -- 1 Sam 7:12-13] spake of the resurrection of the Christ, that neither was he left unto Hades, nor did his flesh see corruption." According to the Lukan understanding, then, Jesus' body was buried in a tomb (Luke 23:50-56; we have noted the reference to Dives' burial in Luke 16:22). God preserved his body from decay (Acts 2:27, 31), and his soul descended into Hades (Acts 2:27, 31). Then God raised him up (Acts 2:32) on the third day (Luke 9:22; 18:33), as a unity of flesh, bones, and spirit (Luke 24:36-43; Acts 10:41). In this uniquely Lukan stress upon the flesh and bones of the Risen Christ we see how far removed Luke is from a Greek anthropology and concept of immortality consisting of a complete liberation from the corrupting body of flesh.[21] Likewise, as we have seen (Chap. III.B.1), the bodies of Dives and Lazarus are on earth and their souls are in the appropriate division of Sheol, where they await the resurrection of the body of flesh for reunification with the soul.

Further light upon Luke's conception of Hades is shed by Acts 2:24, where God raised up Jesus, "having loosed the pangs of death: because it was not possible that he should be held by it." Here Luke conceives of Hades as travailing with countless souls in her womb. When God brought forth Jesus out of the womb of Hades, these travail pangs were loosed or ended and the way was opened for others to follow in the general resurrection at the end of this age.

In short, the NT concept of Hades in general and the Lukan concept in particular indicates that Luke did not platonize apocalyptic eschatology either by adopting the Greek idea of the immortality of the soul or by surrendering the present-future tension between the two ages in favor of a vertical tension between heaven and earth.

The Death and Exaltation of Jesus in Luke-Acts

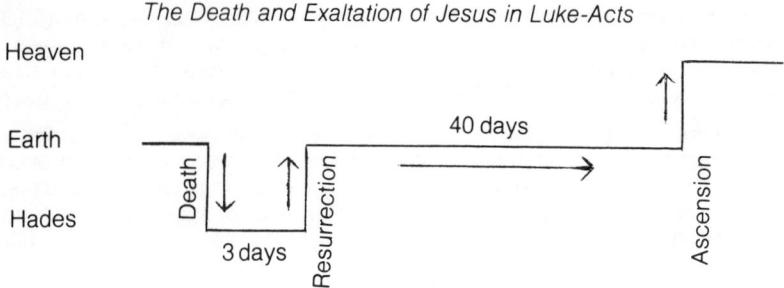

Chart from Cadbury, "Acts and Eschatology," p. 305. Luke has telescoped events at Luke 24:26,51.

---

[20] Job 3:17-19; Ps 16:10-11; 23:4; 88:4-5,10-12; 139:8; Eccl 9:10; Isa 14:9-11; Ezek 32:17-32.

[21] On Luke's view of man and time see further Ellis, *Eschatology*, pp. 8-10.

C. The Thief in Paradise (Luke 23:43)

The other chief passage which has often lent itself to a platonizing interpretation is Luke 23:43: "Today thou shalt be with me in Paradise." The term "Paradise" is a word which the Hebrews borrowed from the Persian language, in which it meant a royal park or garden, the enclosed pleasure-ground of a noble or king, richly wooded, well-watered, and amply stocked with game. "Paradise" appears in Neh 2:8; Eccl 2:5; and Cant 4:13, in the sense of park or pleasure-ground. By Jesus' time various and uncertain ideas of Paradise had become current among the Jewish people, so that it was thought of as an earthly place, sometimes as a heavenly scene, sometimes as a reality of the distant future; above the earth, on the earth, below the earth; now as the intermediate state, now as the final state.

In the NT "Paradise" is found only in Luke 23:43; 2 Cor 12:4; and Rev 2:7. In 2 Cor 12:2 Paul reports that he was "caught up even to the third heaven." Then he goes on to say that he was "caught up into Paradise" (12:4). Thus we may assume that Paul locates Paradise in the third heaven. A similar identification is found in the Secrets of Enoch 8:1-4:

> And those men [angels] took me [Enoch] thence, and led me up to the third heaven, and placed me there; and I looked downwards, and saw the produce of these places, such as has never been known for goodness. 2 And I saw all the sweet-flowering trees and beheld their fruits, which were sweet-smelling, and all the foods borne by them bubbling with fragrant exhalation. 3 And in the midst of the trees that of life, in that place whereupon the Lord rests, when he goes up into paradise; and this tree is of ineffable goodness and fragrance, and adorned more than every existing thing: and on all sides it is in form gold-looking and vermilion and fire-like and covers all, and it has produce from all fruits. Its root is in the garden at the earth's end.

Perhaps Paul would have agreed with those rabbis who thought Paradise was stored in heaven but would descend to earth at the end of days.

In Rev 2:7 the Spirit says to the churches: "To him that overcometh, to him will I give to eat of the tree of life, which is in the Paradise of God." This Paradise would be the new Eden on the new earth in the new age, for in John's vision of the new age he sees a river of water of life and the tree of life, bearing twelve manner of fruits (22:2).

As for the meaning of Paradise in Luke 23:43, the quickest solution would be to follow Marcion in omitting the entire verse. But since there is no other manuscript evidence for such an omission we must accept the verse as an original part of the text.

If Jesus actually spoke these words, it is possible that he may have meant that his death on the cross would compel the general resurrection and the new age to take place at once, so that he and the thief would participate in the new Eden (=kingdom, v. 42) that very day, the Paradise as described by John the Revelator (Rev 2:7; 22:2).[22] But it is unlikely that to Luke the saying meant Paradise as the new Eden of the new age, for the resurrection and new age did not come with the

---

[22] A possibility also raised by Hiers, *Historical Jesus*, pp. 93, 104.

day of crucifixion.

Again, to Jesus Luke 23:43 may have meant that he and the thief would ascend that day to the heavenly Paradise, such as is depicted by Paul and the Secrets of Enoch, possibly as a reward for martyrdom. But Luke would not have thought of the heavenly Paradise, for according to Acts 2:27,31 (as we have seen in Chap.III.B.2), Jesus did not ascend immediately to heaven but went to Hades to await his resurrection and ascension. If Luke had conceived of Paradise as being above, he at Luke 16:22 would probably have referred to Lazarus' being taken *up* into Paradise, as Paul tells of his "being caught *up* into Paradise" (2 Cor 12:4), or as Enoch relates that the angels took him *up* to the third heaven (Secrets of Enoch 8:1). Hence it is most likely that Luke conceived of Paradise, like Abraham's bosom, as being in the happy side of Hades, the intermediate state.[23]

This interpretation receives some support from the rabbinic comment on 1 Sam 28:19, where Samuel, conjured up from Sheol by the witch of Endor, says to Saul: "Tomorrow shalt thou and thy sons be with me." In answer to the question, "What is meant by 'with me'?" Rabbi Jochanan (died 279) said: "With me in my compartment."[24] Thus Luke 23:43 could well be a promise that the thief would join Jesus that very day in the paradisiacal compartment of Sheol, where the righteous dead await the resurrection, judgment, and world-to-come.

Further, in 1 Enoch 37-70 and in the Noachic fragments of 1 Enoch (6-11; 54:7-55:2; 60; 65:1-69:25; 106-107), Paradise (Garden of Righteousness) is the abode of the departed righteous. In 1 Enoch 1-36 these spirits are assigned to a special division in Sheol. Therefore it is possible that Paradise and the happy side of Hades are the same place.[25]

D. Cast into Gehenna (Luke 12:4-5)

If the platonizing of Luke's eschatology cannot be established at Luke 16:19-31 and 23:43, how much less can it be demonstrated in other passages, such as Luke 12:4-5; 12:13-21; and 16:1-9.[26] First of all, let us look at Luke 12:4-5 in comparison with its parallel in Matt 10:28:

Matt 10:28	*Luke 12:4-5*
And be not afraid of them that kill the body, but are not able to kill the soul: but rather fear him who is able to destroy both soul and body in hell.	Be not afraid of them that kill the body, and after that have no more that they can do. 5 But I warn you whom ye shall fear: Fear him, who after he hath killed hath the power to cast into hell; yea, I say unto you, Fear him.

---

[23]Plummer, *Luke*, pp. 393, 536; Browning, *Luke*, pp. 135, 164. Grelot, "Luke 23:43," pp. 202-204, also finds "Abraham's bosom" to be in Paradise, the intermediate state. Aalen, "Enoch," p. 10, rightly points out that Paradise and Abraham's bosom, whether in Hades or not, cannot be taken to represent the final state of blessedness but must refer to an intermediate state of rest and waiting.

[24]Str-B 2.265.

[25]Cf. *APOT*, II, 207.

[26]On Acts 7:55-56 see Chap. VI.G.4; on Acts 14:22 see Chap. IV.G.

Luke eliminates Matthew's reference to killing the soul and substitutes for it a reference to persecutors who can do no more after they have killed the body. God, by way of contrast, not only can kill the body, but after that he has authority to throw into Gehenna (hell).

Dupont contends that Luke here focuses his attention upon that which happens after the death of the individual. To Dupont it therefore seems natural to think that the Gehenna of which Luke speaks is a threatening place not only at the last judgment but also after the death of each individual. And if God is able to dispatch the guilty at death to Gehenna, he is also able to bestow salvation at the close of each individual life.[27]

Against Dupont's individualizing interpretation we may raise several objections. Luke 12:4-5 stands at the beginning of "the Fire upon the Earth Apocalypse" (Luke 12:1-13:35), whose collective, end-time nature is very marked (see Chaps. I.C.3; V.F). Here we shall note especially the immediate context.

Hypocrisy (12:1) is folly, for in the last judgment it will be mercilessly exposed (12:2) and brought to light (12:3). At this final unmasking the Son of Man will serve as advocate of the faithful and as accuser of the unfaithful (12:8-9). "Whatever one may lose now by acknowledging Christ or gain by denying him will be more than made up at the advent of the Kingdom of God. Then the Son of Man shall determine the fate of all in the presence of the angels."[28]

Coming now to Luke 12:4-5 we find that these verses are parallel with 12:46, where the Son of Man at his advent first kills (literally: cuts to pieces, dichotomizes) the unfaithful servant and then puts him with the unfaithful (in Gehenna). This is exactly the same situation as described in 12:4-5. Jesus' friends are to fear only the Son of Man, who, at his parousia, has the authority to kill and then to cast into hell. The context, then, clearly eliminates a Grecized, individualized interpretation of 12:4-5.

E. The Rich Fool (Luke 12:13-21)

We may now consider the individualistic interpretation of the parable of the rich fool as set forth by Dupont:[29]

For Jesus, this parable has been interpreted as teaching a general religious truth (the rich man's attitude is not only foolish but impious, in that he forgets his dependence upon God) or as giving instruction concerning the situation in which Jesus' mission places his hearers (the catastrophe which threatens those who do not receive the message of the Kingdom). But, says Dupont, for Luke the foolishness of the rich man consists not so much in not having thought about death as in forgetting that which comes after death. The rich man considers only the advantages of his riches for the present existence and does not see the advantage he can get out of them for his happiness in the next life. Dupont bases his interpretation upon Luke 12:21 in light of Luke 12:33-34//Matt 6:19-21:

---

[27]Dupont, "Mort," p. 12.

[28]Easton, *Luke*, p. 197.

[29]Dupont, "Mort," pp. 4-7; Michel, "Lukas," p. 111; Schneider, *Parusiegleichnisse,* pp. 79-80.

Luke 12:21.--So is he that layeth up treasure for himself, and is not rich toward God.

Matt 6:19-21

Lay not up for yourselves treasures upon the earth, where moth and rust consume, and where thieves break through and steal: 20 but lay up for yourselves treasures in heaven, where neither moth nor rust doth consume, and where thieves do not break through nor steal: 21 for where thy treasure is, there will thy heart be also.

Luke 12:33-34

Sell that which ye have, and give alms; make for yourselves purses which wax not old, a treasure in the heavens that faileth not, where no thief draweth near, neither moth destroyeth. 34 For where your treasure is, there will your heart be also.

For Luke, then, the way to lay up treasure in heaven is to distribute earthly goods. The folly of the rich man consists in laying up treasure only for himself (Luke 12:21) on earth (Matt 6:19) rather than laying up an unfailing treasure in heaven (Luke 12:33) and being rich toward God (12:21) by distributing his possessions as alms (12:33). Luke's perspective, concludes Dupont, is personal death--the moment when treasures of earth fail (cf. 16:9) and when it is important to have at one's disposal unfailing treasures in heaven (12:33).The true disciple is occupied with the treasure which he will have at his disposal in heaven before God at the moment when God requires his soul (12:20).

As attractive as Dupont's Grecized interpretation is, there are several weighty objections to it. The parable of the rich fool, like Luke 12:4-5 just examined in Section D, is found within "the Fire upon the Earth Apocalypse" (12:1-13:35), with its attention focused upon the eschaton rather than upon the death of the individual (Chap. I.C.3; Chap. III.D; Chap. V.F.3). Further, 12:33-34 and 16:9 refer to the heavenly bank in which accounts are credited when alms are given. But the fact that the accounts are in heaven does not mean that the soul goes to heaven at the moment of death. The passbooks would be opened and audited at the last judgment, as was to be the case for most of Luke's people (Luke 9:26-27). But for that minority which would die before the eschaton a preliminary check of the books would be made before the soul was assigned to the appropriate division of Hades.

The Lukan perspective is most clearly seen when we compare Luke's parable with its parallel in Sir 11:18-19:[30] "There is a man who is rich through his diligence and self-denial, and this is the reward allotted to him: 19 when he says, 'I have found rest, and now I shall enjoy my goods!'he does not know how much time will pass until he leaves them to others and dies." Here the focus is upon the death of the individual and the passing of his goods to heirs. But in Luke the question is: "And the things which thou hast prepared, whose shall they be?" (12:20). And the answer is not, "the heirs," but "they will perish." For Luke, the event which reduces trust in riches to an absurdity is not death but the breaking in of the eschaton: "We are fools like the rich man threatened by death, when we place our trust in earthly goods, for the end is near, when our possessions will perish in the fiery consummation."

---

[30] Adapted from Bartsch, *Wachet*, pp. 101-102.

From this point of view we can understand the introductory logion: "Take heed, and keep yourselves from all covetousness: for a man's life consisteth not in the abundance of the things which he possesseth" (12:15). In the Lukan context it means: No one possesses life through a surplus of goods, for our life is not based upon possessions but upon the will of God, which we should obey by selling our belongings and giving the money to the poor in order to be able to pass safely through the approaching judgment.

Interestingly enough, in the later Gospel of Thomas when the eschatological thrust was no longer understood, the individualistic emphasis returns:

> Jesus said: A rich man had many possessions. He said: I will use my possessions so that I may sow and harvest and plant and fill my barns with fruits, so that I will not be in want of anything. That is what he thought in his heart. And in that night he died. He who has ears, let him hear (Logion 63).

F. The Dishonest Manager (Luke 16:1-9)

Finally, Dupont seeks to individualize the parable of the dishonest manager.[31] As Dupont sees it, the image of the manager relieved of his functions accords less well with eschatological events than with the moment of death when one is compelled to give account of his administration of the goods which have been entrusted to him. Luke 16:9 is another form of 12:33: the best use of money is to make friends for the future, that is, to provide treasure in heaven. It is essential to note also the parallelism between 16:4 and 16:9:

16:4.--I am resolved what to do (*poieō*), that, when (*hina hotan*) I am put out of the stewardship, they may receive me (*dexōntai me*) into their houses.

16:9.--Make (*poieō*) to yourselves friends by means of the mammon of unrighteousness: that, when (*hina hotan*) it shall fail, they may receive you (*dexōntai humas*) into the eternal tabernacles.

In the light of this parallelism, continues Dupont, it is impossible to escape identifying the "friends" with the poor who have benefited from alms. The welcome which the poor give to their benefactors in the eternal tents corresponds to that which the dishonest manager anticipates from the debtors who have profited by his generosity. The perspective is thus that of the death of the individual, as is also indicated by connections with two other accounts with the same outlook, the rich fool (12:13-21) and Dives (16:19-31). The prudence of the manager stands in contrast to the foolishness of the rich fool of chap. 12. The manager's wise use of money also stands out against Dives' blindness.

Dupont also observes that the "eternal tabernacles" (16:9) correspond to the "unfailing treasure" (12:33). "Eternal" refers to duration rather than to eschatological events at the end of time. The tension is not between this world and the world to come but between realities here below and those of heaven above. The "eternal tabernacles" (16:9) are comparable to "Paradise" (23:43).

---

[31]Dupont, "Mort," pp. 12-15; Schneider, *Parusiegleichnisse*, p. 80. Hiers, "Friends," p. 36, treats only incidentally the question of the intermediate versus the final state at death.

The moment when earthly riches give out is that of death, when it is a matter of being received into the eternal tabernacles.

By way of reaction to this platonizing interpretation we note that in 16:9 there is a textual variant as reflected in the KJV: "when ye fail," that is, some late manuscripts use the plural form of the verb rather than the singular, "when it fails." This plural reading is poorly attested and today is almost universally rejected. Metzger's *Textual Commentary* does not even consider it. This variant is important for our purposes, however, for it is the reading which best fits the individualized interpretation. "When ye fail" means " when ye die." Luke 16:9 would then read: "Use mammon, dishonest as it is, to make friends for yourselves so that when you die they may welcome you to the eternal abodes" (Moffatt). If Luke had intended to treat the problem of the fate of the individual after death he surly would have used the second person plural, even as did the later scribes who were unaware of the apocalyptic meaning of the parable.[32]

By far the better attested reading is the singular form, "when it fails," which has the unusually strong support of Papyrus 75 and codices Vaticanus, Sinaiticus, and Bezae. But the question arises, "What is the antecedent of 'it'?" The prevailing answer is "mammon" or "wealth": "when the mammon fails"= "when you die." This interpretation, however, is contrary to the sense of the parable, according to which (16:4,9) wealth does not fail at death but is efficacious to secure one a welcome into the eternal tents.

If, on the other hand, the failure of the money means "when your money gives out" (TEV), then it should be noted that life does not necessarily give out when one's money does, as witness the prodigal son, who spent everything he had (Luke 15:14), yet did not die. Thus the view that "it" refers to money failing or giving out at the death of the individual is untenable, because money, according to the parable, does not fail when life ends, nor does life necessarily end when the money runs out.

We may also observe that the singular verb taken to mean "when the money fails when you die" is equivalent in meaning to the plural form, "when you die." How much simpler it would have been for Luke, if he had intended this meaning, to say so clearly with the plural form.

Because of the difficulties which arise when we take "it" to mean "money," we would do well to look for another possibility. Luke may intend "it" to refer to "mammon" as a symbol of this present evil world: "when mammon (= this world) comes to an end they may receive you into the eternal tabernacles of the new age."[33] This cosmic understanding of "it" (=mammon=old age) has much in its favor. Luke uses the verb "fail" (*ekleipō*) in a cosmic sense to refer to the sun's failing (growing dark, being eclipsed) at the crucifixion (23:45). Another advantage of this cosmic interpretation is that it clarifies the parallelism between 16:9 and 16:4. On the individualistic interpretation "when I am put out of the stewardship" is taken as parallel to "when mammon shall fail at death." But on the cosmic interpretation the manager's "old world" comes to an end when his

---

[32] The plural reading is also adopted by R. Knox: "And my counsel to you is, make use of your base wealth to win yourselves friends, who, when you leave it behind, will welcome you into eternal habitations."

[33] Cf. Creed, *Luke*, p. 205; Aalen, "Enoch," p. 6.

old job is gone (16:4), even as on a large scale the whole world passes away (16:9). The manager then begins a new life in a "new world," even as do those who make friends by means of unrighteous mammon.

This cosmic understanding of 16:9 also accords well with the cosmic interpretation of the parable of the rich fool, according to which all wealth and possessions also perish at the end of the age (12:20). But though money will pass away with this age, the efficacy of money spent as alms will not fail in the world to come (16:4,9; 12:33). And the parallelism between 16:9 and 12:33 speaks in favor of the eschatological interpretation, for we have already seen the eschatological nature of 12:33 (Chap. III.E).

Of much probative force is the fact that a similar usage of the verb "fail" (*ekleipō*) is found in 1 Enoch 100:5, where we are told that the evils and sin of this world will come to an end (*ekleipō*):

> The form of the verb is almost the same (present and aorist subjunctive) in both texts. The view in both cases is also related. Mammon is regarded, in Enoch (v. 6) as well as in Luke, as the symbol of the present age of unrighteousness which is followed by the age of blessedness. And in both texts the verb *ekleipō* indicates the passing of the present evil age.[34]

This two-age dichotomy is explicit in Luke 16:8, where reference is made to "the sons of this world" in contrast to "the sons of light," that is, "sons of the new age." And it is not impossible that the antecedent of "it" (16:9) is "this world (age)" of 16:8: "when this world comes to an end."

If this apocalyptic view of 16:9 is correct, then "the eternal tents" (16:9) are not "heaven" above which the soul enters as a final reward immediately upon death (individualistic interpretation). Rather "the eternal tents" are the tents of **Abraham under the oaks at Mamre magnified into an image of the glorified Canaan of the new age,**[35] or the temporary tents of the wilderness projected as the final eschatological shelter, in contrast to the manager's temporary shelter (cf. Ezek 37:27; Luke 9:33; Acts 15:16; Rev 7:15; 21:3).

NEB's rendition is perhaps an attempt to bring out the cosmic implications of 16:9: "So I say to you, use your worldly wealth to win friends for yourselves, so that when money is a thing of the past you may be received into an eternal home." Once more we see that a Grecized interpretation cannot be established.

G. A Lukan Inconsistency?

If our exegesis of Luke 12:4-5; 12:13-21; 16:1-9; 16:19-31; and 23:43 is correct, then Luke did not adopt the Greek idea of the immortality of the soul or the accompanying Greek conceptions of man and of time. But even if Luke did do so, it does not necessarily follow that he abandoned the apocalyptic framework. Dupont, for example, concludes that Luke's special interest in the fate of the individual after death does not exclude collective eschatology. Luke simply does not seek to harmonize his individual and collective eschatologies, not even by means of an intermediate state nor by positing a Hellenistic particular judgment of each individual at death as a substitute for a final, general judgment.[36]

---

[34]Aalen, "Enoch," p. 6.

[35]Cf. Godet, *Luke*, II, 166.

[36]Dupont, "Mort," pp. 20-21.

We began this chapter by quoting from the Wisdom of Solomon 3:1-6 to illustrate the concept of immortality within Judaism. Yet in 3:7 the author pictures the visible victory of the righteous over the unrighteous: "And in the time of their visitation they shall shine forth, And like sparks among stubble they shall run to and fro." Here the righteous execute judgment on the ungodly; the righteous use the sword to inaugurate the messianic kingdom. Moreover, in 5:17-23 the Lord himself rouses the forces of nature to fight the unrighteous. These verses clash with the view of 3:1-7 that reward and punishment follow immediately upon death. Again, the day of judgment also appears in 3:18 and 4:20-5:13, after which the righteous will receive a glorious kingdom (5:16), which again is inconsistent with the belief that the soul receives its full and final reward immediately after death.

The author of Wisdom thus held a mixture of eschatologies, probably without ever noting their inconsistency.[37] Luke likewise could conceivably have mixed apocalyptic and Hellenistic eschatologies, perhaps being oblivious to the intellectual difficulties involved. If so, Luke was not the first nor the last who failed to work out a consistent eschatology. But the overall impression of a coherent eschatology which one gets from the first page to the last of Luke's two volumes is such as to warn against a too facile acceptance of such inconsistency on Luke's part.

H. Conclusion

Luke nowhere explicitly says that the soul at death goes to its final reward in heaven or punishment in hell. We have tried to show that texts which have been so interpreted fit more naturally into the apocalyptic framework of intermediate and final states.

For Luke, the end is near but not immediate (Chaps. IV, V, VI), that is, Luke is at the point on the apocalyptic timetable when he naturally gives attention to the fate of the individual at the moment of death (Luke 16:19-31; 23:43). Yet the parousia, resurrection, and judgment are near enough that Luke sees no need to abandon the intermediate state in favor of a timeless, eternal, final state at death, for Luke does not envision a very long stay in either the happy or unhappy sides of Hades.

Luke at his juncture in the apocalyptic program finds the concepts of an intermediate state to be followed soon by all of the realistic end-time events to be an adequate framework for his eschatological hopes. Therefore Luke can allow for the death of individuals before the parousia, with preliminary blessing and punishment in the intermediate state, but also he can stress salvation in the kingdom of God and punishment in Gehenna at the end of the world for most of his readers. Luke's eschatological pronouncements are tailored to fit both groups of his people: the minority who will die before the end and the majority who will live to see the end with all of its associated cosmic events.

---

[37]This interpretation of Wisdom is adapted from *APOT*, I, 529, 539, 543. Grelot, "Luke 23:43," pp. 204-205, thinks that entry into full blessedness (3:1-6; 5:15-16) is reserved until the day of visitation (3:8) and the last judgment (5:1-13). Similarly, Aalen, "Enoch," pp. 11-12, finds the righteous dead to be in an intermediate state of rest (4:7) or peace (3:1).

Chapter IV
"Before Long" (Acts 17:31):
The Imminent Expectation in Acts

A. Introductory Considerations

In Chaps. II and III we have sought to refute the views which have it that Luke de-apocalypticized the original tradition by platonizing it and by working out a new three-fold structure of salvation history. Now we turn our attention to the claim that Luke, in view of the delay of the parousia, has given up hope in a quick return of the Lord and has postponed that event to the far distant future.

The study of Luke-Acts today is dominated by the Distant Expectation School (*Fernerwartungsschule*) (Chap. II, note 2), which holds that there is no imminent expectation in Luke-Acts. To establish the lively existence of the *Naherwartung* (imminent expectation) in Luke-Acts, we shall begin with Acts, where the *Naherwartung* is more concealed than it is in Luke's Gospel. If we can demonstrate the presence of the hope of a speedy consummation in the more difficult case, Acts, then, in view of the unity of Luke-Acts, we shall have gone far toward establishing this same hope in the Third Gospel.

Not only has the hope of an early end in Luke-Acts been denied but, surprisingly, the generally accepted unity of Luke-Acts, for some would find the imminent expectation in Luke but not in Acts.[1] Hence if we can find the *Naherwartung* in both volumes we shall have helped to shore up the unity of Luke-Acts.

We call attention to the imminent expectation as expressed in four verses of Acts in Weymouth's translation:[2] 10:42; 17:31; 24:15; 24:25. Behind Weymouth's edition stands the weight of his authority as a Greek scholar. His translation is the fruit of over sixty years' study of Greek, and therefore is not lightly to be cast aside.

B. "Judge of the Living and the Dead" (Acts 10:42)

In Acts 10:42 Peter says: "And He has commanded us to preach to the people and solemnly declare that this is He who has been appointed by God to be the Judge of the living and the dead"(Weymouth). On this verse Hampden-Cook, the editor, notes: "A special reference may be intended to those who were alive at the time Peter spoke. If so the word shows that he expected Christ to return as

---

[1] Wilson, "Lukan Eschatology," pp. 343, 347.

[2] We are using the third edition (1909), edited by Ernest Hampden-Cook. Chap. IV is based on my "Weymouth Reconsidered," which is heavily annotated for those interested in additional references.

King and Judge within the lifetime of that generation."³ This interpretation fits well with other Lukan passages concerning that generation:

> I tell you truly that there are some of those who stand here who will certainly not taste death till they have seen the Kingdom of God (Luke 9:27) (Weymouth).

> For this reason also the Wisdom of God has said, I will send Prophets and Apostles to them, of whom they will kill some and persecute others, so that the blood of all the Prophets, that is being shed from the creation of the world onwards, may be required from the present generation. Yes, I tell you that, from the blood of Abel down to the blood of Zechariah who perished between the altar and the House (Enoch 9:1), it shall all be required from the present generation (11:49-51) (Weymouth).

> You know how to read the aspect of earth and sky. How is it you cannot read this present time? (12:56)(Weymouth).

> If you do not repent you will all perish just as they did (13:5) (Weymouth).

> If after that it bears fruit, well and good; if it does not, then you shall cut it down (13:9)(Weymouth).

> I tell you in solemn truth that the present generation will certainly not pass away without all these things having first taken place (21:32) (Weymouth).

> And it shall come to pass in the last days, God says, That I will pour out My Spirit upon all mankind (Acts 2:17)(Weymouth).

> Yes, and all the Prophets, from Samuel onwards--all who have spoken--have also announced the coming of this present time (3:24)(Weymouth).

> Behold, you despisers, be astonished and perish, because I am carrying on a work in your time--a work which you will utterly refuse to believe, though it be fully declared to you (13:41) (Weymouth).

The Gospel passages will be considered in Chapter V.

Hampden-Cook's observation is also supported by the fact that "to be the Judge of the living and the dead" was perhaps a "fixed formula in a baptismal creed,"⁴ "a very old kerygmatic formula,"⁵ with imminent overtones. This formula is used in 2 Tim 4:1 (see also below, Section F): "I solemnly implore you in the presence of God and of Christ Jesus who is about to judge the living and the dead, and by His appearing and His Kingship: proclaim God's message" (Weymouth). "It might perhaps be that we should understand a sense of nearness here, and that his appearing to judge is not far off."⁶

This formula also appears in 1 Pet 4:5: "But they will have to give account to Him who stands ready to pronounce judgement on the living and the dead" (Weymouth). On this verse Hampden-Cook remarks that "the living" refers to "those who were alive at the time this Letter was written; an indication that Peter expected the Second Advent to take place in the lifetime of his contemporaries."⁷ This understanding of 1 Pet 4:5 harmonizes well with the context, for 1 Pet 4:7 warns that "the end of all things is now close at hand" (Weymouth). Thus it is

---

³Weymouth, p. 343.

⁴Lock, *Pastoral Epistles*, p. 112.

⁵Haenchen, *Apostelgeschichte*, p. 3.

⁶Falconer, *Pastoral Epistles*, p. 94, quoted by Moore, *Parousia*, p. 164.

⁷Weymouth, p. 648.

highly probable that Acts 10:42 is at one with 2 Tim 4:1 and 1 Pet 4:5 in using the same judgment formula to express the *Naherwartung.*

Moreover, the one who has been appointed (*horidzō*) to be judge of the living and the dead (Acts 10:42) is the Son of Man who is appointed (*horidzō*) to come in judgment at the end of the age (17:31).[8] And as we shall shortly see (Section D), the Son of Man expectation was an imminent one, which is further substantiation for the imminent sense of 10:42.

C. The Imminent Hope in Acts 17:31; 24:15; 24:25: General Considerations

1. Weymouth's Translation of *Mellō* in 17:31; 24:15,25

Let us now examine the other three verses in the Weymouth translation:

> But now He commands all men everywhere to repent, seeing that He hath appointed a day on which, before long (*mellō*), he will judge the world in righteousness, through the instrumentality of a man whom He has pre-destined to this work, and has made the fact certain to every one by raising Him from the dead (17:30-31)(Weymouth).

> ... having a hope directed towards God, ... that before long (*mellō*) there will be a resurrection both of the righteous and the unrighteous (24:15) (Weymouth).

> But when he dealt with the subjects of justice, self-control, and the judgement which was soon to come (*mellō*), Felix became alarmed (24:25) (Weymouth).

In the light of today's lively discussion of Lukan eschatology, the significance of Weymouth's translation of the verb *mellō* in these verses can readily be seen. Most translations render *mellō* in these passages by the simple future, as, for example, the American Standard Version of 1900: God "hath appointed a day in which he will judge the world" (17:31); "there shall be a resurrection" (24:15); and as Paul "reasoned of . . . the judgment to come, Felix was terrified" (24:25).

Naturally the *Fernerwartungsschule* denies the *Naherwartung* in these verses. Acts 17:31 is said to be simply good Lukan eschatology, not concerned with the imminent judgment but only with its actuality. 24:15 gives us the resurrection faith in its general Lukan form. 24:25 is a typical Lukan condensation of Christianity: ethics and future judgment.[9]

Weymouth, however, was not the first nor the last to bring out the imminent hope expressed by *mellō* in these three verses. Perhaps the earliest was Matthias Schneckenburger, who noted this hope in Acts 3:19-20; 17:30-31; 26:7; and 24:15,25, but without giving his reasons therefor and without mentioning *mellō*.[10] Since then many authorities have followed suit.[11] Let us now turn to the evidence.

2. The Root Meaning of *Mellō*

In favor of Weymouth's translation of 17:31; 24:15; and 24:25 we may note that he has given us the most obvious and natural translation, were one to come to Acts without any presuppositions as to the Lukan eschatology, for the primary

---

[8]See Lake and Cadbury, *Acts*, p. 122; Macgregor, *Acts*, p. 140.

[9]Conzelmann, *Apostelgeschichte*, pp. 102, 133; Schneider, *Parusiegleichnisse*, p. 87.

[10]Schneckenburger, *Apostelgeschichte*, p. 250.

[11]See my "Weymouth Reconsidered," p. 278.

meaning of *mellō* is "to be on the point to do or suffer something."[12]

3. *Mellō* in Acts

Moreover, in Acts 20, where *mellō* appears five times (vv 3,7,13,13,38), this verb "gives to the whole chapter the tone of looking forward to the immediate future":

> As Paul was *on the point of* taking ship, a plot was laid against him by the Jews (20:3). Paul spoke to the people, for he was *soon* to depart the next day (20:7). We sailed off to Assos, where we would *soon* pick up Paul (20:13), for he was *about* to go by foot (20:13). They grieved at his words that they were *on the point of* seeing him no more (20:38).[13]

By means of this skilful repetition of *mellō* in this action-packed chapter Luke points forward to the even greater excitement of the next chapter, chap. 21, which may be the most exciting chapter in the Bible.[14]

May we not, then, say that the thirty-four appearances of *mellō* in Acts give to the whole book the tone of looking forward to the immediate future? Or, more precisely, especially to the Pauline half of Acts, since thirty of these instances appear in chaps. 13-28? Of the four instances in chaps. 1-12, one (11:28) has to do directly with Paul, and the other three are in Petrine sections long noted to be parallel to Pauline sections (3:3; 5:35; 12:6):

> 3:1-10//14:8-11 (healing of a lame man)
>
> 5:34-39//23:9 (Pharisaic defense)
>
> 12:3-11//16:23-34 (escape from prison)[15]

By this remarkable use of *mellō* Luke has recaptured something of the eschatological urgency of the Pauline mission.

4. An Authentic Pauline Ring

Indeed, Weymouth's translation of our three verses is strongly supported by the fact that this *Naherwartung* fits so well the Paul of the epistles. If 17:31 were given by Paul at the time indicated by Acts, it would be contemporary with his letters to the Thessalonians with their vivid imminent hope:

> For this we declare to you on the Lord's own authority--that we who are alive and continue on earth until the Coming of the Lord, shall certainly not forestall those who shall have previously passed away. For the Lord Himself will come down from Heaven with a loud word of command, and with an archangel's voice and the trumpet of God, and the dead in Christ will rise first. Afterwards we who are alive and are still on earth will be caught up in their company amid clouds to meet the Lord in the air. And so we shall be with the Lord for ever. Therefore encourage one another with these words (1 Thess 4:15-18) (Weymouth).[16]

---

[12]Pickering, *Lexicon*, p. 852.

[13]Rackham, *Acts*, pp. 380, 385.

[14]"Schneckenburger Reconsidered," pp. 115-117.

[15]"Schneckenburger Reconsidered," pp. 110-111.

[16]On this passage Hampden-Cook comments: "The pronouns 'we' and 'you' cannot, as a rule, be used to the total exclusion of the persons speaking or immediately addressed. Therefore here [v 15] and in verse 17 Paul implies that the return of the Lord Jesus would take place in the lifetime of some of the first readers of this Letter" (Weymouth, p. 553).

In the speeches of Acts where Luke lets us hear Paul early (Athens) (17:31) and late (Caesarea) (24:15,25) enunciating his imminent expectation, we perceive an authentic Pauline ring, for this *Naherwartung* is maintained throughout the Pauline epistles (see also 1 Cor 7:26, 29-31; 10:11; 15:51-52; Rom 13:11-12; 16:20; Phil 4:5) (also see the list below of Pauline verses with *mellō* to express the hope of an early advent). In fact, if *mellō* be given its imminent meaning consistently, then the imminent expectation is found from the earliest (1 Thessalonians) to the latest (Pastorals and Hebrews) of the fourteen traditional Paulines.

5. *Mellō* in the New Testament

Weymouth's rendition of 17:31; 24:15; 24:25 is also corroborated by an examination of *mellō* throughout the NT. In the NT as a whole *mellō* has the sense of "soon" sixty times (and is so rendered forty-six times by Weymouth):

Luke-Acts: Luke 7:2; 9:31,44; 10:1; 13:9; 19:4; 22:23; Acts 3:3; 5:35; 11:28; 12:6; 13:34; 16:27; 18:14; 19:27; 20:3,7,13(twice),38; 21:27,37; 22:26,29; 23:3,27; 25:4; 26:2,22; 27:2,10,33; 28:6.

Fourteen Traditional Pauline Epistles: Rom 4:24; 8:13; Gal 3:23; Col 2:17; 1 Tim 1:16; Heb 8:5; 11:8,20.

Other Books: Matt 2:13; 11:14; 17:12,22; 20:17,22; Mark 10:32; John 4:47; 6:6,15; 7:35(twice),39; 12:4,33; 2 Pet 2:6; Rev 3:2; 10:4; 12:4.

And thirty-two times *mellō* is used to indicate the *Naherwartung* (and is so translated twenty-six times by Weymouth):

Luke-Acts: Luke 3:7; 19:11; 21:7,36; 24:21.

Fourteen Traditional Pauline Epistles: Rom 8:18,38; 1 Cor 3:22; 1 Thess 3:4;1 Tim 4:8; 6:19; 2 Tim 4:1; Heb 1:14; 9:11; 10:27; 13:14.

Other Books: Matt 3:7; 16:27; 24:6; Mark 13:4; Jas 2:12; 1 Pet 5:1; Rev 1:19; 2:10(twice); 3:10,16; 6:11; 8:13; 10:7; 12:5; 17:8.

Outside of Acts 17:31; 24:15,25, *mellō* appears 108 times in the NT; ninety-two or eighty-five per cent of these 108 appearances may reasonably be taken to mean "soon" (thirty-two times to indicate the imminent expectation and sixty times otherwise). If, then, *mellō* in the NT in general and in the Lukan-Pauline writings in particular is so frequently used in the sense of "soon" (and often--thirty per cent--to bring out the *Naherwartung*), it seems not unreasonable that it should be so used in Acts 17:31; 24:15,25.

Perhaps *ho mellōn aiōn* should be translated as "the age which is soon to come" (Matt 12:32; Eph 1:21; Heb 6:5), and *hē oikoumenē hē mellou* as "the world soon to come" (Heb 2:5). *Mellō* in the remaining twelve instances deserves further study: John 6:71; 11:51; 14:22; 18:32; Acts 22:16; 23:15,20; 26:23; 27:30; Rom 5:14; Heb 10:1; 2 Pet 1:12.

By means of these general considerations we have sought to establish the possibility, if not the probability, of Weymouth's translation of 17:31; 24:15; and 24:25. Now we shall examine each of these verses separately.

D.*Mellō*, the Son of Man, and the Day of the Lord (Acts 17:31)

According to 17:31, God "will judge the world in righteousness, through the instrumentality of a man whom He has predestined to this work" (Weymouth).

"This is pure 'Son of Man' eschatology."[17] Certainly to Matthew and Mark Son of Man eschatology meant the *Naherwartung*:

> For the Son of Man is soon (*mellō*) to come in the glory of the Father with His angels, and then will He requite every man according to his actions (Matt 16:27) (Weymouth).

> And before long (*mellō*) the Son of Man will be treated by them in a similar way (Matt 17:12) (Weymouth).

> The Son of Man is about to be (*mellō*) betrayed into the hands of men (Matt 17:22) (Weymouth).

> You and others [the judges] will see the Son of Man sitting at the right hand of the divine Power, and coming amid the clouds of the sky (Mark 14:62) (Weymouth).

Weymouth's translation of these Matthean *mellō* verses is supported by W.C. Allen, who remarks on 16:27 that "*mellein*, which here emphasizes the nearness of the coming [of the Son of man], is characteristic of Mt.; cf. 17:12,22 *mellei*."[18] Allen translates *mellō* as "about to" in Matt 2:13; 11:14; 16:27; 17:12,22; 20:22; and 24:6 ("And ye shall be about to hear of wars and rumours of wars").

As we shall see in Section G in connection with Acts 7:55-56, Luke also held that the Son of Man was ready to return. In fact, as 17:31 the Son of Man is even closer to his *parousia* now that the preaching to the Gentiles is so well under way (Chap. VI.H)--this is Paul's second journey and others too have been busy for some time (11:20).

Our contention that Luke in 17:31 has in mind the quick return of the Son of Man receives strong support from the fact that Luke more than once uses *mellō* in connection with the Son of Man to suggest the imminence of coming events. The reference to the Son of Man's coming in glory (Luke 9:26) is followed by the conversation of Moses and Elijah about Jesus' death (*exodus*), which he "was so soon (*mellō*) to undergo in Jerusalem" (9:31) (Weymouth). In 9:44 Luke informs us that "before long (*mellō*), the Son of Man will be betrayed into the hands of men" (Weymouth), within a few months.

In the same breath that Jesus tells his audience that the Son of Man has come to seek and to save that which was lost (19:10), he speaks a parable because they supposed that the kingdom of God was about to appear immediately (*parachrēma mellei*) (19:11). As we shall see later (Chap. VI.D), this passage does not at all imply a *Fernerwartung*, but simply that the imminent end must be preceded by certain eschatological events.

After cosmic woes, men "will see the Son of Man coming in a cloud with great power and glory" (21:27); "deliverance is drawing near" (21:28) (cf. 18:8: "he will soon avenge their wrongs"). "I tell you in solemn truth that the present generation will certainly not pass away without all these things having first taken place" (21:32).Then Jesus warns men to "beware of slumbering;and every moment pray that you may be fully strengthened to escape from all these evils which are on the verge of coming (*mellō*), and to take your stand in the presence of the Son of Man" (21:36).[19]

---

[17]Lake and Cadbury, *Acts*, p. 219.

[18]Allen, *Matthew*, p. 182.

[19]Weymouth is used in this paragraph except for my translation of *mellō* in 21:36.

In Luke 22:22 the Son of Man goes his "pre-destined way" by betrayal, whereupon the disciples "begin to discuss with one another which of them it could possibly be who was about to do this" (*mellō*) (22:23) (Weymouth). The betrayal of the Son of Man is referred to again in 22:48 and his session at God's right hand in 22:69. As we shall see below (Chap. VI.G) this latter verse does not indicate a *Fernerwartung*, in comparison with Mark 14:62, but is Luke's way of preparing for Acts 7:55-56.

In sum, Luke himself points out how imminent his use of *mellō* is in connection with his Son of Man passages. Moreover, the "day" of 17:31 is the day of the Lord, which is also part of Luke's *Naherwartung* (Section G). Hence in 17:31 there are three indications of a speedy end: the day of the Lord, *mellō*, and the Son of Man.[19a]

E. Resurrection before Long (Acts 24:15)

In 24:15 *mellō* appears with a future infinitive: *mellein esesthai*. *Mellō* with the infinitive expresses imminence.[20] In classical Greek *mellō* was regularly used with the future infinitive, but only rarely so in Koine.[21] Hence, Luke may be reverting to classical usage to give emphasis to his sense of urgency.

Mellō with the future infinitive is found only three times in the NT, all in Acts: 11:28; 24:15; and 27:10 (plus a variant reading at Acts 24:25). According to 11:28, Agabus "publicly predicted the speedy coming (*mellein esesthai*) of a great famine" (Weymouth). Luke adds, parenthetically, that it came in the reign of Claudius (11:28), thereby pointing out that this famine did indeed come speedily. Here we have Luke's own interpretation of "speedy coming" (*mellein esesthai*)! By Rackham's chronology, Agabus' prophecy was uttered in 43 or 44 A.D. and the famine occurred in 45 A.D.[22] In this context, "speedy coming" means within a year or two.

We have noted that Paul is the speaker in 17:31; 24:15,25; and is connected with 11:28. And now in 27:10 Paul warns his companions: "I perceive that before long (*mellein esesthai*) the voyage will be attended with danger and heavy loss" (Weymouth). Once more Luke explains what he means by "before long" (*mellein esesthai*): "It was not long before a furious northeast wind . . . burst upon us" (27:14) (Weymouth). Again it is clear that "before long" (*mellein esesthai*) refers to imminent events--in this instance a matter of days.

In view of these striking facts, Weymouth seems fully justified in rendering 24:15 as "before long there will be a resurrection both of the righteous and the unrighteous." To translate *mellein esesthai* here as a simple future would be to violate Luke's own examples of what this phrase means and to ignore the extraordinary conjunction of *mellō*, imminence, and Paul.

To summarize our findings, *mellein esesthai* appears three times in Acts, and only there in the NT. Twice we learn from Luke himself precisely what he means,

---

[19a]Even so conservative a commentator as F.F. Bruce sees that "it is implied, . . . that no long interval is to elapse between this recent act of resurrection and the coming judgement of which it is the pledge" ("The Real Paul," p. 303).

[20]BDF, p. 181.

[21]BAG, pp. 501-502.

[22]Rackham, *Acts*, pp. 172-173, 183.

namely, very soon, speedily. Why, then, should not the third instance, 24:15, be so understood?

F. The Judgment Soon to Come (Acts 24:25)

In 24:25 *mellō* appears as a participle modifying a noun: *tou krimatos tou mellontos* ("the judgement which was soon to come"--Weymouth). In other passages such a construction naturally has an imminent meaning:

Matt 3:7; Luke 3:7: God's wrath that is about to come (TEV).[23]

Rom 8:18: the glory which is soon to be manifested (Weymouth).

Gal 3:23: the faith which was soon to be revealed (Weymouth).

1 Tim 4:8 the Life which is soon coming (Weymouth).

Heb 9:11 the blessings that are soon to come (Weymouth).

Heb 13:14 the city which is soon to be ours (Weymouth).

1 Pet 5:1 the glory which is soon to be revealed (Weymouth).

Rev 3:10 the trial which is soon coming (Weymouth).

2 Tim 4:1 is a striking parallel to Acts 24:25 in construction and meaning: "... Jesus who is about to judge the living and the dead, ... " (Weymouth) (*Iēsou, tou mellontos krinein zōntas kai nekrous*). In Section B we have referred to the imminent sense of this judgment formula. 2 Tim 4:1 may also be of Pauline origin, for it is one of the genuine notes which Harrison finds in the Pastorals.[24] Once more Weymouth is vindicated by these parallels involving *mellō*, imminence, and frequently Paul (directly or indirectly).

The usage of *mellō* in Acts 17:31 and 24:25 to indicate the imminent judgment is borne out by its similar usage in other passages with the verb "judge" (*krinō*) and the noun "judgment" (*krisis*). In addition to 2 Tim 4:1, just noted, *mellō* is so used in Heb 10:27 and in Jas 2:12:

> There remains nothing but a certain awful expectation of judgment, and the fury of a fire which before long (*mellō*) will devour the enemies of the truth (Heb 10:27) (Weymouth).
>
> Thus speak, and thus act, as being about (*mellō*) to be judged by a Law of Freedom (Jas 2:12) (B. Wilson).

These renditions of *mellō* in these two verses fit the mood of expectancy found elsewhere in Hebrews and James: "You can see the day of Christ approaching" (Heb 10:25) (Weymouth), and "the coming of the Lord is now close at hand. ... I tell you that the Judge is standing at the door" (Jas 5:8-9) (Weymouth).

The imminent last judgment may possibly be found also in Acts 23:3, where we again have *mellō* and *krinō*: "Before long (*mellō*), ... God will strike you, you white-washed wall! Are you sitting there to judge (*krinō*) me in accordance with the Law, ... ?" (Weymouth).

The Western text in Latin of Acts 28:31 also connects judgment with imminence (see also Section G): "This Jesus is the Christ, the Son of God,

---

[23]Strangely, Weymouth renders simply as "from the coming wrath." But if anybody preached the *Naherwartung*, John the Baptist did (see Chaps. I.C.1; V.B.).

[24]Harrison, *Pastorals*, p. 117.

through whom the whole world is about to be judged."[25]

We have thus found evidence in connection with each of our three *mellō* verses (Acts 17:31; 24:15,25) that each of them should be translated so as to bring out its sense of eschatological urgency. But we should note too the cumulative force of these arguments. To the extent that the *Naherwartung* can be established in one of these three verses to a similar extent it is also established in the others, for resurrection (24:15) and judgment (17:31; 24:25) go together in the eschatological program. For example, if 17:31 is talking about an imminent judgment, then it is likely that 24:25 is too,'and that 24:15 has to do with an imminent resurrection.

G. The Imminent Expectation in the Rest of Acts

Our contention that the imminent expectation is found in Acts 10:42; 17:31; 24:15; and 24:25 is verified by evidence of the same hope in other passages in Acts.

In the Jerusalem *kerygma* of Acts (Chap. I.F), Dodd detects a "sense of immediacy" equal to that of Paul. In fact, the "announcement of a very speedy advent was even more emphatic at an earlier date" than Paul's earliest epistles. In Acts the *eschaton* was thought of as one great divine event, consisting of the advent of the Messiah, his works and teaching, his death, resurrection, exaltation, the gift of the Spirit, and the parousia. All had taken place except the coming of the Lord to complete that which is already in being. "It was not an *early* advent that they proclaimed, but an *immediate* advent." The world was trembling on the verge of the end.[26] We shall see in Chap. VI that Luke tempers this immediacy by insisting that all conditions must be fulfilled before the end can come.

Turning to specific passages in Acts, we note first of all that the promise of the Spririt (1:5) is an eschatological promise: "In the last days, . . . I will pour forth of my Spirit upon all flesh" (Acts 2:17; Joel 2:28; cf. Isa 32:15; Ezek 39:29). This eschatological promise of baptism with the Spirit (1:5) thus raises the eschatological question of 1:6: "Master, is this the time at which you are about to restore the kingdom for Israel?" (Weymouth). Here the disciples expect the eschatological Davidic kingdom to come "before many days have passed" when they "shall be baptized with the Holy Spirit" (1:5)(Weymouth). The gift of the Spirit and the coming of the kingdom are still regarded as related parts of the eschaton. The outpouring of the Spirit is the dawn of the *eschaton* and not, as the *Fernerwartungsschule* would have it, the beginning of the long period of the church.[27] But in 1:7-8 the answer comes from the Risen Lord that the kingdom does not come immediately, but speedily, since it must be preceded by the Gentile mission (Chap. VI.H) (on Acts 1:6, Chap. VI.F.5.h).

In 1:10-11 the pose of the disciples "gazing into the sky" is an "expression of the Naherwartung" and is reminiscent of Stephen's "looking up to Heaven"

---

[25] Rackham, *Acts*, p. 506.

[26] Dodd, *Apostolic Preaching*, pp. 32-35.

[27] Schubert, "Luke 24," p. 178; Mussner, "Acts 3:19-21," p. 297; Francis, "Eschatology," p. 51. These eschatological manifestations of the Spirit are found in Luke 24:45-49; Acts 1:4-8; 2:1-4,33,38-39; 4:31; 5:32; 8:14-17; 9:17; 10:44-46; 11:16; 19:6.

(7:55).[28] The disciples "gazed after their ascended Lord into heaven in the assurance that he would soon return."[29] The reply of the two men in white garments (1:11) is not a rebuke of the imminent expectation but is an affirmation of the certainty of the parousia when the drama of salvation is shortly completed.

At 2:17 (and 3:24) Luke finds himself in "the last days" prophesied by Joel and "all the prophets," which come immediately before the day of the Lord (2:20; 17:31).

> Joel prophesied for the last days a series of marvels. First would come an outpouring of the Spirit, then heavenly and earthly portents, then darkening of the sun and moon, then the final catastrophe [the day of the Lord]. And Peter tells his pentecostal hearers that these last days have come, the first prediction has been fulfilled, proving that the fulfillment of the others will follow quickly.[30]

More precisely in terms of the entire Lukan program, the beginning of the end has come but the end of the end is yet to come.[31]

Like that of Qumran, the communal living of Acts 2:44-46; 4:34-37 is a reflection of the imminent expectation, as was John the Baptist's preaching on the duty of sharing (Luke 3:10) (Chap. V.B.), or Jesus' stress on lily-like unconcern for possessions (Luke 12:22-34)(Chap. I.C.3; V.F.3), or Luke's advocacy of an eschatological renunciation of property (Luke 14:31-33)(Chap. VIII.E.10.g). "Probably . . . the eager expectation of the Parousia led to improvidence for the future, so that the Jerusalem community was always poor."[31a]

The Lukan summary at 2:47 informs us that "the Lord added to them day by day those that were being saved" (*hoi sōdzomenoi*). The ones being saved are not those who "were gradually being saved by . . . increasing sanctification." Rather this phrase "is a clear reference to Joel 2:32 which has already been quoted in Peter's speech": "Whosoever shall call on the name of the Lord shall be saved" (2:21). "The ones who are being saved" (*hoi sōdzomenoi*) are "the remnant of Israel which is destined to survive the End. They were gradually being selected during the 'Interim' before the End, but they were not being gradually saved."[32] This eschatological meaning of *hoi sōdzomenoi* is verified by its similar usage in Luke 13:23 and 1 Cor 1:18:

> Lord, are those who are being saved few? (NWT)=Sir, are there but few who are to be saved? (Weymouth).
> Unto us who are being saved it [the word of the cross] is the power of God (ASV).

Acts 3:19-21 is another key eschatological passage:

> Repent, therefore, and reform your lives, so that the record of your sins may be cancelled, and that there may come seasons of revival from the Lord, and that He

---

[28]Smith, "History and Eschatology," p. 897.

[29]Stevens, "Eschatology," pp. 668-669.

[30]Easton, "Purpose of Acts," p. 93. "Harnack has suggested that the story of Pentecost was originally even more eschatological than it now appears,--a preaching of the gospel to all nations as the fulfilment of the last preliminary before the end" (Cadbury, *MLA*, p. 287).

[31]Smith, "History and Eschatology," p. 895.

[31a]Macgregor, *Acts*, p. 73.

[32]Lake and Cadbury, *Acts*, p. 30; Cadbury, "Names," p. 383.

may send the Christ appointed beforehand for you--even Jesus. Heaven must receive Him until those times of which God has spoken from the earliest ages through the lips of His holy Prophets--the times of the reconstitution of all things (Weymouth).

In these verses we see expressed the apocalyptic principle, "end time like the first time," that is, the restoration of all things to the original Edenic perfection. "The repentance of Israel in response to the appeal of the apostles will immediately be followed by 'times of refreshing,' by the return of Christ, and by the 'restoration of all things.'"[33] If we interpret 3:19-21 in light of the speedy vindication promised in Luke 18:1-8 ("Yes, He will soon avenge their wrongs"--Weymouth), we have further reason to find the *Naherwartung* expressed in this passage.[34]

Acts 6:10 is an exact fulfillment of Luke 21:15:

And they were not able to withstand the wisdom and the Spirit by which he [Stephen] spake (Acts 6:10).
For I will give you a mouth and wisdom, which all your adversaries shall not be able to withstand or to gainsay (Luke 21:15).

In each verse "withstand" (*anthistēmi*) is coupled with "wisdom" (*sophia*). In this way Acts 6:10 becomes a part of the imminent expectation which we shall find in "the signs in the stars apocalypse" of Luke 21 (chap. VI.H.I).

The narrative about Stephen contains other echoes of end-time urgency. In our discussion of Acts 1:10-11 we have mentioned Stephen's "looking up to Heaven" in imminent expectation (7:55). Years ago Nösgen observed that Stephen's vision of Jesus "standing" marks an advance over Christ's own proclamation of his participation in sovereign authority over the world (Luke 22:69), for Stephen sees the Son of Man already engaged in the exercise of that sovereignty. Jesus has arisen in order to make his enemies his footstool, to make his victory felt.[35]

Owen's interpretation of 7:55-56 also stresses the *Naherwartung*. Similar to Dodd's indivisible seven-fold *eschaton* is Owen's "scheme of messianic progress": the *exodus* of Christ's death, his entering into glory at the resurrection, his being received up into heaven, where he sits at God's right hand, and then, as seen by Stephen, standing in preparation for his parousia. Stephen beholds the Son of Man, who is "about to return," "eager to return," "even now standing in readiness," awaiting only the proclamation of the Gospel to the Gentiles (1:6-11).[36]

There is a perhaps hitherto unnoted anticipation of Acts 7:55-56 in Luke 13:25: the householder (=Messiah), like the Son of Man, arises for the last judgment. Only a short time remains for those who would be admitted (see Chap. V.F.3). A striking parallel is also found in 1 Enoch 100:4: "And the Most High will arise on that day of Judgment, To execute great judgment amongst sinners."

---

[33]Dodd, *Apostolic Preaching*, p. 32.
[34]Francis, "Eschatology," p. 59.
[35]Nösgen, *Apostelgeschichte*, p. 175.
[36]Owen, "Stephen's Vision," pp. 224-226.

Moreover, Stephen sees "the heavens opened" (7:56), "a token of peculiar grace which occurs when the sign concerns not an individual only but the whole people or the whole world. The corporate and all-comprehending significance of the vision is also expressed in the eschatological title 'Son of Man.'" Luke in all likelihood included the account of Stephen's martyrdom "to support or even heighten hope in an early return of Jesus in His glory and power."[37]

In Acts 13:41 the imminent last judgment appears: "Behold, you despisers, be astonished and perish, because I am carrying on a work in your time -- a work which you will utterly refuse to believe, though it be fully declared to you" (Weymouth). The present tense "denotes what God was just *on the point of doing.*"[38] In fact, "to the prophet's hearers the present tense sounded as though God were already busy with that work."[39]

Acts 14:22 reports Paul and Barnabas as saying, "It is through many afflictions (*thlipsis*) that we must make our way into the Kingdom of God" (Weymouth). Here "the eschatological sense is obviously intended: the persecution in Lystra and Derbe was interpreted as part of the 'Woes' which precede the End. Cf. Rev. 1:9."[40] Contrary to a non-eschatological interpretation of *thlipsis* in Acts,[41] Acts 14:22 plus a series of other verses indicate that the great distress is even now on the world. After Stephen's death there arose "a great persecution and tribulation(*thlipsis*) against the church which was in Jerusalem" (8:1, Codex Bezae)(ASV). Believers were "driven in various directions by the persecution (*thlipsis*) which broke out on account of Stephen" (11:19)(Weymouth). The Lord is going to let Paul "know the great sufferings (*paschō*) which he must pass through" (9:16)(Weymouth). In his farewell address to the elders of Ephesus Paul reminds them how he served "the Lord in all humility, and with tears, and amid trials (*peirasmos*)" which came upon him (20:19)(Weymouth). At town after town the Holy Spirit testifies to Paul that imprisonment and suffering (*thlipsis*) await him (20:23). In his epistles Paul also warns of the final tribulation. "We are soon to suffer affliction" (*mellomen thlibesthai*) (1 Thess 3:4) (Weymouth). But tribulation ends in glory: "If indeed we are sharers in Christ's sufferings, in order that we may also be sharers in His glory. Why, what we now suffer I count as nothing in comparison with the glory which is soon (*mellō*) to be manifested in us" (Rom 8:17-18) (Weymouth). Likewise the Lukan Christ experiences the same eschatological suffering and glory: "The Son of Man must suffer much cruelty, . . . and be put to death, and on the third day be raised to life again" (Luke 9:22) (Weymouth). It was necessary for the Christ to suffer and then enter into his glory (24:26).[42] In sum:

---

[37] Smith, "History and Eschatology," pp. 896-897.

[38] Meyer, *Acts*, p. 262.

[39] Lenski, *Acts*, pp. 545-546.

[40] Lake and Cadbury, *Acts*, p. 168.

[41] Conzelmann, *Theology*, pp. 98-99.

[42] These considerations refute Dupont, "Mort," pp. 9-10, who takes *thlipsis* as non-eschatological and who thinks that for Luke individual Christians enter the kingdom at death rather than at the end of time. On Dupont see Chap. III.

It is interesting to note that the church suffered tribulation following the martyrdom of Stephen ... and the chief result, in Luke's mind, of the scattering of the believers was the spreading abroad of the Word of God (8:4; 11:19; 13:51), the preaching of which is itself an eschatological sign. Thus the vision of Stephen at his death, the tribulation of the church that followed hard on his martyrdom, and the resultant missionary preaching are all cut from eschatological fabric and together serve to keep alive hope in an early fulfillment.[43]

Paul's speech in Acts 26 expects the speedy fulfillment of God's promise. We look especially at vv 6-7 and 22-23 (Weymouth):

6 And now I stand here impeached because of my hope in the fulfilment of the promise made by God to our forefathers..7 the promise which our twelve tribes, worshipping day and night with intense devotedness, hope to have made good to them. ... 22 I have stood firm until now, and have solemnly exhorted rich and poor alike, saying nothing except what the Prophets and Moses predicted as soon to happen (*mellō*), 23 since the Christ was to be a suffering Christ, and by coming back from the dead was then to be the first to proclaim a message of light both to the Jewish people and to the Gentiles (23 literally: that the Christ is passible, that (being) (the) first (cf. 1 Cor 15:20; Col 1:18; the firstfruits, the first instance) out of the resurrection of the dead he is about (*mellō*) to announce a light both to the [Jewish] people and to the Gentiles).

Acts 26:7,22 are best read in light of Luke 18:7, where God will soon avenge the wrongs of his people who cry to him day and night. Similarly in Acts 26:7, the "twelve tribes, worshipping day and night with intense devotedness, hope to have" God's promise "made good to *them*." And in 1 Thess 3:9 Paul uses "night and day" to express an imminent desire: "night and day, with intense earnestness, we pray that we may see your faces" (Weymouth).

Mellō in 26:22 also increases the intensity of the expectancy: "... what the Prophets and Moses predicted as soon to happen."

In 26:23 *mellō* is also used with similar effect: "he is about to announce a light both to the people and to the Gentiles." The meaning may simply be that Jesus after his resurrection proclaimed a message of light and salvation to Jews and Gentiles through the disciples.[44] Possibly, however, Luke also has in mind the eschatological light which will summon the nations to Zion, the light of the new age.[45] According to Isa 60:3 nations will come to the light of Jerusalem flooded with the radiance of the divine glory, and kings will tell (following the Dead Sea Scroll of Isaiah) of its rising brightness. Isa 40:5 predicts that "the glory of Yahweh shall be revealed, and all flesh shall see it together." Simeon envisions the Christ as "a light to shine upon the Gentiles, And the glory of thy people Israel" (Luke 2:32) (Weymouth). For Luke, then, the time is at hand for the Risen Lord to announce the blazing forth of the eschatological light, the light which the Lord himself is (Luke 2:32), the light which will illumine the restored Jerusalem (Chap. VI.F), and all flesh will see it (Isa 40:5; Luke 3:6).

---

[43]Smith, "History and Eschatology," p. 897. We shall see in Chap. VI.E.1 that the time of testimony (Luke 21:12-19; Acts 2:17-21), with its accompanying tribulation, is as eschatological as the end-time political upheavals and cosmic disturbances. On Acts 23:3 see Chap. IV.F.

[44]Meyer, *Acts*, p. 469.

[45]Cf. Jeremias, *Promise*, pp. 57, 67, though Jeremias does not consider Acts 26:23.

The *Naherwartung* is reflected again in 26:23, where, as in Rom 1:4, Paul refers to Jesus' resurrection, not as "from the dead" (*ek nekrōn*—1 Pet 1:3), but as "of the dead" (*ex anastaseōs nekrōn*). This remarkable and seldom noticed verbal parallel[46] shows that for Paul in Acts and epistles the resurrection of Jesus and of other men was conceived of as one indivisible event, yet unbroken by the lengthy delay of the parousia into separate events, the resurrection of Jesus "from the dead" and the resurrection of the remainder of the dead at the distant end of the age.

At the close of Acts (28:26-28) a number of prophecies are being fulfilled. As Paul separates himself from his fellow Jews because of their unbelief, he regards their grossness as having been foretold by Isa 6:9-10: "For this people's mind has grown callous" (Weymouth). Paul makes it known that God's salvation is sent to the Gentiles (Acts 28:28), just as Isa 49:6 had foreseen the mission of God's servant to the Gentiles and the spread of God's salvation to the end of the earth. Here too the missionary commands of Luke 24:47 and Acts 1:8 are finding fulfilment, for the Gospel is reaching "the remotest parts of the earth" (Acts 1:8) (Weymouth) as the proclamation of repentance and forgiveness of sins is being made to all the nations (Luke 24:47).

Finally, as noted in Section F, the Western text of Acts 28:31, "the oldest surviving commentary on the ending of Acts,"[47] has caught the contagious *Naherwartung* of Acts, for "the whole world is about to be judged" through Jesus Christ.[48]

We may briefly summarize the results of our study of the imminent expectation in Acts:

> Far from relinquishing hope in a near end, Luke's second volume seeks to nurture that hope.... Jesus Christ, the Son of Man, can come at any time,... Even now the final tribulation is upon the world. Luke-Acts is history in expectation of God's last and universal act.[49]

---

[46]Evans, *Paul*, Vol. 2, 144, 151; Rackham, *Acts*, pp. 471-472.

[47]Smith, "History and Eschatology," p. 898.

[48]Rackham, *Acts*, p. 506.

[49]Smith, "History and Eschatology," pp. 898, 901.

Chapter V
"On the Tiptoe of Expectation" (Luke 3:15): The Imminent Expectation in the Gospel of Luke

More obviously than in Acts, Luke expresses the imminent hope in his Gospel, doing so largely through John the Baptist and Jesus. Since we are primarily concerned with Luke's eschatology we may set aside the question of how accurately Luke represents the thought of John and Jesus. I am persuaded that so far as the imminent expectation is concerned Luke does not basically distort their eschatological message. If anything, he tones it down (cf. Chap. VI). We begin with a quick survey of the key texts.

A. An Overview of the Chief Passages

As crowds come to be baptized by John he warns them of impending judgment: "You snakes!... Who told you that you could escape from God's wrath that is about to come? .... 9 The ax is ready to cut the trees down at the roots; every tree that does not bear good fruit will be cut down and thrown in the fire" (Luke 3:7,9)(TEV).

The eschatological fever of those times is accurately described in 3:15:[1] "People's hopes began to rise; and they began to wonder about John, thinking that perhaps he might be the Messiah" (TEV). The people were living in suspense, "on the tiptoe of expectation" (NEB).

Jesus, after making plain the cost of discipleship (9:23-25), points to the near return of the Son of Man in the Kingdom:

> For whosoever shall be ashamed of me and my words, of him shall the Son of man be ashamed, when he cometh in his own glory, and the glory of the Father, and of the holy angels. But I tell you of a truth, There are some of them that stand here, who shall in no wise taste of death, till they see the kingdom of God (9:26-27).

The much discussed question as to whether Jesus regarded himself as the coming Son of Man need not detain us here, for Luke certainly does make this identification (Luke 17:24-25; Acts 7:55-56), and correctly so, I would think, for otherwise Jesus would have regarded someone else as the ultimate eschatological figure, which, in view of the authority with which he speaks and acts, seems most unlikely.

---

[1] Cf. Selby, "Changing Ideas," pp. 24-25.

The Lord instructs the seventy to proclaim to hospitable towns that "the kingdom of God is at hand upon you" (10:9) (my translation). The evangelists are to warn inhospitable towns that the kingdom of God is at hand (10:11). Jesus will return as a sign to "this generation" (11:30). So urgent are the times that Jesus excludes thought of delay: the servant who says his master "is taking a long time to come back" (12:45) (TEV) will be cut asunder by his returning lord.

Jesus advises debtors to settle matters at once with their creditors out of court, lest they be cast into prison (hell). So too the persons who correctly interpret the signs of approaching judgment will be reconciled to God by repentance now, lest they perish (12:54-13:9). To his oppressed people who cry unto God day and night for help, Jesus promises speedy divine help at the parousia (18:1-8). This promise of fast-approaching eschatological aid leads Jesus to ask about conditions when he returns: "But the Son of Man when he comes will not find faith on earth, will he?" (my translation).

In his eschatological discourse in the temple (21:1-36), Jesus warns of threatening apocalyptic events: wars, revolutions, earthquakes, famines, plagues, persecutions, destruction of Jerusalem, cosmic woes, the appearance of the Son of Man with great power and glory, and the coming of the kingdom of God: "Verily I say unto you, This generation shall not pass away, till all things be accomplished. Heaven and earth shall pass away: but my words shall not pass away" (21:32-33). Jesus then concludes his address on "last things" with the admonition: "Be on the alert, praying at all times for strength to pass safely through all these imminent troubles and to stand in the presence of the Son of Man" (21:36) (NEB). And at the last supper Jesus indicates how really near the kingdom is by refusing to taste wine until the kingdom comes: "I say unto you, I shall not drink henceforth of the fruit of the vine, until the kingdom of God shall come" (22:18).

Joseph of Arimathaea, a disciple of Jesus (Matt 27:57), "was on the lookout for the Reign of God" (Luke 23:51)(Moffatt). Jesus' disciples had "hoped it was he who should redeem Israel" (24:21), that is, eschatologically, even while he was still alive.[2]

As we have seen in Chap. II.B, this imminent sense of these crucial verses has been challenged by the *Fernerwartungsschule*. It has also been disputed by those who would hold to an infallible Bible and/or an infallible and omniscient Jesus. We turn now to these objections.

B. The Approaching Wrath (Luke 3:7,9)

On these verses the Distant Expectation School holds that, though Luke's John proclaims judgment, he does not declare the nearness of the judgment, for Luke has shifted the judgment to the remote future. John preaches only the nearness of the Messiah, who stands at an indeterminate length of time from the last judgment.[3]

How unnatural this interpretation is has already been indicated (Chaps. I.C.; V.A), where reference is made to John's warnings of the impending messianic

---

[2]Selby, "Changing Ideas," p. 27.
[3]Conzelmann, *Theology*, p. 102.

judgment: the Messiah's wrath is soon (*mellō*) (Chap. IV) to come (3:7); even now the Messiah's judgment-ax is being laid and is cutting down unproductive trees (3:9); and already the Messiah's judgment-shovel is in his hand (3:17). All that remains for unproductive trees is felling and burning. "When in 3:9 John says the ax already lies at the roots of the trees that can be understood only as a picture of the exteme nearness of judgment."[4] On this point Streeter has well written:

> On purely critical grounds it is probable that our oldest authority Q represented John as preaching 'the Kingdom of God is at hand'. The phrase is also specially connected with the Baptist in another Q passage 'The law and the prophets were until John: from that time the gospel of the kingdom of God is preached' (Lk. 16:16; cf. Mt. 11:12). But the view that he expected an immediate and catastrophic coming of the Kingdom conceived in the Apocalyptic style does not rest on this one phrase alone. 'Who warned you to flee from the wrath to come' implies an immediate judgement. The metaphor in 'the axe is laid at the foot ot the trees' pictures the farmer throwing down his axe for just a moment while he divests himself of his garment before beginning the *immediate* work of felling. Again, the 'baptism with Spirit and with fire' which is to come after is most naturally interpreted of the Apocalyptic outpouring of the Spirit (Joel 2:28, &c), and the 'purging of the threshing floor' of the Messianic Judgement.[5]

We see, then, that Luke's John, far from thinking of a distant judgment, is rather carried away by his conviction that the end-time is near.[6] In fact, it was John's recognition of the impending judgment of God's wrath that summoned him out of the wilderness.[7] "In the third decade of our era apocalypticism was still on the increase when the Baptist appeared to fan the flame into a white heat."[8] This statement is as true of John in Luke as in the other Gospels. It would be difficult to imagine a stronger apocalyptic message of imminent judgment through the Messiah than Luke's John preaches. The apocalyptic language of Luke 3:7 is impressive:

> "Vipers" throughout the Gospels (Mt 12:34; 23:33) and in the Qumran Literature (Hymns of Thanksgiving 3:1-8) is an eschatological term referring to men under diabolical power at the time of the final struggle; "Who has shown you how to flee from the coming wrath?": This question is also packed with eschatological terminology: "shown" (*hypodeiknymi*) is a technical term for revealing something hidden (Sir 48:25; Lk 12:5); "the coming wrath" contains all the fury of such prophetic words as Is 13:9; 30:27; Zeph 2:2; Mal 3:2; Enoch 90.[9]

We should also note that John's allegedly non-eschatological ethics (Luke 3:10-14) come between 3:7-9 and 3:15-18, in the midst of the "River of Fire Apocalypse" (3:1-20). It is also likely that John's emphasis upon the duty of sharing (3:11) reflects "an expectation of an imminent return of the Lord. Cf. the

---

[4]Michel, "Lukas," p. 106, who notes that Conzelmann passes over this verse in silence.

[5]Streeter, "The Baptist's Preaching," p. 551. We are finding that what Streeter says of the historical John applies to Luke's John. On John as a preacher of the kingdom see Chap. II.E; on Luke 16:16, Chap. II.F.

[6]Moore, *Parousia*, p. 162, also finds 3:9 to mean "that judgement is not far distant"; Creed, *Luke*, p. 52: "the judgement is imminent."

[7]Grundmann, *Lukas*, p. 102. For God's judgment of wrath see also Rom 2:5; 1 Enoch 90:18; 91:7; Wis 5:17-23.

[8]Easton, "Christology," p. 156.

[9]Stuhlmueller, *Luke*, p. 127.

primitive communism in Acts 2:44ff. and 4:32ff."[10] Giving is to be "heedless, in accord with the apocalyptic attitude" of John.[11] John's social teaching, far from being a timeless ethical exhortation, is "the real 'interim ethic,'"[12] that is, emergency norms to live by during the brief interval before the end.

As we have just observed in Section A, this eager expectation is confirmed by Luke 3:15: "The people were in suspense and all were debating in their minds whether John might possibly be the Anointed One" (Weymouth), for "John proclaimed authoritatively the nearness of the Kingdom" and "he employed a rite confirming absolution," all of which was proof to the people that the Messiah and the final salvation were approaching.[13]

Moreover, there is a close link between the expectations of John and Jesus in Luke. As John warns that the ax is ready to cut down the unproductive trees, so too Jesus (Luke 13:6-9), in "a parable in which urgency is the key-note,"[14] tells of the owner of the vineyard who orders his vinedresser to cut down a fruitless fig tree--another warning of the pressing nature of the time (on 13:6-9 see Chap. V.F.3).

C. Seeing the Kingdom (Luke 9:26-27)

1. Luke 9:26-27 and Parallels

To see the issues here it is well to look at Luke in relation to Matthew and Mark:

Matthew 16	Mark 8	Luke 9
27 For the Son of man shall come in the glory of his Father with his angels; and then shall he render unto every man according to his deeds. 28 Verily I say unto you, There are some of them that stand here who shall in no wise taste of death, till they see the Son of man coming in his kingdom.	38 For whosoever shall be ashamed of me and of my words in this adulterous and sinful generation, the Son of man also shall be ashamed of him, when he cometh in the glory of his Father with his holy angels. 9:1 And he said unto them, Verily I say unto you, There are some here of them that stand by, who shall in no wise taste of death, till they see the kingdom of God come with power.	26 For whosoever shall be ashamed of me and of my words, of him shall the Son of man be ashamed, when he cometh in his own glory, and the glory of the Father, and of the holy angels. 27 But I tell you of a truth, There are some of them that stand here who shall in no wise taste of death, till they see the kingdom of God.

---

[10]Leaney, *Luke*, p. 107.
[11]Easton, *Luke*, p. 38.
[12]Manson, *Sayings of Jesus*, p. 545.
[13]Easton, *Luke, pp. 36,40.*
[14]Moore, *Parousia*, p. 86.

The saying of Luke 9:27 and parallels, "which the first three evangelists have with such unanimity preserved in the same connection, was one of the strongest supports of the Apostolic age that there would be a speedy and visible return of Christ."[15] But since the apostolic age came and went without this visible return a number of interpretations of Luke 9:27 have subsequently been advanced.

2. The Transfiguration (Luke 9:28-36)

The view that seeing the kingdom refers to the transfiguration was held by most of the church fathers and by many since then. Indeed, the Synoptists do follow this prediction with their accounts of the transfiguration (Matt 17:1-8; Mark 9:2-8; Luke 9:28-36). Peter, James, and John see the kingdom in the transfiguration, consistently with Luke's view of the kingdom as a reality partly obtainable in the present.[16]

This explanation, however, is nullified by the fact that 9:27 refers to an event distant enough in time to allow for the death of most of Jesus' hearers. Yet the transfiguration, according to all Synoptics, took place about a week later (Matt 17:1; Mark 9:2; Luke 9:28). Thus the prophecy "cannot refer *exclusively* to an event to take place the next week."[17] At most, the transfiguration as a picture of the parousia of the glorified Christ could be but a partial fulfilment of Luke 9:27.

Further, as we shall see in Chap. VII, it is highly questionable that Luke thought of the kingdom as a present reality. Moreover, the Matthean and Markan parallels to Luke 9:27 are clearly references to the coming of the Son of Man and of the kingdom at the end of history. Only by forced exegesis can Matt 16:28 and Mark 9:1 be referred to anything other than the ultimate end of this age.[18] It is possible, of course, that Luke may have altered this apocalyptic meaning of the parallel passages, but the burden of proof is upon those who claim he did. Certainly Luke was not thinking of the transfiguration as the complete fulfilment, for, as just noted, Luke too dates that event within a few days of the sayings in 9:26-27. The transfiguration is not the kingdom of God but the revelation to the three disciples of the true nature of the Son of Man and of the new, transfigured creation which the Son of Man will inaugurate.

3. The Resurrection of Jesus (Luke 24:1-49)

The fulfilment of Luke 9:27 in Jesus' resurrection has been advocated by Cajetan, Calvin, and Beza, and, in the nineteenth century, by Lange, who finds Luke 9:27 and parallels to refer to Christ's coming in the glory of his kingdom

---

[15]Olshausen, quoted by Biederwolf, *Second Coming Bible*, p. 320. Biederwolf summarizes the older literature, as does Plummer, *Luke*, pp. 249-250.

[16]Plummer, *Luke*, p. 250, regards the transfiguration as a partial fulfilment; Grundmann, *Lukas*, p. 191 (9:27 possibly refers to the history of Jesus, especially his transfiguration, death, and resurrection); Leaney, *Luke*, p. 166; Baird, *Luke*, p. 687.

[17]Plummer, *Luke*, p. 250.

[18]An attempt with Mark 9:1 is made by Ellis, "Present and Future," pp. 32-34, and by Nützel, "Eschatologie," pp. 81-89, and with Matt 16:28 by Albright and Mann, *Matthew,* p. 201, who take it to mean some "would not die before the Messiah's passion and resurrection." Summaries of the discussion are in Biederwolf, *Second Coming Bible*, pp. 320-322, 364, and Perrin, *Kingdom of God*, pp. 67-68.

within the circle of his disciples when he arose from the dead and revealed himself.[19]

Against this view is the implication of 9:27 of a more distant event than the resurrection of Jesus, plus the fact that the synoptists themselves do not take the resurrection as the fulfilment of 9:27 and parallels.

4. The Coming of the Holy Spirit at Pentecost (Acts 2:1-4)

According to the French exegete, Godet, Luke 9:27 refers to the coming of the Holy Spirit at Pentecost, which some of those who had been present with Jesus received. They then beheld with the inner eye those wonderful works of God which Jesus calls the kingdom of God (cf. the inward nature of the kingdom in Luke 17:21).[20]

The English scholar, Creed, finds in Acts 1-2 the suggestion that Luke would have been able to recognize a fulfilment of the coming of the kingdom in the coming of the Spirit. Luke's omission of Mark's "come in power" (Luke 9:27; Mark 9:1) makes it easier to adopt such a spiritualized interpretation of Luke 9:27.[21]

Against this view stands the fact that, like the transfiguration and resurrection, Pentecost is not a distant enough event to satisfy Luke 9:27 ("some will not taste death . . ."). Furthermore, if 9:27 is a prediction of Pentecost, it is the only such prediction made by the earthly Jesus in any of the Gospels. Compared with the plain words of the Risen Christ in Luke 24:49 and Acts 1:8 about Pentecost, the words of the earthly Jesus in Luke 9:27 are a darkly veiled prophecy if they refer to Pentecost. Nor does Luke anywhere else equate the coming of the Spirit with the coming or seeing of the kingdom (see the quotation from Manson in #6 below). In Acts 1:1-11 Luke definitely dissociates the outpouring of the Spirit at Pentecost from the coming of the kingdom. The gift of the Spirit is one part of the apocalyptic agenda which precedes the seeing of the kingdom (Luke 9:27) when it appears (19:11). And if, as we shall argue below at #9, the seeing of the kingdom (9:27) includes the coming of the Son of Man (9:26), then 9:27 refers to an objective visible event, not to a spiritualized event perceived with the inner eye. We need but note the physical nature of the parousia in Acts 1:9-11 (and in 2 Thess 1:7-8). Neither would Luke have confused the coming of the Spirit with the coming of the Son of Man, for to Luke both are separate and distinct eschatological events (Acts 1:1-11).

A further indication that Luke and the early church did not equate the coming of the kingdom with the outpouring of the Spirit is found in the variant reading of some minuscule manuscripts and church fathers at 11:2, which instead of "thy kingdom come" read "thy Holy Spirit come upon us and cleanse us." If, as some have maintained, we have here the original Lukan reading,[22] that would mean

---

[19]Lange, *Matthäus*, p. 239.

[20]Godet, *Luke*, I, 422.

[21]Creed, *Luke*, p. 132.

[22]Harnack, "Zwei Worte Jesu," *Sitzungsberichte der preussischen Akademie der Wissenschaften*, Phil.-hist. Klasse, Berlin (1907), pp. 942 ff., cited by Grässing, *Delay*, pp. 109-110.

that Luke himself substituted the coming of the Spirit for the coming of the kingdom, thus indicating that Luke himself did not identify the two events. On the other hand, if, as seems more likely, "it is an early paraphrase that transformed an eschatological petition into one that was related to the immediate needs of the believing community,"[23] then the scribe and/or community which made this change did not themselves understand or take Luke to understand the petition for the coming of the kingdom to refer to Pentecost.

Godet and others who would sunder the apocalyptic advent of the Son of Man in 9:26 from a spiritualized concept of the kingdom in 9:27 find this alleged distinction and antithesis between 9:26 and 9:27 marked by the adversative "but" (*de*) of 9:27, "But I say to you."[24] Luke's *de* replaces Mark's "and" (*kai*). Luke, however, frequently substitutes *de* for Mark's *kai* simply as a matter of style.[25] *De* may also mean "and," and is so rendered here by NEB. Some translations simply ignore the *de* to bring out the continuity rather than the contrast between 9:26 and 9:27 (TEV: "Remember this! There are some here, I tell you, ... ")(Weymouth: "I tell you truly that ... ")(Phillips: "I tell you the simple truth ... ")(Moffatt: "I tell you plainly, ... ")(Goodspeed: "I tell you, ... ")(R. Knox: "Believe me, there are ... "). Hence there is no grammatical necesssity for translating *de* as "but" to indicate a distinction between the events of 9:26 and 9:27. In fact, since 9:18-27 is a closely-knit unity (as we shall see in #9), "and" is to be preferred in 9:27, as in 9:20,23, to express the continuous flow of thought in this unit.[26] Moreover, Luke 9:27 is more closely connected to 9:26 than Mark 9:1 is to Mark 8:38, for Luke 9:27 continues Jesus' direct discourse without interruption, whereas Mark inserts "and he said to them" (9:1).

5. The Beginning of the Church at Pentecost (Acts 2:40-42)

Noting that Luke 9:27 refers only to seeing the kingdom of God, "a simplified expression compared with those in Mt. and Mk.," A.B. Bruce concludes that Luke probably understood thereby "the organization of the church at Pentecost."[27]

This view, like the previous ones, also fails to note that Pentecost was so near to the prophecy of 9:27 that practically all, not some, of those present would have lived to see the beginning of the church at Pentecost. Of even more importance is the fact that for Luke the kingdom of God and the church are not identical. For example, Luke 12:31 is a command to seek God's kingdom. "Kingdom" here cannot mean "church," for Christians do not "seek" the church.[28] In Acts, Philip

---

[23]Gilmore, *Luke*, p. 201. Wellhausen, *Lukas*, p. 56, similarly sees the petition for the Spirit as a later correction of the petition for the kingdom--the Spirit sufficed for a later time, and the parousia was dispensable.

[24]Godet, *Luke*, I, 421-422.

[25]Hawkins, *Horae Synopticae*, pp. 150-152; Creed, *Luke*, p. lxxxi.

[26]Likewise Franklin, *Christ the Lord*, p. 22.

[27]Bruce, *Luke*, p. 531. Similarly Streeter, *Four Gospels*, p. 528. Luke, however, says Streeter (p. 518), still thinks the return of Christ is near but is postponed "until the times of the Gentiles be fulfilled" (21:24).

[28]Easton, *Luke*, p. 202.

(8:12) and Paul (19:8; 20:25; 28:23,31) preach the kingdom, not the church. "It is impossible to substitute 'church' for 'kingdom' in such sayings."[29] So too in Acts 1:3 (Jesus speaking about the kingdom) and 14:22 (entering the kingdom through tribulations) "kingdom" retains its primary meaning of the reign of God which is to supersede this world order.[30]

Returning to Luke's Gospel, we observe that the sayings of Jesus in 18:24-25 about how hard it is for the rich "to enter into the kingdom of God" are in a context which deals with the question of final salvation: "What shall I do to inherit eternal life?"(18:18). The section ends with Jesus' assurance that no one who has left his own "for the kingdom of God's sake, who shall not receive manifold more in this time, and in the world to come eternal life" (18:29-30).

Luke 13:22-30 likewise is concerned with end-time salvation: "Lord, are they few that are saved?" Jesus replies that in the last judgment the condemned will weep when they "see Abraham and Isaac and Jacob in the kingdom of God" (13:28), but the saved will "sit at table in the kingdom of God" (13:29). The messianic banquet of the new age is also the center of concern in the parable of the great supper (14:15-24), which is introduced by the comment, "Blessed is he that shall eat bread in the kingdom of God" (14:15). Thus for Luke the kingdom of God is not the church but the realm of eternal life in the world to come.[31]

6. The Spread of Christianity (Acts)

A number of scholars have seen the fulfilment of Luke 9:27 in the progress and conquests of the Gospel, especially between Pentecost and the fall of Jerusalem.[32] Once more this interpretation encounters the "fatal objection" that "without doubt practically all of them [who heard the prophecy of 9:27] saw at least the beginning of such a fulfilment."[33] Perhaps the best refutation of the views presented thus far has been given by T. W. Manson:

> Against the identification of the coming of the Kingdom with the outpouring of the Spirit and the astonishing progress of Christianity in the first century is to be set the fact that the people who lived through these great events did not make the identification. Paul, who was at the head of the triumphant march of the Gospel through the Empire, still looked for some greater thing. According to the account in the Acts of the Apostles, Peter found in the descent of the Spirit the fulfilment, not of Mark 9:1 (Luke 9:27), but of Joel 3:1f. (EVV 2:28ff).[34]

Also the evangelists themselves "failed to see in the saying a reference to the Resurrection, Pentecost or the era of the Christian Church."[35]

---

[29]Ladd, *Presence*, p. 263.

[30]Cf. Creed, *Luke*, p. lxxii. See also Chap. VII.E.2.b.

[31]These last two paragraphs are adapted from Robinson, *Weg*, p. 62.

[32]Dorner, Erasmus, Farrar, Klostermann, Nösgen, Schenkle, Whedon.

[33]Biederwolf, *Second Coming Bible*, p. 321.

[34]T.W. Manson, *The Teaching of Jesus*, pp. 281-282, quoted with approval by Perrin, *Kingdom of God*, pp. 67-68.

[35]Perrin, *Kingdom of God*, p. 68.

7. The Destruction of Jerusalem, A.D. 70 (Luke 21:20-24)

This view has been popular for several centuries.[36] It fits Plummer's test that "no interpretation can be correct that does not explain *eisin tines* [there are some], which implies the exceptional privilege of some, as distinct from the common experience of all": "The destruction of Jerusalem, witnessed by S. John and perhaps a few others of those present, swept away the remains of the Old Dispensation and left the Gospel in possession of the field."[37]

A modern Roman Catholic takes the same position:

> This isolated saying of Jesus [9:27] shows the Son of Man coming in glory at each decisive moment of history, but especially at the fall of Jerusalem, which some of the apostles would live to see. With the destruction of Jerusalem, Christianity broke irrevocably from the narrow limits of Judaism and reached out to a world-wide Kingdom.[38]

Plummer consciously (and others perhaps unconsciously) prefers this interpretation over that of the final parousia and coming of the kingdom because "none of those present lived to witness it, . . . and we cannot suppose . . . that He uttered a prediction which has not been fulfilled."[39] The question of Jesus' inerrancy is naturally of vital importance to many Christians, but so far as historical criticism is concerned we must proceed to examine the texts as objectively as possible without fear of the consequences to our Christology.

Plummer also argues that the words "who shall in no wise taste of death, till they see the kingdom of God" imply that some will experience death after seeing the kingdom of God, which would not be true of those who live to see the parousia (1 Cor 15:51).[40]

Luke 9:27, however, no more implies the eventual death of those who live to see the kingdom than Luke 21:32 suggests the passing away of "this generation" after all things have been accomplished: "Verily I say unto you, This generation shall not pass away, till all things be accomplished." This verse means that "this generation" will not die out before the end of the world but will still be living when all these things happen. The same Greek phrase (*heos an*) for "till" is used in both verses.[41]

Paul in 1 Cor 4:5 also uses this same phrase when he writes: "Wherefore judge nothing before the time, until the Lord come, who will both bring to light the hidden things of darkness, and make manifest the counsels of the hearts." Paul does not mean that men can judge him after the Lord comes. Rather he is saying that they have no right to pass judgment on him either before or after the parousia.

---

[36] Alford, Biederwolf, Jakob Cappellus, Ebrard, Grotius, Mansel, Morison, Plummer, Plumptre, Stuhlmueller.

[37] Plummer, *Luke*, pp. 249-250.

[38] Stuhlmueller, *Lukan Reading Guide*, p. 83.

[39] Plummer, *Luke*, p. 250.

[40] Plummer, *Luke*, p. 250. We may recall that according to 4 Ezra 7:29 Messiah and all men die after the close of the 400 year messianic kingdom, but such a concept is not found in the NT.

[41] So also Franklin, *Christ the Lord*, p. 22.

Only the Lord can judge the faithfulness of Paul's ministry.

Even more to the point, the parallel verses to Luke 9:27 (Matt 16:28; Mark 9:1) use the same words (*heos an*) when they predict that some of those standing there will not die until they see the Son of Man coming in his kingdom (Matthew) or until they see the kingdom of God come in power (Mark). Here there is no thought that those who are granted this exceptional apocalyptic privilege will die after the parousia and the coming of the kingdom. The Synoptists simply mean that the kingdom will come before all those standing there have died. Several modern translators have brought out this sense of the words unambiguously: "I tell you, some of you who stand here will certainly live to see the Kingdom of God!" (Goodspeed)(Williams). It has even been proposed that the verse should be construed to mean not only will these fortunate ones not die before they see the kingdom but how much less will they die afterward.[42]

But the major objection to equating the seeing of the kingdom by some standing there with the fall of Jerusalem lies in the fact that for Luke the destruction, though an eschatological event (Chap. VI.E), is not identified with the coming of the Son of Man or the coming or seeing of the kingdom. In the Lukan program the fall of Jerusalem will be followed by "the times of the Gentiles" (21:24)(Chap. VI.F). The fall is one necessary step in the eschatological drama which reaches its denouement (21:32) after the fall (21:20-24), the times of the Gentiles (21:24), and the cosmic woes (21:25-26), when the Son of Man comes "in a cloud with power and great glory" (21:27), when heaven and earth pass away (21:33), and when redemption (21:28) and the kingdom arrive (21:31). Luke says more about the destruction of Jerusalem than any other Gospel (Luke 19:39-44; 21:20-24; 23:28-31), yet he nowhere hints that "to see the kingdom" is "to see the destruction of Jerusalem."

8. Perception of the Nature of the Kingdom

A widespread view in scholarly circles today holds that Luke 9:27, which omits Mark's "come with power" (9:1), means to perceive the kingdom as a timeless, transcendent, metaphysical reality. For the idea of the coming of the kingdom Luke substitutes a timeless conception of it. In this way Luke replaces the realistic, futuristic conceptions of Matt 16:28 and Mark 9:1 by a mental understanding of what the nature of the kingdom of God is. Luke does not mean that some of those who heard Jesus will still be alive to witness the wind-up of history and the coming of the eternal kingdom. Rather he declares that some men will come to know the mysteries of the kingdom (cf. Luke 8:10). Whoever looks back at the life of Jesus is able here and now to "see the Kingdom," for its nature has been revealed in the person and work of Jesus. Although for Luke the kingdom remains a future reality, he detaches it from all consideration of time, which is to say that any generation can confirm the fulfilment of the promise of 9:27. Luke's solution therefore does not risk being called into question by the continuation of history.[43]

---

[42]Wordsworth, in Biederwolf, *Second Coming Bible*, p. 321.

[43]Conzelmann, *Theology*, pp. 103-105; Grässer, *Delay*, pp. 136-137; Wilson, "Lukan Eschatology," pp. 338-339 (with reluctance); Ellis, "Present and Future," pp. 30-35; Kaestli, *Eschatologie*, p. 18.

In favor of this interpretation it has been argued that 9:27 cannot refer to the second advent because the words "shall in no wise taste of death, till they see the kingdom of God" implies that these persons will experience death after seeing the kingdom, whereas after the parousia and final manifestation of the kingdom none will die.[44] This point was rejected above at #7, where we found the plain meaning of 9:27 to be that "some ... will certainly live to see the Kingdom of God!"

Does the phrase "to see the kingdom of God" refer to intellectual comprehension? In answer to this question, it is instructive to mark that this phrase appears only three times in the NT: Luke 9:27 (*horaō*=see), parallel Mark 9:1 (*horaō*), and John 3:3 (*horaō*): Jesus tells Nicodemus that "except one be born anew he cannot see the Kingdom of God" (John 3:3). John 3:3 is obviously parallel with 3:5, "Except one be born of water and the Spirit, he cannot enter into the kingdom of God." "To see the kingdom" thus means to John "to enter into the kingdom."[45] The latter refers to future entrance into the kingdom at the end of this age.[46] How remarkable that John, who so predominantly stresses present eschatology, should have included this futuristic statement of 3:3, in which "seeing" does not refer to mental comprehension or to a present experience but to a realistic seeing of the coming kingdom.

It is commonly agreed that Mark 9:1 refers to the final eschatological kingdom.[47] If, then, two of the three NT references to "seeing the kingdom" are apocalyptic, even John 3:3, it seems altogether likely that the usage of Luke the apocalyptist is no different.

Neither does Luke's own usage of the various verbs for "see" (*blepō, horaō, theoreō*), which he apparently uses interchangeably, lend credence to a spiritualized interpretation of 9:27. Luke twice uses "see" to mean "perceive," "understand," "grasp mentally" eschatological teaching:

> Unto you [the disciples] it is given to know the mysteries of the kingdom of God: but to the rest in parables; that seeing (*blepō*) they may not see (*blepō*)[the mysteries of the kingdom] (8:10). And seeing (*blepō*) ye shall see (*blepō*), and shall in no wise perceive (*horaō*):... Lest haply they should perceive (*horaō*) with their eyes (Acts 28:26-27) [Paul's teaching about the kingdom, Jesus, and salvation; 28:23,28,31].

Three times Luke employs "see" to mean "to experience" eschatological realities. It was revealed unto Simeon "that he should not see (*horaō*) death,..." (Luke 2:26). All mankind will "see (*horaō*) the salvation of God" (3:6), that is, they will experience God's saving grace in the kingdom. The time will come when the disciples will wish that they could "see" (*horaō*) one of the days of the Son of man" (17:22).[48]

---

[44] Ellis, "Present and Future," p.32.

[45] Howard, *John*, p. 505.

[46] Kümmel, *Theology*, p. 293.

[47] Otto, *Kingdom of God*, p. 147; Berkey, "Realized Eschatology," p. 187; see also note #18.

[48] The *Einheitsübersetzung* translates *horaō* in 17:22 as *erleben*, experience. On 17:22 see Chap. VI.F.5.g.

But generally Luke uses "see" to signify a realistic witnessing of actual eschatological realities. These realities may be present: Simeon sees (*horaō*) God's salvation (Luke 2:30), that is, the Christ (2:26). Peter, James and John see (*horaō*) Jesus' glory (9:32). Jesus sees (*theoreō*) Satan fall (10:18). The eyes are blessed which see (*blepō*) the things which they see (*blepō*) and which the prophets desired to see (*blepō*) but did not see (*horaō*), namely, Jesus' mighty acts as evidence the new age is near (10:23-24).[49] Stephen sees (*horaō*) the glory of God and then sees (*theoreō*) the Son of Man standing at the right side of God (Acts 7:55-56).

One may also see futuristic eschatological realities: Jesus warns his hearers that they will see (*horaō*) Abraham and companions in the kingdom of God but they themselves will be kept outside (Luke 13:28). Possibly referring to his parousia, Jesus tells the people they will not see (*horaō*) him until they shall say, "Blessed is he that cometh in the name of the Lord" (13:35). In Hades Dives lifts up his eyes and sees (*horaō*) Abraham afar off (16:23). After cosmic woes men will see (*horaō*) the Son of Man coming in a cloud (21:27). When they see (*horaō*) these things coming to pass, they will know that the kingdom is nigh (21:31).[50]

In Acts 1:9-11 are found noteworthy instances of Luke's realistic use of "see" in reference to present (ascension) and future (parousia) eschatological events: While they were looking (*blepō*) Jesus was taken up and a cloud hid him from their eyes. As they looked steadfastly (*atenidzō*) at the sky two men asked them why they were looking (*blepō*) there, and promised that Jesus would come back in the same way as they saw (*theoreō*) him going up into heaven. The physical parousia will be seen with the eyes as surely as was the physical ascension.

In summary, there are only two instances where Luke uses "see" eschatologically in the sense of "understanding," "grasping with the mind," and in these instances Luke makes the meaning clear: understanding the teachings of Jesus and Paul about the kingdom of God (Luke 8:10; Acts 28:26-27). Thrice Luke uses "see" to mean " experience" eschatological things (Luke 2:26; 3:6; 17:22), but here again the meaning is plain from the context. Frequently Luke writes of actual seeing of eschatological realities, both present (Luke 2:26,30; 9:32; 10:18,23-24; Acts 7:55-56) and future (Luke 13:28,35; 16:23; 21:27,31). Furthermore, the aorist tense used for "see" in Luke 9:27 (*idōsin*) "cannot mean .. 'to come to see' or 'to awake to the fact,' for the aorist connotes no such gradual unfolding but rather a definite event to be observed within that generation."[51] Hence the probability is high that when Luke refers to "seeing the kingdom of God" (9:27) he means a realistic seeing of the kingdom when it appears as the final eschatological reality (cf. Luke 19:11). It is also very unlikely that Luke means to see the kingdom as a present reality. Even if Luke thinks of the kingdom as present in this age (see Chap. VII), seeing a realized kingdom would require a vision, as in Luke 9:32; 10:18, or Acts 7:55-56, and there is nothing to indicate that Luke at 9:27 is thinking of seeing the kingdom in a vision. Thus it is most probable

---

[49]Contrast Dodd, *Parables*, p. 31, who takes "see" in 10:23-24 to mean experiencing the coming of the kingdom of God with Jesus himself.

[50]Moore, *Parousia*, p. 131, also finds that the "seeing" in Luke 13:28 and 21:27 clearly refers to the future, final manifestation of the kingdom of God and Son of Man.

[51]Clark, "Realized Eschatology," p. 373.

that Luke at 9:27 means to see the kingdom when it appears at the close of this age.

Mark 9:1 was probably known to Luke and to at least some of his readers. Therefore if Luke did not want to reproduce Mark's meaning he would have had to distinguish much more clearly than he has between his position and Mark's.[52] How improbable, then, that Luke the apocalyptist should be saying here that some men will come to understand the kingdom as a timeless, transcendent, metaphysical reality. Cadbury has forcefully warned against spiritualizing away Luke's concrete eschatological hopes:

> It would be quite contrary to the practice of giving precision of time and place and manner to the divine intervention in history as Luke conceived it. If other Christians ancient or modern have found the primitive emphasis on such a literal future event embarrassing, Luke gives no real countenance to any of their ways of avoiding it.[53]

9. The Coming of the Kingdom of God at the End of the World

According to this final interpretation, which is accepted here, Luke 9:27 points to the final eschatological event: the revelation of the realistic, ultimate kingdom of God, including the apocalyptic advent of the Son of Man (9:26).[54] We have arrived at View No. 9 by eliminating alternative positions Nos. 2 through 8. Some whimsicalities not treated already need only to be stated to be refuted:

> Before this generation has passed away you will see signs that the kingdom of God is on the way.[55]
> Christ's coming in his kingdom at the end of this age is seen in the vision of the disciples at the transfiguration, of Paul in the third heaven, and of John on Patmos.[56]

Several arguments are used by opponents of View No. 9. Some, assuming that Jesus did not err, contend that a direct reference to the end-time kingdom is excluded by the fact that none present lived to witness this event.[57] But, as was pointed out at View No. 7, exegesis cannot be controlled by an a priori assumption of Jesus' inerrancy. There is of course the possibility that we do not have an inerrant report of Jesus' words and meaning, which would allow for Luke's and others' misunderstandings of Jesus' figurative language about the parousia and their attribution of current apocalyptic ideas to Jesus.[58] Our primary concern, however, is with the meaning Luke saw in 9:27.

Others object to View No. 9 on the grounds that Luke cannot have meant the

---

[52] Michel, "Lukas," p. 106.

[53] Cadbury, "Acts and Eschatology," pp. 315-316. Hiers, "Delay," stresses the unmistakable visibility of the parousia, "the real thing" (Luke 3:6; 17:20-21; 21:35).

[54] View No. 9 is also held by Meyer, Olshausen, Holtzmann; Stevens, "Eschatology," pp. 666-667; Gilmour, *Luke*, p. 172; Franklin, *Christ the Lord*, pp. 21-23; Michel, "Lukas," p. 106.

[55] Barclay, *Luke*, p. 123.

[56] Blackstone, quoted by Biederwolf, *Second Coming Bible*, p. 322.

[57] Plummer, *Luke*, p. 250; Biederwofl, *Second Coming Bible*, p. 322.

[58] So Stevens, "Eschatology," pp. 670, 683; Meyer, quoted in Lange, *Matthäus*, p. 239.

parousia-kingdom event happening to some of Jesus' generation, for Luke wrote too late for that. Assuming the earliest date for Luke's Gospel, it is said we can place the end only at the outer limits of Jesus' generation. Yet Luke expected a considerable interval following the destruction of Jerusalem before the end, "until the times of the Gentiles be fulfilled."[59]

In reply to this objection we may say that if Luke wrote before A.D. 70, as is frequently held, then the survival of some of Jesus' hearers until Luke's time and the imminent end is no problem, for the times of the Gentiles need not be a lengthy period.[60] Paul also envisions a "times of the Gentiles" (Rom 11:25-32), which in no way negates his *Naherwartung*.[61] It is instructive to note that Paul, writing to the church at Corinth about A.D. 57, can state that most of the more than 500 brethren to whom Christ appeared are still alive, though some have died (1 Cor 15:6). It could be a considerable time then before only some of them are left. Even if Luke wrote after 70, as many contend, Jesus' generation is not ruled out, for as late as the end of the first century some still expected that at least the Apostle John would live to see the final events (John 21:20-23). Luke himself had contact with some "who from the beginning were eyewitnesses" (Luke 1:2), and thus without difficulty could assume that God would complete the eschatological program during the lifetime of some of Jesus' hearers,[62] and most of Luke's readers. As Michel has pointed out, if Luke were writing about A.D. 80, then 9:27 does not allow for much time before the parousia. To Luke's readers this saying must signal a speedy coming of the kingdom.[63]

Again, some oppose View No. 9 because Luke's removal of Mark's "come in power" is thought to weigh against the apocalyptic interpretation of 9:27. But assuming that Luke knew Mark 9:1,[64] we may reasonably suppose that this change to Luke was only the removal of a redundancy, since in the context of end-time events dealt with in 9:18-27 it would never have occurred to Luke that anyone would ever doubt he had anything less than the parousia-kingdom in mind. He was not concerned to prove to redaction critics two millennia later that he expected the kingdom to come in the near future in a realistic manner. After all, he had referred frequently enough to the coming, appearing, or waiting for the kingdom (Luke 10:9,11; 11:2; 17:20; 19:11; 21:31; 22:16,18; 23:42,51; cf Acts 1:6) that he did not need to be explicit in every instance.[65]

---

[59]Ellis, "Present and Future," p. 30.

[60]See below, Chap. VI.F., and cf. note #27 on Streeter, who dates Luke-Acts about 85-90.

[61]As Ellis himself remarks, *Eschatology*, p. 18.

[62]Likewise Klostermann, *Lukas*, 1929, p. 107; Wilson, "Lukan Eschatology," p. 343; Hiers, "Delay," pp. 152-153.

[63]Michel, "Lukas," p. 106.

[64]Luke's use of Mark is today no longer taken for granted by many. "The use of the source Q by Matthew and Luke and even the priority of Mark are generally admitted to be wide open issues" (Browning, *Luke*, p. 11). It is also suggested that Luke used a preliminary version of Mark's Gospel (Reicke, *Luke*, p. 26).

[65]J. Weiss, *Kingdom of God*, p. 69, notes how Mark 9:1 seems to contrast the "kingdom of God in power," the fulfilled kingdom, to the unfinished earthly one. Could it be that Luke omitted "in power" simply because he had no such contrast in mind? The kingdom for Luke was the fulfilled kingdom of the new age, not a present unfinished reality (see Chap. VII).

Turning to arguments for View No. 9 we find that it fits Plummer's test that the "some" of 9:27 must refer to an exceptional privilege of some as distinct from a common experience of all,[66] for by Luke's time somewhere between A.D. 60-90 the seeing of the kingdom-parousia would because of the inevitable course of nature be an exceptional privilege for those of Jesus' generation.

Of considerable importance is the further consideration that "it is highly improbable that when he speaks of a future coming of the Kingdom Luke means anything other than the parousia."[67] Thus if 9:27 does refer to a future coming of the kingdom, as Views Nos. 2 through 7 agree, it is most probable that it refers to this final eschatological event.

Furthermore, at View No. 4 we have marked the close connection between 9:26 and 9:27 which forbids using *de* ("but," "and") to indicate a contrast between these two verses. Rather, vv 26 and 27 fit as neatly together as do the coming of the Son of Man and of the kingdom of God in one great unified eschatological climax to history (so also Matt 16:28). 9:27 refers to the preceding verses and thus "unambiguously to the parousia."[68] Verse 26 sets forth the certainty of the parousia and verse 27 the nearness of the parousia-kingdom event.

We should also observe that the parallelism of vv 24-27 requires that vv 26 and 27 not be sundered. On the one hand, whosoever would save his life (v 24a) and would gain the whole world (v 25) will be condemned by the Son of Man when he comes in glory (v 26). On the other hand, he who loses his life will save it (24b) in the eternal kingdom, which is to come so soon that some of Jesus' auditors, and most of Luke's people, will still be alive at the time (v 27).

As Luke penned 9:26-27 he was writing not merely as a historian, or as a theologian, or even as a theologically-minded historian, but as a pastor concerned with all sorts and conditions of his people who are longing for God's final intervention.[69] Luke does not write theoretically out of the seclusion of an ivory tower but out of the crucible of a congregation or group of congregations. Since Luke's theological reflections are strongly influenced by a concrete pastoral situation, he may be considered a pastoral or practical theologian.[70] But however we may most appropriately classify Luke, he is stirred by the plight of the poor who are looking for reward in the kingdom (6:20). He is aware of the anxious questionings of Pharisees who would like to know exactly when the kingdom is coming (17:20), of disciples who think the kingdom is to appear immediately upon Jesus' entry into Jerusalem (19:11), of disciples who want to learn when these last things will be (21:7), and of disciples who ask whether the Lord will at this time restore the kingdom to Israel (Acts 1:6). His pastor's heart is moved by the calamities besetting those suffering souls who are crying to God day and night, praying endlessly for the end (18:1-8), some of whom are so earnestly engaged in

---

[66]Plummer, *Luke*, p. 250.

[67]Wilson, "Lukan Eschatology," p. 341.

[68]Bartsch, *Wachet*, p. 87.

[69]Wilson, "Lukan Eschatology," p. 346, finds that both strands in Luke's eschatology, the delay strand and the imminent expectation strand, "are motivated essentially by practical, pastoral problems which faced Luke in the Church of his day."

[70]Cf. Michel, "Lukas," pp. 112-113, and Franklin, *Christ the Lord*, pp. 145, 175-176.

prayer for deliverance that they do not even leave the temple (Luke 2:37). He stands amazed at the sacrifices of those who have forsaken loved ones, even wives, for the sake of the kingdom (18:28-30). He cannot blot out the memory of a penitent thief who cries to Jesus to remember him when he comes in his kingdom (23:42). He admires all those good and righteous men who are looking for the coming of the kingdom (23:51), and wants all those who had hoped Jesus would usher in God's reign to know that Jesus' cause is not lost (24:21). Luke wishes all such persons to "know the full truth of all those matters" (Luke 1:4)(TEV) which they have been taught. He would strengthen the hearts of persecuted disciples by encouraging them to remain true to the faith and by reminding them that only by passing through tribulation can they enter into the kingdom (Acts 14:22). And so he reassures them all, especially any whose faith may be wavering, that the coming of the kingdom cannot be far off, for some of Jesus' own hearers and most of Luke's flock will still be living at the time of the parousia-kingdom event (Luke 9:26-27).

With these broad pastoral concerns in mind, Luke in the unit 9:18-27 focuses his attention on the cost of discipleship in perilous times. We may paraphrase his thought as follows:

> Jesus, having been recognized by Peter as God's Messiah (9:20), announces that he as Son of Man must suffer many things (9:22). Consequently his followers as imitators of Christ must respond by taking up their crosses daily and following after him on the way which leads through suffering to the glory of eternal life in the kingdom of God (9:23,24,27; Acts 14:22). If anyone should refuse the daily suffering of discipleship because he wants to save his life now (9:24) and because he is ashamed of Jesus and his words (9:25), he will lose his life at the parousia, when the Son of Man, coming in incomparable glory, will be ashamed of him (9:26). Even if he has gained the whole world, what will he have profited if he loses himself and is eternally defeated at the last judgment before the Son of Man (9:25-26; cf. 21:36).
>
> On the other hand, he who pays the price of losing his life now will save it forever in the kingdom of God (9:24,27). But in either case the issues are the ultimate ones of life and death; the outcome is sure and certain; and the time is short and urgent, for the Son of Man will soon come to establish God's kingdom of glory and judgment (9:26-27). "Believe me when I tell you the simple truth--there are some standing here today who will certainly live to see the kingdom of God" (9:27).

D. The Kingdom Is at Your Door (Luke 10:9,11)

1. Near or Here?

There are two basic interpretations of these verses, that of realized or present eschatology and that of realistic or futuristic eschatology. The former holds that Luke 10:9,11 mean the kingdom is here, and is reflected in Phillips' translation: "The Kingdom of God has now come to you" (10:9); "The Kingdom of God has arrived!" (10:11).[71] These verses mean that God's reign has come in Jesus, for

---

[71]So Dodd, Montefiore, Bundy, Gilmour, Creed, Flender, Ellis. Phillips even makes a realized eschatologist out of John the Baptist, who started preaching in the desert, "The Kingdom of Heaven has arrived!" (Matt 3:2)(*ēngiken*). Yet years ago C. T. Craig, "Realized Eschatology," p. 20, pointedly observed that Matthew understood the words of Mark 1:15 in the sense of nearness "when he put them on the lips of John, the baptist, for surely no one would hold that John announced the presence of the kingdom." Matthew "certainly did not believe that the Kingdom had come with John" (Campbell, "Kingdom," p. 92).

whose coming the messengers prepare (10:1). Jesus is the kingdom. With him the kingdom comes not only to mankind but to each house and city.[72]

The futuristic view takes these verses to mean the kingdom is chronologically near but not here, and accordingly translates (Weymouth): "The Kingdom of God is now at your door" (10:9); "The Kingdom of God is close at hand" (10:11).[73]

2. The Meaning of *Engidzō* (Luke 10:9,11)

The contention clusters around the translation of the verb *engidzō*, the perfect tense of which is used in both 10:9 and 10:11 (*ēngika*). Does *ēngika* mean "has come" or "is at hand"? "here" or "near"? The realized school has sought a linguistic basis for its understanding in the Greek usage of the Septuagint and in the Hebrew and Aramaic equivalents of *engidzō*. The futuristic school, on the other hand, has read the same evidence so as to support its rendering. The arguments are long and tedious, involving usage in Greek, Hebrew, Aramaic, and other languages.[74] Unfortunately for our purposes the discussion has revolved around the parallel in Mark 1:15, where the same form of the same verb appears: "The kingdom of God (has come?)(is at hand?)(*ēngika*)." Thus we must examine the evidence afresh so as to determine how Luke, not necessarily Mark, Jesus, or the versions understood the verb. Since twenty-four of the forty-two NT occurrences of *engidzō* are in Luke-Acts, *engidzō* may justifiably be called Luke's "favorite."[75]

To ascertain the meaning of the more difficult word, *engidzō*, we may begin with the simpler adverbial form *engus*. This adverb appears thirty-two times in the NT.[76] In every instance ASV takes it to mean "nigh," "near," "at hand." BAG also translates only in the sense of nearness.[77] A check of Vaughan's *Twenty-six Translations* reveals the same remarkable uniformity, with only two exceptions, neither of which is justified:

1) Phillips paraphrases Eph 2:13 to read, you "are with us inside the circle of God's love in Christ Jesus." Kümmel more soberly regards Eph 2:13 as

---

[72]Grundmann, *Lukas*, p. 210.

[73]Thus K. W. Clark, Kümmel, Godet, Hiers, Talbert, Wilson. Conzelmann, *Theology*, pp. 107, 114, 130, feels compelled to recognize the imminent sense of these verses, but not for Luke. The kingdom will be near at a future time after certain stages of salvation history have elapsed!

[74]For summaries of the debate see Perrin, *Kingdom of God*, pp. 64-66, and Berkey, "Realized Eschatology," pp. 177-187. The discussion has often assumed that Mark 1:15 is parallel to Matt 12:28//Luke 11:20: "If I . . . cast out demons, then is the kingdom of God come (*phthanō*) upon you." Those favoring realized eschatology have found both verbs (*engidzō; phthanō*) to mean "has come," whereas advocates of realistic eschatology favor "at hand" for both. See Chap. VII.D.

[75]Plummer, *Luke*, p. 275.

[76]Matt 24:32,33; 26:18; Mark 6:36; 13:28,29; Luke 19:11; 21:30,31; John 2:13; 3:23; 6:4,19,23; 7:2; 11:18,54,55; 19:20,42; Acts 1:12; 9:38; 27:8; Rom 10:8; 13:11; Eph 2:13,17; Phil 4:5; Heb 6:8; 8:13; Rev 1:3; 22:10.

[77]BAG, p. 213, translates Heb 6:8 as "close to being cursed," but then without reason equates this closeness with being "under a curse" (cf. our comment on R. Knox).

emphasizing "the nearness to, in contrast to the distance from, but not the arrival at the place."[78]

2) R. Knox renders Heb 6:8 as "a curse hangs over it." But this is an unjustifiable change in meaning when the original makes good sense: "it is on the verge of being cursed" (Moffatt).

In Luke-Acts and the whole NT, then, the meaning of *engus* is consistent. Kümmel similarly concludes that NT "usage is therefore completely uniform as regards the temporal use of *engus*: it denotes that an event will happen soon, by which it is meant or presumed that there will not be a long time to wait before it happens."[79] Rüstow likewise notes that in connection with *engidzō* every Greek-speaking person correctly thinks of *engus*, which always indicates a distance, be it ever so small, and therefore Matt 3:2 and parallels do not mean the presence but only the nearness of the kingdom.[80]

Engus is found three times each in Luke (19:11; 21:30,31) and Acts (1:12; 9:38; 27:8). This constancy of meaning is significant, because a check of the passages involved shows that Luke uses *engus* and *engidzō* interchangeably. Luke employs *engus* four times to indicate nearness to, but not arrival at, a place: Jesus was nigh to Jerusalem (Luke 19:11); the Mount of Olives is near to Jerusalem (Acts 1:12); Lydda is nigh unto Joppa (9:38), and Fair Havens is near Lasea (27:8). *Engidzō* is likewise used in respect to place to indicate that one comes close to a place without entering into it: one draws near to the gate of the city (Luke 7:12), to heaven (12:33), to the house (15:25), to Jericho (18:35), to Bethpage (19:29), to Jerusalem (19:37,41), to the village (24:28), to Damascus (Acts 9:3; 22:6), to the city (10:9).

Luke uses *engidzō* (but not *engus*) to mean approach toward a person. ASV and RSV render each instance as "draw near" or "come near." Other accurate and vivid translations are:

Luke 15:1   The taxgatherers and sinners were all approaching him to listen to him (Moffatt).

Luke 18:40 When he was quite close, he said to him (Phillips).

Luke 22:47 He approached in order to kiss Jesus (Moffatt).

Luke 24:15 Jesus himself approached and walked beside them (Mofatt).

Acts 21:33 Then the tribune approached and arrested him (Lake and Cadbury).

Acts 23:15 We will be ready to kill him before he ever gets here (TEV).

Thus in each instance *engidzō* means "to approach" rather than "to arrive," though arrival may follow the approach or coming near.[81]

Luke also uses *engus* to indicate nearness to, but not arrival of, a future event: the

---

[78] Kümmel, *Promise*, p. 19.

[79] Kümmel, *Promise*, p. 20.

[80] Rüstow, "Luke 17:20-21," p. 209.

[81] Berkey, "Realized Eschatology," p. 183, overlooks this possibility as he opts for "arrival" at Luke 24:15 and Acts 21:33.

summer is nigh (Luke 21:30) and the kingdom of God is nigh (21:31). "It would be exceedingly difficult, and would demand convincing explanation to translate 21:31 as 'has come.'"[82] So too engidzō: the time (21:8), desolation (21:20), redemption (21:28), feast of unleavened bread (22:1), and the time of promise (Acts 7:17) are at hand or draw nigh but are not yet present. This parallel usage of *engus* and *engidzō* with the coming eschatological events (kingdom of God, time, desolation, redemption) is indeed extraordinary. It strongly suggests that *engidzō* when used with the kingdom of God in 10:9,11 also means "near" rather than "here."

This meaning of *engidzō* in these five passages (Luke 21:8,20,28; 22:1; Acts 7:17) is verified by the context of each verse:

1) "The time is at hand" (Luke 21:8). The correctness of this translation is indicated by the fact that it is accepted by both the Near and Distant Expectation Schools (Chap. VI.E.1.2), as well as by all twenty-six translations.

2) "But when ye see Jerusalem compassed with armies, then know that her desolation is at hand" (Luke 21:20). Jerusalem must first be surrounded by armies and then its destruction is near: "When you see Jerusalem surrounded by armies, then you will know that soon she will be destroyed" (TEV).

3) "But when these things begin to come to pass, look up, and lift up your heads; because your redemption draweth nigh" (Luke 21:28). When the cosmic woes begin to occur, then redemption is at hand, but not actually present until these woes are completed.

4) "Now the feast of the unleavened bread drew near" (Luke 22:1). It is not until verse 7 that Luke says "the day of unleavened bread came." Mark 14:1//Luke 22:1 indicates how near the day was: "Now after two days was the feast of the passover and the unleavened bread."

5) "But as the time of the promise drew nigh which God vouchsafed unto Abraham [to deliver Israel from Egypt--Gen 15:14], the people grew and multiplied in Egypt" (Acts 7:17). The time of deliverance had not yet arrived but was approaching, as indicated by the following verses in Acts 7 and by the fact that the people's growth preceded the exodus.[83]

These observations are confirmed by a check of the eight eschatological usages of *engus* outside of Luke-Acts. *Engus* appears in the parallel passages to Luke 21:30-31 (Matt 24:32-33; Mark 13:28-29): "the summer is nigh," and "he [it] is nigh, even at the doors." In a mini-apocalypse (Rom 13:11-14) Paul declares that final salvation is "nearer (*engus*) to us than when we first believed" (13:11), for "the night [old age] is far spent, and the day [new age] is at hand" (perfect tense of *engidzō*)(13:12). Here Paul uses *engus* and *engidzō* synonymously, as we have seen Luke doing. Later, Paul in prison, eagerly awaiting the coming from heaven of "a Savior, the Lord Jesus Christ: who shall fashion anew the body of our humiliation" (Phil 3:20-21), knows "the Lord is at hand" (*engus*) (Phil 4:5). Phillips attempts to avoid the imminent expectation at Phil 4:5 by giving the saying

---

[82]Clark, "Realized Eschatology," p. 372.

[83]Fuller's analysis of these five verses has led to similar results (*Mission*, pp. 22-23).

a mystical twist: "Never forget the nearness of our Lord." This evasion is prohibited by Phil 3:20-21 and by the meaning of *engus* which we are establishing. Goodspeed and TEV correctly paraphrase: "The Lord is coming soon." John the Revelator begins and ends his Apocalypse with the assurance "the time is at hand" (*engus*) (Rev 1:3; 22:10). Since in Revelation *engus* is thus "used unambiguously to denote the nearness of the end of the world, it is to be presumed ... that this usage is to be found when *engus* is employed in connexion with eschatological events."[84]

Thus far we have checked Luke's six usages of *engus* and twenty-four usages of *engidzō*, and we have found them to mean nearness to a place, person, or event. Other observations on *engidzō* support this conclusion. The perfect tense of *engidzō* is found in Luke 10:9,11; 21:8,20. We have just noted that 21:8,20, being parallel with nearby verses containing *engus*, should be translated "at hand". The fact that the same tense of the verb is used in 10:9, 11 would likewise suggest "at hand" as the meaning in these two verses.[85]

This conclusion is reinforced by a check of the ten appearances of the perfect tense of *engidzō* outside of Luke-Acts. Four of these usages are in verses parallel to Luke 10:9,11 (Matt 3:2; 4:17; 10:7; Mark 1:15: the kingdom is near? here?) and hence must be set aside at this point as being the passages in question. Three of these perfects are used in the Gethsemane account: Jesus' hour (Matt 26:45) and he that betrayeth him (Matt 26:46; Mark 14:42) are at hand. Here the context confirms the imminence rather than the arrival of the hour (of death?) or the person. Mark, thinking of the "hour" (of arrest?) as already having come, uses another verb (*erchomai*) (14:41).[86] Here, where Christological issues are not involved, Phillips does distinguish vividly and accurately between the verbs used by Matthew and Mark: "In one moment (engidzō) you will see the Son of Man betrayed into the hands of evil men ... Look, here comes (*engidzō*) my betrayer!" (Matt 26:45-46). "The moment has come"(*erchomai*) (Mark 14:41).

The three other perfects of *engidzō* are of crucial importance, for they definitely and clearly refer to the imminent arrival of the end:

1) "The day is at hand" (="The day is about to dawn"--Weymouth) (Rom 13:12b). Since the night is not yet past (13:12a), the day has not yet arrived: "The night is nearly over, day is almost here" (TEV).

2) "The coming (parousia) of the Lord is at hand" (Jas 5:8). But it has not yet arrived, for the brethren are to wait for it with patience and hope (5:8), even as a farmer patiently waits for his land to produce precious crops (5:7).

3) "The end of all things is at hand" (1 Pet 4:7). But the end is still a future event, for God "stands ready to pronounce judgement on the living and the dead" (1 Pet 4:5) (Weymouth).

---

[84]Kümmel, *Promise*, p. 20.

[85]Berkey, "Realized Eschatology," p. 183, in favoring "its desolation has arrived" (Luke 21:20) does not take into account the connections between *engus* and *engidzō* being presented here.

[86]Kümmel, *Promise*, pp. 22-23; Fuller, *Mission*, p. 22.

The NT usage of the perfect tense of *engidzō* thus suggests, even requires, that this same verb and tense be translated to mean "at hand" in Luke 10:9,11 and parallels in Matt 3:2; 4:17; 10:7; Mark 1:15. "The perfect *ēngiken* when used of time can only refer to the near future."[87]

Another eschatological passage uses the present tense of *engidzō*: "Ye see the day drawing nigh" (="You see that the Day of the Lord is coming near"--TEV) (Heb 10:25). Not because the day of the Lord is already there but because it is coming Christians are to continue to meet together to encourage one another (10:25). Here again is the imminent, futuristic usage of *engidzō*, and it is so understood by the twenty-six translations.

There remain to be considered the seven remaining NT uses of *engidzō*:

1) 2) "They drew nigh unto Jerusalem" (Matt 21:1; Mark 11:1).

3) "The season of fruits drew near" (Matt 21:34). Kümmel, thinking the servants were sent out before the arrival of the harvest so as to be in time to receive the fruits, translates: "when the time of the harvest had come near."[88] So too other translations: "when vintage time approached" (Berkeley); "when the grapes were getting ripe" (Beck).

4) "Epaphroditus came nigh unto death" (Phil 2:30) =he came to the point of death but did not die.

5) 6) 7) "Draw nigh unto God (Heb 7:19; Jas 4:8) and he will draw nigh to you" (Jas 4:8). One must go out of his way to find it difficult to "draw the line between 'drawing near to' and actual communion with God" in these verses.[89] The twenty-six translations unanimously use such expressions here as "draw near," "come close," or "approach." Clark well says that Hebrews and James "would not have dreamed of writing" "we come to God": "Due reverence for the transcendent and holy God dictated the use" of *engidzō*.[90] Once more the evidence is clear.

We may quote here Clark's conclusions:

> Literally a hundred decisive illustrations can be exhibited from the LXX to demonstrate that in the pre-Christian centures, as well as in the papyri of the second and third centuries A.D., *engidzein* consistently connoted proximity or approach... "It is clear that the LXX affords no good evidence that *ēngiken* ever means 'has come.'"[91] ...In the non-literary and literary papyri of the second and third centuries, in the LXX, the Apostolic Fathers, and the NT, *engidzō* has been employed consistently to mean "to draw near." ....Usage by the three synoptists unanimously agrees with all the above evidence, and no linguistic evidence appears to support the contention that *ēngiken* can mean "has come." ...One may further point out that philology in general observes in *engidzō* no contextual problem and reveals no evidence of changing trend in the connotation of the verb, down to A.D. 1100 at the earliest. In this history of the word no variation in

---

[87]Craig, "Realized Eschatology," p. 20, and Kümmel, *Promise*, p. 24.
[88]Kümmel, *Promise*, p. 23; Fuller, *Mission*, pp. 21-22.
[89]Berkey, "Realized Eschatology," p. 183.
[90]Clark, "Realized Eschatology," p. 370.
[91]Quoted by Clark from Campbell, "Kingdom," p. 92.

meaning has developed, but through all the literature and through the centuries it has consistently been used to mean, "to draw near."[92]

So far as the verb *engidzō* is concerned, then, the translation of Luke 10:9,11 as "the kingdom of God is near but not here" is not only thoroughly justified but any other translation violates the meaning of the verb. A good rendition would be:

The kingdom of God is fast approaching.[93]

3. The Meaning of "Upon You" (Luke 10:9)

Another linguistic problem is found in Luke 10:9 (but not in 10:11 or Matt 3:2; 4:17; 10:7; Mark 1:15), namely, the presence of the words "upon you" or "unto you" (*eph' humas*): "The kingdom of God is come nigh unto you." It is commonly held that the addition of these two words suggests the kingdom may be thought of as already present.[94] Thus, "the Kingdom of God has now come to you" (Phillips). This understanding is undoubtedly influenced by Luke 11:20, where *eph' humas* also appears, and which is often found to have a present meaning (see Chap. VII.D).

Others recognize that the verb in 10:9 refers to the kingdom's coming in the near future. But the phrase *eph' humas* directs attention away from the imminent futurity of the kingdom to the nature of the kingdom which can be perceived in Jesus and in the redemptive work of the seventy. Not the nearness of the kingdom but the nature of the kingdom is the theme of Luke's missionary preaching.[95]

But *eph' humas* also goes well with a futuristic coming of the kingdom. The kingdom of God "is the idea of a world, and indeed of a world which is first of all in heaven. Further, when it is said that the kingdom comes, the idea is always present to some extent that it comes down from above."[96] In Luke 10:9 the kingdom "is naturally [from the apocalyptic viewpoint] thought of as coming 'upon' men, down from above."[97] The same idea is present at Luke 19:11, where the people suppose that the kingdom is just about to appear: the kingdom is to appear when it emerges from concealment above and comes down upon men. Thus Acts 3:19 says that seasons of refreshing are to come "from the face of the Lord," being found with God in heaven and coming down out of heaven from God

---

[92] Clark, "Realized Eschatology," pp. 369, 371, 372.

[93] Albright and Mann, *Matthew*, translate Matt 3:2; 4:17; 10:7 as "the kingdom of heaven is fast approaching." "Our translation attempts to capture the urgency of the Gr. *ēngiken*, which is lost in such English translations as the 'at hand' of the KJ" (p. 25). The four other appearances of *engidzō* in Matthew are translated as follows: "As they approached Jerusalem" (21:1); "When the vintage season approached" (21:34); "See, the hour is almost here" (26:45); "My betrayer is near" (26:46). They render Matthew's three uses of *engus* as: "The summer is near" (24:32); "he is at the threshold" (24:33); "My time is almost here" (26:18).

[94] Creed, *Luke*, p. 146; Flender, *Luke*, p. 149.

[95] Grässer, *Delay*, pp. 140-141; Schneider, *Parusiegleichnisse*, pp. 49-54.

[96] Otto, *Kingdom of God*, p. 54.

[97] Plummer, *Luke*, p. 275.

to earth.⁹⁸ So also John the Revelator sees "the holy city, new Jerusalem [symbolizing the kingdom] coming down out of heaven from God" (Rev 21:2). Luke 10:9 would then read, "The kingdom of God is at hand, [coming down] upon you [from heaven]." Moffatt catches the meaning: "The Reign of God is nearly on you."

4. An Urgent Mission (Luke 10:1-16)

These linguistic conclusions favoring the *Naherwartung* in Luke 10:9, 11 are supported by the apocalyptic urgency of the charge in 10:1-16. "The Lord" sends the seventy "into every city and place, whither he himself was about to come" (10:1). The title "Lord" suggests that the Risen Lord is speaking to his missionary church. Hence Luke is not thinking here of an earthly coming of Jesus to these places nor even of his spiritual coming to the hearts of believers but rather of his imminent parousia. This meaning is further indicated by the non-historical character of the mission of the seventy. Luke's charge to the seventy is drawn from the charge to the twelve as recorded in Matt 9:37-38; 10:1-15; 11:21-23; Mark 6:6-11, as is shown also by Luke 22:35, where Jesus addresses words to the twelve which in 10:4 are spoken to the seventy! "Seventy" symbolizes the Gentile nations of Genesis 10, thus prefiguring Philip's evangelization of Samaria (Acts 8:4-25) and the Gentile mission of Paul and others in Acts. Moreover, "that there was no actual mission may be inferred from the fact that they are no sooner sent out than they return, 10:17, and not a single sign remains of where they went."⁹⁹ Further, Luke is hardly thinking of the earthly Jesus as being about to arrive in thirty-five or more different places prepared by the thirty-five teams. Nor does Jesus appear to follow up the preparations.¹⁰⁰ Again, in 10:1 Luke uses *mellō* ("about to"), a favorite Lukan word with strong apocalyptic overtones (Chap. IV).

If 10:1 does refer to Jesus' imminent parousia, it may be Luke's substitute for Mark 14:28//Matt 26:32, "After I am raised up, I will go before you into Galilee," a verse which may well refer to the Risen Christ's leading his apostles to Galilee where he will be manifested as Son of Man as the kingdom appears.¹⁰¹ Luke 10:1 would then mean that Christ, when the Gentile mission is completed, will return to lead his disciples from town to town from Jerusalem to Galilee for the consummation.

Another indication of the urgency of the mission is found at 10:2, which prays the Lord of the harvest literally to "drive forth" (*ekballō*) laborers into the harvest, for the harvest is great and it is already ripe.¹⁰² Again, 10:2 is "the best

---

⁹⁸Meyer, *Acts*, p. 82. Cf. Rev 3:3: "I will come upon thee" from heaven.

⁹⁹Carpenter, *Gospels*, p. 271. Carpenter thinks of the glorified Messiah's coming "as the kingdom spreads, in the person of his faithful disciples, x.16, or takes up his abode in the believer's soul, cp. Ephes. iii.17." We however are finding it very doubtful that Luke so spiritualizes the kingdom and parousia.

¹⁰⁰Cf. Manson, *Sayings of Jesus*, p. 549.

¹⁰¹Schweitzer, *Quest*, p. 334; *Mysticism of Paul*, p. 246; J. Weiss, *Earliest Christianity*, I, 17-18.

¹⁰²Vincent, *Word Studies*, I, 350.

explanation" of the sayings in the preceding section, 9:57-62. "The seeming harshness of Jesus and his almost brutal thrusting into the background of natural feelings and obligations are due to the overwhelming urgency of His task. The King's business requires haste. He leaves no room for the kind of selfishness that takes shelter behind the plea that charity begins at home. . . . They are few, and the ground to be covered is great, and the time is short."[103]

The Lord at 10:4a instructs the seventy to be encumbered with none of those things travelers ordinarily regard as indispensable, such as purse, bag, and sandals, for "peace-loving" men will supply their necessities (10:7-8). "The command to take no extra provisions . . . is to enable them to make a rapid tour."[104] Nor are the seventy on their rapid journey to lose time with tedious Oriental salutations (10:4b). Just as Elisha commanded his servant Gehazi to salute no one on his way to save the life of the son of the woman of Shunam (2 Kgs 4:29), so too the mission of the seventy is a matter of life-and-death urgency. The missioners are to extend end-time peace only to those who are hospitable (10:5) (on 10:4 see Chap. VIII.E.9).

We have noted in Section C that the sayings in Luke 9:26-27 about the coming of the Son of Man and of the kingdom are in a context of blessing and judgment: those who lose their lives for Jesus will save them in the kingdom, but those who are ashamed of Jesus will be condemned by the Son of Man in the last judgment. Likewise in the charge to the seventy the imminent coming of the kingdom is promised as a blessing to receptive persons (10:8-9), but as a judgment upon the non-receptive (10:10-11). "When the reception is unfriendly, no time is to be wasted. The disciples are to pass on to more promising fields. But before going away they will publicly and solemnly disclaim all responsibility for the consequences of that city's refusal to hear their message." Wiping the dust off their feet is to reckon the city as heathen and its people as no part of the true Israel. "Their blood will be on their own heads in the coming judgement."[105] In addition, "that day" (10:12) is an explicit reference to the impending judgment day, which comes when the kingdom now at their doors (10:9,11) has fully arrived. Then the hardened hearts will be condemned to Hades (10:15). These references to the last judgment prove that Luke understands the kingdom of 10:9,11 as near rather than here, as a threatening future, not as a present reality.[106]

For Luke, this urgent apocalyptic mission of the Risen Messiah's seventy messengers is itself proof that the kingdom of God is at hand. In the Lukan setting, their successful exorcisms induce Jesus to tell of his ecstatic apocalyptic vision of Satan's fall (10:17-18) (Chap. VII.C). Although Luke 10:18 may originally have come out of another setting, in its present location it is connected to the report of the seventy. In this context Luke could have added, as did John after his

---

[103] Manson, *Sayings of Jesus*, p. 367.

[104] Selby, "Changing Ideas," p. 25.

[105] Manson, *Sayings of Jesus*, pp. 367-368.

[106] Kümmel, *Introduction*, p. 101.

vision of Satan's fall (Rev 12), that Satan "hath but a short time" (12:12).[107] The pressing nature of Luke's charge to the seventy results from this nearness of the kingdom. Luke's portrayal of this urgency in 10:1-17 makes it clear that whether 10:9,11 come from Q, Luke, or other source, the imminent coming of the kingdom is hardly there without Luke's approval.[108]

5. The Historical Setting of the Mission

The imminent expectation in Luke 10:9,11 finds support not only in the language used and in the nature of the mission but also in its suitability to various possible settings. If the charge and mission are historical events in the ministry of Jesus,[109] then Luke's seventy could preach the *Naherwartung* even as do Matthew's twelve (Matt 10:7). We have seen in Chap. V.C.9 that this expectation of Jesus' contemporaries was not yet falsified for Luke. It may be that Luke uses the seventy as a prototype of Paul's Gentile mission when the imminent expectation was a living hope.[110] Or, if Luke is thinking of the Gentile mission of the eighties or nineties of the first century he could still picture the missionaries of that period proclaiming the chronological nearness of the kingdom.[111] And it has even been suggested that 10:9,11 mean the imminent coming of the kingdom from the much later point of view of a time after a series of eschatological events has taken place.[112] In short, there is no basis from the vantage point of any of these life-situations to deny an imminent hope in 10:9,11. Thus linguistic, theological, and historical considerations irresistibly suggest that Luke accurately summarizes the message of the seventy in the words:

The kingdom of God is fast approaching!

E. A Sign for the People of His Day (Luke 11:30)

1. Literary Analysis (Luke 11:14-36)

First of all we shall take note of the contrasting Matthean and Lukan orders in the sign pericopes:

---

[107]Kümmel, *Promise*, pp. 113-114, and Ellis, *Eschatology*, pp. 11-12, see at 10:18 a reference to the kingdom as present. Ellis, however, argues from a present meaning at 10:18 back to a present meaning at 10:9,11,since "10:17-18 clearly applies the logion to the mission of the seventy." Even apart from the overpowering linguistic argument based upon Luke's (and NT) usage of *engidzō*, the parallel account in Revelation 12 suggests that Luke 10:18 would have indicated to Luke (and to Jesus) the nearness rather than the presence of the kingdom. See Chap. VII.C.

[108]Cf. Michel, "Lukas," p. 105.

[109]Godet, *Luke*, II, 391.

[110]My "Halévy Reconsidered," pp. 369-371.

[111]Talbert, "Redaction Critical Quest," p. 185; Hiers, "Delay," p. 150.

[112]Conzelmann, *Theology*, pp. 107, 114, 130. This interpretation denies the *Naherwartung* to Luke, but fails to note that Luke sees himself well along the eschatological time-table (Chap. IV). Grässer, *Delay*, p. 190, admits that Luke 10:11 means the nearness of the end, but thinks that Luke simply reproduced his tradition without changing it to suit his own *Fernerwartung*.

Matt 12:22-42	Luke 11:14-36
Healing of a Demoniac (22-23)	*Healing of a Demoniac (14)*
22 Then was brought unto him one possessed with a demon, . . . and he healed him, . . 23	14 And he was casting out a demon that was dumb . . . .
Beelzebub Charge (24)	*Beelzebub Charge (15)*
24 But when the Pharisees heard it, they said, This man doth not cast out demons, but by Beelzebub the prince of the demons.	15 But some of them said, By Beelzebub the prince of the demons, casteth he out demons.
Refutation of Beelzebub Charge (25-37)	*Request for a Sign (16)*
25 And knowing their thoughts he said unto them, Every kingdom divided against itself is brought to desolation; . . .	16 And others, trying him, sought of him a sign from heaven.
Request for a Sign (38)	*Refutation of Beelzebub Charge (17-26)*
38 Then certain of the scribes and Pharisees answered him, saying, Teacher, we would see a sign from thee.	17 But he, knowing their thoughts, said unto them, Every kingdom divided against itself is brought to desolation; . . .
	A Woman's Reaction (27-28)
	27 And it came to pass, as he said these things, a certain woman out of the multitude lifted up her voice, and said unto him, Blessed is the womb that bare thee, . . .
Reply to Request for Sign (39-42)	*Reply to Request for Sign (29-36)*
39 But he answered and said unto them, An evil and adulterous generation seeketh after a sign; and there shall no sign be given to it but the sign of Jonah the prophet: 40 for as Jonah was three days and three nights in the belly of the whale; so shall the Son of man be three days and three nights in the heart of the earth.	29 And when the multitudes were gathering together unto him, he began to say, This generation is an evil generation: it seeketh after a sign; and there shall no sign be given to it but the sign of Jonah. 30 For even as Jonah became a sign unto the Ninevites, so shall also the Son of man be to this generation.

After Jesus casts out a demon (Luke 11:14), some of the people accuse him of being in league with the prince of demons (11:15), whereas others ask him for a sign from heaven (11:16). The request for a sign appears to be "at a very awkward point,"¹¹³ for it separates the Beelzebub charge (11:15) from Jesus' refutation of it (11:17-26), so that the reply to the sign request does not come until 11:29-36. In Matthew, on the other hand, the Beelzebub charge (12:24) is followed at once by its refutation (12:25-37). Then comes the wish for a sign (12:38), with Jesus' immediate answer (12:39-42).

This situation has, of course, occasioned considerable speculation. The separation of the request for a sign (Luke 11:16) from Jesus' reply (11:29-36) is regarded by some as "probably the most important and obvious indication of Luke's hand. . . . The problem this raises is obvious when we read in 11:17 that Jesus 'knowing their thoughts, says..' Why is it necessary to 'know' their thoughts when they have made themselves quite clear by asking for a sign?"¹¹⁴

Others do not hold Luke "responsible for this confusion," but attribute it to Luke's sources in this great non-Markan central section (9:51-19:27).¹¹⁵ Godet however believes that Matthew has separated the two questions and thus Luke's "significant connection" disappears:

> It might seem at first sight that these are two sayings simply placed in juxtaposition; but it is not so. The second is intended to offer Jesus the means of clearing Himself of the terrible charge involved in the first: "Work a miracle in the heavens, that sphere which is exclusively divine, and we shall then acknowledge that it is God who acts through thee, and not Satan.¹¹⁶

Godet's view seems to make good sense of Luke's arrangement, whether Luke found 11:16 at its present location in his sources or shifted it there himself, without eliminating the difficulty created by v 17. The whole section, then, may be coherently outlined as follows:

11:14-36: Exorcisims and Signs

A. 11:14-16 Occasion

 1. 11:14 Cure of a dumb demoniac

 2. 11:15 First challenge to Jesus: the Beelzebub charge

 3. 11:16 Second challenge to Jesus: the request for a sign to disprove the Beelzebub charge

B. 11:17-26 The first discourse: Jesus' reply to the Beelzebub charge

C. 11:27-28 A woman's reaction to the first discourse: the blessedness of Mary

D. 11:29-36 The second discourse: Jesus' reply to the request for a sign¹¹⁷

It is within this Lukan context that our inquiry must now proceed. As we have pointed out, some of the people asked Jesus for a sign from heaven (11:16) to

---

¹¹³Bundy, *Gospels*, p. 347.

¹¹⁴Edwards, *Sign of Jonah*, p. 91.

¹¹⁵Bundy, *Gospels*, p. 347.

¹¹⁶Godet, *Luke*, II, 60.

¹¹⁷Plummer, *Luke*, pp. 308-309, finds no break between 11:32 and 11:33: "Those whose spiritual sight has not been darkened by indifference and impenitence have no need of a sign from heaven."

prove his authenticity. They wanted something more spectacular than the exorcisms which both Jesus and others could work (Luke 9:49; 11:19) (Josephus, *Antiquities* 8.2.5) and which left them in doubt about Jesus' connections with Satan. They desired some overwhelming manifestation of the divine power direct from God, a voice from heaven (*bath qol*), a pillar of fire, a sign in the stars, something which the rabbis could not reproduce. Could he divide the Jordan? or cause the walls of Jerusalem to collapse? or make the sun or moon stand still?

Jesus replied, "This generation is an evil generation: it seeketh after a sign; and there shall no sign be given it but the sign of Jonah" (11:29). Then an interpretation is given, which is peculiar to Luke: "For even as Jonah became a sign unto the Ninevites, so shall also the Son of man be to this generation" (11:30). Only Luke tells us at this point that the Son of Man will be a sign (cf. Matt 24:30). Then follow references to the Queen of Sheba and the people of Nineveh, two OT examples of pagans who demonstrated greater responsiveness to lesser revelations than did Jesus' hearers (11:31-32) (cf. Matt 12:41-42).

2. Jesus' Preaching as the Sign

What is meant by the sign of Jonah? In what sense was the Son of Man to be a sign to that generation? Since 11:32 refers to Jonah's preaching, the sign is commonly thought to be Jesus' preaching. As Jonah proclaimed judgment to the Ninevites in ancient times, so the Son of Man will proclaim it to this generation. Jesus, the preacher of repentance and judgment, is the sign which will be given to this generation.[118]

Several obstacles, however, stand in the way of this view. Whereas Matt 12:39 refers to "the sign of the prophet Jonah," Luke 11:30 mentions only "the sign of Jonah," suggesting that to Luke the main point of comparison was not preaching. Moreover, since Jesus had been preaching for some time, his preaching of repentance can hardly be described by the two future tenses: "there shall no sign be given it" (11:29), and "so shall also the Son of man be to this generation" (11:30). Both futures are to be taken at full value,[119] as if "something else than Christ's ministry, something future in His experience, was the sign. Something is obscurely hinted at which is not further explained, as if to say: wait and you will get your sign."[120] Again, "it is highly unusual to describe the preaching of repentance as a sign, since a sign consists, not in what men do, but in the intervention of the power of God in the course of events."[121]

3. Jesus' Resurrection as the Sign

In order to meet these objections some find the sign to be Jesus' resurrection.

---

[118]Browning, *Luke*, p. 116; Bundy, *Gospels*, p. 350; Conzelmann, *Theology*, p. 192; Edwards, *Sign of Jonah*, p. 95; Gilmour, *Luke*, p. 211; Grundmann, *Lukas*, p. 242; Kümmel, *Promise*, pp. 68-69; Leaney, *Luke*, p. 192; Manson, *Sayings of Jesus*, p. 382; Stuhlmueller, *Luke*, p. 145.

[119]Higgins, *Son of Man*, p. 138; Easton, *Luke*, p. 185.

[120]Bruce, *Gospels*, p. 551.

[121]Jeremias, "Ionas," p. 409.

As Jonah miraculously escaped death and summoned the Ninevites to anticipate the danger before them, so the Risen Jesus will by his disciples proclaim salvation to this generation. This solution harmonizes with that of Matt 12:40, which takes Jonah as a type of the burial and resurrection of Jesus: "For as Jonah was three days and three nights in the belly of the whale, so will the Son of man be three days and three nights in the heart of the earth." If it be wondered why Luke understood the sign to be Jesus' resurrection and yet omitted Matt 12:40, which would have made it all plain, it may be replied that Luke made this omission because Jesus was not in the tomb three days and three nights but only one day and two nights.[122]

Against this view that the sign is Jesus' resurrection we may rejoin that had Luke wanted to keep this meaning he could have altered the three days and nights to bring them into line with the tradition, assuming that this discrepancy bothered him any more than it did Matthew. Moreover, Jesus' resurrection was not a public sign to that generation but only a private one to his followers, and would therefore leave his opponents in doubt as to his authenticity.

4. Jesus' Parousia as the Sign

It would seem that an interpretation must be found which does justice to more of the data than do the above two explanations. Most probably Jesus' parousia as the Son of Man coming in judgment is the sign vindicating his work against the Beelzebub charge.[123] The parousia as a sign from heaven agrees well with the position of the request for a sign (11:16) following immediately the Beelzebub charge (11:15). In this Lukan context the sign must be extraordinary enough to clear Jesus of the charge of complicity with Satan. Ordinary exorcisims are insufficient. But the coming of the Son of Man on the clouds of heaven would cause even his bitterest opponents to acknowledge God's activity through him. No rabbi could reproduce that sign!

This view also fits the two future tenses. "A sign will be given it," and "the Son of man will be a sign to this generation," when Jesus returns as Son of Man. The parousia is also the best possible answer to the request for a spectacular divine intervention: the Son of Man will come "in his own glory, and the glory of the Father, and of the holy angels" (9:26). It coheres too with the request for a sign from heaven. Jesus replies that they shall have only one sign from heaven, that of Jonah, namely, Jesus himself returning from heaven in like manner as he went into heaven (Acts 1:9-11). Luke also depicts the Son of Man as coming down from heaven in Luke 9:26; 12:40; 18:8; 21:27.

The parousia as the sign to "this generation" also harmonizes well with the references to Jonah and the Queen of Sheba. As Jonah came from the far country of Palestine to become a sign to the Ninevites (11:30,32), and as the Queen of the South "traveled halfway around the world to listen to Solomon's

---

[122]Godet, *Luke*, II, 71-72; Plummer, *Luke*, pp. 306-307; Loisy, *Luc*, p. 327 (quoted by Montefiore, *Gospels*, II, 476). Codex Bezae does add the Jonah-fish references at Luke 11:30.

[123]McNeile (cited by Montefiore, *Gospels*, II, 202); Higgins, *Son of Man*, pp. 133-140; Hiers, "Delay," pp. 152, 154.

wise teaching" (11:31) (TEV), so the Son of Man will come from a "far country" (19:12) as a sign from heaven.[124] As Jonah threatened the Ninevites with God's impending judgment, so the Son of Man will bring judgment to his generation.

A judgment motif also links the Ninevites, the Queen of Sheba, and the Son of Man, for each will appear in the judgment to condemn this generation (11:31-32; 12:40; 19:27; 21:36; Acts 10:42; 17:31). When the Son of Man comes in judgment will he find faith (18:8) as that shown by the Queen of the South and the men of Nineveh (11:31-32), or will he find unfaith as in the days of Noah and Lot (17:26-30)? But in either case men will stand before the Son of Man as judge (11:32; 21:36).

The second advent as the sign from heaven also accords with the story of Dives and Lazarus. At Luke 16:31 Abraham tells Dives that if Dives' brothers do not heed Moses and the prophets neither will they be persuaded if one were to rise from the dead: not even Jesus' preaching and resurrection will persuade an evil generation. The parousia from heaven will be the only convincing sign.

The notable similarities between 11:29-32 and 17:20-30, the parousia pericope, further suggest that the parousia of the Son of Man is the sign to "this generation." In both passages there is a concern about signs. Jesus' generation "seeketh after a sign; and there shall no sign be given it but the sign of Jonah" (11:29-30). The kingdom will not come with accompanying signs to be observed (17:20) (Chap. VII.G.8.c), for like the flashing of lightning, all will know when it comes (17:20-24). But the preliminary signs (21:11, 25) will culminate with Jesus' coming as the Son of Man in judgment, the sign to end all signs. Jesus will give no *bath qol* nor call down fire from heaven (9:54-55), but if the people want a sign which is a spectacular demonstration of overwhelming power they will have the sign par excellence when the Son of Man comes in great power and glory (11:30; 21:27).

There is a judgment motif in both 11:29-32 and 17:20-30. Noah's flood came in judgment on that generation "and destroyed them all" (17:27). Fire and brimstone rained from heaven on Lot's generation and "destroyed them all" (17:29). Similarly, Jonah brought judgment to Nineveh, which was to be overthrown (Jonah 3:4), and the men of Nineveh and the Queen of the South will condemn the men of this generation in the last judgment (11:27-30).

Moreover, 11:30 and 17:24,26,28,30 are remarkably parallel in vocabulary, structure ("as....shall be"), and thought:

> For even as Jonah became a sign unto the Ninevites, so shall also the Son of man be to this generation (11:30).

> For as the lightning, when it lighteneth out of the one part under the heaven, shineth unto the other part under heaven; so shall the Son of man be in his day (17:24).

> And as it came to pass in the days of Noah, even so shall it be also in the days of the Son of man (17:26).

> Likewise even as it came to pass in the days of Lot,...after the same manner shall it be in the day that the Son of man is revealed (17:28,30).[125]

---

[124]Bultmann, *Synoptic Tradition*, p. 118.

[125]Edwards, *Sign of Jonah*, pp. 49-50, refers to this "past-future" or "present-future" pattern as "an eschatological correlative."

Finally, an appearance of the Son of Man to "this generation," to Jesus' contemporaries (Chap. V.H.1), is consistent with the imminent expectation in surrounding passages referring to that generation (Luke 9:27; 11:29,30,31; 11:50,51; 12:56; 13:5,9; 21:32; Acts 2:17,40; 3:24; 13:41) (Chap. IV.B).[126]

These results are confirmed by Matt 24:30: "And then shall appear the sign of the Son of man in heaven," the "sign which is the Son of Man,"[127] "a manifest vindication of the Son of Man as one endowed with power and glory."[128] It may be that Luke did not include this statement of Matt 24:30 at 21:26 because he had already referred to the Son of Man in his parousia as a sign at 11:30.

F. Not a Lost Cause: Parables of Watchfulness (Luke 12:35-48)

1. Parousia Parables?

This section contains three parables exhorting to watchfulness: the waiting servants (12:35-38), the thief at night (12:39-40), and the faithful and unfaithful servants (12:41-48). Whether these parables originally referred to the parousia,[129] or to the tribulation preceding the parousia,[130] or to the crisis of the kingdom present in Jesus' ministry,[131] is not our concern here, for it is plain that Luke uses them as parousia parables: "Be ye also ready: for in an hour that ye think not the Son of man cometh" (12:40).[132]

Some however deny that Luke in these parables has in mind the parousia at the end of the world. Rather he is exhorting to readiness for the judgment which is always in process,[133] or to the return of Jesus at the death of each apostle.[134] But such interpretations overlook the many end-time allusions in the surrounding Lukan apocalypse (12:1-13:35) (Chap. I.C.3), to say nothing of Luke-Acts as a whole. We should mark especially the apocalyptic language of the thief motif:

> But know this, that if the master of the house had known in what hour the thief was coming, he would have watched and not have left his house to be broken through (literally: digged through) (Luke 12:39) (Matt 24:43).

---

[126] Similarly Hiers, "Delay," p. 152, who notes that Luke not only has preserved the imminent sayings of Mark 9:1 and 13:30 but adds another, Luke 11:30.

[127] Bruce, *Gospels*, p. 295; Tödt, *Son of Man*, p. 49.

[128] McKenzie, *Matthew*, p. 105. Higgins, *Son of Man*, pp. 108-114, takes Matthew's sign of the Son of Man to be the cross, or at least a premonitory sign.

[129] "This cannot be doubted" (Godet, *Luke*, II, 105); Kümmel, *Promise*, p. 55.

[130] Jeremias, *Parables*, pp. 53-58.

[131] Dodd, *Parables*, pp. 122-139.

[132] "The waiting of the servants in the night [Luke 12:35-38] is the waiting for the eschatological coming of the Son of Man" (Lövestam, *Wakefulness*, p. 93). Lövestam asks, "In the oldest phase of the primitive church that it is possible to reach [1 Thessalonians], the 'thief' simile is thus in fact used about the parousia. What compelling objection then exists for the parable of the thief being originally a parousia parable?" (pp. 98-99). Dodd's reason apparently was his desire to deny parousia teaching to Jesus.

[133] Duncan, *Jesus*, p. 181; C. W. F. Smith, *Jesus*, p. 251; Glasson, *Advent*, p. 95 (cited by Kümmel, *Promise*, p. 55).

[134] A. Feuillet, *RB*, 56 (1949), 89; 56 (1950), 66 (cited by Kümmel, *Promise*, p. 55).

> For yourselves know perfectly that the day of the Lord so cometh as a thief in the night... But ye, brethren, are not in darkness, that the day should overtake you as a thief (1 Thess 5:2,4).
>
> But the day of the Lord will come as a thief; in the which the heavens shall pass away with a great noise, and the elements shall be dissolved with fervent heat, and the earth and works that are therein shall be burned up (2 Pet 3:10).
>
> If therefore thou shalt not watch, I will come as a thief, and thou shalt not know what hour I will come upon thee (Rev 3:3).
>
> ...the great day of God...Behold I come as a thief. Blessed is he that watcheth (Rev 16:14-15).[135]

In light of these passages it would seem quite unlikely that Luke 12:35-48 is concerned with anything other than the final parousia.

2. An Imminent Parousia?

But does Luke at this point presuppose an imminent parousia? A negative answer is frequently given. Luke's church, it is said, is confronted with the problem of the delay of the parousia.[136] Luke anticipates a considerable and incalculable lapse of time before the return of Jesus. The master may not return until the second or third watch (12:38). The servant says in his heart, "My lord delayeth his coming" (12:45). The servant's sin is not in calculating a long absence but in using this delay as an occasion for unfaithfulness. For Luke it no longer matters how long the delay lasts, because he is thinking of the indefinitely extended period of the church's existence. In this fashion Luke solves the problem once and for all.[137]

But surely the object of these parabolic calls to watchfulness is that the end is at hand. The exhortation to watch with constant expectation for the Son of Man implies the imminent expectation or else there would be no point in continual watching. If the end were postponed indefinitely, if it were not likely to occur soon, these admonitions to alertness would lose their urgency. Luke would better have advised his church to adopt another posture than that of vain waiting with girded loins and burning lamps. It may be possible to hold on to the imminent expectation as a formal doctrine to be believed but it is hardly possible to retain a lively *Naherwartung* over long periods of time. Sooner or later an individual or church must return to the normal routine of taking off his girdle (cf. Acts 12:8) and extinguishing his lamp for retirement at night.

---

[135]Godet, *Luke*, I, 106, observes: "Of all the sayings of Jesus, there is not one whose influence has made itself more felt in the writings of the N.T. than this...; it had awakened a deep echo in the heart of the disciples." Lövestam, *Wakefulness*, p. 96, points out that the thief simile is not found "in the eschatological imagery of the Judasim of that [Jesus'] time. In the New Testament, however, this imagery is found in different writings. By all accounts, it then refers back to the teaching of Jesus himself."

[136]Hiers, *Kingdom of God*, p. 74, suggests "it may well be that Jesus himself was puzzled by the delay in the appearance of the Kingdom or Son of man. He had taught his followers to hope and pray that it would come soon, and he and they had gone about proclaiming its nearness. But it did not come. Consequently, it is not simply to be assumed that references to the delay are secondary to the teaching of Jesus himself."

[137]Conzelmann, *Theology*, p. 108 (based upon Klostermann, *Lukasevangelium*, 1929); Stuhlmueller, *Luke*, p. 146; Ellis, *Luke*, pp. 180-181, 210; Schneider, *Parusiegleichnisse*, p. 29.

Yet such relaxation is far from Luke's intention. Luke, by means of the twin motifs of girded loins and burning lamps, counsels constant readiness for a parousia which is pressingly near: the faithful servant sits up all night, if necessary, fights off fatigue, and is ready to run with his garments tucked up at his waist ("loins girded about"), with lighted lamp at hand to greet the master at the gate, so that one may recognize him and he may find the entrance ("lights burning"), when he returns. Luke's picture of the church on the eve of the parousia is reminiscent of Israel on the eve of their liberation: "And thus shall ye eat it [passover lamb]: with your loins girded, your shoes on your feet, and your staff in your hand; and ye shall eat it in haste: it is Yahweh's passover" (Exod 12:11).[138]

Luke's point, then, is this: "At any moment--like a thief at night silently digging through the mud-plaster wall of the home-the Son of Man may appear in glory."[139] Therefore the servant who thinks he has time "to eat and drink and get drunk" (Luke 12:45) (RSV) because his master is delayed in coming will be caught unexpectedly by his returning master, who will hew and hack him to pieces ("dichotomize" him--12:46), like Agag (1 Sam 15:33) (cf. Luke 19:27). Luke thus countenances no thought of an indefinite delay while the church serenely goes about its daily chores. On the contrary, he explicitly excludes thought of delay and warns against complacency (12:45-46). The servant does not know the date of the return (12:46) but he must stay awake (12:37) in full expectation of an imminent event. Otherwise he may share the fate of the unfaithful, that is, in the last judgment he will be excluded from God's kingdom (12:46). Luke addresses the parable to "all" of his people (12:41). They are already standing in the second or third watch (12:38), which means that delay has already occurred (so also 12:45), making the situation all the more urgent. In this manner "Luke makes it clear that the hope of an imminent end was not a lost cause, to be abandoned by the Church."[140]

3. Setting within the Fire upon the Earth Apocalypse (Luke 12:1-13:35)

The imminent expectation in 12:35-48 is right at home within the fiery apocalypse of 12:1-13:35. The fearful consequences of exclusion from the kingdom (12:46-48) are preceded by warnings of being cast into Gehenna (12:5,10). At his parousia the Lord first kills and then casts into hell (12:5,46) (Chap. III.D).[141] The servant who eats and drinks (12:45) is like the rich fool, who, like "a sublimated chipmunk, gloating over his bushels of pignuts,"[142] takes life easy, eats, drinks, and enjoys himself, unaware that the coming judgment is upon him and the world (12:31-21) (Chap. III.E).

The life of continual expectancy of the Lord's return (12:35-48) is best lived

---

[138]Lövestam, *Wakefulness*, p. 94, sees Luke 12:35-37 as alluding to Exod 12:11.

[139]Stuhlmueller, *Lukan Reading Guide*, p. 103.

[140]Wilson, "Lukan Eschatology," p. 341; Kümmel, *Promise*, pp. 54-56; Francis, "Eschatology," p. 58; Franklin, *Christ the Lord*, p. 26.

[141]Contrast Matt 10:28, where God (Satan, according to Grundmann, *Lukas*, p. 253) kills both body and soul in hell.

[142]Rauschenbusch, *Social Principles of Jesus*, p. 118.

with raven- and lily-like unconcern for food and clothing (12:22-34), indeed, without possessions (12:33). Thus Jesus refuses to arbitrate in earthly matters (12:13-14) because property is unneeded in the new age; not even needed now in this age (12:33).[143] Messianic woes and strife will precede the fire and scorching heat of the final consummation (12:49-56). The proper interpretation of the present time (12:56) points to "the imminent eschatological consummation" (21:29-31),[144] when God will give the disciples the kingdom (12:32).[145]

The analogy of the accuser (12:57-59) makes sense in reference to the nearness of the last judgment. The accuser and the accused are "on the way" (12:58) to the judgment,[146] and the way is short.[147] "As one should be reconciled on the way to the judge even at the last moment, so one should know that it is a matter of importance to be ready now at the last moment for the coming judgment."[148] Many, in fact, will not be able to enter the kingdom (13:24). The Son of Man is already rising for the last judgment (13:25-30) (Chap. IV.G; VI.G.4). And unless men repent during the short period which remans (short even with the last limited period of grace wrung from the owner), that generation will perish in the final judgment (13:1-9) (Chap. V.B.).[149] God has already granted his people an unduly long period ("three years," 13:6). Then he allows a final interval, but only one year (13:8-9), the shortest test period possible, meaning that judgment is to fall at the earliest opportunity. The whole tenor of the parable is that of the threatening nature of the time. To regard the year's reprieve for the fig tree as indicating considerable delay in the parousia would be to destroy the meaning of the parable.[150]

The people rejoiced at Jesus' exorcism of the spirit that caused the woman's infirmity (13:10-17), for it is a sign the kingdom is near. A note of imminence may also be found in the parables of the mustard seed and the leaven (13:18-21), intepreted according to 1 Clem 23:

> O fools, compare yourselves with a tree, for instance a grapevine! First it casts off its old leaves, then young shoots arise, then leaves, then blossoms, then the tiny clusters, then the full branch is there. You see how quickly fruit ripens. Verily, quickly and suddenly shall God's decree be accomplished.

4. "Watch!"

Additional evidence for the *Naherwartung* in 12:35-48 is found when we

---

[143]Cf. G. Maier, "Luk. 12:13-15," *Theologische Beiträge*, 5 (1974), 149-158 (*NTA* 19.583); and Jeremias, *Parables*, pp. 164-165.

[144]Kümmel, *Promise*, pp. 21-22.

[145]Hiers, *Kingdom of God*, p. 85.

[146]Hiers, *Kingdom of God*, p. 75. Likewise Wilson, "Lukan Eschatology," p. 342, though Wilson is undecided as to whether the imminent judgment in 12:54-13:9 is the fall of Jerusalem or the final judgment. Easton, *Luke*, p. 213, regards it as the final judgment.

[147]Grundmann, *Lukas*, p. 273.

[148]Kümmel, *Promise*, p. 56.

[149]Similarly Creed, *Luke*, p. 181; Moore, *Parousia*, p. 162.

[150]Cf. Bartsch, *Wachet*, pp. 113-114; Michel, "Lukas," p. 106.

examine Luke's usage of three Greek words for "watch": *gregoreō* (Luke 12:37,39); *agrupneō* (21:36); *prosechō* (21:34). We see that Luke uses these words four times in two eschatological contexts, that is, in 12:35-48 and 21:34-36. It so happens that 12:35-38,41,47-48; 21:34-36 are peculiar to Luke, as is the setting of 12:35-48. Hence we should be coming close to the Lukan mind (see also Chap. V.I.1).

These two units on watchfulness (12:35-48; 21:34-36) are remarkably parallel: both occur within a Lukan apocalypse (12:1-13:35; 21:5-36); both admonish watchfulness for the parousia; both warn against dissipation and drunkenness; both refer to the day (of the Lord); both use expressive figures to illustrate the sudden coming of that day: thief and snare ("a net which all at once encloses a covey of birds peacefully settled in a field"[151]); both mention explicitly the Son of Man; both have to do with final judgment before the Son of Man. These two parallel units are thus a commentary each upon the other. If, as we shall contend below at I in further treatment of 21:34-36, the imminent expectation is found in 21:34-36, then it may well appear in 12:35-48 also.[152]

G. Justice without Delay (Luke 18:1-8)

1. Lukan Touches

The parable of the unjust judge is of crucial importance in the study of Lukan eschatology, for there are many indications of Luke's personal attention to this story. The parable is peculiar to Luke, which suggests that Luke found it particularly meaningful. Luke has not only located it within his own great central section (9:51-19:27) but he also uses it as the climax to one of his unique apocalypses (17:20-18:8), where it serves as the answer to the Pharisees' question as to when the kingdom is coming (17:20). This apocalypse thus ends with the answer to the question with which it begins. Luke's hand is also indicated here by his frequent practice of concluding a discourse with a parable (6:20-49; 10:1-37; 11:14-36; 11:37-12:21; 12:22-48; 16:9-31; 17:20-18:8). In 18:1 (and 5:36; 6:39; 12:6,41; 13:6; 14:7; 15:3; 18:9; 19:11; 20:9,19; 21:29) Luke uses a characteristic formula: "But (he added) and said to them (us, all, some, the people)(a)(this) parable (saying) . . . " Further, "ought" (*dei*) (18:1) is also a favorite Lukan word (Chap. VI.H.2.b). Also 18:8b contains several words frequently used by Luke: "nevertheless" (*plēn*), nineteen of thirty-one NT occurrences in Luke-Acts; *ara* (an interrogative particle expecting a negative response), only in Luke 18:8; Acts 8:30; Gal 2:17; "find" (*heuriskō*), eighty times in Luke-Acts as compared with Matthew, twenty-seven; Mark, eleven; and John, nineteen; and "faith" (*pistis*), Luke-Acts twenty-six times, against Matthew, eight; Mark, five; John, none. And only at 18:1, 9 "is the meaning of a parable put as the preface to it; and in each it is given as the Evangelist's preface, not as Christ's."[153] We cannot be far from Luke's own thinking.

---

[151]Godet, *Luke*, II, 273.

[152]For further illustrations of the watchfulness-imminence motif see Chap. V.I.4 on *agrupneō* (Mark 13:33; Eph 6:18); *gregoreō* (Matt 24:42,43; Mark 13:34,35,37; 1 Thess 5:6,10; 1 Pet 5:8); and Chap. V.F.1 on *gregoreō* (Rev 3:2,3; 16:15).

[153]Plummer, *Luke*, p. 411. Bultmann, *Synoptic Tradition*, p. 193, also traces 18:1 to Luke.

2. The Eschatological Nature of the Parable

This parable of the unjust judge poses two problems for us: What form will God's vindication take? And will this vindication be "sudden" or "soon"?

In regard to the question about the form of God's vindication, does the parable teach that divine help will come now in this age or at the end of this age through the parousia? If the original parable is restricted to vv 2-5 and vv 1,6-8 are regarded as later additions, then Jesus used the parable to teach that "persistence in prayer brings results."[154] There are a number of indications, however, that whatever the parable originally meant Luke uses it to teach that God will vindicate his elect at the second advent. This is clearly shown by v 8b:

> Nevertheless, when the Son of man cometh, shall he find faith on the earth?

"There is not the least reason for understanding any other here than the last coming of the Son of man."[155] How easy it would have been for Luke "to make an editorial conclusion which would bring out the meaning (perhaps the original meaning of the parable anyway) that, in spite of appearances, God is ready to help His servants speedily here and now" in this age![156]

Moreover, since the parable is centered upon the judge (vv 2,6), it could hardly fail to remind readers of the last judgment, when men will stand before the Son of Man (9:26; 18:8; 21:36). The eschatological nature of the parable also shows in its reference to the chosen ones who cry to God day and night, that is, "those whom Rev 6:9 calls 'those who have been slain for the word of God . . .' but who in this passage are still suffering on earth."[157] It is also frequently noted that 18:1-8 "provides a commentary on the petition 'Thy kingdom come', a petition which is fulfilled at the Parousia."[158]

The image of the widow also supports the eschatological interpretation of the parable. In Jewish and Christian thought it is precisely the widow to whom God grants a favorable hearing. The widow is a metaphor for the eschatological community, which according to God's plan will pass through a time of tribulation before the end but will become the bride of the Son of Man when he comes in the near future for the eschatological marriage (cf. Rev. 19:7-9; 21:2,9-10; 22:17). In other words, Luke's community knows itself as the rejected widow. Continual prayer for eschatological vindication gives the oppressed church power to

---

[154]Gilmour, *Luke*, p. 306. Jeremias, *Parables*, p. 156, no longer thinks v 8b is a Lukan addition but is pre-Lukan and Palestinian. Leaney, *Luke*, p. 235, regards 18:6-8 as "either homiletic addition or composed by Luke himself as words of comfort in his own day. He represents the Lord as anticipating these times in such passages as the present section (17:22-18:8) and 21:20-28." Leaney does not comment on 18:8a.

[155]Biederwolf, *Second Coming Bible*, p. 378; Wilson, "Lukan Eschatology," p. 341; Godet, *Luke*, II, 271.

[156]Cranfield, "The Unjust Judge," pp. 299-300.

[157]Leaney, *Luke*, p. 235.

[158]Conzelmann, *Theology*, pp. 123-124. Significantly, Conzelmann hardly notices 18:1-8. Even that treatment is "somewhat lame" (Cranfield, "Unjust Judge," p. 299). Bultmann, *Synoptic Tradition*, p. 193, and Noack, *Luke* 17:20-24, pp. 41-42, also find that "the parable is specifically concerned with prayer for the coming of God's kingdom."

withstand persecution.[159]

It too is significant that 18:1-8 appears at the close of Luke's fire and brimstone apocalypse (17:20-18:8), which is concerned with the coming of the kingdom of God (17:20-21), the parousia of the Son of Man (17:22-37), and cosmic, end-time fires (17:24,29)(Chap. I.C.5). "All of the sayings in 17:20-18:8 have to do with the coming of the kingdom of God and the Son of man, and with the responses men will or should make in the interim and at the time the Kingdom and Son of man are revealed."[160]

Grässer grants that the reference of 18:1-8 to the parousia is strengthened by its position following the parousia discourse of 17:22-37. But this reference of 18:1-8 to the parousia was already in Luke's source. Luke, however, in his characteristic way modified this parousia reference by appending the parable of the publican and sinner (18:9-14), which does not refer to the parousia, to the parable of the unjust judge (18:1-8), thereby making it plain that the real point of emphasis of 18:1-8 is prayer as such and not the parousia.[161]

Grässer's argument is unconvincing, for, as indicated above, if Luke had wanted to change the impression of his sources he could easily have done so editorially. Moreover, the parable of the publican and sinner is directed toward justification in the last judgment, as v 14b indicates: "for every one that exalteth himself shall be humbled; but he that humbleth himself shall be exalted." This verse, like its doublet in 14:11, refers to God's eschatological activity in humbling the proud and exalting the humble in the last judgment. The reverential passives are circumlocutions for the divine name, and the future tenses refer to the coming judgment:[162] in the last judgment God will humble every one who exalts himself, but God will exalt every one who humbles himself.

All of these considerations combine to give us confidence that Luke directs the parable toward the end-time deliverance through the parousia.

3. "Suddenly" or "Soon"?

Now we come to the second question, namely, will this eschatological vindication be "sudden" or "soon"? That is, how is the Greek phrase *en tachei* (18:8) to be translated? Some exegetes, at times with appeal to the usage of *en tachei* in the LXX (Deut 9:3; 11:17; 28:20; Josh 8:18,19; Ps 2:12; Ezek 29:5; Sir 27:3), translate "suddenly," "unexpectedly." God will execute justice suddenly but not necessarily soon. When the moment comes, sooner or later, God will act in the twinkling of an eye, as at the deluge or the destruction of Sodom.[163]

---

[159]Stählin, "Witwe," p. 19; Grässer, *Delay*, p. 37.

[160]Hiers, "'Lo, here!'", p. 383; similarly Noack, *Luke 17:20-24*, p. 40.

[161]Grässer, *Delay*, pp. 37-38.

[162]Jeremias, *Parables*, pp. 142, 192-193.

[163]Godet, *Luke*, II, 202; Ellis, *Luke*, p. 214; Jeremias, *Parables*, p. 155. Jeremias, however, finds the imminent expectation in v 7, which he translates: "Will not God hasten to the rescue of his elect who cry to him day and night, even if he puts their patience to the test?" With "soon" in v 7 and "suddenly" in v 8 the parable would fit well with the basic apocalyptic belief that God will intervene soon, suddenly, swiftly, surprisingly, and spectacularly (Chap. I.B.3).

There are a number of obstacles standing in the way of this translation, however. None of the twenty-six translations reads "suddenly" at Luke 18:8. They generally offer synonymous variations to the KJV-ASV-RSV tradition, "He will avenge them speedily":

> He will soon avenge their wrongs (Weymouth).
>
> He will make haste to provide it (Goodspeed).
>
> He will give them redress with all speed (R. Knox).
>
> He will not delay in seeing justice done (Phillips).

Neither does Septuagintal usage support "suddenly" as the correct translation of *en tachei*. The usage of the Septuagint is not necessarily the same as that of the NT or Luke-Acts, since its Greek is several centuries older. Yet *en tachei* in the Septuagint gives good sense when translated, not with "suddenly," or "unexpectedly," but with "soon," "quickly," and synonyms. Moses promises Israel that the Lord will destroy the nations across Jordan "speedily" (Deut 9:3). Moses warns Israel that if they serve other gods the Lord will withhold rain and they will perish "soon" (Deut 11:17). If Israel forsakes the Lord he will send starvation and thirst until the people have perished "in a hurry" (Deut 28:20). The Lord said that when Joshua would stretch out his javelin as a signal, the ambushers would arise "at once" (Josh 8:18). And when Joshua did so, the men rose "immediately" (Josh 8:19). The Psalmist admonishes conspirators to do obeisance to the king lest they perish when God's wrath is "quickly" kindled (Ps 2:12). Ezekiel prophesies that the Lord will catch Pharaoh, the crocodile, with hooks, bring him up out of the Nile, and "speedily" cast him down (Ezek 29:5). Sirach advises that the house of an irreverent man will be overthrown "at once" (Sir 27:3).[163a]

Nor is the translation "suddenly" or "unexpectedly" borne out by the three appearances of *en tachei* in Luke-Acts (outside of Luke 18:8) and the four in the

---

[163a] The Hebrew behind *en tachei* in Deut 11:17 and Josh 8:19 is *meherah*, and in Deut 9:3; 28:20, *maher*, which Brown-Driver-Briggs defines, with related forms, as "hastily," "quickly," "speedily," "promptly," "swiftly," but not as "suddenly" or "unexpectedly." The Hebrew for *en tachei* in Ps 2:12 is *kimat*, for which Brown-Driver-Briggs gives "lightly," "easily," "quickly."

BAG for *en tachei* and related forms does not give "suddenly" or "unexpectedly" but such words as "at once," "without delay," "soon," "speedily," "shortly," "hastily," "quickly." Liddell-Scott-Jones does not define *en tachei*, but lists it under *to tachos*, "swiftness," "speed." Two columns of small print translate related words as "swiftness," "speed," "soon," "fast," and "quickly," with only the following exceptions: *Tachuthanatos* (Hippocrates, *Aphorisms* 2.44) is said to mean "liable to sudden death," but the text reads, "Those who are constitutionally very fat are more apt to die quicker (earlier, sooner) than those who are thin." Other forms are defined as "sudden," but these too are better rendered otherwise. Thucydides (4.44) says there was no long pursuit nor "hasty flight" (*tacheias phugas*). He (4.55) tells of a war which moved with "swiftness" (*polemon tacheos*), and of a war that was "imminent" (*epi tachei polemō*) and all but upon them (6.45). Sophocles (*Ajax* 833) uses the phrase "at one quick bound" (*tachei pēdēmati*). Euripides (*Hippolytos* 1047) observes that "swift death" (*tachus haides*) is easiest for the wretched. Moschus 3.26 describes Bion's death from poisoning as a "quick doom" (*tachus moros*). Thus even these alleged exceptions of forms related to *en tachei* and used in times distant from Luke do not require that *en tachei* be translated as "suddenly' or "unexpectedly."

rest of the NT:

> Rise up quickly (Acts 12:7)(ASV; KJV; Weymouth).
>
> Get thee quickly out of Jerusalem (22:18)(ASV; KJV; Weymouth)("at once," *Twentieth Century NT*)("with all speed," R. Knox)("as soon as you can," Riece)("without delay," NEB).
>
> He himself was about to depart [to Caesarea] shortly (Acts 25:4) (ASV; KJV) ("very soon," Weymouth) ("before long," Moffatt).
>
> God . . . shall bruise Satan under your feet shortly (Rom 16:20)(ASV; KJV)("before long," Weymouth).
>
> I . . . , hoping to come unto thee shortly (1 Tim 3:14) (ASV; KJV) ("before long," Weymouth).
>
> . . . the things which must shortly come to pass (Rev 1:1; 22:6) (ASV; KJV; Weymouth) ("very soon," Moffatt) (note the urgency of *tachu*--"quickly"--in Rev 22:7,12,20; *engus*--"at hand" in 1:3 and 22:10; and *mellō* in 1:19--the things "which are soon to follow"--Weymouth).

Plummer wisely concludes that these seven verses confirm the meaning "speedily" at Luke 18:8,[164] noting also that *en tachei* is placed last with emphasis.

Grundmann readers *en tachei* as "suddenly" rather than "soon" on the basis of the related word *tacheos* in Luke 16:6.[165] "Suddenly," however, does not fit 16:6, which means "sit down quickly" (ASV), "sit right down" (Goodspeed), or "be quick about it" (NEB). *Tacheos* appears ten times in the NT. For none of these instances does BAG give "suddenly," but rather "quickly," "at once," "without delay," "soon" (Luke 14:21; 16:6; John 11:31; 1 Cor 4:19; Phil 2:19,24; 2 Tim 4:9), or "too quickly," "too easily," or "hastily" (Gal 1:6; 2 Thess 2:2; 1 Tim 5:22). TEV uses "hurry out" (Luke 14:21; John 11:31); "soon" (1 Cor 4:19; Phil 2:19,24; 2 Tim 4:9), "in no time at all" (Gal 1:6), "so easily" (2 Thess 2:2), and "be in no hurry" (1 Tim 5:22).

Linguistically, then, there is no real justification for translating *en tachei* as "suddenly." Luke 18:8 "doubtless refers to the shortness of time before the deliverance is to take place, rather than to the suddenness with which the deliverance takes place when it does come."[166] Years ago Stevens roundly condemned those who "tell us that the synoptic passages do not mean that Jesus' coming was to occur in the near future; 'immediately' means 'suddenly' [Luke 18:8] and 'generation' means 'race' [Luke 21:32]...The dictionary must not impede the good work of harmonizing."[167] Luke 18:8 "declares the speedy advent of the Parousia" and "it is vain to weary oneself and twist about in the vain attempt to explain away this simple meaning of the words."[168]

Cranfield recognizes the "simple meaning of the words" when he concludes

---

[164]Plummer, *Luke*, pp. 414-415. So too Cranfield, "Unjust Judge," p. 299; Moore, *Parousia*, pp. 162-163; Stählin, "Witwe," p. 6; Michel, "Lukas," p. 105; Franklin, *Christ the Lord*, p. 19.

[165]Grundmann, *Lukas*, p. 348.

[166]Biederwolf, *Second Coming Bible*, p. 377.

[167]Stevens, "Eschatology," p. 669.

[168]Meyer, quoted by Biederwolf, *Second Coming Bible*, p. 378.

that for Luke the parable means "the Parousia is near!"[169] But then Cranfield "twists about" and attributes to Luke a watered-down eschatology: "It is near, not in the sense that it must necessarily occur within a few months or years, but in the sense that it may occur at any moment," and that all history after Christ is short, even though it may be long. Such ratiocinations are hardly characteristic of the plain-spoken Luke we are discovering in the passages discussed in Chaps. IV and V. "I say unto you that he will avenge them speedily" is for Luke a solemn statement which, together with admonitions to constant prayer, permits no dilution of the imminent expectation. Speaking of such evasions, Stevens wondered whether they "could ever have obtained the consent and advocacy of candid men in any other realm than that of theology."[170]

4. The Existential Situation

Nor does Luke's existential situation permit any other meaning than "soon." The question of Luke 18:8b does imply a period when the faith of disciples will be sorely tested. But to promise "sudden" relief in the far distant future would be of scant comfort to Luke's suffering flock (cf. Luke 12:32), which apparently is undergoing persecution like that of Acts 9:1-2 or Rev 6:9-11. And how in Luke's mind could God withhold the help for which the elect are crying earnestly day and night? Luke, in fact, has so phrased the question of 18:7 as to require an affirmative answer (*ou me*):[171] "God will vindicate his elect, will he not?" And the positive answer comes that God will not only rescue his own people but will do so soon (18:8).

As just noted, 18:1-8 unavoidably reminds us of Rev 6:9-11, where the souls of the martyrs cry out, "How long, O Master, . . . dost thou not judge and avenge our blood on them that dwell on the earth?" And they were told to "wait patiently for a short time longer" (Weymouth). We think too of the plea of the psalmist after the Gentiles had trampled down Jerusalem: "Delay not, O God, to recompense them on their heads, To turn the pride of the dragon into dishonour" (Pss. Sol. 2:29).

This attitude of praying always (Luke 18:1), of continual coming before the judge (18:3,5), and of crying to God day and night (18:7), is natural for one who passionately longs for the parousia (Rev 6:9-11). There is no justification for understanding stress on persevering prayer as a displacement of the eschatological accent by the ethical in line with Luke's preoccupation with the church's existence in the world.[172] Such an understanding overlooks the appropriateness of continual prayer to an intense expectation.

Luke 18:1-8 "in its eschatological surroundings" has rightly been

---

[169]Cranfield, "Unjust Judge," pp. 300-301.

[170]Stevens, "Eschatology," p. 670. Franklin, *Christ the Lord*, p. 189, rejects Cranfield at this point. On Moore, Cranfield's student, see Chap. V.H.2 and V.J.

[171]BAG, p. 519.

[172]Kaestli, *Eschatologie*, p. 37, is representative of the *Fernerwartungsschule*. And 18:18b, far from tempering the ardent hope of vv 7-8a, directs it to the parousia and judgment, admonishing preparation so as to be able to withstand the day of his arrival (cf. Luke 21:36; Mal 3:1-2).

summarized as "endless praying for the end,"[173] or for revenge.[174] Thus Anna "day and night" worshiped God, "fasting and praying," and speaking "about the child to all who were waiting for God to redeem Jerusalem" (Luke 2:37-38) (TEV). This constant prayer is advocated by Jesus in view of the imminent judgment before the Son of Man (21:36) (Section I): "Be on watch and pray always that you will have the strength...to stand before the Son of Man" (TEV). Just as "there was a continual stream of prayers going up to God from the church" on Peter's behalf (Acts 12:5)(R.Knox), so Luke's church prayed endlessly for the end (Luke 18:1-8) (on Acts 26:7 see Chap. IV.G).[175]

Similarly Paul, thinking of the fast approaching parousia (1 Thess 4:13-18) advises: "Pray without ceasing" (1 Thess 5:17; cf. 1:2f.; 2:13; 3:10). And Paul also gives thanks to God always for the church at Thessalonica (2 Thess 1:3; 2:13) and prays always for them (1:11) that they may be counted worthy "at the revelation of the Lord Jesus from heaven with the angels of his power in flaming fire" (1:7), which revelation is not far off, "for the mystery of lawlessness doth already work" (2:7). Paul always thanks God for the saints at Corinth as they eagerly wait for Jesus to be revealed (1 Cor 1:4-8).

1 Pet 4:7 is also noteworthy: "The end of all things is now close at hand: therefore be sober-minded and temperate, so that you may give yourselves to prayer" (Weymouth).

The prayer in 2 Bar 21:19-25 will serve as a commentary on the type of eschatological prayer recommended in Luke 18:1-8, and may have been composed during Luke's lifetime (A.D. 50-90):[176]

> How long will that which is corruptible remain, and how long will the time of mortals be prospered, and until what time will those who transgress in the world be polluted with much wickedness? Command therefore in mercy and accomplish all that Thou saidst Thou wouldst bring, that Thy might may be made known to those who think that thy long-suffering is weakness.... Bring to an end therefore henceforth mortality. And reprove accordingly the angel of death, and let thy glory appear, ... And now quickly show Thy glory, and do not defer what has been promised by Thee.

We shall return to Baruch's imminent expectation at Section I.4 (Luke 21:34-36).

---

[173]Bundy, *Gospels*, p. 391. So Moore, *Parousia*, p. 162: "As it stands now, this parable speaks not simply of prayer in general (cf. v. 1) but of prayerful longing of the faithful for the Parousia (cf. v. 8b)."

[174]Wellhausen, *Lucas*, p. 98.

[175]Although prayer without ceasing goes hand in hand with the *Naherwartung*, there are NT examples of such praying not so explicitly connected with the end: Acts 2:42; 6:4; 10:2; 12:5; Rom 1:9-10; 12:12; Col. 1:3,9; 4:2,12; 1 Tim 1:3; 5:5; 2 Tim 1:3; Phlm 4; Heb 13:15. It is interesting to note that references to unceasing prayer are found only in Luke-Acts and the Paulines, in both of which the *Naherwartung* is also present. Does Luke's emphasis on constant prayer explain why he does not report Matt 6:5-8 ("In praying use not vain repetitions,...")? In Matthew the Lord's prayer follows immediately upon 6:5-8, whereas Luke gives it another setting (11:2-4) in his great central section (9:51-19:27). Plummer, *Luke*, p. 411, refers to the Jewish doctrine "that God must not be wearied with incessant prayer....A man ought not to pray more than three times a day. Hourly prayers are forbidden."

[176]*APOT*, II, 470.

Likely the parable of the unjust judge should also be understood in terms of a similar passage in Sir 35:18, which promises imminent divine intervention: "And the Lord will not delay, neither will he be patient with them, till he crushes the loins of the unmerciful and repays vengeance on the nations." That is, the Lord will not delay his judgment on the oppressors of his elect people.[177] Interestingly, Sirach in this passage is especially concerned with the plight of widows: "He will not ignore ... the widow when she pours out her story. Do not the tears of the widow run down her cheek as she cries out against him who has caused them to fall?" (Sir 35:14-15).

If these many considerations are pointing in the right direction, then Luke in the parable of the unjust judge has given us a vivid picture of his anticipation that the Son of Man would not delay in returning to see justice done. This parable may truly be "the best clue to Luke's eschatology."[178]

H. The Accomplishment of All Things (Luke 21:32)

1. The Meaning of *Genea*

Luke 21:32 is one of the strongest expressions of the imminent expectation in Luke-Acts. Yet its meaning is much disputed, especially the translation of *genea*. Those who find the *Naherwartung* in Luke-Acts naturally translate it as "generation," as do those who think the verse predicts the destruction of Jerusalem:

> Verily I say unto you, This generation shall not pass away, till all things be accomplished (ASV).

> Remember this! All these things will take place before the people now living have all died (TEV).

Others, however, who for one reason or another reject the *Naherwartung* or the reference of the verse to Jerusalem render *genea* as "race": "Jewish race";[179] "human race" (mankind in general);[180] "Jewish nation".[181] Some prefer a qualitative meaning: "this type of faithless generation."[182]

Sometimes one of these renditions is arrived at by process of elimination. The prophecy, it is said, cannot refer to the fall of Jerusalem, for " all things" includes the end of the world. But it cannot mean the end of the world in Jesus' generation because the world obviously still continues, and "the view that this prophecy has failed is of course not to be thought of." Therefore *genea* must mean "race" in

---

[177]*APOT*, I, 439.

[178]Wilson, "Lukan Eschatology," p. 340.

[179]Biederwolf, *Second Coming Bible*, p. 347; Marxsen, *Markus*, p.133(but"generation" at Mark 13:30!).

[180]Conzelmann, *Theology*, p.131; Kaestli, *Eschatologie*, pp. 53-54; Leaney, *Luke*, p. 263; Browning, *Luke*, p. 152 (the human race "will survive until the End without losing the tradition of Jesus' words"); Grundmann, *Lukas*, p. 385 (mankind or the disciples who survive the catastrophes); Schneider, *Parusiegleichnisse*, pp. 59 61.

[181]Schniewind, *Markus*, p. 167; Meinertz, *Theologie*, I, 61 (cited by Kümmel, *Promise*, p. 61).

[182]Michaelis, *Verheissung*, p. 30; Danker, *Luke*, p. 216.

some sense or other.[183]

Others, because of their view that Luke has abandoned Mark's imminent expectation (Mark 13:30), choose "Jewish race,"[184] or "human race" (humanity in general),[185] or "non-Christian humanity."[186] "In view of Luke's reinterpretation and deliberate extension of the times of the end, 'generation' cannot for him mean one generation of history, as it does for Mark: Luke has forced it to bear the meaning 'mankind.'"[187] In olden times also as the church was settling down in the world and adjusting "its thinking to the indefinite continuance of the historical order, 'this generation' was interpreted to mean either 'the race of mankind' or 'the company of the faithful.'"[188]

In favor of "race" it is pointed out that this is the root meaning of *genea*,[189] which is a valid claim.[190] It should be noted, however, that BAG cites no instances where *genea* means "race." Moreover, the Greek *genea* may mean "race," but not the Hebrew (*dor*) or Aramaic (*dar*) words for "generation."[191] This debate, however, cannot be settled without examining each of the thirty-eight instances of *genea* in the NT outside of the three instances in Luke 21:32//Matt 24:34//Mark 13:30. We shall devote special attention to those sayings which refer to "this generation," the phrase used in Luke 21:32.

a. "This Generation" Sayings in Luke-Acts

1)*Luke 7:31//Matt 11:16.*--"Whereunto then shall I liken the men of this generation?" ("the people of this day?"--TEV), a reference to the contemporaries of John the Baptist and Jesus, who received John as demonic and Jesus as gluttonous.

2)*Luke 11:29//Mark 8:12 (cf. Matt 12:39).*--"This generation is an evil generation" ("How evil are the people of this day!"--TEV), that is, Jesus' contemporaries, being evil, seek a sign.

3)*Luke 11:30.*--The Son of Man will be a sign to "this generation" ("the people of this day"--TEV), Jesus' contemporaries.

4)*Luke 11:31//Matt 12:42.*--The Queen of the South will condemn "this generation" ("the people of today"--TEV), that is, Jesus' contemporaries because they were less willing to hear wisdom than she was.

5) *Luke 11:32//Matt 12:41.*--The men of Nineveh will condemn "this generation" ("you"--TEV), that is, Jesus' contemporaries, for the Ninevites were more responsive than Jesus' hearers.

---

[183]Biederwolf, *Second Coming Bible*, pp. 347-348.
[184]Marxsen, *Markus*, p. 133.
[185]See Note #180.
[186]Robinson, *Weg*, p. 65.
[187]Leaney, *Luke*, p. 263.
[188]Gilmour, *Luke*, p. 370.
[189]Biederwolf, *Second Coming Bible*, p. 347.
[190]BAG, p. 153.
[191]Jeremias, *Theology*, p. 135.

6) Luke 11:50-51//Matt 23:36--The blood of the prophets will be required of "this generation" ("the people of this time"--TEV), that is, Jesus' contemporaries. "We have the authentic commentary on this saying [21:32] in Luke xi.50,51, where Jesus declares that it is the very generation which is to shed His blood and that of His messengers, which must suffer, besides, the punishment of all the innocent blood shed since that of Abel down to this last."[192]

7) Luke 17:25.--Jesus must be rejected by "this generation" ("the people of this day"--TEV), that is, by his contemporaries. Keck finds 17:25 to be a Lukan redaction and therefore indicative of what Luke understands (or at least can understand) *genea* to mean, namely, Jesus' contemporaries who reject him. The term is primarily temporal but has a secondary pejorative connotation.[193]

8) Luke 21:32//Matt 24:34//Mark 13:30.--"This generation will not pass away until all things have taken place." In line with the other sayings about "this generation" we are maintaining that the meaning here is also Jesus' contemporaries ("the people now living"--TEV).

9) Acts 2:40.--Peter admonishes his hearers to save themselves from the punishment coming upon "this crooked generation," that is, "this wicked people" (TEV) then living to whom Peter was speaking.

Our review shows that in every instance in Luke-Acts (apart from Luke 21:32, the verse in question), "this generation" means "contemporaries," the people living at that time, the hearers of Jesus and Peter. The presumption is strong, then, that Luke has not used "this generation" with any other meaning in 21:32.

b. Other Appearances of *Genea* in Luke-Acts

1) Luke 1:48.--From henceforth all generations will call Mary blessed, that is, all sets of fathers and sons who have ever lived and are living. "All generations" refers to past and present rather than future generations, as at Acts 14:16; 15:21; Col 1:26.[194]

2) Luke 1:50.--"His mercy is unto generations and generations on them that fear him," that is, he shows mercy to one set of fathers and sons after another.[195]

3) Luke 9:41//Matt 17:17//Mark 9:19.--"O faithless and perverse generation!" Jesus calls his contemporaries ("you people"--TEV) ("people of the times"--Williams) faithless because of their powerlessness against demons.

4) Luke 16:8.--The sons of this age are wiser than the sons of light because

---

[192]Godet, *Luke*, II, 271.

[193]F. Keck, "Farewell Address," p. 289. Moore, *Parousia*, p. 136: "Lk 17, 25, against Conzelmann, means the contemporaries under whom the Son of Man suffered." Kümmel, *Promise*, pp. 70-71, thinks 17:25 authentic, for it contains no mention of Jesus' resurrection; so indefinite a statement could hardly be a *vaticinium ex eventu*.

[194]Hiers, "Delay," p. 152.

[195]Moore, *Parousia*, p. 136, remarks that "Lk. 1:48,50 would support Conzelmann, except that the problem of compilation (cf. e.g. Creed, *Luke, ad loc*) makes this indecisive for specific Lukan usage," that is, this hymn may not have been Luke's composition and he may not have felt free to change it or even have seen any need for doing so. Conzelmann has ruled out Luke 1-2 (Chap. II).

they know better how to adapt themselves to "their own generation," that is, to their contemporaries.

5) *Acts 8:33*.--"His generation who shall declare?" The meaning here is not clear, and is variously rendered as "posterity," "descendants," "family," or "origin."[196] "No one will be able to tell about his descendants, For his life on earth has come to an end" (TEV).

6) *Acts 13:36*.--David served God in his own generation, that is, in the time of his contemporaries.

7) *Acts 14:16*.--"In the generation gone by" (= in times past) God allowed the nations to go their own way.

8) *Acts 15:21*.--Moses has been preached "from generations of old," that is, "for a very long time" (TEV), to one set of fathers and sons after another for a long time.

In all these instances *genea* has a temporal rather than ethnic or qualitative meaning, referring to contemporaries or various sets of fathers and sons. Luke-Acts is consistent in its usage of *genea*, especially in the "this generation" sayings, and *genea* should therefore be so translated in Luke 21:32.

We can see in the light of Luke 1:48,50 that the singular "this generation" (21:32) cannot be rendered as if it were the plural "all generations" (1:48) or "unto generations and generations" (1:50). If Luke had wanted to say something like "the whole human race" or "mankind" at 21:32 he would have written, "All generations will not pass away," or "Generations and generations will not pass away," for only at 1:48,50 does Luke come close to using *genea* as "human race." Thus 1:48,50 as good as proves that *genea* in 21:32 must be translated "this generation"=the people then living. "But of all the other uses of this word [*genea*] in Luke-Acts [outside of Luke 21:32], only two [Luke 1:48,50] could be cited as possible parallels to this meaning ["the whole human race," "mankind"], and neither this nor any other attempt to give *hē genea* a meaning other than Jesus' contemporaries carries any conviction."[197]

c. "This Generation" Sayings outside of Luke-Acts

1) *Matt 12:45*.--"This evil generation" (=Jesus' contemporaries), who at first showed some appreciation of him, is now relapsing, so that its last state will be worse than its first. "This is the way it will happen to the evil people of this day" (TEV).

2) *Mark 8:38*.--In the judgment the Son of Man will condemn those of "this adulterous and sinful generation" (=Jesus' contemporaries) who were ashamed of him "in this godless and wicked day" (TEV).

3) *Heb 3:10*.--God was displeased with "this generation" (=Moses' contemporaries).

---

[196]BAG, p. 153.

[197]Wilson, "Lukan Eschatology," p. 343. Wilson also rejects Ellis' attempt (*Luke*, p. 247) to expand *genea* of Luke 21:32 to mean several lifetimes, as does "the last generation" in 1 Qp Hab 2.7 and 7.2. Wilson finds the Qumran phrase not sufficiently close to "this generation" of Luke 21:32. At any rate, Ellis goes on to admit that "the public revelation of the kingdom is just around the corner" (p. 247).

Here again we find the temporal meaning of "this generation."[198]

d. The Remaining Appearances of *Genea* in the New Testament

1) Matt 1:17.--Matthew reckons forty-two generations from Abraham to Jesus, that is, forty-two "sets of fathers and sons" (TEV).

2) Matt 12:39//Mark 16:4 (cf. Mark 8:12; Luke 11:29).--"An evil and adulterous generation seeketh after a sign" ("How evil and godless are the people of this day!"--TEV). Jesus' evil and godless contemporaries ask for a miracle.

3) Eph 3:5.--The mystery of Christ was not revealed to "other generations," that is, to other sets of fathers and sons in times past.

4) Eph 3:21--God's glory is to be unto "all generations," that is, "to the last generation of eternity" (R. Knox).

5) Phil 2:15.--God's children are to shine like lights in the midst of "a crooked and perverse generation" (=in the midst of the evil people contemporaneous with Paul).

6)Col 1:26.--The mystery has been hidden for ages and "generations," that is, "for long ages and through many generations" (NEB).

Once more we find the temporal meaning of *genea* in every case. Of the thirty-eight appearances of *genea* apart from Luke 21:32//Matt 24:34//Mark 13:30 all have the temporal meaning, primarily that of "contemporaries." Our check of every instance in the NT verifies Olshausen's contention that *genea* is not once used in the NT in the sense of "race."[199] Hence *genea* in Luke 21:32 and parallels should be translated "generation," the contemporaries of Jesus.[200] Thus the contemporaries of Luke 21:32 are the same as "those standing here" of Luke 9:27.

The temporal meaning of *genea* in 21:32 is also supported by the presence of chronological notices in surrounding verses: "your redemption draweth nigh" (21:28); "summer is now nigh" (21:30); and "the kingdom of God is nigh" (21:31).

2. Other Evasions of the Imminent Expectation in Luke 21:32

In addition to translating *genea* as something else than "generation" there are other attempts at avoiding the *Naherwartung* in 21:32.

a) One way is to refer the verse to the fall of Jerusalem, perhaps as a type of the end of the world.[201] Some hold that Jesus at 21:28 returns to the subject of the destruction of Jerusalem. "Deliverance" (v. 28) then means the emancipation of

---

[198]Like the Son of man sayings, all of the "this generation" sayings in the Gospels are on the lips of Jesus. This fact would speak in favor of their authenticity.

[199]He also claimed that *genea* is not so used by profane writers and only once in the LXX (quoted by Biederwolf, *Second Coming Bible*, p. 347). TEV takes the plural "generations" of Col 1:26 as equivalent to "mankind": "the secret he hid through all past ages from all mankind." But then one must recognize that, as at Luke 1:48,50, this translation prohibits rendering the singular "this generation" of Luke 21:32 as "mankind" or "human race."

[200]Godet, *Luke*, II, 271; Bruce, *Gospels*, p. 622; Plummer, *Luke*, p. 485; Kümmel, *Promise*, p. 61; Jeremias, *Theology*, p. 135; Moore, *Parousia*, p. 135.

[201]Plummer, *Luke*, p. 485.

the Jewish-Christian church from Jewish persecution. The coming of the kingdom of God (v 31) is the preaching of the Gospel among the Gentiles, and Jesus' generation (v 32) will see the fall of Jerusalem.

Several objections to this view make it untenable. "All things" (v 32) certainly include not only the fall of Jerusalem (vv 20-24) but also the coming of the kingdom (v 31), redemption (v 28), the Son of Man (v 27), and the cosmic woes (vv 25-26). And with these events "heaven and earth shall pass away" (v 33).[202]

Moreover, there is nothing in the text to lead one to believe that the subject changes at v 28 from the parousia to the fall of Jerusalem. Not only is the subject of the parousia "quite too solemn when once mentioned to be treated as a purely accessory idea,"[203] but Luke, by interpreting the "he" or "it" of Mark 13:29 as the kingdom of God, makes it plain that for him the coming of the Son of Man (v 27), redemption (v 28), and the kingdom of God (v 31) are all parts of one great apocalyptic event.[204]

b) Another evasion of the imminent expectation in 21:32 is made by interpreting "this generation" to mean the generation when the cosmic woes of 21:25-26 happen, whenever that may be. This is the generation that will see all things consummated.[205] A variation of this view has it that *genea* is "the generation of the end time...from pre-resurrection mission to the parousia."[206] These views are pure makeshifts, ignoring the clear evidence cited above that "this generation" means those who lived when Jesus did, not hundreds or thousands of years thereafter.

c) A similar expedient is to take "this generation" as the generation which sees the signs of the end but not the end itself. Moore strives valiantly to avoid a "delimited expectation" (Section J) at Mark 13:30//Matt 24:34//Luke 21:32.[207] He begins with Mark, outlining the chapter as follows: signs of the end (13:5-23);

---

[202]Herder, p. 96, refers "all things" to vv 20-24; Keck, "Farewell Address," p. 288, to vv 12-24; Geldenhuys, pp. 538-539, to vv 10-24; Moore, *Parousia*, pp. 135-136, evidently to vv 8-24. The variety of these answers suggests their subjectivity. Keck, "Farewell Address," pp. 286-294, thinks the subject changes at v 32 from the nearness of the kingdom (v 31) because of the solemn introduction, "Truly I say to you" and because of the omission of *tauta* ("these things"), which refers to the immediately preceding events (coming of the kingdom, final judgment, and the Son of Man in vv 27-31). Against Keck, such a weighty introductory formula is more appropriate to all events of the discourse, and the omission of *tauta* would, if anything, broaden rather than restrict *panta* ("all things"). It is possible that Luke omitted *tauta* simply for stylistic reasons (Moore, *Parousia*, p. 136; Wilson, "Lukan Eschatology," p. 342), for Luke follows Mark's *tauta* at Mark 13:29//Luke 21:31 but drops it at Mark 13:30//Luke 21:32. Matthew however has "all these things" (*panta tauta*) in both instances. We might add that Luke does use *tauta panta* in 21:36: to flee all these things which are about to happen. Luke thus uses Mark's *tauta* at 21:31 and *panta* at 21:32, "thereby retaining the overall sense of *tauta panta*" (Moore, *Parousia*, p. 136). TEV translates 21:32 "all these things."

[203]Biederwolf, *Second Coming Bible*, p. 386.

[204]Bruce, *Gospels*, p. 622.

[205]Hahn, *Das Evangelium des Lucas*, 1892-1894, referred to by Bruce, *Gospels*, p. 622.

[206]Ellis, *Luke*, p. 247, though Ellis thinks that the public revelation of the kingdom was "just around the corner" (p. 247)(see Note #197).

[207]Moore, *Parousia*, pp. 131-136.

the end (13:24-27); time of the signs of the end (13:28-31); time of the end (13:32-37). In other words, 13:30 refers back to 13:5-23, the signs of the end which were to come upon that generation within the immediate future, though not necessarily exhausted then. 13:32 thus refers to the unknown time of the end.

This interpretation of Mark seems dubious. How unlikely for an apocalyptist to split up the end events so that the signs of the end occur in his generation but the end itself is to arrive at a lengthy interval thereafter, perhaps hundreds or thousands of years later. Moreover, Moore's outline of Mark 13 is subject to question. He refers to other possibilities, such as that of Lightfoot and Lohmeyer:[208] the beginning of the consummation (13:5-13); the consummation itself (13:14-27); warnings regarding the consummation (13:28-37). If 13:30 refers to 13:5-23, as Moore supposes, then it, on the outline of Lightfoot and Lohmeyer, refers to both the beginning of the consummation and to the consummation itself, which seems more in line with verses such as 13:17-20. We may also point out that the *Huck-Lietzmann Synopsis* entitles #221 (Mark 13:30-32//Matt 24:34-36//Luke 21:32-33) "The Time of the Parousia."

As for Matthew, which Moore likewise interprets, even so conservative a commentator as Biederwolf says that "all these things" (Matt 24:34) "look back to the preceding verses, and however far back it might seem necessary to carry their reference, the words of verses 29-31 must be included in it."[209]

We are concerned with Moore's treatment of Mark and Matthew only to show how weak is the foundation upon which he builds his understanding of Luke 21:32. He admits that if "all things" is "an expression for the entire sweep of salvation history," it "would appear to embrace the events of vv. 27-28, and so to delimit the End also to the contemporary generation!" But he regards Luke's omission of "these things" (*tauta*) as probably stylistic (Note #202), "signifying no alteration of Mark's meaning, namely that the *signs* of the End will come upon that generation."[210]

Moore does not elaborate his interpretation of Luke, but it would seem to be as follows: signs of the end (Mark 13:5-23//Luke 21:8-24); the end (Mark 13:24-27//Luke 21:25-28); the time of the signs of the end (Mark 13:28-31//Luke 21:29-33); the time of the end (Mark 13:32-37). This scheme breaks down for several reasons: 1) Luke has no parallel to Mark 13:32-37, which means that Luke leaves the all-important question of the time of the end dangling in mid-air. 2) If Luke 21:32 refers back to Luke 21:8-24//Mark 13:5-23, it refers not only to the signs of the end but also to the end itself in 21:11: earthquakes, famines, pestilences, terrors and great signs from heaven (outline of Luke 21 in Chap. VI.E.1). 3) If, as Moore claims, Mark 13:30 ("all these things") refers to 13:29 ("these things"), which in turn refers to 13:5-23, that is, only to the events preceding the end itself, then Luke 21:32 must refer back to Luke 21:31//Mark 13:29. But, as we have shown, 21:31 (kingdom) is parallel with 21:28 (redemption) and 21:27 (parousia). This parallelism forbids limiting "all things" of 21:31 to the signs

---

[208]Lightfoot, *Gospel Message*, p. 49, and Lohmeyer, *Markus*, p. 267, cited by Moore, *Parousia*, p. 134.

[209]Biederwolf, *Second Coming Bible*, p. 347.

[210]Moore, *Parousia*, p. 136.

preceding the end. It also seems likely that "all things" does include the entire sweep of salvation history and therefore does involve a "delimited expectation."[211]

d) One more way out of the *Naherwartung* at 21:32 is found by accenting Luke's omission of "these things" (*tauta*). Luke simply has "all things" (*panta*) in contrast to "all these things" (*tauta panta*) of Matt 24:34//Mark 13:30. This change is taken to mean that Luke, who has given up the imminent hope anyway as part of his reconstruction of eschatology, no longer regards v 32 as a declaration the end is near at hand but is here referring to the entire process of salvation history which will extend into the distant future and culminate with preceding signs and the end. "Humanity in general," not Jesus' generation, will live to see it all.[212]

Against this interpretation, we have already suggested that "all things" includes the final events of the preceding verses. If anything, the whole sweep of salvation would be even broader. "All things" of 21:32 may be the same as "all things" of Acts 3:21--"all things" of which God spoke by his prophets (Chap. VI.F.5.i). Yet all is to come to pass in that generation, unless *genea* can be proved to mean the whole human race. But in view of the evidence about "this generation" presented above, we can say only that to take "this generation" as meaning "mankind in general" simply "exemplifies the capacity of the exegete to bend the evidence to fit a preconceived interpretation."[213] How odd it would be for Luke to let Jesus utter the mere tautology that God will bring to pass the divine plan in its entirety before the human race is extinct. Neither Luke nor his people would have regarded that as "good news" to proclaim (Chap. I.E). Such a prediction fits nothing in apocalyptic in general nor in Luke 21 in particular. Can we imagine Luke on the one hand exhorting his people to pray endlessly for the end (18:1-8; 21:34-36), and on the other telling them that God in his own leisurely time will wind things up before the human race disappears? As we are seeing in the key passages treated in Chaps. IV and V the exciting thing for Luke was that God was about to complete his whole divine plan before Jesus' generation had died out and while most of Luke's generation was still living.

Upon the basis of linguistic evidence and theological considerations, as well as by process of elimination of alternative views, we conclude with an impressive group of critics that "Luke does not give a date, but in his Gospel too Jesus says, 'the present generation will live to see it all!' (21:32)."[214]

---

[211]Franklin, *Christ the Lord*, p. 189, also rejects Moore's attempts to refer v 32 to the signs of the parousia rather than to the parousia itself.

[212]Conzelmann, *Theology*, p. 131; Leaney, *Luke*, p. 263; Stuhlmueller, *Luke*, p. 148. Keck, "Farewell Address," p. 286, finds Luke's omission of *tauta* to be of decisive significance: "If Luke understood this logion in the same sense as Mark 13:30 that would contradict all that we know about his eschatological views; above all in Acts there is not a single logion that even intimates such a *Naherwartung*." It would be difficult to find a better statement of the position of the *Fernerwartungsschule*.

[213]Hiers, "Delay," p. 152.

[214]Bartsch, "Eschatology," p. 397; Talbert, "Redaction," pp. 184-186; Hiers, "Delay," pp. 152-153; Wilson, "Lukan Eschatology," pp. 342-343; Michel, "Lukas," p. 106; Franklin, *Christ the Lord*, p. 14.

I. "That Great and Terrible Day of the Lord" (Luke 21:34-36)

1. Lukan Features

This little pericope is one of the most remarkable of Luke's peculiar traditions:

> 34 But take heed to yourselves, lest haply your hearts be overcharged with surfeiting and drunkenness, and cares of this life, and that day come on you suddenly as a snare: 35 for so shall it come upon all them that dwell on the face of all the earth. 36 But watch ye at every season, making supplication, that ye may prevail to escape all these things that shall come to pass, and to stand before the Son of man.

Luke's favorite words and phrases in this unit include: "take heed to yourselves" (*prosechete heautois*) (Luke 12:1; 17:3; 21:34; Acts 5:35; 20:28); "come upon" (*ephistēmi*) (only in Luke-Acts-Paulines: Luke 2:9,38; 4:39; 10:40; 20:1; 21:34; 24:4; Acts 4:1; 6:12; 10:17; 11:11; 12:7; 17:5; 22:13,20; 23:11,27; 28:2; 1 Thess 5:3; 2 Tim 4:2,6); "upon the face of all the earth" (Luke 21:34; Acts 17:26); "make supplication" (*deomai*) (Luke 5:12; 8:28,38; 9:38,40; 10:2; 21:36; 22:32; Acts 4:31; 8:22,24,34; 10:2; 21:39; 26:3; elsewhere only in Matt 9:38 and Paulines); *mellō* (Chap. IV). Here we stand in the very presence of the mind of Luke.

2. Accentuating the Ethical

The *Fernerwartungsschule* finds that characteristic Lukan eschatological features appear in Luke 21:34-36 in profusion. Once again Luke's emphasis is upon ethical exhortation regulating the practical life of Christians rather than upon a call to repentance in view of the approaching kingdom (Mark 1:15). Luke no longer reckons with a short period before the end but advises adjustment to a long time in this world. Luke also underscores the sudden and unforeseeable character of the final irruption, thereby cutting off all apocalyptic speculation about the date of the end. Men will stand before the Son of Man, not at the time of the imminent parousia, but at the general resurrection of the dead, an event which is independent of a definite date. The ethical stress, plus accentuation of the resurrection and judgment, means that 21:34-36 is absolutely independent of every consideration of time. Thus this little pericope shows how Luke because of the delay of the parousia sketches an eschatological program with a completely different accent from that of primitive apocalyptic.[215]

3. The Pressing Nature of the Times

Contrary to the Distant Expectation School, we have seen that although Luke opposes setting of precise dates he does so without eliminating an imminent hope. We are also finding that for Luke ethics and imminence go together. A number of considerations suggest that this Lukan ending to the synoptic apocalypse (21:34-36) contains the imminent expectation. In the first place, the key word *mellō* appears in 21:36, so that this verse should be translated: "... all these things that are about to take place." Several translations bring out this imminent sense: "all these disasters that are on their way" (Rieu); "all these

---

[215]Grässer, *Delay*, pp. 167-168; Kaestli, *Eschatologie*, pp. 54-55.

impending events" (Berkeley); "all these imminent troubles" (NEB); "all these things being about to occur" (B. Wilson). It is a strong indication of Luke's awareness of the pressing nature of the times that he begins (21:7 --"what shall be the sign when these things are about to come to pass?") and ends (21:36) his apocalyptic discourse with *mellō*.

The word "come upon (*ephistēmi*) ("that day come upon you suddenly," 21:34) also has imminent overtones. In Acts 28:2 the barbarians received Paul's group kindly "because it threatened to rain" (*ephistēmi*),[216] or was about to rain. In 2 Tim 4:6 Paul says, "The time of my departure is imminent" (*ephistēmi*).[217] A non-canonical passage reads, "The fates of death are close at hand" (*ephistēmi*).[218] Thus the meaning of Luke 21:34 likely may be: "and the day come upon you soon and suddenly."

Further, the admonition to pray "every moment" (Weymouth) is the appropriate reaction for one who thinks the end is near: "With expectation prayer is naturally conjoined under the influence of that grave feeling which is produced by the imminence of the expected advent."[219]

Moreover, 21:34-36 is set within an immediate context of impending events. We have just noted the *mellō* framework (21:7,36). We also saw on Luke 10:9,11 (Chap. V.D.) that Luke uses *engus* and *engidzō* four times in chapter 21 to express imminence (21:8,20,28,31). And we have also found the *Naherwartung* unmistakably present in 21:32.

4. Impressive Parallels

The likelihood that the imminent expectation is found in 21:34-36 is increased by the parallels this unit has with other units which express this hope.

a) The incipient apocalypse of Isaiah 24-27, especialy 24:17, may have been Luke's model, which he paraphrases. The verbal parallels in italics are impressive:

Luke 21:34-36	Isa 24:17-20 (LXX)
34c. . . and that day come *upon you* (*eph' humas*) suddenly as a *snare* (*pagis*);	17 Terror and a pit and a *snare* (*pagis*) are *upon you* (*eph' humas*) who dwell *upon the earth* (*epi tes ges*).
35 for so shall it come *upon* (*epi*) all them that dwell *on* (*epi*) the face of all *the earth* (*tēs gēs*).	18 . . . he who *fleeth* (*pheugō*) the terror shall fall into the pit; and he that

---

[216]BAG, p. 331.

[217]BAG, p. 331.

[218]Liddell and Scott, *Abridged Lexicon*, p. 294.

[219]Godet, *Luke*, II, 273. Easton, *Luke*, p. 315, says that "at every season" belongs to "watch ye, praying" taken together. Lövestam, *Wakefulness*, pp. 122-132, has an illuminating section on 21:34-36 but never alludes to the *Naherwartung*, though he does find "the eschatological orientation" of 21:34-36 and related passages to be "clear and obvious." He points out that the orientation of the concept of spiritual wakefulness in the NT epistles is "clearly eschatolgical" and that "in the Synoptic Gospels the exhortations to keep awake are located in Jesus' eschatological teaching" (p. 78).

36 ... that ye may *prevail* (*katiskeuō*) to *escape* (*ekpheugō*) all these things that shall come to pass, and to *stand* (*histēmi*) before the Son of man.

34b ... lest haply your hearts be overcharged with *surfeiting* (*kraipalē*), and *drunkenness* (*methē*), and cares of this life.[220]

cometh up out of the pit shall be caught by the *snare* (*pagis*).

20 The earth shall be shaken like the hut of a gardenwatcher; it reeled to and fro like a *drunkard* (*methuō*) when *intoxicated* (*kraipalō*), and it will fall, and not be able to *rise* (*anhistēmi*), for lawlessness hath *prevailed* (*katiskeuō*) over it.

Both passages use the image of the snare to depict the universal last judgment. Both describe cosmic woes and terrors. Both mention those who seek to escape the final terrors. And for Isaiah the end is at hand: "Come, my people, enter thou into thy chambers, and shut thy door; hide thyself for a little moment, until the wrath of the Lord is past. For behold, the Lord cometh forth out of his holy place bringing his wrath upon the inhabitants of the earth" (26:20-21).[221]

b) In the Apocalypse of 2 Baruch, dated A.D. 50-90,[222] there are notable parallels: unceasing prayer that the righteous may be prepared for the last judgment and that they may prevail and not be prevailed upon; proper disposition of the heart; the coming to pass of all these things; and the imminent consummation:[223]

> If ye prepare your hearts, so as to show in them the fruits of the law, it shall protect you in that time in which the Mighty One is to shake the whole creation (32:1).
>
> And at all times make request perseveringly and pray diligently with your whole heart that the Mighty One may be reconciled to you (84:10).
>
> If therefore we direct and dispose our hearts, We shall receive everything that we lost, And much better things than we lost by many times (85:4).[224]
>
> Let us prepare our soul That we may possess, and not be taken possession of, And that we may hope and not be put to shame (85:9).[225]
>
> For the youth of the world is past, And the strength of the creation already exhausted, And the advent of the times is very short, yea, they have passed by; And the pitcher is near to the cistern, And the ship to the port, And the course of the journey to the city, And life to its consummation. And again prepare your souls, so that when ye sail and ascend from the ship ye may have rest and not be condemned when you depart. For lo! when the Most High will bring to pass all these things ... (85:10-12).

---

[220]"There can hardly be any doubt that *kraipalē kai methē* here alludes to *ho methuon kai kraipalon* in Isa 24:20 (LXX)" (Lövestam, *Wakefulness*, p. 124).

[221]Note also Isa 27:1 ("In that day Yahweh with his hard and great and strong sword will punish leviathan") and Luke 12:12 (the lord "shall cut him asunder"). Cf. Lke 22:36,38 (Chap. VIII.E.8).

[222]*APOT*, II, 470.

[223]See Chap. V.G (Luke 18:1-8) on 2 Baruch 21:19-25 and prayer for a speedy consummation.

[224]Cf. Luke 9:24-25--"For whosoever would save his life shall not lose it." See Chap. VIII.E.10 for the eschatological doctrine of manyfold rewards.

[225]Cf. Luke 9:26.--"For whosoever shall be ashamed of me..."

For truly my redemption has drawn nigh, and is not far distant as aforetime (23:7).[226]

The consummation which the Most High will make is very nigh, and His mercy that is coming, and the consummation of His judgment, is by no means far off (82:2).

c) There are also interesting contacts between Luke 21:34-36 and other passages in Luke-Acts. 21:34-36 takes us back to 9:23-27, with its imminent expectation, warnings against undisciplined living, and judgment before the Son of Man (Chap. V.C.). 21:34 also contains the phrase "upon you" (*eph'humas*), as does 10:11, which, as we noted in Chap. V.D.3, indicates the kingdom of God is about to come down upon men from heaven, like the snare (21:35) coming down upon a covey of birds (Note #151), "like a falling trap" (Weymouth). The parallels between Luke 21:34-36 and 12:35-48 have been noted above (Chap. V.F.4).

21:34-36 also recalls 18:1-8 (Chap. V.G.): continuous prayer (18:1; 21:36), the day of the Son of Man (18:8b; 21:36c), when the Son of Man comes speedily and men stand before him in judgment,[227] and concern whether disciples will be prepared to withstand that day (18:8b; 21:36). Each unit concludes an apocalypse (17:20-18:8; 21:5-36).[228]

Luke 21:34-36, with its expressions "that day," "all who dwell upon the face of the whole earth," "all these things which before long (*mellō*) will happen," and "to stand before the Son of man," calls to mind similar words and phrases in the Areopagus address:

> He made of one every nation of men to *dwell on all the face of the earth* (Acts 17:26) (ASV).... But now He commands all men everywhere to repent, seeing that He has appointed a *day* on which, *before long* (*mellō*), He will judge the world in righteousness, through the instrumentality of a *man* whom He has predestined to this work (17:30-31) (Weymouth).

Here we see remarkable parallels: mankind as those dwelling upon all the face of the earth; the Day of the Lord; universal judgment before the Son of Man; and *mellō*, indicating that these things are on the verge of happening (Chap. IV.C.D).

d) It is of considerable significance that although each evangelist has his own ending to the synoptic apocalypse each nevertheless concludes with appeals to watchfulness (Matt 24:42-51; Mark 13:33-37; Luke 21:34-36). Thus Matthew and Mark illustrate the appropriateness of watchful perseverance to an ardent hope.[229]

---

[226]Cf. Luke 21:28.--"Your redemption draweth nigh"; also Rom 13:11.

[227]21:36c indicates in the judgment, as is shown by 11:32 ("The men of Nineveh shall stand up in the judgment with this generation").

[228]Higgins, *Son of Man*, p. 94, observes: "It is clear, therefore, that in 21:34-36 the same eschatological theme is presented as in 17:22ff. and 18:1-8." Hiers, "Delay," p. 154, also points up this relationship: "It is not accidental that these two verses [18:8; 21:36] conclude Luke's two apocalyptic sections: 17:20-18:8; 21:6-36. Both indicate that for Luke the main point of the two apocalyptic discourses was that Christians should be ready for the Parousia at all times, for the Son of man could now come at any time!"

[229]Other Lukan parallels to Mark 13:33-37 are Luke 12:38-40 (Chap. V.F) and 19:12-13 (Chap. VI.D).

e) The parallels in thought and language between Luke 21:34-36 and the Paulines have often been noted.[230] Luke's admonition against drowsiness, dissipation, drunkenness, and the anxieties of life reminds us of Paul's warning against sleep, revelling, drunkenness, chambering, wantonness, strife, and jealousy, in view of the nearness of the new age (Rom 13:11-13).

In Ephesians Paul "ceases not to give thanks" (1:16). He admonishes the Ephesians not "to be drunken with wine" and to give "thanks always for all things" (5:18,20). The Ephesians are to pray "in every season" (*en panti kairō*; only Luke 21:36; Eph 6:18) and to watch (*agrupneō*--only Mark 13:33;[231] Luke 21:36; Eph 6:18; Heb 13:17). The *Naherwartung* in Ephesians is generally overlooked, but is probably found in 5:16 ("redeeming the time, because the days are evil"), which suggests the hope and urgency of a speedy end,[232] and in 1:21, "the age which is about to come" (*mellō*). Thus in Ephesians we find the conjunction of ceaseless praying, sobriety, and the imminent expectation.

Phil 4:5-6 also combines the imminent parousia with exhortation to prayer and freedom from the cares of this life: "The Lord is coming soon. Don't worry about anything, but in all your prayers ask God for what you need, always thanking him with a thankful heart" (TEV).

We mark also the parallels with 1 Thess 5:1-4,6-7,17:

> Exhortation to take heed, watch, keep awake (21:34,36; 5:6,10); warning against drunkenness (21:34; 5:6,7); reminder that the day of the Lord comes upon

---

[230]Bultmann, *Synoptic Tradition*, p. 119, in line with his conviction that Paul had little interest in or access to the Gospel tradition, observes that in Luke 21:34-36 the terminology is "so characteristic and akin to Paul's that one could hazard a guess that Luke was here using a fragment from some lost epistle written by Paul or one of his disciples." Dodd, *Parables*, p. 123, finds that "the general similarity of the two passages [Luke 21:34-36; 1 Thess 5:2-8] is striking, and the similarity extends to the actual language. That Paul is quoting from the Gospel is impossible. That the evangelist had heard Paul give such teaching is possible. The probability is that both passages represent a common type of early Christian preaching, at least in missions to the Gentiles." Lövestam, *Wakefulness*, p. 123, remarks that Luke 21:34-36 and 1 Thess 5:2ff. "are possibly manifestations of a common primitive Christian tradition, which--in the words of J. A. T. Robinson [*Jesus and His Coming*, p. 114] 'has strong claim to embody elements of the teaching of Jesus himself.'" Perhaps Luke, who is creative, but seldom *de novo* composed 21:34-36 upon the basis of his tradition about Jesus' imminent expectation, Isa 24:17, Acts 17:26,30-31, and his personal knowledge of Paul's teachings. If so, this would be another instance where Luke has conformed his account of Jesus in his Gospel to that of Paul in Acts, in the interest of his Jesus-Paul parallelism. For other examples see my "Evans Reconsidered," pp. 37-40 (Luke 9:51-19:44//Acts 15:3, Samaritan journey; Luke 10:19//Acts 28:3-6, serpents; Luke 20:38//Acts 17:28, live in him; Luke 21:18//Acts 27:34, hair; Luke 22:41//Acts 21:5, kneeling; Luke 23:6-16//Acts 25:13-26:32, trial before Herod; Luke 24:47; Acts 1:8//Acts 17:30; 13:47, world mission). Of these seven examples, it is striking that three are found in close proximity to Luke 21:34-36, namely, Luke 20:38; 21:18; 22:41. Luke 21:12-19 is also conformed to the history of Acts, including Paul. Moreover, three of these parallels are found in Acts 17:26-31 (Luke 20:38; 21:34-36; 24:47).

[231]Luke's use of this rare word suggests he had his eye on Mark 13:33 and Mark's imminent expectation.

[232]Moore, *Parousia*, p. 161.

(*ephistemi*) (21:34; 5:3)²³³ men suddenly (*aiphnidios*; in NT only in 21:34; 5:3) as a snare (or thief) (21:34,35; 5:2,3,4); reference to season(s) (21:36; 5:1); encouragement to pray ceaselessly (21:36; 5:17); desirability of escaping the final woes (*ekpheugō*) (21:36; 5:3).

Paul's *Naherwartung* in 1 Thessalonians, especially 4:13-18, is forceful.

f) In 1 Pet 4:7 and 5:7-8 we also find the motifs of sobriety, prayer, watchfulness, freedom from anxieties, and the imminent end: "The end of all things is now close at hand: therefore be sober-minded and temperate, so that you may give yourselves to prayer (4:7) (Weymouth) (see Chap. V.G.)....Throw all your worries on him, for he cares for you. Be alert, be on watch!" (5:7-8) (TEV).

g) Luke 21:36 also contains an exact verbal parallel with Rev 6:17 (to stand=stathēnai): "For the great day of their wrath is come; and who is able to stand?" At Luke 21:34-36 (indeed, all of Luke 21) we are breathing the same apocalyptic air as at the sixth seal (Rev 6:12-17), with its cosmic woes and men seeking to escape from the wrath of God and the Lamb on the imminent day of the Lord. The only question under such circumstances is, "Who is able to stand?" So too Luke, after describing dreadful cosmic woes and men fleeing with fear (21:25-26), advises men to pray that they may escape all these things about to happen on that day and be able to stand before the Son of Man.

Luke 21:34-36 should be read together with the best commentaries upon it, those treated here: Isaiah 24-27; 2 Bar 21:19-25; 23:7; 32:1; 84:10; 85:5-12; Luke 9:23-27; 10:11; 12:35-48; 18:1-8; Acts 17:26-31; Matt 24:42-51; Mark 13:33-37; Rom 13:11-13; Eph 1:16; 5:18,20; 6:18; Phil 4:5-6; 1 Thess 5:1-17; 1 Pet 4:7; 5:7-8; Rev 6:12-17. These passages share the motif of imminence with various combinations of the motifs of continuous prayer, watchfulness, sobriety, anxiety-free living, snare, woes, flight, judgment, Son of Man, and day of the Lord. Since Luke 21:34-36 has all of these latter motifs, it would be quite strange if it lacked the motif of imminence. It is as if Luke made a noble and successful attempt to capsulize all of these apocalyptic motifs in the grand climax to his version of the synoptic apocalypse.

Against the background of this weighty evidence we may reasonably paraphrase 21:34-36 as follows:

> Never let your guard down, lest your hearts and minds be heavy and lose their sensitiveness because of crapulous headaches and drunkenness and the anxieties of the daily grind, and that great and terrible day of the Lord come down from heaven upon you soon and suddenly, for that day of reckoning, like a net falling suddenly upon an unsuspecting covey of quail, will likewise fall upon all men sitting at ease, eating and drinking, upon the face of all the earth. But keep awake! Fight off fatigue! And pray every moment that you may be strong and victorious to escape in the eschatological flight all these dreadful disasters which are on the verge of taking place, that you may prevail when you shall soon stand with all men in the last judgment before the Son of Man.

J. Jesus' Vow of Abstinence (Luke 22:18)

When Jesus at the last supper had passed the cup to his disciples he said, "I

---

²³³*Ephistēmi* appears only in Luke-Acts-Paulines. Possibly also in 1 Thess 5:3 its imminent overtones should be recognized: "soon and suddenly destruction cometh on them."

say unto you, I shall not drink from henceforth of the fruit of the vine, until the kingdom of God shall come" (22:18). Some have understood the kingdom here to refer to the church. Luke does not visualize an eschatological reunion of Christ and his disciples at the parousia but rather the promise of the coming of the Spirit in the church.[234] This view is inconsistent with Luke's concept of the kingdom as a futuristic eschatological reality (Chap. V.C.5).

Others have found at 22:18 an expression of the *Nächsterwartung*, but more on the part of Jesus than of Luke. "If Jesus refuses to taste wine 'until the kingly reign of God comes' (Luke 22:18), then this coming must be really near."[235]

> One might expect to drink wine again, a common beverage at any meal, as early as the next day, and at any rate on the next Sabbath (which, acording to Jeremias, would have been the next day). Was the vow also parallel, then, to the petition he had taught his disciples, "Give us our bread for tomorrow today" (Matt. 6:11)? Here he says in effect, "Give us the wine of the messianic table by tomorrow."[236]

This may have been the original meaning of the logion, which probably originated in a situation of intense apocalyptic expectation.[237] But again this view would hardly have been Luke's understanding, for we have seen that he does not attribute an immediate expectation to Jesus.

Another possibility is that Luke thinks here of an "undelimited parousia hope," that is, Jesus and/or Luke holds forth the possibility that the kingdom may come at any moment but it need not necessarily come within a few years.[238] But this distinction between a "delimited" and an "undelimited" expectation is a false one, for apocalyptists, even when not setting dates, were certain that the end was chronologically near. They believed the last things "must (*dei*)happen very soon" (Rev 1:1), which for John the Revelator was about A.D. 100.[239] No NT author says the end *may* come soon. Flat statements are used, as "the end of all things is now close at hand" (1 Pet 4:7). Sometimes these prophecies are introduced by solemn formulae: "But I tell you of a truth, ... " (Luke 9:27); "I say unto you, ... " (18:8); "Verily I say unto you, ... " (21:32; Matt 10:23). The speaker may even bind himself by a solemn oath: the angel "swore by him who lives for ever and ever, ... that there should be no more delay" (Rev 10:6) (RSV). We have already examined Luke's earnest expectations for "this generation" (9:27; 11:30; 21:32) (Chap. IV.B; V.C.E.H.).

An everyday example may help to clarify matters. We generally eat supper at 6 p. m. sharp. But to make sure I may ask my wife a few minutes before six when we are going to eat. She, busy in the kitchen, preparing the meal, replies, "We shall eat at 6:00." Then I know things are exactly on schedule. But sometimes she answers, "We'll eat soon," which means a few minutes after 6:00, probably by 6:10, but certainly not 6:30 or 7:00, to say nothing of several hours or days later.

---

[234]J. Wellhagen, *Anden och ricket*, 1941; V. Taylor, *The Formation of the Gospel Tradition*, 1933 (cited by Kaestli, *Eschatologie*, p. 59).

[235]Jeremias, *Theology*, p. 137; Grässer, *Delay*, pp. 53-54, 76.

[236]Hiers, *Historical Jesus*, p. 97.

[237]Cf. Kaestli, *Eschatologie*, p. 59.

[238]Moore, *Parousia*, pp. 138, 182. See Chap. V.G.3 on Cranfield, Moore's teacher.

[239]Rist, *Revelation*, p. 365.

"Soon" for her, as for apocalyptists, means a delimited period, only slightly less limited that 6:00 p.m. sharp. Apocalyptists knew God was, so to speak, busy in the kitchen preparing the messianic banquet, and whether they said it would be served within 3½ years, within that generation, or soon, they had in mind a delimited period of time. Even if God were to wait out of graciousness toward sinners (Luke 13:6-9) it would be a wait of short duration (Chap. V.F.3). God might even reduce the days (Mark 13:20). Even in John 16:16 there is a definite promise without qualification (Chap. VI.A).

The Distant Expectation School claims more support for its position in Luke 22:18. When Jesus speaks of eating and drinking with his disciples in the kingdom of God (22:16,18), he means, according to Luke, a future blessing coming after a long fasting time, during which Jesus does not drink. Luke indicates this lengthy period by his characteristic "from henceforth" (*apo tou nun*) (as in 12:52; 22:69). During that extended interval between passion and parousia the disciples receive the supper not only as a foretaste of that future salvation but, like the Spirit, as a substitute for the promised salvation during the period of the church. Spirit and meal empower the church to endure persecution and opposition in a godless, continuing world.[240]

That Luke's "from henceforth" does not imply a distant expectation will be shown in connection with 12:52 (Chap. VIII.B) and 22:69 (Chap. VI.G.3). The same phrase appears at 5:10 ("From henceforth thou [Peter] shalt catch men") and at Acts 18:6 ("From henceforth I [Paul] will go unto the Gentiles"), but in neither instance is there thought of a lengthy church age. Matt 26:29//Luke 22:18 also contains "henceforth" (*ap' arti*), but without denying the nearness of the messianic banquet.[241] Most likely, then, Luke at 22:18 is thinking, as elsewhere, not of an immediate or distant but of an imminent expectation: the kingdom of God comes[242] speedily (18:8) but not immediately (21:9). Jesus' vow of abstinence will not be a long one.

K. The Eschatological Urgency of Luke-Acts: Summary

Luke nowhere says nor reports anyone else as saying that God has postponed the end to the distant future or that the time of the church will last very long. This he could easily have done if it had been his intention to transform primitive eschatology. But not only has he failed to give us such a statement--he has even neglected to expunge those passages which we have examined in Chaps. IV and V. Luke nowhere suggests that people are to live as if the parousia would happen, "even though they knew in their hearts that it would not. Luke has not yet embraced such a compromise. He still believes in the return and does not expect it to be long delayed."[243]

---

[240]Conzelmann, *Theology*, pp. 80, 115; Grässer, *Delay*, pp. 55-56; Kaestli, *Eschatologie*, p. 59; Ellis, *Luke*, pp. 252-253.

[241]On "from henceforth' in Luke 1:48 see Chap. V.H.1.b, and on the Spirit as an eschatological gift see Chap. IV.G. Note *ap' arti* in Rev 14:13.

[242]It should be noted that Luke speaks here of the coming of the kingdom, whereas the parallels have "in my Father's kingdom" (Matt 26:29) or "in the kingdom of God" (Mark 14:25).

[243]Franklin, *Christ the Lord*, p. 14.

Moreover, Luke adds a mission of the seventy, who are twice instructed to announce that the kingdom of God is fast approaching in blessing and judgment (10:9,11). Only Luke says that the Son of Man will come as a sign to this generation (11:30). Only Luke points out that the eschatological urgency is not only for the first disciples but for all (12:41). Luke alone relates the stories of the deaths of the Galileans and of the eighteen and tells the parable of the fig tree to point up the nearness of judgment (13:1-9), already prophesied with a similar figure by John the Baptist (3:9). Only Luke has "already" in the invitation to the great supper: "Come; for all things are already ready" (14:17), that is "the Kingdom is coming sooner than you expect it."[244] Only Luke tells us that the Son of Man will come speedily to vindicate his suffering elect (18:1-8). And Luke has a unique ending to the synoptic apocalypse (21:34-36), Luke alone among the gospel writers exhorting to constant prayer (18:1; 21:36) in order to escape all the woes which are on the brink of coming (21:36). Only Luke has so much apocalyptic material (Chap. I.C) permeated with the imminent hope. Only Luke follows his Gospel with an "Acts of the Apostles," in which he continues to set forth the eschatological program and the near consummation (Chap. IV). And over forty percent of the occurrences in the NT of Luke's favorite words--"approach" (*engidzō*), "near" (*engus*), and "be about to" (*mellō*)--are in Luke-Acts, words which Luke skillfully uses to give his message an unmistakable note of eschatological urgency.[245]

That Luke's imminent hope could be denied is one of the marvels of modern criticism:

> The Distant Expectation School is hard-pressed to maintain that Luke re-worked his material consistently. They have to admit that reference to the nearness of the kingdom in 10:9,11 is extraordinary, and they try to explain it away as instruction for the future; they urge that Luke "carefully eradicated" any connection between Elijah and John the Baptist, but admit that such a connection appears in 1:16-17,76 and 7:26-27; they resort to the futile theory that "this generation" (21:32) means "humanity in general," and they have no explanation for the promise of speedy vindication in 18:1-8.[246]

---

[244] Easton, *Luke*, p. 228.

[245] *Engidzō* (24 of 42 occurrences); *engus* (6 of 32 occurrences); *mellō* (47 of 111).

[246] Adapted from Hiers, "'Lo, here!'", pp. 379-380.

Chapter VI
"Day by Day" (Luke 11:3):
Speedily But Not Immediately

A. "Changing Ideas in New Testament Eschatology"

Two decades ago there appeared a little-noted article on the chronological development of eschatological ideas within the NT.[1] Since this article provides a framework within which the passages of this present chapter may best be understood, we shall summarize it here, largely in the author's own words:

> The NT eschatological development may be divided into four periods, each with its own stratum of materials. Period A comprises Jesus' public ministry and ends abruptly with the crucifixion. This was a time of extreme expectancy, when the eschaton was expected momentarily. Nothing remained yet to be fulfilled before the coming of the end. The mood of Period A is expressed by Mark 1:15 ("The time is fulfilled, and the kingdom of God is at hand; repent, and believe in the gospel") and by Matt 10:23 ("Ye shall not have gone through the cities of Israel, till the Son of man be come"). Jesus' followers saw in him and in his message the signal that the time for the eschaton had come. Their hope rose to a feverish pitch, but instead of the eschaton came the cross.
>
> Period B begins abruptly with the resurrection experience. Peter's announcement that he had seen the Lord and the subsequent experience with the Risen Lord revived the eschatological hopes that had been dashed by the crucifixion. Jesus was exalted to the position from which he could come as the eschatological Son of Man. During Period B the eschatological ideas of Period A are corrected and the failure of the expectations of Period A are explained. The distinctive characteristic of Period B is the notion that with the crucifixion and/or exaltation the conditions for the coming of the eschaton have finally been fulfilled. The notion of the parousia was developed in this connection. The momentary expectation of the end was revived. Again there is a cry to repent as though the very hour had arrived. The end was not yet, but it was casting heavy shadows before it.
>
> With the failure of the hopes of Period B came the reassessment by Period C. The essential characteristic of Period C is the arrangement of systems of further conditions upon the fulfilment of which the coming of the eschaton depends. The end begins to recede and there is a marked increase in the more mundane

---

[1] Selby, "Changing Ideas," pp. 21-36.

problems of the church. Conversely, details of apocalypticism become more prominent in some quarters, as in the synoptic apocalypses (Matthew 24; Mark 13; Luke 21), and the sayings that place the times and the seasons in the Father's hands (Acts 1:7; Mark 13:32) are useful during Period C. Ethical teaching becomes more concerned with day-to-day problems rather than with last-minute preparation for judgment. There arises the vision of the world mission of the church in "this generation," at the end of which the appointed hour will arrive (cf. Mark 13:10).

Period D is characterized by a more drastic reorientation of eschatology. In some quarters there grew up a different approach to "last things" from that of Periods A, B, and C. We may call it the "Eternal Life" school. Eternal life was contrasted with life "in the world" as a quality of life as well as immortality, especially in the Johannine writings. But in none of the four periods is the eschaton lost sight of. Period D still looks forward to this hope but now in a much more formal and less vivid way.[2] The place of the church in this world and individual immortality become the central interests. Yet, as today, there were attempts to revive the earlier apocalyptic hope, as in II Peter and Revelation.

It should be noted that the periods subsequent to the crucifixion overlap and vary in different localities and with different writers. Often various lines of thought move side by side in the same general time. The temporal sequence here described is only a general pattern of development.[3]

In this chapter as we observe some of the eschatological adjustments made by Luke we shall see that Luke's eschatology belongs to Period C.

B. Heroic Living (Luke 9:23)

"If any man would come after me, let him deny himself and take up his cross daily, and follow me." Luke is sometimes thought to have added the word "daily" (*kath' hēmeran*) in the interest of his *Fernerwartung* (distant expectation). The original saying (Matt 16:24; Mark 8:34), with its call to martyrdom in the imminent tribulation, has been toned down by Luke to direct attention merely to the burdens of ordinary life. The heroic days of the *Nächsterwartung* (immediate expectation) and *Naherwartung* (imminent expectation) are past and the church now faces an extended period of routine existence and commonplace trials. "Luke makes it clear that Christians face a long, continuous testing."[4]

---

[2] We may add that the imminent expectation appears even in the Fourth Gospel: "A little while, and ye behold me no more; and again a little while, and ye shall see me" (16:16). Here is a reference not only to Jesus' death and resurrection but also to his departure and parousia. See Moore, *Parousia*, pp. 161-162.

[3] Oberlinner, "Terminworte," pp. 65-66, outlines a process of eschatological development similar to that of Selby's, though Selby would be more hesitant in ascribing an immediate or imminent expectation to Jesus himself: 1) Jesus expects the full manifestation of the kingdom in the very near future. 2) Jesus' death and resurrection intensify hope in the imminent coming of the kingdom of God. 3)The delay of the parousia produces a new strengthening of the *Naherwartung* by the assurance that, though some have died, others will live to see the parousia (Mark 9:1). 4) Further delay of the end brings about a shift of focus from the parousia to the present as the decisve time.

[4] Cf. Stuhlmueller, *Luke*, p. 118.

We should observe, however, that this saying fits well within its context of imminent expectation, 9:18-27 (Chap. V.C.9). In the next unit on 11:3 we shall find that a similar addition of "daily" does not de-eschatologize the third petition of the Lord's prayer. Again, the Q form of 9:23 does appear in Luke 14:27 (Matt 10:38): "Whoever doth not bear his own cross, and come after me, cannot be my disciple." Moreover, "daily" appears in a strongly eschatological verse, Acts 2:47 (Chap. IV.G): "And the Lord added to them day by day those that were being saved" (cf. Acts 16:5).

Finally, Luke's taking up of the cross daily is no more inconsistent with the imminent hope than is Paul's daily dying (1 Cor 15:31; cf. Rom 8:36; 2 Cor 4:10; Gal 6:17). Paul, in fact, stands "in jeopardy every hour" (1 Cor 15:30)(ASV). He runs "the risk of danger every hour" (TEV). He lives "dangerously every moment" (Berkeley). He faces "death every day!" (TEV). "Not a day" passes when he is not "at death's door" (Moffatt). May not Luke's daily cross-bearing reflect, like Paul's daily dying, not merely the burdens of everyday life, but the daily, even hourly, perils of heroic, eschatological living? Several times we have had occasion to note the plight of Luke's people (Chap. IV.G--14:22; V.C.9; V.G.4). Daily taking up of the cross may thus indicate a heightening rather than diminution of the eager expectation.

C. Eating Bread in the Kingdom of God (Luke 11:3)

1. The Apocalyptic Interpretation of the Lord's Prayer (Matt 6:9-13)

"Give us day by day our daily bread" (Luke 11:3). To grasp the eschatological significance of this petition in its Lukan form we must look briefly at the apocalyptic interpretation of the Lord's prayer as it appears in Matt 6:9-13.[5] In this prayer Jesus asks his disciples to pray for nothing else than the content of the kingdom of God: the hallowing of God's name, the rule of God's will, and the forgiveness of sins. "Thy kingdom come" does not mean, "Let thy church triumph," or "Let there be a just social order on this earth." It is not a prayer for the "reign of grace" (*regnum gratiae*), the kingdom of God which gradually spreads through the Word and in the mission as an order of moral, social and religious life.[6] Rather it is a plea that the "reign of glory" (*regnum gloriae*),[7] God's apocalyptic kingdom of the new age, may come soon, today, immediately. The aorist imperative form of "come" (*elthatō*) in Matt 6:10//Luke 11:2 expresses "the hope for a definite coming of the Kingdom in the near future."[8] This imminent expectation is also found in an ancient Aramaic prayer, the *Qaddish* ("Holy"),

---

[5] Adapted from Schweitzer, *Mysticism of Paul*, pp. 239-241, and Jeremias, *Lord's Prayer*, pp. 21-31.

[6] Origen, *De oratione* 25.1, and the Greek fathers.

[7] Tertullian, *De oratione* CSEL 20.180-207, and the Latin fathers. This and the preceding reference cited by Grässer, *Delay*, p. 98. Chrysostom, *Matth. Homil.* 19 on Matt 6:10 (*PG* 57, col. 279), and Luther, WA 30.1, p. 200, combine the two views. But as Grässer, *Delay*, p. 98, comments, not a word of this twofold coming stands in the text.

[8] Clark, "Realized Eschatology," p. 372. Conzelmann, *Theology*, pp. 123-124, rightly observes that Luke 18:1-8 "provides a commentary on the petition 'Thy Kingcome come', a petition which is fulfilled at the Parousia." But he fails to note that this commentary means the kingdom-parousia is coming speedily (Chap. V.G.3).

which concluded the synagogue service and which Jesus undoubtedly knew from childhood:

> Exalted and hallowed be his great name
> in the world which he created according to his will.
>
> May he rule his kingdom
>
> in your lifetime and in your days and in the lifetime
>
> of the whole house of Israel, speedily and soon.
>
> And to this, say: amen.[9]

The expectation is not that God's will shall ever be done on this earth, for the earth is to pass away, but on the new earth, to which the heavenly kingdom descends.

The request for "daily bread" does not mean ordinary bread at all, whether thought of as "continual bread," or "bread for our need," or "bread for today." It means "the coming bread," "tomorrow's bread," the food of the messianic banquet in the kingdom of God. "Give us today the food of the kingdom of God!" "Let thy kingdom immediately come, in which we shall eat the food of the messianic feast."

Jerome, in his commentary on Matt 6:11, reports: "In the gospel called according to the Hebrews, for 'substantial bread' I found '*mahar*,' which means 'of the morrow'; so that the sense is: our bread of the morrow, that is, of the future, give us this day."[10]

In late Judaism "tomorrow" (*mahar*) meant not only the next day "but also the great Tomorrow, the final consummation":

> Accordingly, Jerome is saying, the "bread for tomorrow" was not meant as earthly but as the bread of life. Further, we know from the ancient translations of the Lord's Prayer, both in the East and in the West, that in the early church this eschatological understanding—"bread of the age of salvation," "bread of life," "heavenly manna"—was the familiar, if not the predominant interpretation of the phrase "bread for tomorrow." Since primeval times, the bread of life and the water of life have been symbols of paradise, an epitome of the fulness of all God's material and spiritual gifts... The eschatological thrust of all the other petitions in the Lord's Prayer speaks for the fact that the petition for bread has an eschatological sense too, i.e., that it entreats God for the bread of life.[11]

Still with eyes riveted upon the imminent kingdom the petitioners ask God to forgive their debts without their passing through the tribulation and receiving forgiveness thereby, even as they forgive without satisfaction from their debtors.

---

[9] From Jeremias, *Lord's Prayer*, p. 21.

[10] Quoted in *Gospel Parallels*, p. 25. For a convenient summary of the attempts to translate this rare word *epiousios*, which appears only in Matt 6:11//Luke 11:3 and in the Lord's prayer in Didache 8:2, see BAG, pp. 296-297. We do not have "any other clear example of its use in the whole of Greek literature" (John Reumann, in Jeremias,*Lord's Prayer*, p. x).

[11] Jeremias, *Lord's Prayer*, pp. 24-25, and *Weltvollender*, p. 246.

"And lead us not into temptation" (*peirasmos*), that is, not temptation to sin, but rather allow us to escape the pre-messianic tribulation. *Peirasmos* (Matt 6:13; Luke 11:4) also appears in Rev 3:10: "I also will keep thee from the hour of trial, that hour which is to come upon the whole world, to try them that dwell upon the earth." Since this tribulation will be brought about by Satan at the end, the prayer concludes with the urgent desire for deliverance, not from abstract evil, but from the Evil One, from Satan, who will make one last effort to keep his power on earth, the tribulation.

This apocalyptic interpretation of the Lord's prayer would seem to be substantially correct because of the unity which it finds in the prayer and because of the way it fits with the apocalyptic background and atmosphere of the Gospels.

> While in the Old Testament there are many vivid pictures which paint the glory of the final kingdom, in the words of Jesus there is only one, which is drawn many times, the picture of the marriage feast or the king's feast, of eating and drinking or reclining at table with the patriarchs, in Abraham's bosom, and the pictures of harvest or sowing only serve to show the great context in which "our bread" is situated. One might almost say that from this point of view to pray for the coming of the kingdom and to pray "Give us our bread today" amounted to the same thing.[12]

If anything, the Matthean version of the Lord's prayer expresses, not the *Naherwartung*, but the *Nächsterwartung*, the expectation that the kingdom is to come immediately. The Lukan version contains similar apocalyptic requests for the quick coming of the kingdom, its bread, forgiveness of sins, and deliverance from the tribulation. Luke's form has in fact been found to be even more apocalyptic than Matthew's in that Luke does not reduce the force of the eschatological note "thy kingdom come" by reference to doing the will of God on earth.[13] It is questionable, however, whether Matthew has so compromised the apocalyptic meaning here, for "earth," as already indicated, means "new earth."

2. Lukan Variations in the Third Petition (Luke 11:3//Matt 6:11)

In the third petition of Luke 11:3 are two significant variations from the Matthean version:

1) Matthew has the aorist imperative of the verb "give" (*dos*), which means to give once for all, a single act of giving. Luke has the present imperative of the same verb (*didou*), which means "keep on giving," "continually give."[14]

2) Matthew has "today" (*sēmeron*), whereas Luke reads "day by day," "every day," "each day," "daily," "day by day" (*to kath' hēmeran*) (*to kath' hēmeran* also appears in Luke 19:47; Acts 17:11). With these two deviations from Matthew, Luke's petition reads: "Continually give us day by day our coming bread."

---

[12]Lohmeyer, *Lord's Prayer*, p. 148.

[13]Baird, *Luke*, p. 689. Dibelius, *Evangelium und Welt* (Göttingen, 1929), pp. 66ff., and Vielhauer, *Verkündigung und Forschung* (1949-1950), pp. 221-222, hold that Luke preserves the original apocalyptic suspense of the Lord's prayer better than Matthew (cited by Grässer, *Delay*, pp. 97, 107).

[14]See, e.g., Nunn,*Syntax*, p. 84.

These differences do not mean that for Luke the eschatological interpretation has yielded to more pressing daily problems.[15] But they do imply that the present age will continue for a while. The net effect of these changes is a shift from the immediate to the imminent expectation. The disciples are to pray, not for the one ultimate gift of bread in the messianic banquet (Matthew), but rather for a day-by-day supply of bread during the interval between the beginning of the end and the end of the end (for this contrast see Chap. IV.G on Acts 2:1 f, and the chart on p. 25).

3. Luke's Understanding of Bread

The Lukan version thus seems to modify the Matthean petition so as to refer to the ordinary bread needed for physical nourishment. This emphasis would fit well with Luke's concern for the poor and hungry in this age: "When thou makest a dinner or a supper, call not thy friends, nor thy brethren, nor thy kinsmen, nor rich neighbors; lest haply they also bid thee again, and a recompense be made thee. But when thou makest a feast, bid the poor, the maimed, the lame, the blind" (Luke 14:12-13). Luke varies from Matt 4:3, where the devil asks Jesus to command these "stones" to become loaves of bread; in Luke 4:3 Jesus is to command this "stone" to become a loaf. Apparently Luke is here concerned with Jesus' own personal hunger (Luke 4:2) rather than with the messianic feast of Matthew.[16] Luke holds that the law may be abrogated when persons, such as David and his men or Jesus and his disciples, hunger (6:1-5).

Only Luke notes that John came eating "no bread!" Jesus, by way of contrast, came eating (7:33-34). Only Luke tells of the midnight traveler who hungers for bread (11:5-8), and of Jesus' going into a Pharisee's house to eat bread (14:1). Only Luke describes the plight of the prodigal, who "would fain have filled his belly with the husks that the swine did eat: and no man gave unto him. But when he came to himself he said, How many hired servants of my father's have bread enough and to spare, and I perish here with hunger!" (15:16-17). Only Luke tells us that on such occasions it is meet to "eat and make merry" (15:23,32). Also unique to Luke is the beggar Lazarus "desiring to be fed with the crumbs that fell from the rich man's table" (16:21).

Luke advocates that the church be properly organized to feed its widows (Acts 6:1-6). He marks how Paul broke his fast, took food, and was strengthened (9:19). Peter, before his vision about eating unclean foods, "became hungry and desired to eat" (10:10), and did eat with uncircumcised men (11:3). Paul and Barnabas proclaim that God "gives you rain from heaven and crops at the right times; he gives you food and fills your hearts with happiness" (14:17)(TEV). In an atmosphere of great joy the Philippian jailer sets food before Paul and Silas (16:34). Luke knows from first-hand experience the good cheer that food brings to fasting, storm-tossed sailors (27:36). Luke writes as one who himself had at times almost perished of hunger and no one would give him so much as a bean

---

[15]Stuhlmueller, *Luke*, p. 144; Grässer, *Delay*, pp. 107-108. Grässer, *Delay*, p. 108, also interprets the fourth petition in terms of the delayed end: "In the still continuing time we shall again and again forgive our debtors." Luke's change of Matthew's aorist tense ("we have forgiven"--ASV) to present ("we forgive"--ASV) suits exactly Period C rather than a distant expectation, as Grässer would hold.

[16]Bacon. "Autobiography of Jesus," p. 556.

pod. Rackham well observed that "Luke gives great attention to the thought of bodily nourishment (more than his medical training would account for)."[17]

Luke's hearty interest in bread and his pleasure in enjoying and savoring good food would make it most unlikely that he could pray his third petition for continual, day-by-day provision of bread without thinking of man's need of ordinary bread. How appropriate this petition for the twelve as they traveled without taking along bread (Luke 9:3). Luke too is concerned with the "daily distribution" of bread (Acts 6:1), a further indication that he, like James (2:15- "daily food") and the church, is familiar with the idea of "daily bread."

And yet Luke knows too that "man shall not live by bread alone" (Luke 4:4). He realizes that men will be truly filled in the new age (6:21). He longs to be one of those faithful servants, "whom the lord when he cometh shall find watching," for the lord "shall gird himself, and make them sit down to meat, and shall come and serve them" (12:37). Only Luke tells us how "blessed is he that shall eat bread in the kingdom of God" (14:15). Luke alone notes the tragedy that "none of those men that were bidden shall taste of my supper" (14:24). Only at 22:16 does Jesus inform his disciples that he will never eat the passover again "until it be fulfilled in the kingdom of God" (22:16). After Jesus takes bread, gives thanks, breaks it, and gives it to the twelve (22:19), he appoints unto them a kingdom, that they "may eat and drink at my table in my kingdom" (22:29-30). Only in Luke does the Risen Christ sit down "with them to meat," take the bread, bless it, break it, and give it to them, thereby becoming known to them in the breaking of bread (24:30,35). Only Luke pictures the Risen Lord as eating a piece of broiled fish in Jerusalem before the disciples (24:41-42), and as eating with them during the forty days between resurrection and ascension (Acts 1:4--ASV margin). Yet a third time Luke reminds us that the disciples "ate and drank with him after he rose from the dead" (10:41). In view of these passages, Luke in his third petition must surely be thinking, like Matthew, of the "coming bread," "tomorrow's bread," the food of the messianic feast in the kingdom of God.

Yet in these passages there are also unmistakable eucharistic overtones. The pattern at the last supper of taking bread, giving thanks, breaking it, and giving it (Luke 22:19) reappears at the feeding of the multitudes (9:16), the meal on the Emmaus road (24:30), the repast at Troas (20:7,11), and at sea (27:35). The church fathers may have gone too far in identifying the bread of the Lord's prayer with that of the developed Eucharist of their day,[18] yet such an association cannot be ruled out completely. "Everywhere [in the ancient church] the Lord's Prayer was a constituent part of the celebration of the Lord's Supper."[19] Moreover, Marcion's version asks for "thy bread," which may be a reference to the eucharistic passage of John 6:33,[20] and probably to the Lord's supper.[21] The Didache, parts of which may go back to the first century, perhaps presupposes a similar connection, for in Chap. 8 it quotes the Lord's prayer, which is immediately followed by Chap. 9, which begins, "Now about the Eucharist . . ." Luke was surely mindful of such Jewish meals as the *Kiddush* (a religious meal eaten

---

[17] Rackham, *Acts*, p. 37.
[18] As Cyprian, "The Lord's Prayer," 18.
[19] Jeremias, *Lord's Prayer*, p. 2.
[20] Nestle, *Novum Testamentum Graece*, p. 181.
[21] Jeremias, *Lord's Prayer*, p. 3.

together by devout Jews) and the *Haburah* (=fellowship; a meal enjoyed together by friends on special days). Must not Luke also have in mind the fellowship meals of the primtive church? The disciples "continued steadfastly...in the breaking of bread and the prayers" (Acts 2:42). One of these prayers could have been the Lord's prayer, with its third petition for the baker's bread so necessary for existence until the parousia, when the Lord would himself serve his waiting servants (Luke 12:37), but a petition which would also refer to the bread of these fellowship meals. That Luke has this meaning in mind is further indicated in Acts 2:46, where the phrase "daily" (*kath' hēmeran*) is again used as in 11:3: "And day by day, continuing steadfastly with one accord in the temple, and breaking bread at home, they took their food with gladness and singleness of heart."

The extent to which these daily fellowship meals were eucharistic is impossible to detemine, but that they were more than secular meals goes without saying. The church came out of a rich background of table fellowship and sacred meals whose meaning would spill over into practice and belief. Probably Luke is referring to communal meals consisting of the agape or love feasts (cf. Jude 12; 2 Pet 2:13; 1 Cor 11:34) followed by the Lord's supper. At Troas the disciples gathered together to break bread (no article before "bread"), probably an agape meal ("fellowship meal"--TEV). Then after an interval Paul broke *the* bread, that of the holy communion (Acts 20:7,11).[22] The phrase "breaking of bread" (Luke 22:19; 24:30,35; Acts 2:42,46; 20:7,11; 27:35) is probably a veiled expression referring to the sacrament of the Lord's supper.[23] It is quite likely that Luke's version of the third petition grew up in these early circles of disciples meeting day after day for fellowship meals in anticipation of the Lord's return. "Each of the evangelists transmits to us the wording of the Lord's Prayer as it was prayed in his church at that time...No author would have dared to make such alterations in the Prayer on his own."[24]

How, then, should we translate or paraphrase Luke's third petition? An adequate rendering must include references to common bread, to the bread of the coming apocalyptic banquet, and to the day-by-day meals held in anticipation of that supremely great feast. The following attempt to catch something of all these connotations may be offered: "Keep on giving us day after day the bread of the fellowship meals[25] not only as physical nourishment until the Son of Man comes in glory but also as a foretaste of the messianic banquet which we shall soon eat in the kingdom of God."

As the disciples recited this petition at these fellowship meals they would unavoidably look back to Jesus' feeding of the 5,000 (Luke 9:10-17), to the last supper in the upper room (22:14-38), to the repasts with the Risen Lord (24:30-42; Acts 1:4; 10:41), and they would look forward to the messianic banquet when the Son of Man would serve them (Luke 12:37) at the celebration of completed redemption in the kingdom of God (22:16).[26] Luke thus gives us a form of the

---

[22] Rackham, *Acts*, p. 378.

[23] Jeremias, *Weltvollender*, p. 78.

[24] Jeremias, *Lord's Prayer*, p. 10.

[25] TEV renders "the breaking of bread" (Acts 2:42) as "the fellowship meals."

[26] Franklin, "Ascension," p. 199, likewise finds that in Luke one "anticipates the eschatological banquet in the Eucharistic meal (22.16,18,29-30), and prays for a daily anticipation of the eschatological food (11.3), an anticipation that can be realised only as daily one takes up the Cross and follows in the way of Jesus (9.23)."

Lord's prayer which basically is no less apocalyptic than the Matthean. Yet the Lukan circles have adapted the original to meet the needs of their time in Period C when a *Naherwartung* rather than a *Nächsterwartung* was in order.

D. Good Servants and Rebellious Citizens (Luke 19:11-27)

1. Literary Analysis

This eschatological unit contains the familiar parable of the pounds plus, as seems likely, a political parable, that of the rebellious citizens. This latter has been reconstructed as follows:[27]

> 12 A certain nobleman went into a far country, to receive for himself a kingdom, and to return... 14 But his citizens hated him, and sent an ambassage after him, saying, We will not that this man reign over us. 15a And it came to pass, when he was come back again, having received the kingdom, that he commanded.... 17b Have thou authority over ten cities.... 19b Be thou also over five cities....27 But these mine enemies, that would not that I should reign over them, bring hither, and slay them before me.

Luke thus gives us an allegorized parable which reflects many details about Jesus, church, and kingdom. These allegorical features include: Matthew's "man" (Matt 25:14) has become a "nobleman" or "prince," that is, Jesus, high-born as son of David and Son of God (Luke 1:26-34); he departs from his own land to receive a kingdom from the hands of the superior power (cf. Luke 22:29); he is resisted and rejected by his own people; the church has been formed, and is administered and expanded by disciples through the Gentile mission; he returns as king in his kingdom and punishes the Jews for their unbelief.[28]

Luke has placed the combined parables toward the end of his great central section (9:51-19:44) within a Jerusalem framework of vv 11 and 28:

> 11 And as they heard these things, he added and spake a parable, because he was nigh to Jerusalem, and because they supposed that the kingdom of God was immediately to appear.[29]

> 28 And when he had thus spoken, he went on before, going up to Jerusalem.

We find here a number of indications of Luke's hand. The eager expectancy is akin to that of the disciples on the Emmaus road, who had hoped Jesus would redeem Israel while he was still alive (Luke 24:21), and to that of the apostles, who wanted Jesus to restore the kingdom to Israel at once (Acts 1:6). Another Lukan touch is seen in the connection between the account of Jesus as house-guest and ensuing parables: cf. Luke 5:33 as the link between 5:27-32 (Jesus in Matthew's house) and 5:34-39 (parables), and 19:11 as the connection between 19:1-10 (Jesus in Zacchaeus' house) and 19:12-27 (parables).

The following Lukanisms occur in 19:11: the skilful phrasing, "and as they heard these things" (similarly Luke 20:45); "he added (*prostithēmi*--Luke-Acts,

---

[27]Bundy, *Gospels*, p. 413.

[28]Cf. Montefiore, *Gospels*, II, 565-566; Stuhlmueller, *Luke*, p. 152.

[29]The "appearing of the kingdom" is probably meant to include the parousia--cf. "appearing" in connection with the parousia in 2 Thess 2:8; 2 Tim 4:1.

thirteen times; entire NT, eighteen) and spake a parable" (Chap. V.G.1); *dia to* (because) with infinitive (Matthew, twice; Mark, three; John, once; Luke-Acts, fourteen); *einai* (to be) after a preposition and article (*dia to . . . einai*) (Luke-Acts, ten times; Paulines, nine; John, once; James, once); Jerusalem (spelled *Ierousalēm*)(Luke-Acts, sixty-three times; rest of NT, five); immediately (*parachrēma*)(Matthew, twice; Luke-Acts, sixteen); *mellō* (Chap. IV); appear (*anaphainō*)(Luke-Acts, twice); the kingdom of God (Luke-Acts, thirty-eight times; rest of NT, twenty-nine).[30]

The immediate occasion is the Zacchaeus incident (19:1-10). Jesus' words about salvation (vv 9-10) give rise to speculation about the nearness of the realm of salvation, the kingdom of God. Possibly Luke intends us to picture Jesus as speaking the parable in the house of Zacchaeus. At any rate, Jesus "added" a parable to the conversation there. But what does Luke wish the parable to teach about the imminent expectation? Several interpretations have been advanced.

2. "Be Ready to Wait"

According to the *Fernerwartungsschule*, Luke at 19:11-27 rejects the imminent expectation. As Jesus draws near to Jerusalem, the disciples and possibly others present sense an immediate climax to the eschatological drama: the kingdom will expel the darkness with magnificent splendor. But the parable is a warning to those of Jesus' day as well as those of Luke's time who have an over-eager expectation of the parousia. As the nobleman went to a far country and was therefore gone for a long time, so too Jesus' absence will be an extended one, during which there will be abundant time for service, testing, and rebellion. There will be no immediate triumph but, after the Lord's departure, a long period of probation followed by Jesus' return and the last judgment. The parousia is removed beyond the lifetime of that generation. This period of anticipation might in fact stretch out into countless years. The parable is thus a summons to be ready for a long period of waiting. Luke, under the pressure of the delay of the parousia, substitutes salvation history for the imminent expectation.[31]

For a number of reasons, however, it appears unlikely that Luke is here rejecting the *Naherwartung*. There is little reason to suppose that the nobleman's journey to a far country represents a *Fernerwartung*. The parable of the rebellious citizens possibly alludes to the journey of Herod Archelaeus to Rome to receive his kingship, he too being opposed by a delegation of irate citizens (Josephus, *Antiquities* 17.9; 17.11; *Wars* 2.2). But even though Archelaeus' journey was a long one, it occupied no extensive period of time. We may also call to mind Paul's far-flung travels of no little rapidity. Luke, being himself well-traveled, knew first-hand of the comparatively short period of time involved in a long trip. In the parables themselves both the servants and rebellious citizens are alive and well when the nobleman returns. Again, if 19:11-27 does express a

---

[30]From Jeremias, *Parables*, pp. 99-100, and Hawkins, *Horae Synopticae*, pp. 30,39.

[31]Baur and Zeller, in Biederwolf, *Second Coming Bible*, p. 379; Godet, *Luke*, II, 219; Plummer, *Luke*, p. 444; Conzelmann, *Theology*, p. 113; Grässer, *Delay*, pp. 115-117; Stuhlmueller, *Lukan Reading Guide*, p. 125; Kaestli, *Eschatologie*, pp. 38-40; Schneider, *Parusiegleichnisse*, pp. 38-42.

distant expectation it is contrary to our findings in Chaps. IV and V.³²

3. No Instant Eschatology

As the *Naherwartungsschule* sees it, Luke by means of 19:11-27 rejects the immediate expectation.³³ B. Wilson's translation of 19:11 is suited to bring out the position which Luke here seeks to refute: "The Kingdom of God was about immediately to appear." In the Greek the two words "immediately" (*parachrēma*) and "about to" (*mellō*) appear first in the sentence for emphasis. By this means Luke is telling us exactly what he wants to say: he is rejecting an immediate expectation but affirming an imminent expectation. Luke "vigorously supported the imminence of the end while denying its immediacy."³⁴ In other words, Luke's arrangement of words in his introductory sentence expresses the view against which the parable is directed: the enthusiastic crowds think that when they get to Jerusalem contact will be made which will set the end-time events into motion. We find ourselves in Period A. Luke in Period C lets Jesus tell the parable at this juncture to show that the expectation is false that "immediately about to appear is the kingdom."

Luke frequently uses "be about to" (*mellō*) to indicate an imminent hope (Chap. IV). At 19:11 he uses it with the even more urgent "immediately" (*parachrēma*), the only such combined usage in the NT. As we have already noted, *parachrēma* is found twice in Matthew and sixteen times in Luke-Acts.³⁵ All but two or three of these instances have to do with instantaneous miracles, such as: "He laid his hands upon her: and immediately she was made straight" (Luke 13:13); "Jesus said unto him, Receive thy sight: . . .And immediately he received his sight" (Luke 18:42-43). What the disciples are expecting is the greatest of all miracles, the instantaneous appearance of the kingdom in spectacular demonstration (19:11): "Instantly was the kingdom of God to shine forth" (Rotherham).

How, then, does Luke dampen this excessive eschatological enthusiasm? He does so by indicating through his allegorical parable that certain events must take place before the miraculous consummation. Jesus must depart (through death, resurrection, and ascension--Luke 18:31-34; 9:51) to the far country of heaven to receive his kingdom. During his absence his disciples must see how much they can earn, that is, they must win more followers through missionary activity. Then, while some of Jesus' hearers (9:27; 21:32) and most of Luke's people are living the Lord will return in judgment to reward the faithful with rulership over the cities of the kingdom and to slay the rebellious citizens (his own people) who did not want him to rule over them. There will, then, be a delay in the

---

³²It is interesting to observe that whereas Matt 25:19 states that the master returned "after a long time," Luke 19:15 simply says he returned. Nevertheless at Luke 20:9 the householder goes into another country "for a long while," a phrase not found in Matthew 21:33 or Mark 12:1. Yet the householder returns that same season.

³³Easton, *Luke*, pp. 279-280; Wilson, "Lukan Eschatology," p. 337; Francis, "Eschatology," pp. 58-59; Franklin, *Christ the Lord*, p. 26.

³⁴Francis, "Eschatology," p. 59.

³⁵Matt 21:19,20; Luke 1:64; 4:39; 5:25; 8:44,47,55; 13:13; 18:43; 19:11; 22:60; Acts 3:7; 5:10; 12:23; 13:11; 16:26,33.

consummation. But it will not be long. The end will come speedily (18:8) but not immediately (19:11).

4. Jesus' Resurrection as Parousia

According to H. W. Bartsch,[36] Luke at 19:11 rejects the Gnostic view that the resurrection of Jesus was his parousia, that the parousia and end had already happened with the death and resurrection of Christ: his day had come with his resurrection. There is therefore nothing left to be expected in the future. This was the earliest primitive Christian position, that of the disciples and of Luke's readers. It is the understanding Luke is correcting at 19:11-27. It is incorrect to suppose, as do the Distant and Imminent Expectation Schools, that primitive Christianity began with the expectation of the parousia in the near future. A sample of this earliest eschatology is found in 2 Tim 2:18, according to which our resurrection has already taken place. But very soon this primitive view was corrected not only by Luke but by the whole gospel tradition. Luke holds that the passion ended with the ascension and that the parousia will happen after the ascension. Luke does not fix a precise date but he too thought it would come in that generation. In short, says Bartsch, Luke rejects the belief that the end has come directly with Jesus' death and resurrection (19:11; 21:9,12), but he also renounces the opinion that the parousia would be long delayed (12:45). He admonishes constant expectation of the sudden irruption of the eschaton.

In response to Bartsch's position, we may observe that Gnosticism is a most controversial subject, especially as to its impact upon the NT. It may be briefly described as a system of salvation which claimed to impart secret, divinely revealed knowledge or *gnosis*, which would deliver the soul from the miseries of its material existence in an evil material world which was created by an inferior deity. The true God lives beyond the seven planets in a realm of light, from which man's soul has fallen. But with the divine revelation provided by Gnosticism the soul is enabled to find its way back at death to its own element. Expressed another way, salvation is the release of the divine spark of light (soul) imprisoned in man so that it can escape the prison of the body and return to the light-world from which it originally came.[37]

In respect to eschatology, Gnostics denied apocalyptic thought as being too physical in character and adopted instead a spiritualized eschatology which saw the "last things" as realized in this age rather than in the new age on a new earth.

Gnosticism reached its full development in the third century, but it is commonly held that the roots of the later systems go back to the first century or even earlier. The undeveloped thought of these early antecedents should probably be referred to as incipient or proto-Gnosticism. It is generally agreed that the Pastoral and Catholic epistles are directed against various types of incipient Gnosticism combined with Jewish and Christian beliefs.

---

[36]Bartsch, *Wachet*, especially pp. 7-9, 106-123, and "Eschatology," pp. 392-393. Bartsch bases his views on the studies of Ernst Lohmeyer, *Galiläa und Jerusalem*, 1936; Walter Bauer, *Rechtgläubigkeit und Ketzerei im ältesten Christentum*, 1934; and C. H. Dodd's realized eschatology as found in his *History and the Gospel*, 1938; *The Parables of the Kingdom*, 1953; *The Apostolic Preaching and Its Development*, 1954.

[37]Adapted from Selby, *Introduction*, pp. 271-272.

Bartsch's theory, however, is not that later NT writings contain a polemic against Gnostic heresies. He claims that Christianity began with a Gnostic eschatology, a spiritualized, realized eschatology, which saw the "last things" as present here and now. But there is widespread agreement that Jesus' teaching included a futuristic eschatology.[38] If Bartsch is correct, then one so early as Paul was not only wrong in his imminent expectation but also in his claim that "the word of the Lord" (1 Thess 4:15) was the authority for his belief. Some would be willing to grant that Paul strayed from the earliest eschatology when he expected realistic future events to occur soon and traced his hope back to Jesus. But if Luke and the entire gospel tradition have buried the original Christian eschatology so deeply as Bartsch holds, then we may as well despair of recovering any facts about primitive Christian beliefs. A course of development such as that proposed by Selby and Oberlinner (Chap. VI.A) appears to be much more likely, that is, Christianity began with an eager expectation of the early end.

The problem for the primitive community was this: How does the one who was crucified and dead become the one who will come in glory? The answer: through his resurrection and exaltation as Lord. Jesus' resurrection was the connecting link between his death and his parousia, the *conditio sine qua non* of the parousia, but not the parousia itself. The coming one was not expected out of the grave but out of the clouds of heaven.[39]

Until Bartsch can produce more convincing evidence for his interpretation we would do well to stay closer to the NT documents. To his credit, though, Bartsch has long recognized and stressed Luke's strong apocalypticism and imminent expectation.

5. Jesus' Ascension as Parousia

As Charles Talbert sees it, Luke by means of 19:11-27 is rejecting the Gnostic view that the ascension of Jesus was his parousia, that is, Luke here polemizes against a spiritualized, completely realized eschatology.[40] The end has already occurred. The parousia is actualized entirely in the present.

If, says Talbert, we begin with the principles of redaction criticism that narratives reflect the interests and problems of the author and of his community, then Luke 19:11-27 shows us an eschatological problem agitating Luke and his church rather than the historical Jesus and the disciples. If 19:11 is read in light of its context in Luke 9:51-Acts 1:11, then we see that Luke's focus is upon the ascension of Jesus to take place in Jerusalem:

> And it came to pass, when the days were well-nigh come that he should be received up, he steadfastly set his face to go to Jerusalem (9:51).

> Moses and Elijah . . . appeared in glory, and spake of his decease (margin: departure; Greek: *exodos*) which he was about to accomplish at Jerusalem (9:31).

> Ye men of Galilee, why stand ye looking into heaven? this Jesus, who was

---

[38]Craig, "Teaching of Jesus," p. 153; Ladd, *Presence*, p. 123.

[39]This paragraph is adapted from Grässer, *Delay*, p. 32. Kaestli, *Eschatologie*, p. 95, is also unconvinced by Bartsch's reconstruction.

[40]Summarizing Talbert, "Redaction," pp. 171-222.

received up from you into heaven, shall so come in like manner as ye beheld him going into heaven (Acts 1:11).

Luke 19:11 against this background reveals that the problem in Luke's community is a misunderstanding of Jesus' ascension. The disciples (=Luke's church) wrongly suppose that Jesus' ascension which is shortly to take place in Jerusalem is to be identified with the appearance of the kingdom of God, the parousia. The problem of Luke's community is not that of a delayed parousia, as views Sections 2 and 3 presuppose, but rather is an erroneous identification of Jesus' being received up in Jerusalem and the coming of the kingdom.

Luke, continues Talbert, combats this error in two ways: 1) He sets up three stages in the chain of eschatological events: a) the nobleman's departure to receive kingly power; b) the period of trading by his servants; c) the nobleman's return and his judgment of servants and enemies. In other words, Luke distinguishes Jesus' ascension from his parousia in the kingdom. 2) Luke also makes plain that the parousia involving the destruction of Jesus' enemies will be a physical, visible event which has not yet occurred. The very nature of the parousia indicates it is a future, not a present, event, though it is an imminent event.

Similar Gnostic views are rejected in the writings of the church fathers and even in the NT, that is, before, during, and after the Lukan period: 2 Tim 2:17-18, the resurrection has already come to pass; 1 Cor 4:8, Christians already reign in the kingdom of heaven; 2 Thess 2:2, the day of the Lord is already here. These writings refute these eschatological errors in the same manner as does Luke, namely, by setting up stages and by depicting the physical, universal nature of the end events.

Turning now to a critique of Talbert's reconstruction, we find that certain aspects of it are well-taken. 19:11-27 must be read against the background of Luke-Acts. Luke is concerned with eschatological problems in his own church. He does set up stages and depict the realistic nature of the final events, while still affirming the *Naherwartung*. And Talbert would seem to have the edge over Bartsch, for whereas Bartsch thinks of an over-realized eschatology as the original view of primitive Christianity, Talbert regards it as a later heresy, which is a much more likely course of development and which does not entail such a drastic revision of the NT documents.

There are a number of considerations, however, which render Talbert's view not a little suspect. a) It is not certain that 9:51 and 9:31 refer to the ascension. "Taking up" (*analēmpsis*) (9:51) could mean death or resurrection, though it is more naturally understood of the ascension as concluding or including these three events.[41] Weymouth and TEV take *exodos* (9:31) to mean Jesus' death rather than his ascension.

b) It is difficult to see how Talbert leaps from the fact that Luke is concerned with Jesus' ascension to the claim that the disciples (Luke's church) therefore identified the ascension with the parousia-kingdom event. It seems more likely that Luke is stressing the ascension because there were those in Jesus' day who thought that the kingdom would come without the ascension and other stages: it was about to come immediately (*parachrēma mellei*). Some of the disciples may

---

[41]Cadbury, "Acts and Eschatology," p. 306.

have looked for the kingdom to appear at once upon Jesus' messianic entry into Jerusalem, or when he cleansed the temple, or they may have thought that Jesus' symbolic enactment of the messianic banquet would induce God to cause his kingdom to come, or that it would be manifested when they retired to the Mount of Olives, or that perhaps God would send deliverance while Jesus was on the cross but before he died. Against this background of eager expectation Luke stresses the ascension, not because some were identifying it with the parousia, but because some were leaving it out of consideration altogether.[42] Luke thus corrects this error of Period A, namely, that this instant eschatology did not take into acount all of the events on the apocalyptic agenda which must take place before the kingdom can come.

While seeking out Luke's own theological problems and answers, we must not forget his historical interests. There seems every reason to suppose that Luke at 19:11 has correctly reported the excited mood of the disciples as they approached Jerusalem. Luke 19:11 may well be Luke's summary of Mark 10:35-45, which does reflect such an expectancy. "The narrative of the request of the sons of Zebedee which Lk. has omitted from Mk. shewed that the disciples at this time entertained high hopes of the immediate appearance of the kingdom, and perhaps that narrative has indirectly influenced Lk. here."[43] Possibly this same instant eschatology is seen in Matt 26:58, where Peter sits with the guards "to see the end" (*to telos*). This verse may mean "to see how it would all come out" (TEV), but then again it may express Peter's primitive hope in Period A.[43a] Grässer holds on the basis of Mark 11:10 that Luke 19:11 reflects Jesus' own *Nächsterwartung*.[44] Similarly Hiers finds that the behavior of Jesus and his disciples afterward shows they still held such a hope.[45] Loisy says that "the old historic tradition, still recognizable in Mark, though corrected even there, that Jesus came to Jerusalem to establish the Kingdom had to be contradicted and effaced by Luke to satisfy the exigencies of faith."[46] Wellhausen sums up the situation well by commenting that 19:11 is from Luke but the idea that Jesus would establish the kingdom in Jerusalem is hardly invented by Luke.[47] The important thing for us is that Luke is here dealing first of all with an historical situation, not only with problems in his own community. Luke 19:11 "gives the parable a definite historical setting in the light of which it is intended to be understood."[48]

If 19:11 does give us the attitude of the disciples as they approached the royal city,[49] we need not say therefore that the pericope is only of historical interest to

---

[42]Cf. Hiers, *Historical Jesus*, pp. 96, 97, 105.

[43]Creed, *Luke*, p. 233.

[43a] This possibility becomes more likely if *to telos* in Jas 5:11 also refers to the parousia. See R. P. Gordon, "James 5:11," *JTS*, 26 (1975), 91-95 (*NTA* 20.218).

[44]Grässer, *Delay*, pp. 24-28.

[45]Hiers, *Historical Jesus*, p. 79.

[46]Loisy as quoted by Montefiore, *Gospels*, II, 565.

[47]Wellhausen, *Lucas*, p. 106.

[48]Franklin, *Christ the Lord*, p. 26.

[49]This could be so even though the framework of a Samaritan journey in 9:51-19:44 is fictitious (see, e.g., my "Halévy Reconsidered") and even if Jesus did not speak the parable on this particular occasion.

Luke. On the contrary, it would be most relevant to Luke's audience. Luke's readers were repeatedly asking questions about the coming of the kingdom (Luke 17:20; 19:11; 21:7; Acts 1:6). But this repeated questioning means that for Luke's people the kingdom had not yet come and that past events had not fulfilled their expectations.

In Luke's own church there would be the problem of the delay which among some gives rise to over-heated apocalyptic expectations. Luke (in Period C) points out to these enthusiasts that they are making the same error as did the disciples (in Period A) as they drew nigh to Jerusalem: they expect too much too soon. The Lord has a program which must be fulfilled, a program including Jesus' departure, reception of sovereignty, world mission, and return in judgment.

It may be too that some of Luke's friends were claiming rightly or wrongly that Jesus himself expected the kingdom to display itself instantly, perhaps without death, resurrection, and ascension. To show that Jesus was not wrong, even if the disciples were, Luke has Jesus tell the conflated parables of 19:11-27.[50]

Again, perhaps some of Luke's people were asking, "He promised to come, didn't he? Where is he?" (2 Pet 3:4) (TEV). The problem of the delay of the parousia had arisen as early as 1 Thess 4:13-18 and "was essentially the same when 2 Peter was written."[51] If the young community at Thessalonica had questions about the delay, it seems even more likely that such questions had already arisen in the older Palestinian churches where they had been waiting for some twenty years.[52] It would be strange if this widespread concern had not reached Luke's readers, who, like the Thessalonians (1 Thess 4:13-18), may have puzzled over the unexpected development that brethren were dying before the parousia. Possibly it is out of Luke's interest in the state of departed brethren that he addresses himself to the intermediate state of Abraham's bosom, Hades, and Paradise (Luke 16:19-31; 23:43) (Chap. III). And the account of Ananias and Sapphira may be an attempt to explain the first deaths in the Christian community. To reassure these doubters that Jesus would truly return Luke uses this parousia parable of 19:11-27 most effectively. The situation is that of Period C and the adjustments being made at that time because of the delay of the parousia.

Further, Luke uses this means to let his readers know that Jesus regarded the interval between ascension and parousia as a time of testing and trading during which more disciples are to be brought into the church, thus fulfilling the "time of the Gentiles" (21:24) (Chap. VI.F) as a pre-condition of the kingdom. Finally, this parable would reassure and warn Luke's people that there will surely be a strict and severe last judgment with generous rewards and stern punishments.

c) Although Luke's argumentation may have proved useful to later anti-Gnostic church fathers that does not mean that it originated as a polemic against a gnostic front, a front which may not have existed as early as Luke-Acts. How Luke's materializations may have helped later anti-Gnostics may be indicated by two textual variants at Luke 24:42-43. According to these later readings, the disciples gave the Risen Jesus not only a piece of boiled fish, as in

---

[50]Cf. Hiers, *Historical Jesus*, p. 79.

[51]Owen, "Stephen's Vision," p. 226.

[52]Manson, *Sayings of Jesus*, p. 628.

the older texts, but also "of an honeycomb" (Luke 21:42)(KJV). Then Jesus not only took it and ate it before them (earlier reading), but also "gave the rest to them" (23:43). Apparently an anti-Gnostic (or anti-docetic) scribe added these features to prove that the Risen Lord had a real body--after all, Jesus left his teeth marks in the honeycomb from which he ate and then returned the remainder to the disciples.[53]

But even these later proofs of Jesus' corporeality may not have arisen out of an anti-Gnostic polemic. "Since in parts of the ancient church honey was used in the celebration of the Eucharist, ... copyists may have added the reference here in order to provide scriptural sanction for liturgical practice."[54]

d) Another difficulty with Talbett's view is this: If Luke had wanted to refute over-realized eschatologists would he not have had various persons say "The kingdom has come," or "the ascension is the parousia"? Luke is capable of presenting his concerns in a relatively straight-forward manner, such as his interest in the poor, women, prayer, missions, Peter, and Paul. In the instance before us, Luke is alleged to have his characters who represent over-realized eschatology express the opposite, that is, over-realistic eschatology: "God's Reign would instantly come into view" (19:11) (Moffatt). How unlikely for Luke to expect his readers to take these over-realistic eschatologists and by mental legerdemain transform them into over-realized eschatologists by projecting the alleged viewpoints of Gnostics of Luke's time back into the characters of Luke's story who express the opposite view to that which they are supposed to represent! How amazing that those persons who look for the kingdom in the future are really those who look for it in the past. It seems most improbable that Luke would so have hidden his message under a bushel of puzzles, parables, and riddles.

e) Luke's stress on the ascension has other purposes than that of showing it is different from the parousia. For Christians of every type he wants to portray vividly Jesus' enthronement as Lord (Luke 24:52). He uses it as a vehicle to present the missionary command of Acts 1:8, which literarily speaking serves as an outline of the Book of Acts, and which eschatologically speaking presents the world mission as a part of the apocalyptic agenda (as hinted in the parable of the pounds)(19:11-27). "Jesus' exaltation is the basis of their faith; his commission in Acts 1:8 is unthinkable without it. The end has not come, but the Church must go on living and expanding."[55]

f)It should be noted also that the parallel parable of the talents in Matt 25:14-30 outlines three stages: 1) the merchant's departure; 2) the period of trading by servants; 3) the merchant's return and judgment of his servants. The use of stages is part of apocalyptic without reference to Gnosticism. Stages also appear in 2 Thess 2:1-12, where Paul seeks to cool over-heated apocalyptists, not by denying the imminent parousia, but by indicating the events which must precede the end. The error which Paul refutes (2 Thess 2:2) is most likely that of claiming "the day of the Lord is just at hand" (ASV) rather than the day has

---

[53]Jeremias, *Weltvollender*, p. 271.

[54]Metzger, *Textual Commentary*, p. 188.

[55]Wilson, "Lukan Eschatology," p. 337. See also Franklin, "Ascension," pp. 191-200, and *Christ the Lord*, pp. 29-41.

already come.⁵⁶ Or perhaps Paul's opponents were thinking that the "day of the Lord hath set in" (Rotherham), that is, the final period had already begun and the futuristic events were just beginning to come to pass. Or the Thessalonians may have held the mistaken view that Jesus had already returned secretly (cf. also Luke 17:22-37; Mark 13:6,21). To combat such a misconception Luke stresses the public nature of the parousia.⁵⁷ Contrary to Talbert, then, the Thessalonian error may not be that of a spiritualized eschatology at all.

g) The delay motif is too deeply imbedded in Luke-Acts to be disposed of altogether, as Talbert apparently tries to do. Even if the Gnostic key should unlock the door to a passage or two, other keys will be needed for other passages. Viewing Luke-Acts against the background of Period C seems to account better for the evidence.

6. Conclusion

Of these four understandings of Luke 19:11-27 Interpretation Number 3 of the *Naherwartungsschule* seems to be the most natural and least forced. It gives a convincing explanation in the original setting in Jesus' ministry as well as in Luke's community. It fits comfortably into the general course of NT eschatological development, that is, Period C correcting Period A. Here, as in Mark 13 and 2 Thessalonians 2, we see excessive apocalyptic enthusiasm mitigated by a list of events which must precede the end.⁵⁸ Interpretation Number 3 accounts for Luke's use of two of his favorite words in the emphatic position: "immediately" (*parachrēma*) and "be about to" (*mellō*). It meshes well with what more and more seems to be Luke's eschatology: not instant, not distant, but imminent expectation.

E. "Not Immediately the End" (Luke 21:7-13)

1. Literary Analysis

Another important section where Luke allows for a delay of the parousia is the beginning of his version of the synoptic apocalypse, which we compare with the Matthean and Markan parallels:

Matt 24:3-9	Mark 13:3-9	Luke 21:7-13
3 And as he sat on the mount of Olives, the disciples came unto him privately, saying, Tell us, when shall these things be? and what shall be the sign of thy coming, and of the end of the world? 4And Jesus answered	3 And as he sat on the mount of Olives over against the temple, Peter and James and John and Andrew asked him privately, 4 Tell us, when shall these things be? and what shall be the sign when these things	7 And they asked him, saying, Teacher, when therefore shall these things be? and what shall be the sign when these things are about to come to pass? 8 And he said, Take heed that ye be not led astray: for

---

⁵⁶Vincent, *Word Studies*, IV, 63.

⁵⁷Cf. Ellis, *Luke*, p. 210.

⁵⁸Cf. Thompson, "Gentile Mission," p. 20.

and said unto them, Take heed that no man lead you astray. 5 For many shall come in my name, saying, I am the Christ; and shall lead many astray. 6 And ye shall hear of wars and rumors of wars; see that ye be not troubled; for these things must needs come to pass; but the end is not yet. 7 For nation shall rise against nation, and kingdom against kingdom; and there shall be famines and earthquakes in divers places. 8 But all these things are the beginning of travail. 9 Then shall they deliver you up unto tribulation, . . .	are about to be accomplished? 5 And Jesus began to say unto them, Take heed that no man lead you astray. 6 Many shall come in my name, saying, I am he, and shall lead many astray. 7 And when ye shall hear of wars and rumors of wars, be not troubled: these things must needs come to pass; but the end is not yet. 8 For nation shall rise against nation, and kingdom against kingdom; there shall be earthquakes in divers places; there shall be famines: these things are the beginnings of travail. 9 But take heed to yourselves: for they shall deliver you up to councils; and in synagogues shall ye be beaten; and before governors and kings shall ye stand for my sake, for a testimony unto them.	many shall come in my name, saying, I am he; and, *The time is at hand*: *go ye not after them*. 9 And when ye shall hear of wars and tumults, be not terrified: for these things must needs come to pass first; but the end is not *immediately*. 10 Then said he unto them, Nation shall rise against nation, and kingdom against kingdom; 11 and there shall be great earthquakes, and in divers places famines and pestilences; and there shall be terrors and great signs from heaven. 12 *But before all these things*, they shall lay their hands on you, and shall persecute you, delivering you up to the synagogues and prisons, bringing you before kings and governors for my name's sake. 13 It shall turn out unto you for a testimony.

In Luke 21:7 certain disciples or hearers ask Jesus the time and sign of the destruction of the temple. Thus some scholars hold that Luke's discourse deals exclusively with that subject, Luke having treated the parousia in chapter 17.[59] It may be observed that the question in Matt 24:3 refers both to the destruction of the temple and the parousia at the end of the world. Others find it impossible to disentangle the two subjects.[60] Yet others contend that the discourse answers the question of 21:7 by placing the destruction of the temple within the context of the entire series of events leading up to the parousia and the end of the world.[61]

---

[59]Godet, *Luke*, II, 257-258; Stuhlmueller, *Lukan Reading Guide*, p. 133.

[60]Plummer, *Luke*, pp. 477-478.

[61]Montefiore, *Gospels*, II, 578; Talbert, "Redaction," p. 182; Francis, "Eschatology," p. 57.

Because the outline of this latter group seems to make good sense of the Lukan discourse we present a modified form of it here:

A. Time of the eschaton, accompanied by warning (8).

   B. Political upheavals (9-10).

      C. Cosmic disturbances (11).

         D. Time of testimony (12-19).

   B.[1] Political upheavals (20-24).

      C.[1] Cosmic disturbances (25-26).

A.[1] Time of the eschaton, accompanied by warning (27-36).

Luke at 21:12 helps with the outline, for he (different from Matthew//Mark) says "but before all these things," that is, before the political and cosmic woes of 21:9-11 comes the time of testimony (21:13). He also says "first" (21:9) to emphasize the precedence of political woes. Moreover, the fall of Jerusalem depicted in 21:20-24 would be an example of the political troubles of 21:9-10. Luke himself in 21:9-13 really supplies his own outline as follows:

1) Time of testimony (21:12-19), as illustrated in Acts.

2) Political upheavals (21:9-10), such as the fall of Jerusalem (21:20-24).

3) Cosmic disturbances (21:11,25-26).

4) The eschaton (21:8, 27-36).

With the structure of the Lukan version of the synoptic apocalypse thus in view, we may proceed to look at several other distinctive Lukan features which are of importance to our study. Only in Luke 21:8 do the false messiahs announce "the time is at hand." Only there does Jesus say, "go ye not after them." Only Luke reads, "Not *immediately* the end" (*ouk eutheos to telos*) (21:9), emphasizing "not immediately" by placing these words first in the sentence. Matt 24:6//Mark 13:7 reads, "Not yet the end." Although these differences may seem to be insignificant, they are the basis for the opposing interpretations of the *Fernerwartungsschule* and the *Naherwartungsschule*.

2. The Parousia Indefinitely Delayed

According to the former school, these changes indicate an indefinite delay of the parousia. The real heresy is the belief that the end is coming soon. To say in Luke's day "the end is near" is a mark of deception; indeed, Luke magnifies his warning against the preaching of the nearness of the end by ascribing the proclamation of "the time is at hand" to pseduo - messiahs. Luke thereby not only dissociates himself from all bogus messiahs but decisively rejects all preaching of the near approach of the end. Luke pushes the time (*kairos*) forward to a distant advent. In v 12, "before all these things" further postpones the parousia by moving the persecution to a position before the signs. Christians must adjust themselves to a long period of waiting and persecution.[62]

3. "Not Immediately the End"

As the *Naherwartungsschule* sees it, those false prophets who use the formula "I am" (*egō eimi*) are thereby claiming to be the Son-of-Man-Messiah making his return (cf. Jesus' answer in 22:70, *egō eimi*). Thus only the grandiose consummation of the end events would remain and it would be right at the door: "the time is at hand." According to Luke, these bogus Son-of-Man-Messiahs err in defining the "time" (*kairos*) too narrowly, limiting it to the parousia and the apocalyptic wind-up of history. In the Lukan program the *kairos* includes the whole end-time agenda, from "the beginning of the end" to "the end of the end": time of testimony (21:12-19), political upheavals (21:9-10, 20-24), and cosmic woes (21:11, 25-26). Because these stages must take place before the end of the end or the eschaton proper (21:27-36), Luke warns not to become a disciple ("go behind"--*opisō*) of those who would circumvent the correct apocalyptic time-table. "Not *immediately* is the end" of the end (21:9). But the beginning of the end has begun, for Luke's people are living in "the last days" (Acts 2:17). The time of testimony is well under way (Acts) and the fall of Jerusalem is about to occur or already lies in the past (depending when one dates Luke-Acts). And so the entire process of salvation history will speedily be consummated in that generation (21:31-32) (see Chap. V.G.H) but not immediately (21:9).

The situation here is similar to that of 19:11, where the disciples who expect the kingdom of God to appear when they enter Jerusalem are told there will be a period of trading between the master's departure and return. Thus this interpretation appears to account better for the Lukan evidence which repeatedly rejects immediacy in favor of imminency.[63]

F. "The Times of the Gentiles" (Luke 21:24)

1. Literary Analysis

For purposes of study we may divide Luke 21:24 into four parts:

a) And they shall fall by the edge of the sword,

b) and shall be led captive (*aichmalōtidzō*) into all the nations:

c) and Jerusalem shall be trodden down (*pateō*) of the Gentiles,

d) until the times of the Gentiles be fulfilled.

This verse is peculiar to Luke, and the phrase, "the times of the Gentiles," is found only here in the Bible.

2. A Non-Eschatological Period

Here again the *Fernerwartungsschule*[64] finds evidence of Luke's lengthened

---

[62]Baird, *Luke*, p. 700; Conzelmann, *Theology*, pp. 127-128; Creed, *Luke*, pp. 254-255; Danker, *Luke*, pp. 210-211; Gilmour, *Luke*, p. 362; Keck, "Farewell Address," p. 99; Montefiore, *Gospels*, II, 579; Stuhlmueller, *Luke*, p. 154; Kaestli, *Eschatologie*, p. 44.

[63]Wilson, "Lukan Eschatology," p. 340; Francis, "Eschatology," p. 57; Talbert, "Redaction," pp. 182-186.

[64]Godet, *Luke*, II, 412; Flender, *Luke*, p. 14; Kaestli, *Eschatologie*, p. 50; Danker, *Luke*, p. 213; cf. Chap. V, notes #59-#61.

perspective. Luke offers this verse instead of Matt 24:22//Mark 13:20 ("those days shall be shortened"), for a reference to the shortening of days might suggest a hastening of the end. Luke adds "the times of the Gentiles," which, with its plural "times," makes the parousia chronologically distant from the fall of Jerusalem. Hence the period of "the times of the Gentiles" is not eschatological (contrary to Rom 11:25), a fact which accords with Luke's historicizing purpose.

Over against this position we should note that Luke says nothing as to the length of this hiatus separating the fall of Jerusalem from the parousia.[65] He uses the plural "times" because each nation has its "time." This period must be interpreted in light of Luke's imminent hope as set forth in Chaps. IV and V. To such an intepretation we now address ourselves.

3. Gentile Lordship over Jerusalem

By "the times of the Gentiles" Luke surely means first of all the period when Gentiles would physically possess Jerusalem, would exercise political lordship over it, and would with their barbarous rule serve as instruments of God's wrath against unbelieving Israel (Luke 19:41-44).[66]

Luke evidently was mindful of the Gentile king of Dan 7:25 who would "wear out the saints of the Most High; . . . and they shall be given into his hand until a time and times and half a time" (*heōs kairou kai kairōn kai heōs hēmisous kairou*). Luke would have been thinking of the voice of the holy one in Dan 8:13 who asks, "How long shall be . . . the sanctuary and the host of the heavens trampled under foot?" (*sumpateō*) (American). Luke would have in mind too the man clothed in linen of Dan 12:7 who answers, "It shall be for a time, times, and a half (*eis kairon kai kairous kai hēmisu kairou*); and when they have made an end of breaking in pieces the power of the holy people, all these things shall be finished" (*panta tauta suntelesthesetai*) (ASV). Nor would Luke have overlooked Ezek 30:3, "The day of Yahweh is near; it shall be . . . a time of the nations." Similarities of thought and language also suggest that Luke may well have known something like the widely circulated prophecy which is now preserved in Rev 11:2, where John is commanded to measure the temple but not the temple court, "for it hath been given unto the nations (*tois ethnesin*): and the holy city shall they *tred* under foot (*pateō*) forty and two months."[67]

Luke too may have been acquainted with Psalms of Solomon 2 about Pompey's conquest of Jerusalem in 63 B.C. This Psalm was probably written shortly after Pompey's death in 48 B.C.[68]

> 20 For the nations reproached Jerusalem, trampling it down; Her beauty was dragged down from the throne of glory.
> 24 And I saw and entreated the Lord and said, Long enough, O Lord, has Thine hand been heavy on Israel, in bringing the nations upon (them).
> 25 For they made sport unsparingly in wrath and fierce anger;
> 28 Pouring out their wrath upon us with a view to rapine.

---

[65]Wilson, "Lukan Eschatology," p. 339. Streeter, *Four Gospels*, p. 518, finds that Luke thinks Christ's return is near, but it is postponed until the times of the Gentiles are fulfilled. See also Harnack, *Date of Acts*, pp. 121-122: Luke "could only have thought of weeks or months."

[66]Bruce, *Gospels*, p. 621.

[67]So Streeter, *Four Gospels*, pp. 517-518, on the prophecy of Rev 11:2 as known to Luke.

[68]*APOT*, II, 630.

4. Salvation for the Gentiles

But as appropriate to scriptural background as is this interpretation which takes "the times of the Gentiles" to be a period of Gentile lordship over Jerusalem, it does not exhaust Luke's meaning at this point. The word "times" (*kairoi*) has, as we have seen, its antecedents in Dan 7:25; 12:7. But this word has richer overtones than mere chronological time (*chronos*). It can also mean "opportunity," "eschatological opportunity," "the time of crisis," "the last times."[69] Hence the phrase "times of the Gentiles" would seem to refer to more than their allotted time to occupy Jerusalem. It would include the "eschatological opportunities" which the Gentiles have to accept the Gospel.[70]

Luke's familiarity with the Pauline ideas in Rom 11:25 is suggested by similarities in thought and language:

> A hardening in part hath befallen Israel, until the fulness of the Gentiles be come in (Rom 11:25)(ASV)=The stubbornness of the people of Israel is not permanent but will last only until the complete number of Gentiles comes to God (TEV) (*achri hou to plērōma tōn ethnōn eiselthē*)... until the times of the Gentiles be fulfilled (*achri hou plērōthōsin kairoi ethnōn*) (Luke 21:24d).

Paul also writes: "Now is the acceptable time (*kairos*); behold, now is the day of salvation" (2 Cor 6:2). Luke 21:24d, like Rom 11:25, likely refers to the time of the Gentile mission when salvation is offered to the Gentiles.[71]

A glance at a synopsis shows that Luke has omitted Mark 13:10: "And the gospel must first be preached to all nations" (similarly Matt 24:14). With Luke's strong interest in the Gentile mission as an eschatological pre-condition of the end (Chap. VI.H), it is striking he should not include Mark 13:10. This non-inclusion is only partly accounted for by the fact he has a similar statement in Acts 1:8. It may be that he compensates for Mark 13:10 by his unique reference to Gentile conversion in 21:24d, "until the times of the nations be fulfilled."[72]

Moreover, Israel did not know the "time" (*kairos*) of its visitation (Luke 19:44), that is, "the time when God came to save you!" (TEV). *Kairos* denotes the "season when God visits people with the offer of salvation."[73] Thus the *kairos* of Israel corresponds to that of the Gentiles.

---

[69]Cf. BAG, pp. 395-396.

[70]Most commentators do not regard these two interpretations (Gentile domination; Gentile mission) as mutually exclusive. See Plummer, *Luke*, p. 483; Creed, *Luke*, p. 257; Bruce, *Gospels*, p. 621; Keck, "Farewell Address," p. 228; Grundmann, *Lukas*, pp. 383-384.

[71]Walvoord, "Times of the Gentiles," p. 5, says "there are just as many divergent views" of the term "the fullness of the Gentiles" as there are of the expression "the times of the Gentiles." Walvoord finds "the times of the Gentiles" to be a period of physical, political, Gentile lordship over Israel. It begins with Nebuchadnezzar in 600 B.C. and ends at the parousia, when Israel will permanently gain political control of Jerusalem.

[72]Kaestli, *Eschatologie*, p. 47, supposes that Luke omits Mark 13:10 because the world mission is already completed (Acts 28:30-31; Col 1:6,23). If that is the case, the end must truly be near (Chap. IV.G on Acts 28:26-28), contrary to Kaestli's *Fernerwartung*.

[73]Godet, *Luke*, II, 412.

5. The Restoration of Israel

If our analysis of Luke 21:24 is correct, we have the following motifs in this verse: 1) death by the sword; 2) being led captive into all nations; 3) trodding down of Jerusalem by Gentiles; 4) Gentiles as God's instrument of punishment upon Israel; 5) fulfilment of a limited time of punishment; 6) conversion of Gentiles to the Lord. We have found several of these motifs in Ezek 30:3; Dan 7:25; 8:13-14; 12:7; Psalms of Solomon 2; Rev 11:1-2; Rom 11:25-26; 2 Cor 6:2; and Luke 19:44. Let us now look at other key passages with the same themes.

a) In the incipient apocalypse of Ezekiel 38-39, Israel, after its Babylonian exile, and while dwelling in security in the Holy Land, is invaded by Gog and his Gentile hordes from the North, whom God destroys with fire and brimstone, that the nations may know "that the house of Israel went into captivity (*aichmalōtidzō*) for their iniquity; because they trespassed against me, and I hid my face from them: so I gave them into the hand of their adversaries, and they fell all of them by the sword" (*kai epesan pantes machaira*) (39:23). Here are parallels, even verbal parallels, to Luke 21:24 in connection with themes Number 1 (death by the sword), Number 2 (captivity), and Number 4 (Gentiles as God's instrument of punishment upon Israel). Then Ezekiel turns to theme Number 5 (fulfilment of a limited time of punishment), and promises that God will "bring back the captivity of Jacob, and have mercy upon the whole land of Israel" (39:25), and will bring "them back from the peoples" and gather them "out of their enemies' lands" (39:27):

> 28 And they shall know that I am Yahweh their God, in that I caused them to go into captivity among the nations, and have gathered them unto their own land; and I will leave none of them any more there; 29 neither will I hide my face any more from them; for I have poured out my Spirit upon the house of Israel.

Ezekiel 40-48 then proceeds to describe a new age with a new temple in a new Jerusalem. Thus we find here two additional motifs, 7) God's restoration of his people to their land, and 8) rebuilding of the temple and city, a new Jerusalem. Ezekiel thinks of Gentile punishment upon Israel in the form of destruction of Jerusalem and exile, followed by the restoration of Israel to their land, a second attack by ungodly forces, followed by the new Jerusalem in a new age. Is it possible that Luke follows a similar pattern of events?

b) When we analyze Tobit 14 (second century B.C.) we also find interesting parallels to Luke 21:24 in Tobit's farewell address:

> 4 Our brethren will be scattered (*aichmalōtidzō*, Codex S) over the earth from the good land, and Jerusalem will be desolate. The house of God in it will be burned down and will be in ruins for a time (*mechri chronou*). 5 But God will again have mercy on them, and bring them back into their land; and they will rebuild the house of God, though it will not be like the former one until the times of the age are completed (*heōs plerōthōsin kairoi tou aiōnos*). After this they will return from the places of their captivity, and will rebuild Jerusalem in splendor. And the house of God will be rebuilt there with a glorious building for all generations for ever, just as the prophets said of it. 6 Then all the Gentiles will turn to fear the Lord God in truth, and will bury their idols. 7 All the Gentiles will praise the Lord, and his people will give thanks to God, and the Lord will exalt his people. And all who love the Lord God in truth and righteousness will rejoice, showing mercy to our brethren.

Tobit gives expression to motifs Number 2 (captivity amongst the nations), Number 3 (destruction of Jerusalem), Number 5 (fulfilment of a limited time of punishment), Number 6 (conversion of Gentiles), Number 7 (restoration of Israel to their land), and Number 8 (rebuilding of the temple and city, a new Jerusalem). Motifs Number 1 (death by the sword) and Number 4 (Gentiles as God's instruments of punishment upon Israel) may be inferred.

In view of the motifs and language common to Luke 21:24, Ezekiel 38-39, and Tobit 14:4-7, it would seem probable that Luke was informed by these or similar passages.[74] Are we justified in supposing that Luke also thinks of motifs Number 7 (restoration of Israel to their land) and Number 8 (new Jerusalem)? There are several indications which support such a supposition.

c) We have already observed Luke's probable familiarity with the thought of Rom 11:25. But 11:26 predicts that "all Israel shall be saved," Paul's spiritualized version of motifs Numbers 7 and 8. It is beginning to look as if Luke at 21:24 is thinking not only of the salvation of the Gentiles, but, like Ezekiel, Tobit, and Paul, each in his own way, of the salvation of Israel. We find remarkable confirmation of this possibility in other portions peculiar to Luke-Acts.

d) In the infancy narratives, Gabriel (Luke 1:32-33) describes Jesus as the Davidic Messiah of the popular Jewish hope: "The Lord God shall give unto him the throne of his father David: and he shall reign over the house of Jacob for ever; and of his kingdom there shall be no end." The common view has it that "Luke must have interpreted this promise very broadly and 'spiritually,' as it did not represent his own theology at all."[75] But as we examine the relevant passages we are finding reason to question this dominant opinion.

The same theme of national deliverance is repeatedly sounded by Zacharias, who speaks of "redemption for his people" (Luke 1:68), "a horn of salvation for us" (1:69), "salvation from our enemies" (1:71, 74), and "salvation unto his people" (1:77), as God "spake by the mouth of his holy prophets that have been from of old" (1:70).

Simeon expects "the consolation of Israel" (2:25). Anna and many others are "looking for the redemption of Jerusalem" (2:38).

e) Jesus says, "He hath sent me to proclaim release to the captives" (*aichmalōtos*) (4:18). Can these captives include the captives of 21:24b? In the NT, the noun "captive" appears only in Luke 4:18, and the related verb "to make captive" (*aichmalōtidzō*) only in Luke 21:24, outside of figurative use in Rom 7:23; 2 Cor 10:5; 2 Tim 3:6. Possibly Luke thinks of Jesus through missionaries preaching release to those taken prisoner during the fall of Jerusalem. Their message would include "salvation from our enemies, and from the hand of all that

---

[74]Similar motifs, plus imminent fulfilment, are also found in these passages: "Through the wickedness of your works shall ye provoke him to anger, And ye shall be cast away by Him unto the time of consummation" (Testament of Zebulun 9:9). "And when the humiliation of Sion shall be complete, And when the Age which is about to pass away shall be sealed, . . . And it shall be whosoever shall have survived all these things that I have foretold unto thee, he shall be saved and shall see my salvation and the end of my world" (4 Ezra 6:18-25). "Then the Most High regarded his times--And lo! they were ended; And his ages--(and) they were fulfilled" (4 Ezra 11:44), that is, the predetermined time is fulfilled, for all apocalyptists stand at the end of the age (*APOT*, II, 611).

[75]Easton, *Luke*, p. 9.

hate us" (1:71), "to grant unto us that we being delivered out of the hand of our enemies should serve him without fear" (1:74). The enemies of 1:71 are the heathen, whose domination prevents Israel from serving God without fear (1:74) during the times of the Gentiles (21:24d). If Luke were familiar with the thought of Rev 11:1-2 he may even have considered a prophesying by supernatural witnesses Moses and Elijah (Rev 11:3), who had already appeared (Luke 9:30-31), and were to appear before the end to preach repentance (Mal 3:1; 4:4-6). Thus Israel, at the end of "the times of the Gentiles," would experience both physical and spiritual deliverance.

f) Jesus also was anointed "to proclaim the acceptable year of the Lord" (Luke 4:19). This year has been understood as the twelve-month period of Jesus' public activity,[76] or as "the center of salvation history."[77] But the OT background points in another direction. "The year when the Lord will save his people" (Luke 4:19) (TEV) is "the year of the Lord's favor" (Isa 61:2), a year of grace, of jubilee (Leviticus 25), the time of salvation, the greatest of sabbaticals, the grandest of jubilees, when the holy land would be returned to Israel, even as in an ordinary year of jubilee all possessions were returned to the original owner (Lev 25:10). Possibly Luke is thinking of this time of social restoration as a brief one, perhaps a year in length, but a sufficient fulfilment of Israel's glorious destiny. The background passage, Isaiah 61, also speaks of a new promised land rising from the ruins of Nebuchadnezzar's destruction as recompense for past sufferings.

g) This intepretation is corroborated by Luke 17:22-37. The understanding of this section is however impeded by the alternation of the singular and plural of "day":

> 17:22.--The days will come,[78] when ye shall desire to see one of the DAYS of the Son of man, and ye shall not see it.[79]
>
> 17:24.--For as the lightning, when it lighteneth out of the one part under the heaven, shineth unto the other part under heaven; so shall the Son of man be in his DAY.[80]
>
> 17:26.--And as it came to pass in the days of Noah, even so shall it be also in the DAYS of the Son of man.
>
> 17:30.--After the same manner shall it be in the DAY that the Son of man is revealed.
>
> 17:31.--In that DAY, he that shall be on the housetop . . . let him not go down to take them away.

The parallel verses in Matt 24:27,37 refer to "the parousia of the Son of Man."

---

[76] Noack, *Luke 17:20-24*, p. 48.

[77] Grundmann, *Lukas*, p. 121, following Conzelmann, *Theology*, p. 37.

[78] A favorite Lukan expression: Luke 5:35; 19:43; 21:6; 23:29.

[79] "And ye shall not see it" (17:22) has been taken to imply "a long and vain waiting for the Advent. To see the first day of it would be a comfort, . . . but they must not hope for this" (Montefiore, *Gospels*, II, 550; similarly Grässer, *Delay*, p. 170; Grundmann, *Lukas*, p. 343). Luke's statement, however, is not absolute but means that only some (9:27) of Jesus' disciples will see it, and they not so soon as they would like. During this delay they will be "open to temptation through false readers of the times encouraging delusive hope" (Bruce, *Gospels*, p. 595; Easton, *Luke*, p. 262).

[80] "In his day" is omitted by a very strong group of manuscripts: Papyrus 75, Vaticanus, and Codex Bezae, and is given a "C" rating (a considerable degree of doubt on a scale of A-D) in Metzger, *Textual Commentary*, p. 167.

The term, "the day of the Lord," appears often in the OT (Amos 5:18; Obad 15; Zephaniah 1:7),[81] and forms the background for "the day of the Son of Man," the day when the Son of Man will come in judgment. "The day of the Lord" (Acts 2:20; Joel 2:31), "that day" (Luke 10:12; 21:34), and "a day" (Luke 12:46) also refer to the same event. "The last days" (Acts 2:17), "those days" (Acts 2:18), and "these days" (Acts 3:24) are the period before "that great and notable day" (Acts 2:20).

But what is meant by the plural peculiar to Luke, "the days of the Son of Man"? According to a long series of interpreters evidently going back to Codex Bezae's reading, "one of these days," the disciples are nostalgic for one of the good old days when the Son of Man was on earth.[82] But this view does not fit the futuristic orientation of the context, especially v 26.

Another possibility is that Luke mistook an Aramiac adverb meaning "very much" for the numeral "one." The original of 17:22 read, "You will greatly desire to see the day of the Son of Man." The plural in 17:26 would have been formed by Luke on the analogy of "the days of Noah."[83] Another view has it that 17:24 and 17:26 are old, originally independent detached sayings which referred both originally and in Luke to the parousia, so that there is no difference in meaning between the singular and plural of "day."[84] But these two views fail to do justice to Luke's concern to present a reasonably coherent eschatological program. The chances are good that Luke used the singular and plural to point up something of importance on the apocalyptic agenda. Moreover, the singular "day" means the moment of the parousia, as in Acts 2:20, whereas the plural "days" in this context refers to a period:

> "The days of the Son of man" in verse 26 must, on the analogy of "the days of Noah", denote a *period*, of which the term is the coming of the Son of man. Just as the days of Noah ended with the flood, so the days of the Son of man will culminate in his sudden advent.[85]

This latter objection also stands in the way of the opinion that the plural "days" means one of the days of the new age after the Son of Man has been revealed.[86] Luke is thinking of a period before, not after, the parousia.

Others think that the plural "days" indicates a plurality of appearances of the Son of Man:

> Each great manifestation of the Son of Man--his birth (2:9) or his transfiguration (9:28 ff.); his resurrection; the fall of Jerusalem; the death of each individual--is a *day* of Jesus' messianic triumph . . . The great eschatological moment can no longer be imagined as one self-contained event. It extended through Jesus' earthly ministry and is still awaited as the Church relives the mysteries of transfiguration, cross, resurrection, and Pentecost.[87]

---

[81]Cf. also Rom 2:16; 1 Cor 1:8; 5:5; 2 Cor 1:14; Phil 2:16; 2 Tim 4:8.

[82]Alford, Bengel, Kuinoel (cited by Biederwolf, *Second Coming Bible*, p. 373); Kaestli, *Eschatologie*, p. 31.

[83]C. C. Torrey, *The Four Gospels*, p. 312 (cited by Higgins, *Son of Man*, p. 87).

[84]Kümmel, *Promise*, pp. 37-38.

[85]Higgins, *Son of Man*, p. 87; Manson, *Sayings of Jesus*, p. 435.

[86]Creed, *Luke*, p. 220.

[87]Stuhlmueller, *Lukan Reading Guide*, pp. 117-118; *Luke*, pp. 150-151.

Such a view runs the danger of spiritualizing Luke's eschatology and making it too much like that of John 1:51, where the Son of Man is pictured as coming repeatedly instead of only once in judgment at the end of the age: "Verily, verily, I say unto you, Ye shall see the heaven opened, and the angels of God ascending and descending upon the Son of man."

A variation of this plurality view which is less guilty of spiritualization and is grounded more securely in the texts contends that Luke means by the "days" of the Son of Man a number of "glorious days": the transfiguration (Luke 9:28-36), the resurrection-ascension (Luke 24; Acts 1:1-11), the appearances to Stephen (Acts 7:55-56) and to Paul (9:3-9), the restoration of Jerusalem and Israel (Luke 2:25,38; 17:30; 21:27-28; 23:51; Acts 1:6), and the final consummation (Luke 9:26; 21:34). The "days of the coming of the Son of Man" constitute the coming of the kingdom of God on earth (21:31) before the final parousia and last judgment. The "days" of the Son of Man=the kingdom of God also comprise the "seasons of refreshing" and "restoration of all things" (Acts 3:20).[88]

There is much in this novel interpretation to commend it, including the stress on the restoration of Jerusalem and Israel during a messianic period before the final consummation. But it is most questionable that Luke 17:30; 21:27-28 should refer to this temporary period rather than to the eternal kingdom in the new age.

Our examination of these various views of Luke 17:22-37 leads to these conclusions: For Luke the distinction between "day" and "days" is important, the latter denoting a period during which key eschatological events occur before the parousia on the day of the Son of Man. These "days" are not the kingdom of God but are the days of the year of jubilee (Luke 4:19), the days of the consolation of Israel (Luke 2:25) and the rebuilding of Jerusalem (2:38), the days of the kingdom of David (1:32-33), which the disciples during coming days of tribulation will desire to see (17:22).

h) The two disciples on the road to Emmaus had been hoping Jesus would redeem Israel before his death, that is, free her from foreign rule and from evil.[89] Luke does not reject their hope but rather postpones it: this hope was not to be fulfilled during Jesus' life on earth but after his resurrection and ascension, as based upon Moses and all the prophets and all the scriptures (24:27). No wonder that their hearts burned like fire within them as Jesus opened unto them the scriptures (24:32).

i) If Luke closes his gospel with an expression of the nationalistic messianic hope (Luke 24:21), he opens his second volume on the same note when the apostles ask the Risen Jesus, "Dost thou at this time restore the kingdom to Israel?" (Acts 1:6). Here, as in the other similar passages which we are now examining, this hope is not repudiated. Cadbury correctly remarks that the question of Acts 1:6 "is not corrected by any hint of present partial realization, as it is not by any hint of a less nationalistic character."[90] Jesus does not rebuke the apostles, saying, "How foolish you are! How slow you are to understand that the

---

[88]Leaney, *Luke*, pp. 68-72.

[89]Easton, *Luke*, p. 260.

[90]Cadbury, "Acts and Eschatology," p. 315.

kingdom of God is in your hearts."⁹¹ On the contrary, it seems quite likely that Luke is thinking of the restoration to the holy land after "the times of the Gentiles."

Here we may have the solution to an old exegetical puzzle. If Jesus had instructed the apostles for forty days about the universal kingdom of God (Acts 1:3), their question about restoring the glorious Davidic empire appears to be quite stupid. But from Luke's point of view the restoration of the kingdom to Israel is not a narrow nationalistic idea to be rejected but a valid eschatological hope soon to be fulfilled. Luke would be contradicting himself were he to have Jesus reject the idea of the restoration of Israel at Acts 1:6 and yet have Peter proclaim it at 3:19-21.⁹² Luke stands by the prophecies from of old that God will restore the kingdom to Israel: "I will cause the captivity of Judah and the captivity of Israel to return, and will build them, as at the first" (Jer 33:7) (similarly Ps 14:7; 85:1; Hos 6:11). Elijah is ready "to restore the tribes of Jacob" (Sir 48:11).

Here we must also consider Isa 49:6b: "I will also give thee for a light to the Gentiles, that thou mayest be my salvation unto the end of the earth" (*heōs eschatou tēs gēs*). Luke has employed Isa 49:6 in the song of Simeon (Luke 2:32), where it refers to the Christ and his universal mission; in the remarks of Paul and Barnabas to the Jews of Pisidian Antioch (Acts 13:47), where it refers to the Gentile mission of Paul and Barnabas; and in the speech of Paul to Agrippa (Acts 26:23), where it again refers to Christ and his world mission:

> A light for revelation to the Gentiles, And the glory of thy people Israel (Luke 2:32).
> I have set thee for a light of the Gentiles, That thou shouldest be for salvation unto the uttermost part of the earth (*heōs eschatou tēs gēs*) (Acts 13:47).
> . . . how that he [Christ] first by the resurrection of the dead should proclaim light both to the people and to the Gentiles (Acts 26:23).

Hence it is not surprising that Luke at Acts 1:8 should again use Isa 49:6 in connection with the Gentile mission: ". . . and ye shall be my witnesses . . . unto the uttermost part of the earth (*heōs eschatou tēs gēs*)."

But Luke is not so pre-occupied with the Gentile mission that he forgets the servant's mission to Israel: the Lord formed the servant "to bring Jacob again to him, and that Israel be gathered unto him" (Isa 49:5): "Yea, he saith, It is too light a thing that thou shouldest be my servant to raise up the tribes of Jacob, and to restore the preserved of Israel" (49:6a). Each of the four times Luke uses Isa 49:6 he is much concerned with the mission to Israel. This interest stands out in Acts 1:6-8, where, as in Isa 49:5-6, the Lord is expected to restore his people Israel. Luke's high regard for Isa 49:5-6, then, is another indication that he strongly asserts Israel's national hope.

The expectation that Jesus would redeem Israel (Luke 24:24) and restore the kingdom to her (Acts 1:6) was thus still the hope of Luke and his community. "The kingdom of our father David" was not to come at once as the excited crowds anticipated (Mark 11:10--omitted by Luke), but come it would at the time set by the Father (Acts 1:6). Luke's people were often asking, "Does Jesus at this time restore the kingdom to Israel?" "Wasn't he the one who was to redeem Israel?" "Is the old hope still valid or is it a lost cause?" Luke, with his pastor's heart, is profoundly moved by the pathos of these questions, whose poignancy pierces

---

⁹¹Cf. Luke 24:25 (TEV), and Noack, *Luke 17:20-24*, p. 45.
⁹²Cf. Mussner, "Acts 3:21," p. 298.

his soul like a sword (cf. Luke 2:35).

j) Just how literally Luke thinks of this restoration of Israel and rebuilding of Jerusalem is difficult to say. Luke's tendency to materialization is evident: the descent of the Spirit in bodily form (Luke 3:22); the flesh and bones and ability to eat of the Risen Jesus (Luke 24:39-43; Acts 10:41); the physical ascension and parousia (Acts 1:9-11); the tongues as of fire at Pentecost, perceptible to the senses (Acts 2:3).[93] Because of Luke's concrete way of thinking we should be cautious about spiritualizing his eschatology. It seems likely that Luke is thinking of a fulfilment which will be objective, tangible, and material, and not of one which will be recognizable only in faith.[94] But whatever form it may take, Luke apparently does have in mind some kind of salvation for Israel as part of God's eschatological program. In this light let us look at Acts 3:19-21:

> 19 Repent ye therefore, and turn again, that your sins may be blotted out, that so there may come seasons of refreshing from the presence of the Lord; 20 and that he may send the Christ who hath been appointed for you, even Jesus: 21 whom the heaven must receive until the times of restoration of all things, whereof God spake by the mouth of his holy prophets that have been from of old.

Numerous interpretations of this passage have been offered. The "seasons (times) of refreshing" have been understood as the time of rest after death (Schulz), deliverance from the yoke of the ceremonial law (Kraft), the putting off of penal judgment on the Jews (Barkey), the sparing of Christians amidst the destruction of the Jews (Grotius), and the glorious condition of the Christian church before the end of the world (Vitringa).[95]

Instructive parallels, however, suggest that "the seasons of refreshing" are much more eschatological in nature than these interpretations allow:

> And so the whole earth, freed from thy violence [=of the world-empire], shall be refreshed again, and hope for the judgment and mercy of him that made her [=the rule of God] (4 Ezra 11:46).
> An hour of refreshing in the future world is better than an entire life in this world (Rabbi Jaakob, c. A.D. 170).[96]

Frequently "the seasons of refreshing" and "the times of restoration of all things" are taken synonymously to refer to the new age after the parousia. The restoration of all things affects believers as times of refreshing.[97] Others take "the seasons of refreshing" to refer to a pause in the suffering of the messianic woes before the parousia and "the times of restoration of all things."[98] Another possibility is that "the restoration of all things" means the restoration of all moral conditions before the parousia, which is followed by "the times of refreshing" from God, blessed rest and refreshment for the people of God.[99] Or one could

---

[93] Cf. Cadbury, "Acts and Eschatology," p. 304.

[94] Against Mussner, "Acts 3:21," p. 305. Also contrary to Mussner I am distinguishing between "the seasons of refreshing" and "the times of restoration of all things." Yet Mussner's study is most informative.

[95] See Meyer, *Acts*, pp. 81-84.

[96] Str-B 2.626.

[97] Haenchen, *Apostelgeschichte*, p. 168.

[98] Bauernfeind, quoted by Haenchen, *Apostelgeschichte*, p. 168.

[99] Meyer, *Acts*, pp. 81-84.

think of "the seasons of refreshing" as the gift of the Holy Spirit and incorporation into the eschatological community, whereas "the restoration of all things" is the restoration of the kingdom to Israel following the parousia.[100]

We would prefer to regard the "seasons (*kairoi*) of refreshing" as a period separate from "the times (*chronoi*) of restoration of all things," even as we distinguished between "the days of the Son of Man" (Luke 17:22,26) and "the day of the Son of Man" (17:24,30,31). "Restoration" (*apokatastasis*) is a technical medical term denoting complete restoration of health; the restoration of a dislocated joint to its place.[101] "The times of restoration of all things" would thus be a fitting expression for the new age, when "last things become like first things" (Chap. I.B.8), when there will be a universal renewal of the world into paradisiacal glory (cf. Matt 19:28; Rom 8:18-30; 2 Pet 3:13).

The "seasons of refreshing" would then be a breathing space (literally=cooling, reviving with fresh air) in the suffering of the messianic woes before the parousia. The "seasons of refreshing" would be "the days of the Son of Man," when the hope of Israel (Acts 26:6; 28:20) is realized as Israel is restored to the holy land, and the kingdom restored to Israel (Acts 1:6). This period of rest would be followed by the cosmic woes (Luke 21:11, 25-26) and "the times of restoration of all things."

This interpretation finds some support in Deut 30:1-9, an OT parallel to Acts 3:19-21.[102] Moses undoubtedly would be one of the "holy prophets" of Acts 3:21 who spoke long before of repentance, return of captives to the holy land, and of good times which are veritable "seasons of refreshing":

> God has dispersed his people among all the nations (30:1). But if they turn back to him and obey him the Lord will also bring back their captives, show them mercy, and collect them from all the peoples (30:3), and bring them into the land of their fathers, and do them good and multiply them (30:5), and grant them prosperity (30:9).

k) Our view is strikingly confirmed by James' address at the council of Jerusalem (Acts 15:15-18). James lends his support to the Gentile mission by finding it prophesied in Amos 9:11-12 (LXX):[103]

> 16 After these things I will return, And I will build again the tabernacle of David, which is fallen; And I will build again the ruins thereof, And I will set it up: 17 That the residue of men may seek after the Lord, And all the Gentiles, upon whom my name is called.

This prophecy envisions God's building the temple, walls, and city, as well as God's re-establishment of the Davidic theocracy in the messianic age, with the result that the Gentiles will be converted to the Lord. Here we see once again motifs Number 6 (conversion of Gentiles) and Number 8 (rebuilding of the city and

---

[100] Franklin, *Christ the Lord*, p. 102.

[101] Vincent, *Word Studies*, I, 463.

[102] Cf. Mussner, "Acts 3:21," pp. 295-296.

[103] For our purpose of ascertaining Luke's thought, it is not necessary for us to solve the problem of James' supposed use of the LXX to prove his point. However, if Luke has put the Greek text in James' mouth we would indeed be close to the Lukan mind.

temple). Motif Number 1, death by the sword, is found in Amos 9:10.[104]

It is significant that the peculiar Lukan phrase, "from of old" (*ap' aiōnos*) occurs in the NT only in Luke 1:70, Acts 3:21, and 15:18:

> As he spake by the mouth of his holy prophets that have been from of old (Luke 1:70).
> ... whereof God spake by the mouth of his holy prophets that have been from of old (Acts 3:21).
> Saith the Lord, who maketh these things known from of old (Acts 15:18).

Here we have Luke's deliberate linking of three passages: Luke 1:68-75, Acts 3:19-21, and 15:16-18. Two of these three passages are explicitly nationalistic (Luke 1:68-75; Acts 15:16-18). We have argued in the preceding section that Acts 3:19-21 also contains a strong national emphasis. This argument is supported by Luke's own linking of these three passages: if the first and third express the Israelite hope then the second probably does so too. God has made the hope of Israel known through his prophets long ago. The same idea (but without the words "from of old") also appears at Luke 24:27, where the hope of Israel's redemption is based upon Moses, all the prophets, and all the scriptures; at Luke 4:18-21, which fulfills Isa 61:1-2; and at Acts 26:6, hope of the promise made by God unto the fathers.[105]

1) Acts closes with Paul bound in chains "because of the hope of Israel" (28:20), which hope, like the hope of Israel in 26:6, is "the Messianic national hope."[106] If Luke begins and ends each of his two volumes with this same hope (Luke 1:32; 24:21; Acts 1:6; 28:20), he must be serious about it. Luke, who so stresses this hope and relates it so sympathetically (Luke 1:32-33; 1:68-75; 2:25; 2:38; 4:18; 24:21; Acts 1:6-8; 3:21; 15:15-18; 26:6; 28:20) through the mouths of Gabriel, Zachariah, Simeon, Anna, the earthly and heavenly Jesus, Peter, James and Paul, must himself have hoped that these Jewish dreams would soon find a happy fulfilment.

On the one hand, we recognize that Luke has not explicitly defined "the times of the Gentiles," and therefore our interpretation remains hypothetical. On the other hand, Luke has said that the events connected with the destruction of Jerusalem are taking place "that all things which are written may be fulfilled" (Luke 21:22). We have sought to show that Luke is especially concerned with the fulfilment of key eschatological passages in Ezekiel, Daniel, Amos, and Tobit. As noted, Luke emphasizes this fulfilment at Luke 1:70; 4:18-21; 24:27; Acts 3:21; 15:18; and 26:6 in connection with the hope of Israel.

---

[104]Our view has some precedent in Borgen, "Paulus," p. 146, who thinks Luke presupposes the idea of a new Jerusalem (Luke 21:24; Rom 11:25-26); in Flückiger, "Luke 21:20-24," pp. 385-390, who, on the basis of Ezek 39:21-29, suggests the restoration of Israel to Palestine; and in Franklin, *Christ the Lord*, pp. 13, 81, 102, 130, 204, who finds that the restoration of Jerusalem and of the kingdom of Israel are parts of Luke's hope. See also Leaney at Note 88. These works are only beginnings, however.

[105]Mussner, "Acts 3:21," pp. 299-301, takes the rebuilt tabernacle of David (Acts 15:15-18) to mean the NT people of God rather than the political kingdom of David. But Mussner does not consider the connection of Acts 15:15-18 with such nationalistic passages as Luke 1:68-75; 4:18-21; Acts 26:6.

[106]Meyer, *Acts*, p. 503.

It may be objected that Luke regards the conclusion of Acts as the conclusion of the mission to the Jews, who henceforth are rejected without hope of salvation.[107] But it should be noted that in Acts (13:46-47; 18:4-6; 28:25-28) Paul repeatedly turns from Jews to Gentiles, yet continues to preach to Jews. Even at the close of Acts some Jews are convinced (28:24). And Paul continues to welcome all who come to see him (28:28), Jews not excluded.[108]

> Whether Luke himself was a Jew must remain an open question. At any rate, however, he must have been one who was influenced supremely by the Jewish faith, one who loved "our nation," who was moved by its law and captivated by its Scriptures, one who was led to see in Jesus a fulfilment of its hopes and a widening of its promises. It is scarcely conceivable that one such as Luke who was so immersed in the Old Testament could ever have turned his back upon the nation whose hopes it recorded.[109]

Now we can see more clearly why Luke insists that the kingdom is not immediately about to appear (Luke 19:11) and that the end does not come immediately (21:9). Yet "all things," including the times of the Gentiles (21:24d) and the jubilee year (4:19), "will take place before the people now living have all died" (21:32)(TEV). Luke says "all things" instead of "all these things" because the eschatological program contains more than is explicitly found in Luke 21, namely, all those things included in the redemption of Israel. Yet the whole program will be accomplished speedily, for it is the Lord who effects it: "I [God] will return . . . I will build . . . I will set it up" (Acts 15:16-18).[110] "What is impossible with man is possible with God" (Luke 18:27). As indicated above, supernatural witnesses may also be used, and, as hinted by the term "the acceptable year," the interregnum would be a short one. Luke's program for the salvation of Jews and Gentiles, like that of Paul (Rom 11:25-26), is consistent with his imminent hope.

G. "At the Right Hand of God" (Luke 22:69)

1. Literary Analysis

This verse, which suggests a delay of the parousia, must be seen in relation both to its synoptic parallels and to its OT background:

Matt 26:64. -- Nevertheless I say unto you, Henceforth ye shall see the Son of man sitting at the right hand of power, and coming on the clouds of heaven.	Mark 14:62. --And ye shall see the Son of man sitting at the right hand of Power, and coming with the clouds of heaven.	Luke 22:69. --But from henceforth shall the Son of man be seated at the right hand of the power of God.

---

[107] For example, Keck, "Farewell Address," p. 222.

[108] Similarly Mary Moscato, "Critique of Jervell," p. 163.

[109] Franklin, *Christ the Lord*, p. 79.

[110] The words "I will return" are not in the Hebrew or LXX texts of Amos 9:11, which Luke quotes at Acts 15:16.

Ps 110:1.--Yahweh saith unto my Lord, Sit thou at my right hand, Until I make thine enemies thy footstool.

Dan 7:13.--I saw in the night-visions, and, behold, there came with the clouds of heaven one like unto a son of man, and he came even to the ancient of days, and they brought him near before him. 14 And there was given him dominion, and glory, and a kingdom, that all the peoples, nations, and languages should serve him: his dominion is an everlasting dominion, which shall not pass away, and his kingdom that which shall not be destroyed.

The NT writers saw Ps 110:1 fulfilled in Jesus' session in the place of honor at God's right hand (*sessio ad dexteram Dei*) (Matt 22:44; 26:64; Mark 14:62; Luke 20:42; 22:69; Acts 2:33-34; Heb 1:13; 10:12). The NT frames the parousia of the Son of Man in terms of the Danielic vision of 7:13 (Matt 24:30; 26:64; Mark 13:26; 14:62; Luke 21:27; Acts 1:9-11; Rev 1:7).

Luke has made several changes in the Markan text:[111]
1) Surprisingly, Luke and Matthew agree against Mark, beginning with "henceforth" or "from now on" (Matt 26:64: *ap'arti*) (Luke 22:69: *apo tou nun*).[112] Mark simply has "and" (*kai*).[113]
2) Luke drops "ye shall see" (*opsesthe*) for "he will be" (*estai*).
3) Luke adds "of God'" (*tou theou*) to "the Power."
4) Luke drops "and coming with the clouds of heaven."

2. An Irrefutable Prophecy

The Distant Expectation School, which sees in Luke 22:69 another example of Luke's lengthened perspective, explains these changes as follows:[114]

1) "From now on" points to a lasting situation, the era of Christ's elevation, that is, the era of the church, in contrast to Mark 14:62, where it is a matter of the irruption of the eschatological event.

2) "He will be" describes the permanent state of the exalted Lord, in contrast to Mark's climactic apocalyptic event which the members of the Sanhedrin "will see." Luke makes no reference to what the Sanhedrin will see, for Luke knows that the judges are all dead and will not see the parousia. Luke thus changes an unfulfilled prophecy into one that could be fulfilled and could not be disproved. The vision of the Son of Man coming with the clouds is hidden from hostile eyes and reserved for eyes of faith, especially martyrs, as Stephen (Acts 7:55-56).

3) This change is of no eschatological significance. Mark's "the Power" is a Jewish euphemism for "God," which Luke clarified for his Gentile readers by adding, redundantly, "of God."

---

[111] Assuming Luke knew Mark 14:62, which is not at all certain, as he may have used another source for Luke 22:66-71 (see Bundy, *Gospels* p. 523).

[112] BAG, pp. 109, 548, translates both *ap' arti* and *apo tou nun* as "from now on." Apart from 2 Cor 5:16, the latter is used in NT only by Luke (Luke 1:48; 5:10; 12:52; 22:18,69; Acts 18:6).

[113] In this "and" Schweitzer, *Mystery*, p. 80, sees a causal connection between Jesus' death and the coming of the kingdom, that is, the death would compel the kingdom to come.

[114] Conzelmann, *Theology*, pp. 57, 109, 116; Danker, *Luke*, p. 230; Kaestli, *Eschatologie*, p. 21; Stuhlmueller, *Luke*, p. 160; Schneider, *Parusiegleichnisse*, p. 69.

4) Luke omits reference to "coming with the clouds of heaven" because for him that wondrous event remains in the distant future.

According to the Distant Expectation School, then, Luke, in conforming 22:69 to Ps 110:1 (session) over against Dan 7:13-14 (parousia), has de-apocalypticized Mark 14:62 and set it within the context of redemptive history, a period of incalculable length until the parousia.

3. Alternative Explanations

But are there not more likely explanations of these Lukan modifications of Mark 14:62? It seems very probable that Luke here does recognize a certain delay in the eschatological program, as is characteristic of Period C, but as in other passages positing a delay Luke rejects immediacy in favor of imminency. Before the Son of Man can return he must go to heaven to receive his kingly authority, as indicated by the parable of the pounds (19:11-27)(Chap. VI.D). Moreover, Matt 26:64 also reads "henceforth" without any diminution of his hope that the Son of Man will soon come on the clouds of heaven.[115] Likewise Luke simply means that the Son of Man will "henceforth" be seated at God's right hand until he stands, ready to return (Acts 7:55-56) (see Section 4).

We should also note that Luke, with all of his interest in the *sessio ad dexteram Dei* (Luke 20:42; 22:69; Acts 2:31-35; cf. 5:31), has by no means forgotten about the Son of Man's advent at the end of history:

> For whosoever shall be ashamed of me and of my words, of him shall the Son of man be ashamed, when he cometh in his own glory, and the glory of the Father, and of the holy angels (Luke 9:26) (Chap. V.C).
> For even as Jonah became a sign unto the Ninevites, so shall also the Son of man be to this generation (11:30) (Chap. V.E).
> Be ye also ready: for in an hour that ye think not the Son of man cometh (12:40) (Chap. V. F).
> For as the lightning, when it lighteneth out of the one part under the heaven, shineth unto the other part under heaven; so shall the Son of man be in his day.... after the same manner shall it be in the day that the Son of man is revealed (17:24,30)(Chap. VI.F.5.g).
> Nevertheless, when the Son of man cometh, shall he find faith on the earth? (18:8) (Chap. V.G).
> And then shall they see the Son of man coming in a cloud with power and great glory (21:27) (Chap. V.H.2).
> But watch ye at every season, making supplication, that ye may prevail to escape all these things that shall come to pass, and to stand before the Son of man (21:36) (Chap. V.I).
> This is he [Son of Man] who is ordained of God to be the Judge of the living and the dead (Acts 10:42) (Chap. IV.B).
> He hath appointed a day in which he will judge the world in righteousness by the man [Son of Man] whom he hath ordained (Acts 17:31) (Chap. IV.C.D).

Not only is Luke thus continually mindful of the parousia of the Son of Man but all of the above passages treated in Chaps. IV and V are part of his imminent

---

[115] On Matthew and the Son of Man see Chap. IV.D. On "henceforth" in Luke 1:48; 12:52; and 22:18 sees Chaps. V.H.1.b; VIII.B; and V.J.

expectation strand. It is precisely because Luke has so hammered home his point that the Son of Man is coming soon that he is free to make alterations at 22:69.

Again, at 22:69 Luke anticipates the ascension (which he alone in the NT describes in some detail) (Luke 24:50-52; Acts 1:1-11), the great missionary command (Acts 1:8) for a growing church (Acts 2:47), and the session of Jesus at God's right hand (Luke 20:42; 22:69; Acts 2:33-34; 5:31). Luke wants to confirm his people's faith in Christ's heavenly reign, which some may have questioned because of the delay of the end. That is, if he has not yet come, it may be that he is not exercising sovereign power either.[116] "Let all the house of Israel therefore [because of Jesus' session, vv 33-35] know assuredly that God hath made him both Lord and Christ, this Jesus whom ye crucified" (Acts 2:36).

Luke also highlights the session because it is necessary for the outpouring of the Spirit at Pentecost, whose power is needed for witnessing (Luke 24:45-49; Acts 1:8): "Being therefore by the right hand of God exalted, and having received of the Father the promise of the Holy Spirit, he hath poured forth this, which ye see and hear" (Acts 2:33).

The Son of Man's *sessio ad dexteram Dei* must also be viewed in light of the predictions about his suffering:

> The Son of man must suffer many things, and be rejected of the elders and chief priests and scribes,and be killed, and the third day be raised up (Luke 9:22).
> For the Son of man shall be delivered up into the hands of men (9:44).
> But first he [Son of man] must suffer many things and be rejected by this generation (17:25).
> Behold, we go up to Jerusalem, and all the things that are written through the prophets shall be accomplished unto the Son of man. For he shall be delivered up to the Gentiles, and shall be mocked, and shamefully treated, and spit upon: and they shall scourge and kill him: and the third day he shall rise again (Luke 18:31-33).
> The Son of man must be delivered up into the hands of sinful men, and be crucified, and the third day rise again (24:7) (cf. also Luke 9:31; 12:50; 13:32-35).

It is fitting that Luke, having thus emphasized the Son of Man's sufferings, should create a balance by stressing God's vindication of the Son of Man, who "from now on" sits at God's right hand.

Further, since Jesus' accusers are thinking of him as a political messiah (Luke 22:67, 70), Luke must assert Jesus' transcendent majesty at the side of God.[117]

4. Luke's Scheme of Messianic Progress

The chief reason, however, for Luke's modifications of Mark 14:62 is that Luke at 22:69 is looking ahead to Stephen's vision: "But he, being full of the Holy Spirit, looked up steadfastly into heaven, and saw the glory of God, and Jesus standing on the right hand of God, and said, Behold, I see the heavens opened, and the Son of man standing on the right hand of God" (Acts 7:55-56).

But why is the Son of Man standing? Since Chrysostom many have held that Christ has risen to greet his first martyr, and such a thought should probably not

---

[116]Cf. Wilson, "Lukan Eschatology," p. 337, and Flender, *Luke*, p. 101.

[117]Cf. Flender, *Luke*, p. 45.

be ruled out altogether. Others contend that the Son of Man is standing to come individually for Stephen himself, as distinct from the universal parousia of the last day:

> Luke saw that for the individual Christian death was truly an *eschaton* (though not *the eschaton* . . .) marked by what we may term a private and personal parousia of the Son of man. That which was to happen in a universal sense at the last day, happened in individual terms [at death].[118]

This view collides with the imminent, collective, cosmic thrust of Luke's eschatology, which we have had occasion to observe again and again. Moreover, Luke does not write that Stephen "departed" or "was carried up into heaven" but Luke follows the idiom of Jesus and the early church in saying that Stephen "fell asleep" (Acts 7:60; cf. Luke 8:52-54; John 11:11; Acts 13:36; 1 Cor 11:30; 15:18; 1 Thess 4:13-15; 5:10).[119] In view of our conclusions in Chap. III on the fate of the individual after death, we may assume that Stephen, according to Luke, has gone to the happy side of Hades, if not directly to heaven as a special reward for his martyrdom, as in Rev 6:9-11.

Some students think that the Son of Man is not sitting as judge (cf. Matt 25:31) but standing like angelic intercessors to serve as Stephen's advocate, that is, to give testimony in behalf of his witness on earth.[120] This advocate theory is in line with Luke's ideas about the work of the Son of Man: "Every one who shall confess me before men him shall the Son of man also confess before the angels of God: but he that denieth me in the presence of men shall be denied in the presence of the angels of God" (Luke 12:8-9). In 12:8-9 the Son of Man is not functioning as judge (Matt 16:27; Mark 8:38; Luke 9:26) but rather as advocate of the faithful before God at the last judgment.[121] The Son of Man would then be serving as Stephen's advocate so that Stephen may receive a martyr's reward of direct access of the soul to heaven.

But the interpretation which most beautifully fits all the data of Luke-Acts is that the Son of Man is standing ready to return upon the proclamation of the Gospel to the Gentiles (Chap. IV.G). Although other explanations "are not to be rejected lightly and can hardly be disproved it seems more natural to explain the word ["standing"] by placing it in an eschatological context."[122] Luke has presented "Christ's career from the Cross to Second Coming through a series of words . . . which, taken together, constitute a highly imaginative picture":

1) His death is an *exodos* (Luke 9:31).

2) He "entered into" his glory at the resurrection (24:26).

3) After forty days he was "received up" into heaven (Acts 1:2, 11, 22).

4) In heaven he "sits" at God's right hand (Luke 20:42; 22:69; Acts 2:34).

5) He "stands" at God's right hand (7:55-56).

---

[118] Barrett, "Son of Man," pp. 35-36, followed by Schneider, *Parusiegleichnisse*, pp. 89-90.

[119] Ellis, *Eschatology*, p. 6.

[120] Higgins, *Son of Man*, pp. 144-146.

[121] Creed, *Luke*, p. 172.

[122] Adapted from Owen, "Stephen's Vision," pp. 224-226. See also Chap. IV.G.8.

6) He will "come" again in triumph to judge the world (Luke 9:26; 12:36-38; 18:8; 19:23; 21:27; Acts 1:11).

Luke's original scheme of messianic progress uses the first three words to define the climax of Jesus' earthly ministry and the last three to indicate his exaltation and return. The distinctive meaning of "standing" now emerges. It is midway between "sitting" (4) and "coming" (6). Christ rises in preparation for his parousia. The Son of Man in Stephen's vision is the Christ who is about to return.

In Chap. IV.G we have already sought to show how this interpretation is of a piece with Luke's imminent expectation, and with Luke 13:25, where the master rises in judgment. But now we wish to bring out more confirmatory evidence. At 10:1-16 we have seen the Risen Lord speaking of his impending parousia when the Gentile mission is completed (Chap. V.D.4). At 18:8 the Son of Man comes speedily to avenge his persecuted elect, who cry unto him day and night. Likewise at Acts 7:55-56 the Son of Man is anxious to return to avenge his martyr Stephen.

Stephen, giving expression to his imminent expectation as he looks up into the sky (7:55) and sees the heavens opened as an indication of the cosmic import of his vision (Chap. IV.G), probably has similar expectations as Taxo the Levite, who, with his seven sons, fasts and goes into a cave to die for his faith, saying "If we do this and die, our blood shall be avenged before the Lord. And then His kingdom shall appear throughout all His creation, . . . for the Heavenly One will arise from His royal throne, And He will go forth from His holy habitation With indignation and wrath on account of His sons" (Assumption of Moses 9-10) (A.D. 7-30).[123] Taxo and sons evidently expected their deaths would fill up the predestined measure of their fathers' sins (cf. Matt 23:32; 1 Thess 2:16; Rev 18:5) and the predestined number of martyrs (Rev 6:11; 1 Enoch 47:4; 4 Ezra 4:36; 2 Baruch 23:4-5), and thus set the end events in motion. Similarly Luke wrote of Stephen's death and of the killing of the righteous:

> I will send unto them prophets and apostles; and some of them they shall kill and persecute; that the blood of all the prophets, which was shed from the foundation of the world, may be required of this generation; from the blood of Abel unto the blood of Zachariah, who perished between the altar and the sanctuary: yea, I say unto you, it shall be required of this generation (Luke 11:49-51).

Luke, then, at Luke 22:69 points up the session of the Son of Man so that at Acts 7:55-56 he may show him standing in readiness for his parousia. "Now the Lord will stand up for judgment" (Isa 3:13, LXX). Luke's changes do not indicate a rejection of apocalypticism but a desire to hold to that frame of reference in Period C.

H. "To the Ends of the Earth" (Acts 1:6-8)

1. Mission or Imminence?

When the apostles met together with Jesus after the resurrection they asked him:

---

[123]*APOT*, II, 421. Collins, "Political Perspective," pp. 246-252, argues that in the Assumption of Moses and the Apocalypse of John martyrdom helps to bring about the end.

> 6 Lord, dost thou at this time restore the kingdom to Israel? 7 And he said unto them, It is not for you to know times or seasons, which the Father hath set within his own authority. 8 But ye shall receive power, when the Holy Spirit is come upon you: and ye shall be my witnesses both in Jerusalem, and in all Judaea and Samaria, and unto the uttermost part of the earth (Acts 1:6-8).

The *Fernerwartungsschule*[124] declares that here Luke has decisively renounced the *Naherwartung*. Whereas the earliest church lived in daily expectation of the parousia, Luke substitutes for the imminent establishment of the kingdom the gift of the Spirit, which will empower the disciples to persevere during the extended course of church history and to carry on a program of world missions, a program which is no longer a part of eschatology but rather of redemptive history. In this manner Luke replaces the apocalyptic expectation of the primitive community with the descent of the Spirit and the progressive evangelization of the world.

Contrary to this view we have already seen that for Luke the Spirit remains an eschatological phenomenon (Chap. IV.G). Nor does the missionary command push the parousia into the background, for "the promise of the Parousia standing here at the outset of the church's life and work serves rather as a constant reminder that the history being narrated is to come to an end, that the opportunity for mission is temporary, and therefore the missionary task of the church is urgent, forbidding idle wistfulness and lethargic sorrow."[125] And the program of discipling the nations no more implies for Luke the surrender of the imminent hope in the consummation of all things than it does for Matthew, Mark, or Paul:

> And this Good News about the Kingdom will be preached through all the world for a witness to all mankind--and then will come the end (Matt 24:14)....All these things will happen before the people now living have all died (Matt 24:34)(TEV). The gospel must first be preached to all peoples (Mark 13:10)... All these things will happen before the people now living have all died (13:30) (TEV).
> The stubbornness of the people of Israel is not permanent, but will last only until the complete number of Gentiles comes to God. 26 And this is how all Israel will be saved (Rom 11:25-26)(TEV)(cf. 1 Thess 4:15-18; Rom 16:20 for the imminent expectation).

2. The Eschatological World Mission

Neither has Luke de-eschatologized missionary work, any more than have Matthew, Mark, or Paul. That Matthew, Mark, and Paul regarded the mission of the church as a necessary precondition of the end is sufficiently indicated by the passages just quoted from the synoptic apocalypse and from Paul's comprehensive philosophy of history in Romans 9-11.[126] That the same is true for Luke is proved by the following considerations:

---

[124]Conzelmann, *Theology*, pp. 121, 136; Grässer, *Delay*, pp. 205-207; Haenchen, *Apostelgeschichte*, pp. 111-112; Kaestli, *Eschatologie*, pp. 60-61.

[125]Moore, *Parousia*, p. 148.

[126]See especially Cullmann, "Missionary Task," pp. 210-245; Munck, *Paul*, pp. 36-68; and Thompson, "Gentile Mission," pp. 18-27. These writers treat Luke-Acts incidentally. Hiers, "Delay," p. 154, asserts that the world mission in Acts "had eschatological importance of the highest order, for it was understood that this mission must take place before the end of the age"; likewise Mussner, "Acts 3:21," p. 297. Bartsch, *Wachet*, pp. 120-121, and "Eschatology," p. 392, suggests that for Luke the mission is not an eschatological condition of the end, not because the end is distant, but because Luke thinks the end may come before the mission is completed!

a) The Mission as a Part of the Eschatological Program

Luke, like Matthew 24, Mark 13, and Romans 9-11, sets forth missions as one of the stages on the apocalyptic agenda. By means of the combined parables of the pounds and of the rebellious citizens (19:11-27) Luke shows that the kingdom cannot appear upon the arrival of Jesus' party in Jerusalem, for Jesus must first depart to heaven, be enthroned, and, after the world mission (time of "trading" when disciples are to be gained through evangelistic work), return in judgment (Chap. VI.D).

As we have also seen (Chap. VI.F), "the times of the Gentiles" (21:24) includes the world mission. As such, the mission is one indispensable part of the end-time program, including testimony, social and cosmic woes, and the end (Chap. VI.E). This conclusion is confirmed by the fact that Luke's "times of the Gentiles" is the equivalent of Matt 24:14//Mark 13:10 and Rom 11:25-26 (Chap. VI.F). Since these latter three passages regard the church's mission as an eschatological necessity, it seems most likely that Luke's equivalent is no different.

Acts 1:1-11 also presents the world mission as one of the essential stages of the end-times: ascension, outpouring of the Spirit, world mission, and parousia. Before God will establish the kingdom, the disciples must spread the Gospel over the world. Acts 3:19-21; 10:42; and 17:30-31 also remind us of the necessity of preaching repentance and Jesus as judge before the end can come:

> Repent ye therefore, and turn again, that your sins may be blotted out, that so there may come seasons of refreshing from the presence of the Lord; 20 and that he may send the Christ who hath been appointed for you, even Jesus; 21 whom the heaven must receive until the times of restoration of all things, whereof God spake by the mouth of his holy prophets that have been from of old (3:19-21).
> And he charged us to preach unto the people, and to testify that this is he who is ordained of God to be the Judge of the living and the dead (10:42).
> The times of ignorance therefore God overlooked; but now he commandeth men that they should all everywhere repent; 31 inasmuch as he hath appointed a day in which he will judge the world in righteousness by the man whom he hath ordained; whereof he hath given assurance unto all men, in that he hath raised him from the dead (17:30-31).

Here again the preaching of the Gospel is a part of the eschatological drama and an indispensable condition for the coming of the messianic era.[127]

If Owen's interpretation of Stephen's vision is correct (chap. VI.G.4), there is also at Acts 7:55-56 an indication of the place of the church's mission in the eschatological program: the Son of Man is standing ready to return, awaiting only the completion of the Gentile mission.

b) The Mission as an Eschatological Necessity

That Luke regards the world mission as eschatological is further indicated by his use of the word "be necessary," "must" (*dei*). *Dei* appears 102 times in the NT, forty-two of which are in Luke-Acts (cf. eight in Matthew and six in Mark). *Dei* represents one of Luke's central theological concepts and is a favorite word

---

[127]Cullmann, "Missionary Task," pp. 234-235; Munck, *Paul*, pp. 39-40.

among apocalyptists to show that God himself is committed to these plans:[128] "The Revelation of Jesus Christ, which God gave him to show unto his servants, even the things which must (*dei*) shortly come to pass" (Rev 1:1). Significantly, Mark 13:10 uses *dei* to show the divine necessity of the missionary task: "And the gospel must (*dei*) first be preached unto all the nations." Thus Mark 13:10 indicates that "the world mission is just as much a prelude to the end as apocalyptic motifs such as wars and the Messianic Woes (cf. 13:7)."[129]

Luke also uses *dei* in his synoptic apocalypse (Luke 21:9//Mark 13:7): wars and tumults "must needs (*dei*) come to pass first." He repeatedly uses the *dei* of divine necessity in connection with missions. Jesus "must (*dei*) go" on his way (through Samaria) toward Jerusalem (13:33), a mission which may be a foreshadowing of the later Gentile mission.[130] The Risen Christ grounds the world mission in the divine necessity when he says "all things must needs (*dei*) be fulfilled, which are written . . . that repentance and remission of sins should be preached in his name unto all nations" (24:44-47).

Again and again Paul's mission is anchored in the divine *dei*, not only by way of spillover from Luke 13:33 and 24:44-47 but also directly: the Lord informs Ananias that Paul is "a chosen vessel" to bear his name "before the Gentiles and kings, and the children of Israel," and that for his sake Paul "must" (*dei*) suffer many things (Acts 9:15-16). Paul tells the Jews of Pisidian Antioch that "it was necessary (*dei*) that the word of God should first be spoken to" them, but since they rejected it, the Lord set Paul for a light of the Gentiles, "for salvation unto the uttermost part of the earth" (13:46-47). At Ephesus Paul "purposed in the spirit, when he had passed through Macedonia and Achaia, to go to Jerusalem, saying, After I have been there, I must (*dei*) also see Rome" (19:21). The Lord cheers Paul with the assurance that as Paul testified concerning Jesus at Jerusalem, so must (*dei*) he bear witness also at Rome (23:11). And again the same compulsion of carrying the Gospel to Rome is reaffirmed by an angel: "Fear not, Paul; thou must (*dei*) stand before Caesar: and lo, God hath granted thee all them that sail with thee" (27:24). The task before the emperor was God's foremost aim, that of saving 276 lives secondary![131] This surprising order or priorities serves to point up the urgency of the eschatological mission. And Acts 16:6-7, where the Holy Spirit and Spirit of Jesus forbid Paul to go to Asia and Bithynia, likely preserves an accurate memory, namely, that Paul as missionary is only the organ of an eschatological plan fixed in all its details.[132] Hence for Luke as for Mark the world mission is as eschatological as the social and cosmic woes.

c) The Mission as Eschatological Tribulation

Eschatological missions are characterized not only by being one stage in the apocalyptic program and by standing under the divine necessity but also by messianic sufferings. The mission of Mark 13:10, for example, involves beatings in synagogues, hatred, betrayal, and death (13:9, 12-13). Likewise Paul in the

---

[128]Thompson, "Gentile Mission," p. 23; Grundmann, *dei*, pp. 21-25; and my "H. H. Evans Reconsidered," pp. 26-27.

[129]Thompson, "Gentile Mission," p. 23.

[130]My "Halévy Reconsidered," p. 373.

[131]Munck, *Acts*, p. 251.

[132]Cullmann, "Missionary Task," pp. 239-240.

same breath refers to the world mission and to his sufferings therein (Col 1:23-24). So too in Acts, Paul's mission is linked with messianic sufferings at 9:15-16 (quoted above) and at 14:22: "Through many tribulations we must (*dei*) enter into the kingdom of God." It is significant that in 9:15-16 and 14:22 are found world mission,*dei*, and eschatological tribulation.[133]

d) The Mission as Eschatological Testimony

Another motif found in connection with eschatological missions is that of testimony before councils, governors, and kings, as in Mark 13:9. But the same motif is also present in Luke 21:12-13; Acts 23:11; and 27:24, with *dei* in the latter two verses (quoted above). Also at 25:10 Paul stands before the emperor's own court, where it is necessary (*dei*) for him to be tried, for Paul's testimony in Rome is on God's agenda.

e) The Mission as Ecumenical

Yet a fifth theme occurs with end-time evangelization, namely, worldwide scope: "into all nations" (Mark 13:10), "the fulness of the Gentiles" (Rom 11:25), "this gospel which has been preached to everybody in the world" (Col 1:23)(TEV). In Luke-Acts we have already looked at Luke 24:47; Acts 1:6-8; 13:46-47; 17:30-31; 19:21; and 23:11. We may also observe that in 17:30-31 we find imminence (Chap. IV.C.D), ecumenical scope, and stages (world-wide preaching preceding imminent judgment).

Luke reiterates these five motifs to accentuate the eschatological necessity of the mission to the nations. Luke has not de-eschatologized the process of spreading the good news. He has not lifted it up out of eschatology and put it down in redemptive history. It is as apocalyptic as wars and woes, not simply a part of the uneschatological past history of the church which Luke describes as one aspect of the extended era of the church. The missions of Peter, Paul, and others depicted in Acts are no less a pre-condition of the imminent end than those of Matt 24:14; 28:18-20; Mark 13:10; Rom 9-11; Col 1:23-24. As Luke sees it, the object of the world mission is to make disciples everywhere so that when the Son of Man speedily returns he will find faith on earth (18:8).

I. Conclusion

In Luke-Acts we have seen evidence of "the changing ideas in NT eschatology." During Period C Luke reassesses and recasts traditional eschatology but does not jettison apocalypticism. By adding conditions which must be fulfilled before the end can come he frequently tones down the immediate expectation in favor of an imminent hope.

Disciples are to take up their crosses "daily" as they face the perils of heroic eschatological living (Luke 9:23). While participating in fellowship meals (Acts 2:42, 46) they pray for a day-to-day supply of bread (Luke 11:3) in anticipation of the messianic banquet in the kingdom of God (12:37; 22:16). Those disciples who thought the kingdom would appear immediately upon their entrance into the royal city erred, for they had over-simplified the Lord's end-time program, which was to include Jesus' departure, enthronement, world mission, and return in judgment (19:11-27).

---

[133]On eschatological tribulation see also Chap. IV.G on Acts 14:22.

Again Jesus had to remind the disciples that the end does not come immediately (21:8) but must be preceded by testimony and by social and cosmic woes (21:8-36). Before the Son of Man can come in great power and glory (21:27), Jerusalem will be destroyed and its people slain by the sword or taken captive until the times of the Gentiles be fulfilled (21:24) and the kingdom is restored to Israel (Acts 1:6) during the ultimate year of jubilee (Luke 4:19).

At first Jesus will sit at God's right hand (22:69), from whence he will pour out the Spirit (Acts 2:33) to empower the church, whose members are increasing every day (2:47), for its world mission (Luke 24:45-49; Acts 1:8), propelled by the compulsion of the divine necessity (Luke 24:44). Stephen sees the Son of Man standing (Acts 7:55-56), ready to return speedily to avenge his elect (Luke 18:8), when their eschatological mission is complete (Acts 1:6-8).[134]

---

[134]Professor Selby comments: "The Church eventually came, of necessity, to a position not unlike that which Conzelmann *et al.* ascribe to Luke, but the route to that position was longer and far more complex than they suppose" (letter, 4 October 1976).

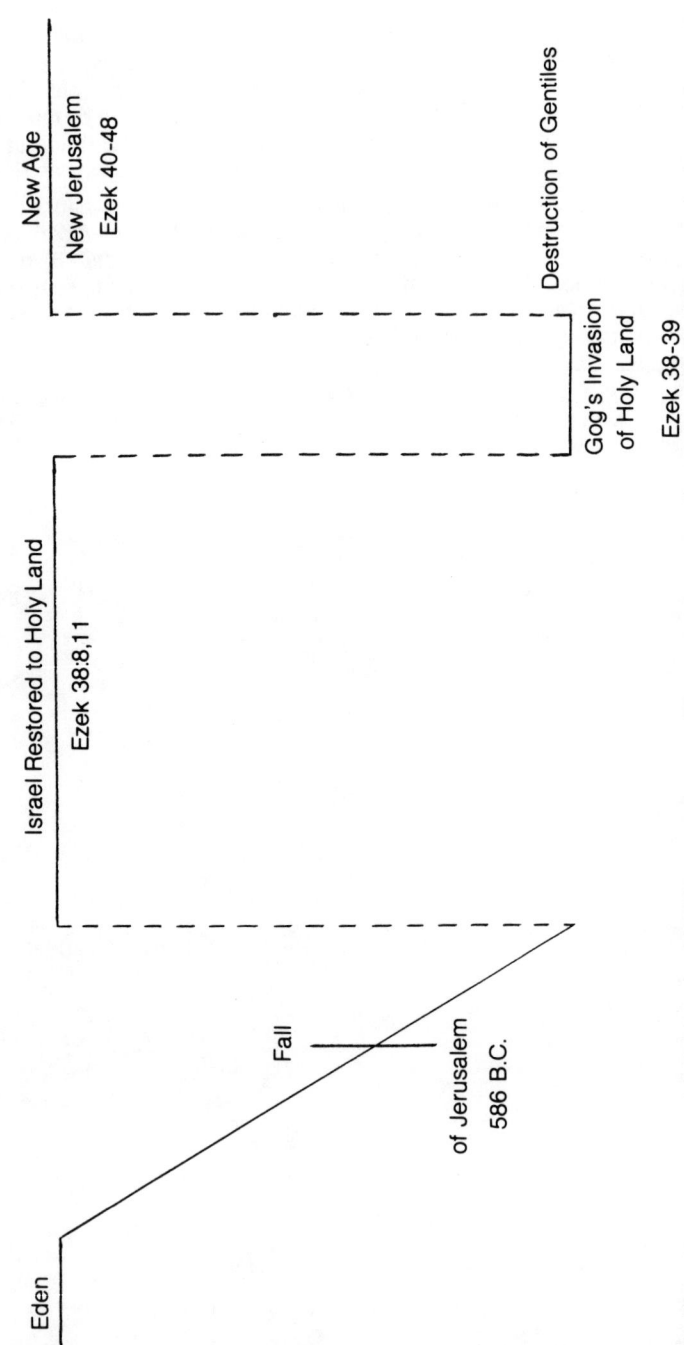

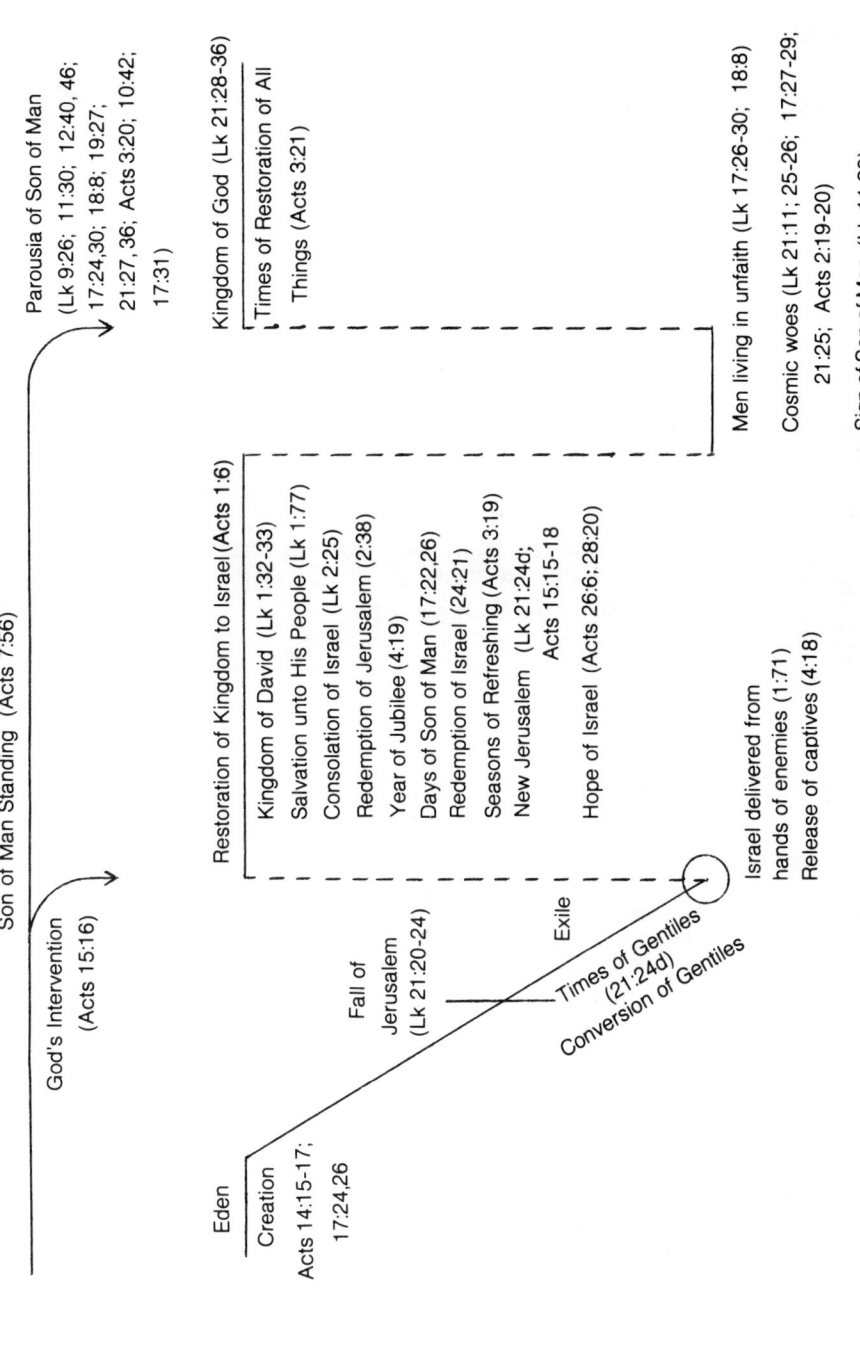

Chapter VII
"In the Midst of You" (Luke 17:21): The Kingdom a Present Reality?

A. The Relevant Texts

Probably all critics would agree that in Luke-Acts the kingdom of God is a future reality to come at the end of this age. There is also a widespread consensus that for Luke the kingdom is in addition a present reality now in this age. This latter view is based largely upon the following verses:

> *Luke 7:28.*--I say unto you, Among them that are born of women there is none greater than John: yet he that is but little [Greek: lesser] in the kingdom of God is greater than he.

> *Luke 10:18.*--And he said unto them, I beheld Satan fallen as lightning from heaven.

> Luke 11:20--But if I by the finger of God cast out demons, then is the kingdom of God come upon you.

> *Luke 13:18-21.*--18 He said therefore, Unto what is the kingdom of God like? and whereunto shall I liken it? 19 It is like unto a grain of mustard seed, which a man took, and cast into his own garden; and it grew, and became a tree; and the birds of the heaven lodged in the branches thereof. 20 And again he said, Whereunto shall I liken the kingdom of God? 21 It is like unto leaven, which a woman took and hid in three measures of meal, till it was all leavened.

> *Luke 16:16.*--The law and the prophets were until John: from that time the gospel of the kingdom of God is preached, and every man entereth violently into it.

> *Luke 17:20-21.*--20 And being asked by the Pharisees, when the kingdom of God cometh, he answered them and said, The kingdom of God cometh not with observation: 21 neither shall they say, Lo, here! or, There! for lo, the kingdom of God is within you (or, in the midst of you).

The *Fernerwartungsschule*, however, maintains that for Luke-Acts the kingdom will not come until the parousia in the distant future. The kingdom cannot be present before then because salvation history is non-eschatological in nature and all eschatological events are relegated to the ultimate end of the world.[1] For different reasons, some of the *Naherwartungsschule* also regard the kingdom for Luke as reserved for the new age. The kingdom may exist in the

---

[1] Cf. Conzelmann, *Theology*, pp. 107, 119, 122-124.

transcendent world but it is not a reality in this age or on this earth.² Because of this marked disagreement as to whether the kingdom is present we must now examine carefully each of the six passages cited above.

B. Greater in the Kingdom (Luke 7:28)

1. The Kingdom of God as Present

a) *The Prevailing View.*--Luke 7:28 is commonly regarded as showing that the kingdom is present in Jesus' ministry and that Jesus' followers are already in it, experiencing now the blessings of messianic salvation. It is a greater thing to hear the good news and to receive the healing and life of the kingdom than to be a prophet as great as John. "He who is least in the kingdom of God is greater than John (who is not in the kingdom)."³

Against this view is the fact that it eliminates John from the kingdom. Certainly Luke would not exclude John from either a present or future kingdom, for as we have seen in our discussion of 16:16 (Chap. II.E.F) John preaches the good news of the kingdom and is himself a part of the era of fulfilment which will culminate in the kingdom. Moreover, Abraham, Isaac, and Jacob will be in the kingdom (13:28), an indication that Luke would hardly leave out one who is more than a prophet (7:26).

b) *Schweitzer's Assumption.*--Schweitzer is dissastisfied with "the usual explanation, that Jesus expressed in these words [Matt 11:11//Luke 7:28] a criticism of the Baptist and placed him at a lower level than the believers in his teaching who were assembled round him as adherents of the Kingdom of God, ... for these believers were also born of women." Since the verse contrasts the Baptist with members of the kingdom, Schweitzer was driven to the assumption that it takes "into account the difference between the natural world and the supernatural, Messianc world."

> As a man in the condition into which all men enter at birth the Baptist is the greatest of all who have ever lived. But members of the Kingdom of Heaven are no longer natural men; through the dawn of the Messianic Kingdom they have experienced a change which has raised them to a supernatural condition akin to that of the angels. Because they are now supernatural beings the least among them is greater than the greatest man who has ever appeared in the natural world of the age which is now passing away. John the Baptist does, indeed, belong to this Kingdom either as a great or a humble member of it. But a unique greatness, surpassing that of all other human beings, is his only in his natural mode of existence.⁴

Surprisingly, Schweitzer, who attributes a thoroughly futuristic eschatology to Jesus, here at Matt 11:11//Luke 7:28 thinks of the kingdom as already having begun in Jesus' ministry. In the natural world, John is the greatest of natural men

---

²Hiers, "'Lo, here!'", p. 384; Francis, "Eschatology," p. 61; Franklin, "Ascension," p. 198, and *Christ the Lord*, pp. 11-25, 42. Ellis, *Luke*, pp. 12-15, regards the kingdom in Acts as futuristic only.

³Easton, *Luke*, p. 102; Creed, *Luke*, p. 107; Manson, *Sayings of Jesus*, p. 362; Gilmour, *Luke*, p. 138; Ellis, *Luke*, p. 121; Baird, *Luke*, p. 684; Ladd, *Presence*, pp. 199-205.

⁴Schweitzer, *My Life, pp. 12-13.*

born of women, but the least of the supernatural beings, not born of women, who are now in the supernatural world of the kingdom, are greater than John as a natural being. It would appear on Schweitzer's view that the Baptist is at one and the same time out of the kingdom as a natural man yet in the kingdom as a supernatural person.

2. The Kingdom of God as Future

a) Schweitzer's View Modified.--To avoid these difficulties it would seem advisable to adapt Schweitzer's view to a futuristic interpretation as follows:

> John is the greatest natural man born of woman who has ever lived. But in the coming kingdom all members will be supernatural beings like the angels, not born of women. Hence even the least of these supernatural persons in the future kingdom will be (apocalyptic "is") greater than even the greatest of the natural persons is now in this age.

Therefore all the people "justify God" (Luke 7:29-30), that is, "recognise and proclaim by word and deed the excellence of His ways for the salvation of men."[5] The people, by being baptized with John's baptism, are assured of entering the kingdom, of being transformed into supernatural persons, and of thereby becoming even greater than is John in his natural state.

b) "Those Born (Only) of Women."--Like Schweitzer, Hiers stresses the phrase "born of women."[6] If "those born of women" means "born *only* of women" and if such are not yet in the kingdom, then those who enter into the kingdom must be "born again" (John 3:3-5) of God or become as little children (Matt 18:3; Luke 18:17) now and at the end of the age in the cosmic rebirth (Matt 19:28). Thus there is as yet no one in the kingdom, but in the new age those in the kingdom will be greater than John is now, even though he is the greatest man of this age. The least in the age to come will be greater in blessings than the most righteous man of this age.

But, continues Hiers, if we do not supply the word "only," then there is an exclusive contrast between "those born of women" and those in the kingdom, the latter being angels, who of course are not born of women and who are in the kingdom of heaven, which is waiting to come down out of heaven at the end of this age (Chap. V.D.3). Therefore John, the greatest of those born of women, is not so great as the least of the angels in heaven.

Hence there may be a temporal contrast between the present period when even the forerunner, the greatest of men, awaits rebirth at the end, on the one hand, and the future state of those in the kingdom, on the other. But there may also be a spatial contrast, between men now on earth and angels now in the heavenly kingdom. Hier's futuristic interpretation is interesting, but his attention is focused primarily on Matt 11:11 and he does not seek to gain Lukan support for his view.

c) A Simpler View.--Others who hold the futuristic interpretation make nothing of the supposed contrast between those born and not born of women. They simply render quite plausibly: "Among them that are born of women there is none

---

[5]*Godet, Luke*, I, 352.
[6]Hiers, *Kingdom of God*, pp. 57-65.

greater than John; yet he who in the (future) kingdom of heaven is least (will be)(apocalyptic "is") greater than John (is now)."[7] But here again there is no stress on Luke's own view of the matter.

d) Chrysostom's Solution.--A quite different solution was proposed by Chrysostom:[8] "But he who is less in age and fame [=Jesus] is greater than John in the kingdom of God." At first glance this paraphrase seems so odd as to be unworthy of note except as an exegetical curiosity. But since it was accepted by such worthies as Hilary, Ambrose, Theophylactus, Euthymius, Erasmus, Luther, and Fritzsche, it may deserve some consideration.

In the first place, it gives a literal translation of the first three words of the Greek: "But he who is less" (*ho de mikroteros*), *mikroteros* being the comparative, not the superlative, form. Nor does this translation do violence to the structure of the Greek sentence as a whole, which literally reads: "The Lesser One, in the kingdom of God greater than he is." It is simply a matter of reading "greater in the kingdom" instead of "the lesser one in the kingdom." "Greater" rather than "the lesser one" is linked to the kingdom.

It is of course possible that Jesus (assuming he spoke 7:28) did not have Chrysostom's meaning in mind, for "Christ's main concern was not to get people to think highly of Himself, but to have high thoughts of the kingdom. What he says, therefore, is that any one in the kingdom, though of comparatively little account, is greater than John."[9] But whether or not Jesus spoke the words, or regardless of what he may originally have meant by them, our concern is what they meant to Luke. Is Chrysostom's interpretation possible for Luke?

It so happens that only Luke informs us that Jesus was younger than John (Luke 1:24-38).

> It seems to be one of Luke's obsessions to prove that John was the *temporal* predecessor of Jesus. The incentive was already present in the Malachi and Isaiah passages used at the opening of Mk. But Luke alone relates the legends of John's birth, significantly dating John's birth before that of Jesus.[10]

Conceivably Luke could also have thought that Jesus in the kingdom as the pre-existent Son of Man would be greater than John in age (cf. John 8:58: "Before Abraham was born, I am").

It is rather doubtful that Luke thought of Jesus as less in fame, even in this age, than John. The multitudes, including Jesus, were baptized by John (Luke 3:7,21; Acts 1:21-22; see Chap. II.D.1). And "all men reasoned in their hearts concerning John, whether haply he were the Christ" (Luke 3:15). John preached to all the people of Israel (Acts 13:24). He was known as far as Alexandria (Acts 18:24-25) and Ephesus (Acts 19:1-3). Yet Jesus' fame would surpass that of John. "The multitudes sought after" Jesus (Luke 4:42; 5:1; 7:24). The news about him spread throughout Galilee (Luke 4:14). "And he taught in their synagogues, being glorified of all" (Luke 4:15). Whereas John worked no miracles, Jesus fed the five thousand (Luke 9:10-17) and "went about doing good, and healing all that were

---

[7]Cf. Allen, *Matthew*, pp. 115-116.
[8]Homilies on Matthew 37; see Bruce, *Gospels*, p. 172.
[9]Bruce, *Gospels*, p. 172.
[10]Grobel, "He That Cometh After Me," p. 400.

oppressed of the devil" (Acts 10:38; Luke 4:33-39; 5:1-26; 6:6-10; 7:1-17; 8:22-56; 9:37-43; 13:10-17; 14:1-6; 17:11-19; 18:35-43; 22:50-51). Thus we should omit "fame" from Chrysostom's suggestion and read: "He who is less in age is greater than John in the kingdom of God."

  e) F. Dibelius' Proposal.--Is it possible to modify further Chrysostom's suggestion so as to find a more significant point of comparison than that of age? F. Dibelius has made such an attempt,[11] basing his view upon the then recently developed futuristic approaches of J. Weiss and A. Schweitzer, though, as we have seen, Schweitzer was apparently unable to hold to a futuristic interpretation of Matt 11:11//Luke 7:28. Dibelius points out that the ususal translation does not agree with 7:28a, "Among them that are born of women there is none greater than John," for after such a statement one could not add that nevertheless there is a whole host of men greater than John, unless those in the kingdom are not born of women. And if one takes kingdom here in the futuristic sense, as Dibelius does, then John is excluded from the kingdom, which is an impossible thought. These difficulties disappear when we render: "The Lesser One is greater in the kingdom of God than he." "The Lesser One" refers to a definite person, Jesus, who is lesser now than John, but "the Lesser One" Jesus, will be greater in the kingdom. Jesus, continues Dibelius, is clearly saying that he regards himself as less than John. But this statement does not contradict Jesus' knowledge of himself as Messiah, for the Messiahship, like the kingdom, is futuristic. Jesus is now lesser than John, but when the kingdom comes Jesus will be Messiah, king of the kingdom, and therefore greater than the greatest of all men.

  The present tense "is," continues Dibelius, says nothing against this interpretation, for prophecy is often spoken in the present tense (Matt 27:63; Luke 12:40; 1 Thess 5:2-3). That Jesus should speak of himself in the third person is understandable, for in such matters he is reserved. Jesus says "*the* Lesser One," not "*a* lesser one," whereby he lets it be known that he, though less than John, is only a little less, for Jesus is the only one being compared with John.

  The question, "Who is greater, John or Jesus?", must have been in the minds of many, and it forms the background of 7:24-28 (at this point Dibelus could have added a reference to Luke 3:15, "... all men reasoned in their hearts concerning John, whether haply he were the Christ"). At 7:24-28 Jesus is speaking to former enthusiastic followers of John who now regard Jesus as the greater and are inclined therefore to berate the Baptist. Jesus rejects this evaluation of himself and defends John. He reminds them of their former opinion: "What went ye out into the wilderness to behold? a reed ...? ... a prophet? Yea, I say unto you, and much more than a prophet.... He is the greatest of all men" (7:24-28). Softly, as if incidentally and understandable only to the initiated, he adds: "But the Lesser One is greater in the kingdom of God than he."

  Dibelius concludes by pointing out that his understanding is supported by the exposition of the ancient church (Section 2.d). Today's prevailing view apparently did not appear before Jerome. We may paraphrase Dibelius' proposal as follows:

> The one who is less than John now will one day as Messiah be greater than John when the kingdom appears, for he will be king of the kingdom.

---

[11]F. Dibelius, "Worte," pp. 190-192.

f) Another Angle.--Thus far we have concluded that 7:28 may refer to Jesus as less than John in respect to age (Chrysostom) and to rank (Dibelius). Can we find yet another point of comparison even more firmly based in Luke's accounts? To do so we should examine the passages where Luke compares Jesus with John:

> John answered,...I indeed baptize you with water; but there cometh he that is mightier than I, . . . : he shall baptize you in the Holy Spirit and in fire (Luke 3:16). John indeed baptized with water; but ye shall be baptized in the Holy Spirit not many days hence (Acts 1:5; 10:16). John had first preached before his coming the baptism of repentance to all the people of Israel. And . . . John . . . said, What suppose ye that I am? I am not he. But behold, there cometh one after me the shoes of whose feet I am not worthy to unloose (Acts 13:24-25).

These passages suggest that Luke's dominant concern is to contrast John's baptism with that of Jesus. But Jesus' baptism with Holy Spirit and fire (Acts 2:34; 10:44; 19:6) was not to occur until after Jesus had ascended into his kingdom (Luke 19:12; 23:42; Acts 1:9-11):

> Being therefore by the right hand of God exalted, and having received of the Father the promise of the Holy Spirit, he hath poured forth this, which ye see and hear (Acts 2:33).

In other words, Jesus in respect to baptism during his earthly ministry was less than John, who baptized the multitudes. But in the kingdom of God, when he pours out his baptism of Spirit and fire, culminating with his cosmic baptism of fire (Luke 12:49-50; Chap. VIII), he will be greater than John, even in respect to baptism. Hence we may render Luke 7:28 so as to bring out Luke's meaning:

He who on the earth is lesser as a baptizer will in the kingdom be greater as a baptizer than John is now.

Amazingly, this interpretation is borne out by the next two verses, 7:29-30:

29 And all the people when they heard, and the publicans, justified God, being baptized with the baptism of John. 30 But the Pharisees and the lawyers rejected for themselves the counsel of God, being not baptized of him.

These verses are found only in Luke and interrupt the direct discourse of 7:24-28 and 7:31-35. Hence some translations, such as RSV, enclose vv 29-30 in parentheses. The verb "justify" (*dikaioō*) occurs five times in Luke and twice in Acts but not at all in Mark and John and twice in Matthew (all other occurrences are in the Paulines and James). "The baptism" (*to baptisma*) is found ten times in Luke-Acts and ten times in the rest of the NT. "Lawyer" appears in the NT ten times, of which seven are in Luke. The combination "Pharisees and the lawyers" occurs only in Luke. "The counsel of God" is peculiar to Luke-Acts in the NT (Luke 7:30; Acts 13:36; 20:27; cf. Acts 2:23; 4:28). "Counsel" appears thirteen times in the NT, ten of which are in Luke-Acts. Thus we probably have "Luke's own comment on the reaction of Jesus' audience to his discourse."[12]

Luke reports, then, that the people and the publicans, by being baptized with John's baptism, acknowledge God's program of salvation as excellent, just, right, and true. This excellent program includes John's water baptism as a preparation for Jesus' greater baptism in Spirit and fire. The Pharisees and the lawyers, on the

---

[12]Gilmour, *Luke*, p. 139.

contrary, by refusing John's baptism will not receive Jesus' baptism of Spirit and fire and thereby reject God's program of salvation. All that remains for them is Jesus' cosmic baptism of fire at the end (Luke 12:49-50).

Thus understood Luke 7:28-30 forms a perfect unity. 7:28 tells us that Jesus pouring out his baptism of Spirit and fire from the kingdom will be even greater as a baptizer than John, who baptized multitudes in water. The people and the publicans respond by proclaiming the excellency of this plan, whereas the Pharisees and lawyers reject it. Men either proclaim the excellency of this plan or reject it, depending upon their reception or rejection of John's baptism.

Our understanding gains some support from John 3:30: "He must grow greater, but I must grow less" (Weymouth). In the Gospel of John too the context is one of baptism, as the Baptist's disciples tell him that Jesus is also baptizing and everyone is going to Jesus. John's importance, especially as a baptizer, will decrease, whereas Jesus' importance as a baptizer will increase. Jesus will become the greater and John the lesser one. That is also the message of Luke 7:28, except for Luke it is a contrast between John's baptism administered on earth and Jesus' baptism administered from the transcendent kingdom.

The likelihood that Jesus is "the lesser" (*ho mikroteros*) of 7:28 is enhanced by the fact that he is also the lesser (*ho mikroteros*) of 9:48 ("he that is lesser among you all, the same is great"), the younger (*ho neōteros*) and the one that serveth (*ho diakonōn*) (22:26; 12:37). Thus 7:28 is only one of several verses where Jesus appears as "the lesser one." Although Jesus, who is the standard of humility and service, may refer to himself as "the lesser one," John the Baptist appropriately refers to him as "the stronger one" (*ho ischuroteros*) who will baptize in Spirit and fire (3:16).

Another advantage of this understanding of 7:28 is that it does not exclude John from the kingdom. In short, if this view of 7:28 is correct, 7:28 does not mean that the kingdom is a present reality into which Jesus' followers enter here and now. Rather the kingdom as here pictured is above ready to descend to the new earth after Jesus has poured forth his baptism of Spirit and fire.

C. "Like a Lightning-Flash" (Luke 10:18)

1. The Beginning of the New Age

Luke 10:18 is often regarded as "the most important passage illustrating the fact that the Kingdom of God was present not only in Jesus but also in his disciples, both in the smaller circle of the twelve and in the larger circle of the Seventy."[13] Jesus sees the defeat of Satan accomplished in the fight he is waging victoriously against demons and therefore the kingdom is a present reality in his ministry. Successful exorcisms are evidence that the evil forces are dethroned and the new age has already begun.[14]

2. The Beginning of the End for Satan

a) A Prophetic Vision.--A number of interpreters regard Jesus' vision as prophetic: it represents what is to take place in the future, like the visions of

---

[13]Ladd, *Presence*, p. 257.

[14]In addition to Ladd: Manson, *Sayings of Jesus*, p. 550; Jeremias, *Weltvollender*, p. 60; Gilmour,*Luke*, p. 189; Flender, *Luke*, p. 103; Ellis, *Luke*, p. 155.

Micaiah (1 Kgs 22:17) and John (Rev 20:10).[15] Since Satan continues to be active (Luke 11:14; 22:3,31), the vision refers to Satan's future fall, especially if "fall" means "defeat" or "ruin." But "fall" may also mean "arrival in power," as in Rev 12:7-17, to inaugurate the period of final woes upon earth. The disciples report their success against demons (10:17). Jesus warns against premature optimism by saying Satan has come down to reinforce his troops (v 18). But despite Satan's arrival the disciples will prevail against "all power of the enemy" (v 19).

There is, however, a slight balance of probability that 10:18 describes Satan's ultimate defeat (=cast down to Hades; cf. Hades in 10:15), says Hiers. Jesus is then arming his band in preparation for future dealings with demonic forces (v 19). It is possible that 10:18 (cf. 11:20) means that exorcisms can be performed because Satan has been defeated and the kingdom of God is present. But since Satan continues to be active and the coming of the kingdom is regularly regarded as a future event, it is more plausible to conclude that Jesus understood that through his own success and that of the disciples against demons Satan's power is being overcome. Satan's kingdom will end and soon the kingdom of God will be established.

b) Satan's Counter-Attack.--Some years ago F. Spitta made a valuable contribution to the study of this pericope.[16] As Spitta sees it, 10:18 is not Jesus' report of Satan's overthrow, since it is too dry and incomplete for such a catastrophic event as that. Neither can one appeal to John 12:31 to support the view that Luke 10:18 refers to Satan's defeat and the consequent arrival of the kingdom of God. John 12:31 reads: "Now is the judgment of this world: now shall the prince of this world be cast out." This verse points not to a present but to a future event, as is shown by 12:32: "And I, if I be lifted up from the earth, will draw all men unto myself."

Moreover, argues Spita, the authority of the seventy over demons (10:19) is not based upon Satan's downfall but upon a communication of power from Jesus (10:19). Again, Luke 11:21-22 (contrary to the parallels in Matt 12:29; Mark 3:27) does not speak of the binding of Satan, for Luke's passion narrative is regarded in the light of satanic hostility (22:3,31). The picture of "falling like lightning" also weighs against the idea that 10:18 speaks of Satan's overthrow, for we must distinguish between the fall of a star, which is abnormal (Isa 14:12; Matt 24:28; Mark 13:25), and the fall of lightning, which is normal (Matt 28:2; 24:27; Luke 17:24). Thus in John 12:31 and Rev 12:9 Satan is "cast out," whereas in Luke 10:18 he "falls (*piptō*) (intransitive), which means that 10:18 does not envision a forceful expulsion of Satan out of heaven.

The literature often speaks of lightning or fire falling from heaven:

> Fire fell (*piptō*) from the Lord out of heaven and consumed the burnt-offering (1 Kgs 18:38).

Job 1:6 is especially important:

> Fire fell (*piptō*) out of heaven and burned up the sheep. After Satan had received permission to torment Job, God's fire fell and consumed his herds. In

---

[15]Plummer, *Luke*, p. 278; Fuller, *Mission*, pp. 26-27; Hiers, *Kingdom of God*, pp. 50-56; this section is based on Hiers.

[16]Spitta, "Blitz," pp. 160-163.

the apocryphal Testament of Job this passage has it that Satan himself comes down as fire, appearing like lightning (cf. Ps 104:4; Heb 1:7). Against this background, says Spitta, we can see that Satan's fall like lightning from heaven described in Luke 10:18 is to be understood, not as Satan's overthrow, but as Satan's attempt to do harm on earth. Jesus understood this fall exactly as in John 14:30, where he speaks of a coming of Satan directed against him:

> The prince [Satan] of the world cometh: and he hath nothing in me (=he has no power over me).

And that is what Jesus tells the seventy (Luke 10:19) when they report the demons are subject to them (10:17). In other words, continues Spitta, Jesus had observed that, when he sent forth the seventy in the interests of the coming kingdom, Satan responded with his own attack. But the disciples received from Jesus the power to overcome Satan's messengers, the demons.

In conclusion, Spitta notes that his interpretation settles the problem as to when Jesus saw Satan fall.[17] Also the common view that Satan was overthrown and the kingdom of God has therefore come is refuted. There remains for Spitta only the question whether Jesus' speech was linked to an actual flash of lightning or whether he expressed his inner certainty figuratively.

c) *Satan Comes in Power.*--Spitta has made a good case for interpreting Luke 10:18 in light of the books of Job, but we would like to underscore important connections with Rev 12:7-17:

> Satan is called "serpent" (Rev 12:9); the disciples are given power over serpents (Luke 10:19). In both passages Satan comes down from heaven. In each account Christ shows his authority (*exousia*) (Rev 12:10; Luke 10:19). Disciples win a victory over Satan by the word of their testimony (Rev 12:11; Luke 10:5,9,11,17), and are "willing to give up their lives and die" (TEV)(Rev 12:11; Luke 10:3,19). Satan's fall is terrible for the earth (Rev 12:12; Luke 10:19; 21:26) and for the sea (Rev 12:12; Luke 21:25). And when Satan comes to earth he persecutes the church (Rev 12:13-17; Luke 10:19; 22:3,31; cf. Acts 5:3; 10:38; 14:22). Those who dwell in the heavens are to rejoice (Rev 12:12), even as the disciples on earth are to rejoice because their names are written in heaven (Luke 10:20). The ground of rejoicing in each case is that heaven is no longer the abode of Satan, from which he exercises full power (cf. 1 Cor 8:5; Eph 6:12). His coming to earth signifies the beginning of the end of his reign.[18]

Against this background of Job and Revelation we may understand Luke 10:17-20 as follows: The disciples return joyfully because through the incantation of Jesus' name they have exorcised demons. The jubilant report induces Jesus to tell of the ecstatic vision or visions he has been having of Satan's fall (cf. his visions at his baptism and transfiguration).

> There is no doubt of the possibility that Jesus had such experiences. And the wording of the saying with its comparison of Satan's fall in its swiftness and conspicuousness to a flash of lightning suggests a visionary experience more strongly than a figure of speech.[19]

---

[17]Webster, "Luke 10:18," p. 52, notes three views: the occasion was Jesus' sending out the disciples (Mayer); the vision was coincident with the success of the disciples (Plummer), or refers to the incarnation (some Roman Catholic commentators).

[18]Cf. Easton, *Luke*, p. 162; Bultmann, *Synoptic Tradition*, p. 161.

[19]Kümmel, *Promise*, p. 114. Cf. Num 12:6.

Jesus was "looking away, gazing into that dark realm to which His thoughts had just been directed" by the mission of the seventy.[20] As he was looking, he saw Satan fall like a blaze of lightning from heaven.

Many attempts have been made to bring out the nuances of the imperfect tense of "see" and the aorist tense of "fall":

> I have been seeing Satan, that he fell as lightning that falleth from heaven (Syriac).
>
> I watched Satan's fall; it was like lightning for swiftness.[21] Satan fell like lightning: I was there beholding.[22]
>
> I kept my eyes on Satan, he replied. He fell, like lightning from the sky (Rieu). I have had visions of Satan, fallen, like lightning from the heavens (Twentieth Century NT).
>
> I was looking on when Satan was hurled like a lightning-flash out of Heaven (Weymouth margin).[23]

The correct implication of the aorist tense ("fallen") evidently is that "we are not to think of him [Satan] as lying where he had fallen,"[24] or "lying in a huddled heap as a result of his fall."[25] We may, therefore, picture Satan as falling from heaven, not in final defeat, but "having great wrath, knowing he hath but a short time" (Rev 12:12). Like Satan in the Testament of Job, Satan falls to do harm on earth. He launches a counter-attack against Jesus and his disciples.[26] Satan is "destructive as lightning, swift, fatal, devouring."[27]

Because Jesus sees Satan's counter-attack in all its severity, he warns his disciples against premature optimism by reporting that Satan has arrived in power to reinforce his troops (10:18).[28] In view of this crisis Jesus bestows a special charismatic charm on his band to give them immunity against the attacks of half-demonic serpents and scorpions and all the power of Satan (10:19-20).[29] But great as this power is, the disciples are to rejoice, not because of it, but because their names are written in the book of life,[30] which means they are destined for the bliss of the coming kingdom.[31] Here again the reference is to the world to come, not to a present reality on earth.

Luke 10:18 is, therefore, best understood to mean, not that Satan has already been defeated and the kingdom has already come in Jesus and his disciples, but that Satan has come in power to direct the final attack against the forces of the

---

[20]Cf. Webster, "Luke 10:18," p. 52.

[21]Clarke, "Luke 10:18," p. 103; the translation of the Syriac is also from Clarke.

[22]Thomson, "Luke 10:18," p. 191.

[23]"Was hurled" is hardly correct for "fall" (see Spitta above). For discussion of these tenses see the articles by Thomson, Lewis, Clarke, and Webster.

[24]Webster, "Luke 10:18," p. 53.

[25]Clarke, "Luke 10:18," p. 103.

[26]Cf. Spitta, summarized above.

[27]Lewis, "Luke 10:18," p. 233.

[28]Cf. Hiers, summarized above.

[29]Cf. Otto, *Kingdom of God*, p. 367; Gilmour, *Luke*, p. 189.

[30]Exod 32:32; Ps 69:29; 87:4-6; Dan 12:1; Phil 4:3; Heb 12:23; Rev 3:5; 13:8; 17:8.

[31]Cf. Manson, *Sayings of Jesus*, p. 551.

approaching kingdom.

D. "By the Finger of God" (Luke 11:20)

1. The Kingdom of God as Dynamic Presence

At Luke 11:20//Matt 12:28 Jesus says: "But if I by the finger of God cast out demons, then is the kingdom of God come upon you." By far the prevailing interpretation of this saying is that the kingdom is present.[32] The classic statement of this position is set forth by Dodd.[33]

> Here the Kingdom of God is a fact of present experience, . . . Something has happened, which has not happened before, and which means that the sovereign power of God has come into effective operation. . . . It is a matter of being confronted with the power of God at work in the world. In other words, the "eschatological" Kingdom of God is proclaimed as a present fact, . . . In the ministry of Jesus Himself the divine power is released in effective conflict with evil. . . . The ministry of Jesus [is] "realized eschatology," that is to say, . . . the impact upon this world of the "powers of the world to come" in a series of events, unprecedented and unrepeatable, now in actual process.

Otto puts more emphasis upon the cosmic warfare being waged between two present kingdoms:[34]

> The Kingdom of God pushes forward its boundaries against the Kingdom of Satan in Christ's activity as exorcist. It expands its realm through eschatological warfare. . . . Jesus works by the finger--the Spirit--the dynamis, charisma of God, the dynamis of the Kingdom of God. This charisma and charismatic activity of his is nothing other than the coming of the Kingdom of God.

Ladd, who finds that in Luke 11:20 "the Kingdom of God is unambiguously present among men in this age," stresses the powers of the kingdom at work:[35]

> If the Kingdom has in some way reached men, then it is present. If in fact the evils of present existence are in process of being transformed, it can be nothing else but the powers of the Kingdom, and therefore the Kingdom of God itself--if the Kingdom of God by definition is the dynamic reign and rule of God.

2. The Meaning of *Phthanō*

Before we accept or reject this interpretation of "realized eschatology," we must examine the meaning of the word which ASV translates as "is come" (*phthanō*).

a) *Clark's Study of Phthanō.*--Since Clark's study of *phthanō* is often not readily available, we may summarize his results:[36]

---

[32]J. Weiss, "Luke 11:14-26," pp. 565-568, and *Kingdom of God*, pp. 66-67; Creed, *Luke*, p. 161; Kümmel, *Promise*, pp. 105-109; Gilmour, *Luke*, p. 207; Flender, *Luke*, p. 149; Ellis, *Luke*, p. 165, though some of these writers are more concerned with the meaning of the saying for Jesus than for Luke.

[33]Dodd, *Parables*, pp. 28-29, 35; Martin, "Messianic Age," pp. 272-273.

[34]Otto, *Kingdom of God*, pp. 97-104.

[35]Ladd, *Presence*, p. 141.

[36]Clark, "Realized Eschatology," pp. 374-383.

Phthanō appears twenty-six times in LXX for the Aramiac *metah* (reach, attain) or Hebrew *nagah* (touch, reach, extend to). Without exception *phthanō* is used in LXX to describe either the action of approaching or the precise point of contact, but not the participation in some ensuing experience. In the non-literary papyri, in the instances where *phthanō* means "to arrive," the term conveys the idea of just reaching, thus bringing *phthanō* and *engidzō* into synonymity. As late as A.D.709 the connotation of *phthanō* is still limited to the point of attainment, and in modern Greek it has never come to mean anything different. It is likewise in the contemporaries of the evangelists, Philo and Plutarch. Thus from LXX to modern Greek, when *phthanō* means "to come," "to arrive," it means "to reach" in the sense of straining after and attaining. It describes arrival upon the threshold of fulfilment and accessible experience, not the entrance into that experience. In the NT, *phthanō* retains the older meaning, "to precede," at 1 Thess 4:15, but the other six occurrences all involve the newer meaning, "to reach." Thus we have found no instance anywhere in the Greek language which requires translating Matt 12:28//Luke 11:20, as does Dodd, "The kingdom of God has come upon you as realized experience, as a series of events now in actual progress." On the contrary, general usage insists that we translate here, "The kingdom of God has just reached you."

Among all the instances reviewed herein, we may list all those illustrating precisely the same construction and meaning as Luke 11:20:

Judg 20:34: Disaster overtakes them (*phthanei ep' autous*).

Judg 20:42: The battle pressed them close (*ephthasen ep' autous*).

Dan 4:28: Now all these things befell Nebuchadnezzar (*ephthasen epi Nabouchadonosor*).

Eccl 8:14: The experience which belongs to the wicked overtakes them (*phthanei ep' autous*).

Philo, *Creation* 8: He attained the very summit of philosophy (*ep' autēn phthasas*).

1 Thess 2:16: But God's wrath has overtaken them at last (*ephthasen de ep' autous*).

In all these passages the sense of reaching after to make contact or to overtake persists as the connotation of *phthanō*. Disaster is about to eventuate: the battle pursued the refugees; prophesied events overtook Nebuchadnezzar; punishment confronts the wicked; Moses obtained an objective; God's wrath is about to be vented. In each instance fulfilment of events is future, and *phthanō* denotes their imminence. These contexts afford no precedents by which to find in Matt 12:28//Luke 11:20 "realized eschatology." Thus *engidzō* and *phthanō* are synonymous in the meaning "to draw near, even to the very point of contact," but the experience which draws near is still sequential. Therefore Luke 10:9 and 11:20 should be translated alike: "The kingdom of God has reached you." It is quite unjustifiable to hold that *engidzō* and *phthanō* must, or even may, be translated "has come as a fact of present experience, in a series of events now in actual progress."

In this way Clark seeks to refute Dodd and all those who hold that Luke 11:20 means the kingdom has come and its redeeming powers are working in the present. Let us check his results by examining some of the evidence in greater detail.

b) *Phthanō in the New Testament.*--*Phthanō* appears only five times in the NT outside of Luke 11:20//Matt 12:28, and all of these five occurrences are in Pauline epistles:

1) All commentators are agreed that at 1 Thess 4:15 *phthanō* has its older meaning of "precede." Paul, in writing about the fate of those who have died before the return of Christ, declares that the living and the dead in Christ will enter the kingdom together: "We who are alive on the day the Lord comes will not go ahead (*phthanō*) of those who have died" (TEV).

2) The earlier meaning of "precede" or "come before another" probably remains in 2 Cor 10:14. Paul tells the Corinthians that, unlike those intruders who had come to Corinth in Paul's sphere, he does not carry on his mission beyond the territory assigned him by God. In fact, Paul had to come to Corinth as a pioneer missionary: "We were the first to come (*phthanō*) all the way to you with the gospel of Christ" (RSV). But the later meaning of *phthanō* is present and perhaps even dominant: to reach, overtake, come up to, attain, arrive at; draw near, even to the point of contact: "For we came even as far as unto you in the gospel of Christ" (ASV). Whether, however, we translate with RSV or ASV Paul is referring to his initial contact, to his reaching the Corinthians with the Gospel, but not to his subsequent work in Corinth. That work is mentioned in the next two verses, 15-16: "We hope . . . that we may be able to do a much greater work among you. . . .Then we can preach the Good News in other countries beyond you" (TEV). Paul in v 14 thus writes of "his coming even to" the Corinthians, an objective "which served as the threshold before the door opening upon his subsequent ministry to them." But *phthanō* "neither refers to nor describes the activity subsequent to the point of his arrival."[37]

3) In Rom 9:31 Paul finds that Israel was pursuing a law that could give righteousness but they did not arrive at one. Here Paul refers only to the point of arrival at a goal but not to any subsequent efforts after the point of arrival or non-arrival. "Israel, straining after a law that should bring uprightness, did not come up (*phthanō*) to it" (Goodspeed) ("never attained to it"--NEB).

4) At Phil 3:16 Paul exhorts, "Whereunto we have attained (*phthanō*), by that same rule let us walk" (ASV). *Phthanō* directs attention only to the point of attainment, to the Christian's present condition. Subsequent activity beyond that level requires another verb, "let us walk." "But whatever be the point that we have already reached, let us persevere in the same course" (Weymouth).

5) At 1 Thess 2:16 Paul declares that the Jews of Judea had killed Jesus and the prophets and had hindered Paul and the Gentile mission, but now "God's wrath has overtaken (*phthanō*) them at last" (Goodspeed). God's wrath has reached the Jews, but Paul mentions nothing beyond the point of contact.

> Some have held that this statement is an interpolation referring to the later destruction of Jerusalem. Such an emendation is unnecessary since *phthanō* does not envisage particular events already being experienced, but only the immediate anticipation of such a sequel. The divine wrath which at last reached the Jews threatens the imminent condemnation which God is expected to pronounce upon the unbelieving now that his Kingdom is ready to be revealed.[38]

---

[37]Clark, "Realized Eschatology," p. 380.
[38]Clark, "Realized Eschatology," p. 380.

Campbell prefers to stress the imminence of God's wrath rather than its bare arrival. He observes in connection with the aorist tense of *phthanō* (as in Luke 11:20 and 1 Thess 2:16) that it may be a "timeless aorist" with a future reference. Luke 11:20 would then read, "The kingdom of God will be upon you immediately." The aorist of 1 Thess 2:16 "almost demands this interpretation":

> How could Paul, writing about A.D. 50, say that the divine wrath had already come upon the Jews? But if he meant only that it would come upon them immediately, there is no difficulty. And there is one passage in the LXX where this interpretation also seems to give the best sense.- Dan 4:24, 'It is the decree . . . which is about to come upon my lord the king.'[39]

6) In light of the above Pauline passages where *phthanō* means at the most "reach," "come into contact," but without reference to any process, experience, or activity after the point of contact, Luke 11:20//Matt 12:28 would appear to mean: "The Kingdom of God has overtaken you" (Goodspeed). But Luke does not describe the kingdom here as a present reality in which the powers of the kingdom are at work following its initial contact. Rather, Jesus' successful activity as exorcist precedes this drawing near of the kingdom to the point of contact: "But if it is with the finger of God that I am driving the demons out, *then* (*ara*) the Kingdom of God has overtaken you" (Goodspeed). "Then" (*ara*) here means "then, as a result."[40] It is a result of Jesus' exorcisims that the kingdom has overtaken them. The exorcisms are thus signs of the proximity of the kingdom rather than of its presence.[41] The seventy on their mission preach the nearness rather than the presence of the kingdom (10:9,11) (Chap. V.D), yet cast out demons (10:17), which means that for Luke exorcisms precede the coming of the kingdom.

This interpretation of the exorcisms is supported by the allusion of the symbol "finger of God" (11:20) to Exod 8:19, where the Egyptian magicians describe the plagues as wrought by "the finger of God." Just as the plagues were preliminary to the exodus, so Jesus' exorcisms point forward to the final deliverance.[42]

c) *Phthanō as Synonymous with Engidzō*.--At least twice in the various Greek translations of the OT *phthanō* and *engidzō* are used to translate the same Aramaic word, *metah* (reach, attain). In Dan 4:11 Nebuchadnezzar dreams of a great tree whose height "reached" (*phthanō*) (Theodotion's Greek version, second century A.D.) or "came close" (*engidzō* in the LXX) unto heaven.

Again in Dan 4:22 Nebuchadnezzar's greatness, like the greatness of that tree, "reached "(*phthanō*, Theodotion) or "came close" (*engidzō*, LXX) unto heaven. "It is evident in this context that *phthanō* means at most 'to touch,' but not 'to break into' heaven."[43] If we stress the literal meaning of *engidzō* (Chap. V.D.2) then *phthanō* here would mean "come near." Thus Campbell can remark that "if one wishes to indicate that a tree was of enormous size it matters little whether it is said to have reached to heaven or only to have come close to

---

[39]Campbell, "Kingdom," pp. 92-93.

[40]BAG, p. 103.

[41]Fuller, *Mission*, pp. 26-27; Hiers, *Kingdom of God*, pp. 33-34.

[42]Fuller, *Mission*, pp. 37-38.

[43]Clark, "Realized Eschatology," p. 377.

heaven."[44]

d)Judg 20:34 and 20:42--We now examine more closely the two texts from Judges which Clark isolates as being parallel to Luke 11:20. In Judges 20 the Lord commands Israel to go out against the Benjaminites. Israel sets men in ambush about Gibeah and craftily draws the unsuspecting Benjaminites away from their base, the latter not knowing that "disaster was close upon them" (*phthanō*) (20:34) (RSV) ("evil was coming upon them") (Bagster; Thomson-Muses), as it truly was, for Israel destroyed 25,100 of them that day (20:35).

The battle continues and follows hard after the Benjaminites, pressing them close (*phthanō*) (Clark) (20:42). Then the Israelites enclose the Benjaminites and kill another 25,000 of them (20:46). "This is precisely the form and syntax" of Luke 11:20, "and the context makes plain beyond all doubt the sense of pursuit and imminent contact, rather than the idea of an actual conflict."[45] This sense is clearly seen in ASV: "The battle followed hard after them; and they that came out of the cities destroyed them." In both Judg 20:34 and 20:42 *phthanō* indicates imminent contact, the subsequent contact and action being described by other verbs. These two parallels from Judges 20, then, suggest the following translation of Luke 11:20:

The kingdom of God has come close upon you.[46]

In Judg 20:34,42 *phthanō* is used in a context of a threatening future: disaster is ready to descend upon the Benjaminites. This same threatening atmosphere surrounds Luke 11:20. Jesus is having a confrontation with his opponents, who want to trap him (11:16). Jesus uses "upon you" (*eph' humas*) as a threat, to warn his adversaries that the kingdom, of which they are enemies, will surprise and crush them. Like the Benjaminites, Jesus' adversaries are unaware that disaster "is close upon them," for the kingdom, like the Israelites pursuing the Benjaminites, has caught up with them and soon will cut them down (cf. Luke 12:46; 19:27). This sense of threatening catastrophe indicates the kingdom is thought of as an imminent future reality, whose coming, like the judgment of 11:30-32, 50-51, is "bad news for Jesus' accusers."[47]

e) Further Evidence for the Imminent Sense of Phthanō.--It seems likely that *phthanō* also means "draw near" in Ezra 3:1 (=2 Ezra 3:1, LXX) and Neh 7:73 (=2 Ezra 17:73, LXX):

> In both passages the context makes it clear that the meaning cannot be, 'When the seventh month was come' (KJV and ASV), unless we are to suppose an incredible amount of activity in the early hours of the first day of that month. The meaning plainly is, 'When the seventh month drew near.'[48]

---

[44]Campbell, "Kingdom," p. 92. These passages cast doubt upon the validity of Kümmel's observation that there can be "no question of *phthanō* ever being used as a real synonym" for *engidzō* (*Promise*, p. 107).

[45]Clark, "Realized Eschatology," p. 377.

[46]Campbell, "Kingdom," p. 92.

[47]Hiers, *Kingdom of God*, p. 31; Godet, *Luke*, II, 55, also stresses the threat involved here, but still regards the kingdom as present.

[48]Campbell, "Kingdom," p. 92.

The activitiy mentioned in Ezra 3 appears to include traveling to Jerusalem, building the altar, setting it on its base, and offering burnt- offerings morning and evening. Dodd replied to Campbell, suggesting that for the writer of Ezra the first day of the month had arrived and the other events had already taken place.[49] But the narrative reads much more naturally if 3:1 means "when the seventh month drew near." Then there is time to complete preparations for offering burnt-offerings on the first day of the month (Ezra 3:6). Here too we may compare Matt 21:34 (Chap. V.C.1): "The season of fruits drew near" (engidzō). Once again *phthanō* and *engidzō* are synonymous.

The same is true of Dan 4:24 (Theodotion), which ASV renders, "It is the decree of the Most High, which is come (*phthanō*) upon my lord the king." "This may perhaps mean that the decree has already come upon the king, but it would be the more natural to say 'which is about to come upon my lord the king,' especially since the divine judgment is actually pronounced by a voice from heaven twelve months later, and is then fulfilled at once upon him (4:28-33)."[50] Some translations also reproduce this sense of imminence:

> The decree of the Most High . . . is about to come upon my lord the king (Thomson-Muses).
> There is a decision of the Most High, which has gone out against my lord the king, . . . (American).
> The decree of the Most High is that which must befall my lord (NWT).

"And in Dan 8:7, where the Hebrew means explicitly 'coming close to,' Theodotion has *phthanonta heōs*."[51] "I saw him indeed coming up to the ram" (Thomson-Muses). "I saw him come close unto the ram" (ASV). With these verses in mind we may again best represent the aorist of *phthanō* used in Luke 11:20 by an English perfect: "The kingdom of God has come close upon you."[52]

f) *Phthanō in the Testaments of the Twelve Patriarchs.*--In this pseudepigraphical book, written about 109-107 B.C.,[53] *phthanō* is used three times in the sense "to reach," "to attain to."[54] According to Reuben 5:7 the angels or watchers who had changed themselves into men appeared to the women as "reaching (*phthanō*) even unto heaven"[55] or "to the sky."[56] Naphtali 6:9 tells of a ship which, after the storm ceased, "reached (*phthanō*) the land as it were in peace."[57] Levi 6:11 has it that because of the wickedness of the men of Shechem "the wrath of the Lord came upon them to the uttermost"[58] or "reached and smote them."[59] It is possible that Paul adopted this verse at 1

---

[49]Dodd, "Kingdom of God," pp. 138-142.
[50]Campbell, "Kingdom," p. 93.
[51]Campbell, "Kingdom," p. 92.
[52]Campbell, "Kingdom," p. 92.
[53]*APOT*, II, 290.
[54]Fitzer, "*Phthanō*," pp. 89-90.
[55]*APOT*, II, 207.
[56]Fitzer, "*Phthanō*," p. 89.
[57]*APOT*, II, 338; Fitzer, "*Phthanō*," p. 89.
[58]*APOT*, II, 308.
[59]Fitzer, "*Phthanō*," pp. 89-90.

Thess 2:16.[60]

g) Ladd's Five Sayings.--Ladd refers to five sayings containing *phthanō* in support of his interpretation of Matt 12:28//Luke 11:20 to mean the dynamic presence of the kingdom. "In all of these sayings, something actually arrives, not merely comes close."[61] But Ladd fails to observe that these sayings, referring as they do at most to the point of arrival and nothing subsequent to that, do not support his thesis that Luke 11:20 means the kingdom is present as dynamically active among men in the mission of Jesus and his disciples and continuing active until the end of time. Let us examine these five verses:

1) 2 Chron 28:9.--"Ye have slain them in wrath, and it has reached even to heaven" (Bagster; Thomson-Muses; ASV), or "towered up to heaven" (NEB). Here *phthanō* indicates nothing beyond the point of contact, not even entrance into heaven.

2) Cant 2:12.--"The pruning season is come" (*phthanō*) (Thomson-Muses), that is, has just arrived, or, better, "is coming" (NEB), but the verse does not describe the pruners at work after the season has begun. We may compare Ezra 3:1 ("When the seventh month drew near") and Matt 21:34 ("The season of fruits drew near").

3) Dan 6:24.--"And before they [Daniel's accusers and families] reached (*phthanō*) the floor of the pit the lions were upon them and crunched them up, bones and all" (NEB; similarly Bagster; Thomson-Muses). A more vivid illustration of *phthanō* in the sense of contact, but nothing after that, could not be imagined. Before the victims could so much as touch the bottom of the den the lions had the mastery of them.

4) Dan 7:13.--"He came on (*phthanō*) to the Ancient of days, and was brought near to him" (Basgster). *Phthanō* indicates at most the bare arrival of the Son of Man and is followed by another verb for the subsequent presentation. He "advanced toward the Venerable One, and was brought near his presence" (American).

5) Dan 7:22.--"The time came on (*phthanō*), and the saints possessed the kingdom" (Bagster). Here again *phthanō* suggests only the point of arrival; the possession takes place thereafter.

Ladd, then, is hard pressed to find support in these verses for his contention that *phthanō* in Luke 11:20 can be stretched to include activity following the bare arrival of the kingdom, activity evidently extending for thousands or more years, if necessary, until the apocalyptic kingdom breaks in. The use of *phthanō* in these five verses would rather suggest the following translation of Luke 11:20:

> The kingdom of God has approached toward you, coming down out of heaven upon you.

h) A Modern Greek Waiter.--To support his realized eschatology, Dodd cites the modern use of the aorist tense of *phthanō*. "If you call a waiter, I am told, he will say, as he bustles up, '*ephthasa, kurie!*' ('Here I am, sir!')."[62] But Campbell

---
[60]*APOT*, II, 308.

[61]Ladd, *Presence*, p. 143.

[62]Dodd, *Parables*, p. 28.

finds the correct meaning to be, "Just coming, sir!"[63] A possible translation of Luke 11:20 would then be:

> The kingdom of God is just coming down out of heaven upon you.

i) Summary.--Since writers often do not distinguish clearly enough among the three basic meanings of *phthanō* which have emerged in the lengthy discussions summarized above, we shall recapitulate the results of our survey to this point.

1)*Phthanō*=precede, come before, come first, reach before, come sooner, go ahead of:

> 1 Thess 4:15: We ... will not go ahead of those who have died (TEV).
>
> 2 Cor 10:14: We were the first to come all the way to you (RSV).

Vincent seeks to convey this sense of *phthanō* by rendering Luke 11:20 as "it has come upon you before you expected it."[64] *Phthanō* does at times carry the idea that an event is not foreseen but comes as a surprise.[65] We recall that Luke 14:17 also suggests   surprise at the speedy coming of the kingdom (Chap. V.K).

2)*Phthanō*=reach, arrive at, attain, just arrive, come up to, overtake, come into contact:

> 2 Chron 28:9: A rage hath reached up into heaven (ASV) (Bagster) (Thomson-Muses).
>
> Eccles 8:14: The experience which belongs to the wicked overtakes them (Clark).
>
> Dan 4:28: All these things befell Nebuchadnezzar (Clark).
>
> Dan 6:24: Before they reached the floor of the pit (NEB) (Bagster) (Thomson-Muses).
>
> Dan 7:22: The time came on, and the saints possessed the kingdom (Bagster).
>
> Reuben 5:7: Angels reached unto heaven (*APOT*).
>
> Naphtali 6:9: A ship reached the land (*APOT*).
>
> Levi 6:11: Wrath reached them (Fitzer).
>
> Philo, *Creation*, 8: He attained the very summit of philosophy (Clark).
>
> Rom 9:31: Israel never attained to it (NEB).
>
> 2 Cor 10:14: For we came even as far as unto you (ASV).
>
> Phil 3:16: ... the point that we have already reached (Weymouth).

The aorist tense of *phthanō*, as in Luke 11:20, appears in each of the above verses except Eccl 8:14 (present) and 2 Chr 28:9 (perfect). These verses would support those translations of Luke 11:20 which bring out the sense of bare contact:

> The kingdom of God has overtaken you (Goodspeed).
>
> The kingdom of God has just reached you (Clark).

---

[63]Campbell, "Kingdom," p. 93.

[64]Vincent, *Word Studies*, I, 72.

[65]Fitzer, "*Phthanō*," p. 89.

3) *Phthanō*=come near, come close, draw near, approach, advance toward, be about to:

> Judg 20:34: Evil was coming upon them (Thomson-Muses).
>
> Judg 20:42: The battle pressed them close (Clark).
>
> Ezra 3:1; Neh 7:73: When the seventh month drew near (Campbell).
>
> Cant 2:12: The time of pruning is coming (NEB).
>
> Dan 4:11, 22: Tree (greatness) came close to heaven (Campbell).
>
> Dan 4:24: The decree is about to come upon the king (Campbell) (Thomson-Muses).
>
> Dan 7:13: He came on the Ancient of days and was brought near to him (Bagster).
>
> Dan 8:7: I saw him close unto the ram (Campbell).
>
> 1 Thess 2:16: God's wrath will come upon them immediately (Campbell).

The aorist tense of *phthanō* appears in each of the above verses except Judg 20:34 and Dan 8:7 (present) and Cant 2:12 (perfect). These verses would support those translations of Luke 11:20 which bring out the sense of imminent contact: "The kingdom of God will be upon you immediately," or "has come close upon you" (Campbell), or "is about to come down out of heaven upon you" (cf. Dan 4:24). But neither the translations sanctioned by 2) bare contact, or by 3) imminent contact, gives support to the thesis of realized eschatology that for Luke the kingdom is a present process at work in this age on this earth.

j) The Prophetic Past Tense (Aorist).--We have been trying to establish upon the basis of linguistic evidence that the kingdom at Luke 11:20 is an imminent future reality or has at the most made initial contact. It is possible, however, to agree with the School of Realized Eschatology that 11:20 should be translated as "the kingdom of God has arrived upon you" and yet hold to the futuristic meaning of the kingdom in this verse. This possibility is based upon the so-called "prophetic past tense" (aorist), which means that here Jesus and/or Luke is so certain of the coming of the kingdom that he speaks of it as if it had already come:

> The certainty of the event is so overwhelming, the signs of its impendingness so sure, that it is said to have occurred, or to be occurring already....The fact that the demons are yielding to his exorcisms is for Jesus so overwhelming proof, so vivid a sign, of the proximity of the Kingdom, that he speaks of it as though it had arrived already.[66]

In other words, even if we have misinterpreted the meaning of *phthanō* there is still no necessity for finding realized eschatology in Luke 11:20.

3. The Lukan Context

This futuristic understanding of 11:20 fits well its context in Luke 9-11, where Luke stresses the kingdom, parousia, and judgment as future events:

> Jesus, having solemnly declared that some of his hearers will live to see the kingdom of God (9:27), sends out the seventy to heal the sick (10:9), presumably

---

[66] Fuller, *Mission*, p. 25, who likewise interprets 1 Thess 2:16.

to cast out demons (9:2; 10:17), and to announce that "the kingdom of God is nearly upon you" (10:9), and "is fast approaching" (10:11). Elated by their mastery of demons (10:17), the seventy report their success to Jesus, who alerts them to the fact that Satan has arrived in power to bolster his forces (10:18). Jesus then teaches his followers to pray for the speedy coming of the kingdom (11:2) and for the eschatological gift of the Spirit (11:13). In reply to the Beelzebub charge (11:15), Jesus warns his opponents that, if he is casting out demons by the finger of God, then the kingdom of God is threateningly close upon them, even to the point of contact (11:20). The final battle between God and Satan is underway. Jesus, as God's exorcist, is freeing Satan's captives as a sign the kingdom is at hand (11:21-22). Jesus' hearers, like the Benjaminites (Judg 20:34), are unaware that disaster is close upon them. As connoted by the early meaning of *phthanō* ("come before"), it is coming upon them before they had expected, for the Son of Man, in answer to the urgent petition for a speedy consummation (11:2,13), will come in judgment as a sign to this very generation (11:30-32), which is the last and worst of all generations (11:49-51).

We have seen, then, that the futuristic interpretation of 11:20 best fits not only the linguistic evidence but also the Lukan theological context as well as the Lukan stress on exorcisms as preliminary to the coming of the kingdom.

E. "Blessed Assurance": Twin Parables of the Kingdom (Luke 13:18-21)

1. Literary Analysis

The parable of the mustard seed appears in Luke 13:18-19 in Q form, in Mark 4:30-32 in Markan form, and in Matt 13:31-32 in a conflation of Mark and Q forms, whereas the parable of the leaven (Matt 13:33) is almost identical with the Q form in Luke 13:20-21:

Matt 13:31-33	Mark 4:30-32	Luke 13:18-21
Another parable set he before them, saying, The kingdom of heaven is like unto a grain of mustard seed, which a man took, and sowed in his field: 32 which indeed is less than all seeds; but when it is grown, it is greater than the herbs, and becometh a tree, so that the birds of the heaven come and lodge in the branches thereof.	And he said, How shall we liken the kingdom of God? or in what parable shall we set it forth? 31 It is like a grain of mustard seed, which, when it is sown upon the earth, though it be less than all the seeds that are upon the earth, 32 yet when it is sown, groweth up, and becometh greater than all the herbs, and putteth out great branches; so that the birds of heaven can lodge under the shadows thereof.	He said therefore, Unto what is the kingdom of God like? and whereunto shall I liken it? 19 It is like unto a grain of mustard seed, which a man took, and cast into his own garden; and it grew, and became a tree; and the birds of the heaven lodged in the branches thereof.
33 Another parable spake he unto them;		20 And again he said, Whereunto shall I

The kingdom of heaven is like unto leaven, which a woman took, and hid in three measures of meal, till it was all leavened.	liken the kingdom of God? 21 It is like unto leaven, which a woman took and hid in three measures of meal, till it was all leavened.

The chief differences between the Lukan (Q) and Markan forms of the parable of the mustard seed are that Luke mentions neither the smallness of the seed nor the greatness of the size of the herb, though Luke does call the fully-grown plant a "tree" rather than a herb. Luke also has the man casting the seed into his own garden in contrast to Matthew's field and Mark's earth.

2. Parables of Growth?

The chief problem in determining what these twin parables mean to Luke is this: What is the analogue? Is it growth, contrast, or miraculous results? Those who find the point of comparison in the process of growth are disagreed as to whether the kingdom is growing in society or in the church.

a) The Kingdom Growing in Society

Some think of the kingdom of God as present and growing in society: In opposition to the superficial notion that one wave of the magic wand will establish Messiah's kingdom in the twinkling of an eye, these two parables set forth the idea of a moral development which works by spiritual means and takes account of human freedom. This growth is therefore slow and progressive. The spiritual life enclosed in the gospel must penetrate the whole of human life, thereby the family, and through it society.[67]

Against this view it is often pointed out that the idea of the kingdom of God conquering the world by gradual permeation is foreign to biblical and Jewish thought. To Luke and everyone else in the apostolic age the kingdom and the world were in irreconcilable opposition, and the world was not thought of as developing into the kingdom.[68]

Moreover, the oriental mind does not concentrate upon the process of growth:

> The modern man, passing through the ploughed field, thinks of what is going on beneath the soil, and envisages a biological development. The people of the Bible, passing through the same plough-land, look up and see miracle upon miracle, ... on the one hand the dead seed, on the other, the waving corn-field, there death, there, through the divine creative power, life. . . . nothing less than resurrection from the dead.[69]

b) The Kingdom Growing in the Church

Others hold that the kingdom is present in the church as a growing institution,

---

[67] Godet, *Luke*, II, 122.
[68] Cf. Easton, *Luke*, p. 216; Ladd, *Presence*, pp. 236-238.
[69] Jeremias, *Parables*, pp. 148-149.

in full expansion, gradually but inevitably developing into a church for all nations, transforming the world as it grows. Jesus sowed the seed, thereby inaugurating a movement whose victorious march nothing can stop. The marvellous diffusion of the gospel message in the world manifests the power of the ferment which Jesus introduced. An irrepressible force is at work as is seen in the expansion of the church.[70]

In opposition to this view stands not only the Oriental's lack of interest in the process of growth but also the fact that Luke does not equate the kingdom with the church (Chap. V.C.5). That Luke does not think of the growth of the church as synonymous with the growth of the kingdom is further indicated by the fact that his own summary statements never refer to the growth of the kingdom but only to the growth of the church:

> Acts 2:47: The Lord added to them day by day those that were saved.
>
> Acts 4:4: Many of them that heard the word believed.
>
> Acts 5:14: Believers were the more added to the Lord.
>
> Acts 6:1: Now in those days, when the number of disciples was multiplying, . . .
>
> Acts 6:7: The word of God increased; and the number of disciples multiplied in Jerusalem exceedingly; and a great company of the priests were obedient to the faith.
>
> Acts 9:31: So the church . . . was multiplied.
>
> Acts 11:21: A great number that believed turned unto the Lord.
>
> Acts 11:24: Much people was added unto the Lord.
>
> Acts 12:24: The word of God grew and multiplied.
>
> Acts 13:49: The word of the Lord was spread abroad throughout all the region.
>
> Acts 16:5: The churches were strengthened in the faith, and increased in number daily.
>
> Acts 19:10: All they that dwelt in Asia heard the word of the Lord.
>
> Acts 19:20: So mightily grew the word of the Lord and prevailed.

For Luke, then, the analogue is not the process of growth, either in society or in the church.

3. Parables of Contrast?

Certain scholars stress the contrast between the small beginning and the great end-result. Here again opinion bifurcates.

a) Movement and Kingdom

Some find the point of contrast to be between the small moral movement begun by Jesus and the vastness of the coming apocalyptic kingdom of God:

> Small as is the circle which he [Jesus] gathers about himself in comparison with

---

[70]Easton, *Luke*, p. 216; Gilmour, *Luke*, p. 244; Kümmel (for Q), *Promise*, pp. 129-131; Dupont, "Parables," pp. 903, 909.

God's Kingdom, it is none the less certain the Kingdom will come as a result of this moral renewal, restricted as it is in scope.... Watch not only for the harvest, but watch for the Kingdom of God, for the next earthly harvest will be the last and will coincide with the heavenly harvest when the Lord will cause his harvest to be reaped by the angels. The Kingdom of God is at hand.[71]

b) Present Kingdom and Future Kingdom

According to others, the contrast is between the kingdom present in Jesus' ministry and the greatness of the final kingdom. In Jesus' ministry the eschatological sphere of salvation has broken in and is present in a tiny form which one day will be a great tree, the kingdom in the new age.[72]

In regard to both varieties of the contrast theory we may say that since Luke does not mention the smallness of the seed and the largeness of the tree it is questionable that for him the contrast in size is the point of comparison.

4. Parables of Miraculous Results?

This interpretation sees the analogue in the fully-grown tree and the fully-leavened loaf. But here also there are two possibilities:

a) The Kingdom Has Come

The birds are flocking to find shelter in the shade of the tree; the dough is leavened; the kingdom of God has now come; it is present in the ministry of Jesus.[73] But against this and the other views which regard the kingdom as somehow present is the lack of evidence we have found thus far for a realized eschatology in Luke-Acts.

b) The Certainty of the Results

Others think that the analogue is the certainty with which the gardener trusts in the growth of the tree or with which the woman trusts in the working of the sourdough. Luke expresses this same certainty in the powerful, irresistible coming of the future kingdom. Those who know what is happening in the church may anticipate the coming of the kingdom with assurance.[74] That we have at last found the meaning of the twin parables intended by Luke is indicated not only by the objections already raised against alternative views but also by a number of positive considerations.

1) The correct translation of the introductory formula should not be the kingdom is "like unto a grain of mustard seed," but "It is the case with the kingdom

---

[71]Schweitzer, *Mystery*, pp. 108-110, 256; *Quest*, pp. 355-356; Schweitzer is concerned with the meaning of the parables for Jesus, not for Luke; Franklin, *Christ the Lord*, p. 24, also regards these as parables of contrast rather than of growth, parables which point to the final manifestation of the kingdom which is not present on earth, even in Jesus' ministry.

[72]Otto, *Kingdom of God*, pp. 123-125; Ladd, *Presence*, pp. 235-238; neither Otto nor Ladd is concerned primarily with Luke's meaning.

[73]Dodd, *Parables*, pp. 152-154; Dodd is concerned with Jesus' meaning.

[74]Hiers, *Historical Jesus*, p. 16, and *Kingdom of God*, pp. 66-67; cf. Maisch, "Botschaft," pp. 33-36.

of God as with a grain of mustard seed," that is, the kingdom is not compared to the grain of mustard seed but to the tree in whose branches the birds lodge, the tree which shelters the birds being a common metaphor for a kingdom which protects its subjects (Ezek 31:1-9). Similarly, the kingdom of God is not like leaven but is like the risen dough, dough being a metaphor for God's people (Rom 11:16).[75]

2) This futuristic interpretation is underlined by the eschatological overtones of the tree and the great mass of dough. The mustard plant is not a tree and not many housewives would bake some forty-five pounds of bread, sufficient to feed over a hundred persons. These exaggerated features suggest the abundance of the new age, when every man will sit under his own vine and fig tree (Mic 4:4; cf. the tree of life in Rev 22:2). Possibly we have here the reason for Luke's statement that a man planted a grain of mustard seed in his own garden (Matt 13:31, field; Mark 4:31, ground). Luke is alluding to the security and abundance of the new age and new Eden as pictured by Micah and John the Revelator.

Moreover, the tree is a traditional symbol of the new age. The Lord plants a tree upon a "lofty mountain," a tree which shall "bring forth boughs, and bear fruit, . . . and under it shall dwell all birds of every wing; in the shade of the branches thereof shall they dwell" (Ezek 17:22-24; Dan 4:11-12). The birds symbolize Gentiles taking refuge in the kingdom (so also 1 Enoch 90:30-37). Luke's parable is thus saying the same thing as Luke 13:29 states openly:[76] "And they shall come from the east and west, and from the north and south, and shall sit down in the kingdom of God." The fact that the kingdom in 13:29 is futuristic increases the likelihood that the kingdom in the parallel verse 13:19 is also future.

3) This apocalyptic understanding also fits Luke's life situation. As we have noted (Chap. VI.D.5.b), some of Luke's community must have had doubts about the coming of the kingdom. The old faith for them had grown weak. Luke reassures them by pointing to the tree with the birds nesting in its branches and the mass of leavened dough. As the gardener trusts that power is available to cause a tree to grow out of a seed, or, better, creative power to bring life out of death; or as a woman has full confidence in the power of leaven to permeate the dough, so too the Christian of Luke's time may also be absolutely confident that God's mighty action will bring in the eternal kingdom.

At this point we see why Luke does not stress the contrast between the smallness of the seed and the largeness of the tree, for in Luke's time it was no longer a contrast between a handful of Jesus' personal band of followers and the coming of the universal kingdom, for Luke can repeatedly report that the churches are increasing in numbers daily, as we have observed above. But since these numbers would pale in comparison with the might of evil forces in the Mediterranean world the growing size of the church would not prevent many from losing hope. Hence Luke finds the two parables of confidence, as we may call them, to be useful to his eschatological purpose of restoring hope in the coming of the kingdom.

4) This stress upon the kingdom as future rather than as present also fits the context of 13:18-21, which is "heavy with the sense of terrible urgency."[77] In

---

[75] Jeremias, *Parables*, pp. 101-102, 147.

[76] Cf. Manson, *Sayings of Jesus*, p. 415.

[77] Cf. Manson, *Sayings of Jesus*, p. 415.

13:10-17 Jesus looses a woman bound bound eighteen years by Satan, thereby triumphing not only over Satan but also over his human adversaries who oppose healing on the Sabbath. Jesus' double victory over his opposition presages the coming final mighty triumph of the kingdom as symbolized by the tree and the risen dough.

Here we have the explanation of Luke's "therefore" of 13:18, "He said therefore," which we may spell out as follows:

> You people are rightly rejoicing (13:17) over the power which you have seen displayed over Satan and his servants in the synagogue. Therefore let me tell you that this power is like the creative power which you see changing a seed into a tree or leaven into a bushel of dough. This power is a preview of the final victory of the kingdom of God, which will be like a tree sheltering all men, including Gentiles, or like a fully-leavened mass of dough, symbolizing the plenty of the new age.

Further, the very idea of the sabbath also points forward to the new age, which is a sabbath rest. "The sabbath is the image of the world to come" (Genesis Rabbah17; Heb 4:1-11). Moreover, the twin parables are followed by a question about salvation in the future kingdom of God (13:22-24): "Lord, are they few that are saved? And he said . . . , many . . . shall seek to enter in, and shall not be able."

Luke 13 contains an element of imminence, as we have already noted in 13:1-9 (Chap. V.A.F.3) and in 13:22-30, where the householder (=Messiah) rises for the last judgment (13:25) (Chap. IV.G.8), preceding the messianic banquet in the kingdom (13:28-29). The woman (13:10-17) who had been rheumatic for eighteen years could have waited a few more hours until the sabbath was past. But Luke may have thought of Jesus as desirous not only to make a point about sabbath observance but also as wishing to illustrate the urgency of the times by healing at once to underline exorcisms as signs the kingdom is at hand.

This sense of urgency is continued in the parables, for the mustard plant grows quickly to its height of ten feet, being an annual plant, and the leaven works overnight. If Luke and/or Jesus had wanted to illustrate a slow, gradual growth the acorn and oak would have been more apt (cf. Amos 2:9). These parables contemplate at most only a brief process of growth, not one lasting through centuries.[78] Similarly 1 Clement 23 uses a grapevine to indicate the imminence of God's judgment (quoted at Chap. V.F.3).

All of these considerations lead us to conclude that Luke uses the twin parables of confidence to teach, not that the kingdom is present, but that it is surely and speedily coming.

F. Storming into the Kingdom (Luke 16:16c)

1. Literary Analysis

We begin this unit by comparing Luke 16:16 with Matt 11:12-13 in their respective contexts:

---

[78]Craig, "Teaching of Jesus," p. 148; Easton, *Luke*, p. 217.

Matt 11:11-14	Luke 16:14-18
Verily I say unto you, Among them that are born of women there hath not arisen a greater than John the Baptist; yet he that is but little in the kingdom of heaven is greater than he. 12 And from the days of John the Baptist until now the kingdom of heaven suffereth violence (*biadzetai*), and men of violence take it by force. 13 For all the prophets and the law prophesied until John. 14 And if ye are willing to receive it, this is Elijah, that is to come.	And the Pharisees, who were lovers of money, heard all these things; and they scoffed at him. 15 And he said unto them, Ye are they that justify yourselves in the sight of men; but God knoweth your hearts: for that which is exalted among men is an abomination in the sight of God. 16a The law and the prophets were until John: b) from that time the gospel of the kingdom of God is preached, c) and every man entereth violently (*biadzetai*) into it. 17 But it is easier for heaven and earth to pass away, than for one tittle of the law to fall. 18 Every one that putteth away his wife, and marrieth another, committeth adultery: and he that marrieth one that is put away from a husband committeth adultery.

In Matt 11:12 the kingdom of heaven suffers violence; in Luke 16:16 the kingdom of God is preached (*euangelidzō*). Luke's hand is seen here, for *euangelidzō* ("preach the good news") occurs twenty-five times in Luke-Acts, once in Matthew (11:5), and not at all in Mark and John. "To preach the good news of the kingdom of God" is found in the NT only in Luke 4:43; 8:1; 16:16; and Acts 8:12.

The form *biadzetai* may be either middle or passive voice. In Matt 11:12 *biadzetai* is usually taken as passive voice: the kingdom of heaven "suffers violence," or "is violently treated," or "is stormed," or "is taken by force." Some linguists however regard it as middle voice: "the kingdom of heaven exercises force."[79]

In Luke 16:16c *biadzetai* is generally taken as middle voice: every man "entereth violently," or "presses his way into it by force,"[80] or "throws himself into it."[81]

Matthew gives the impression that after John the kingdom of heaven is there! After John there will be no more prophecy because then is the time of fulfillment. But for Luke, after John the kingdom of God is preached. The Lukan formulation takes into account the delay of the parousia.[82]

---

[79]Otto, *Kingdom of God*, p. 108.

[80]Otto, *Kingdom of God*, p. 111.

[81]Godet, *Luke*, II, 172-173.

[82]Bartsch, *Wachet*, p. 82; Kaestli, *Eschatologie*, pp. 25-26.

Matt 11:12-13 and Luke 16:16 appear in different contexts in each gospel. In Matthew, these verses are in Jesus' remarks about John after the departure of John's emissaries (Matt 11:7) and follow directly upon 11:11, "Among them that are born of women . . ." Luke's non-inclusion of Matt 11:14 has already been discussed (Chap. II.C.D).

In Luke, 16:16 is part of a bridge of sayings (16:14-18) between the parables of the dishonest manager (16:1-13) and Dives and Lazarus (16:19-31). This context is the despair of commentators, who have regarded it as an "awkward bridge" or as a "rag-bag collection of sayings." Some conclude that since we can no longer ascertain the connection of 16:16 to its context we must interpret it apart from its immediate context.[83] The three sayings of 16:16-18 appear to be united by the theme of the law, and were perhaps found by Luke already so grouped.

Numerous interpretations of Matt 11:12 have been offered:

> 1) Jesus and the twelve are the men of violence who through exorcisms, especially on the mission of Matthew 10, compel the kingdom to come.[84]
>
> 2) Zealots are the men of violence who have sought to establish the kingdom by force.
>
> 3) The men of violence are those who persecute the church=kingdom of heaven.
>
> 4) The men of violence are enthusiastic, unorthodox people, like the publicans and harlots, who are storming the kingdom.[85]
>
> 5) Demons are the violent ones.[86]
>
> 6) The kingdom exercises force against Satanic forces without man's help; yet men must press into it.[87]

Many would agree that Matt 11:12 is "hopelessly obscure," and is, therefore, the original version of the saying which Luke has tried to explain and adapt.[88] Others find Matt 11:13 as less original than Luke 16:16a. Matthew has reversed "law and prophets" to fit his context about prophets; 16:16b,c are secondary.[89] At any rate, Matt 11:12-13 is of little help in interpreting Luke 16:16.

2. The Kingdom as a Present Realm

Most commentators understand Luke 16:16 as directing attention to the kingdom of God as a present realm or sphere into which men are now entering. The old legalistic barriers are down and the gates of the kingdom are open. All sorts and conditions of men, even the lowest of publicans, are free to press their way into it by responding to the universal preaching of the good news of the kingdom. But the presence of the kingdom demands radical, violent conduct--the

---

[83] Kümmel, "Luke 16:16," p. 404.
[84] Schweitzer, *Mystery*, p. 144.
[85] Box and Allen, in Montefiore, *Gospels*, II, 164.
[86] Dibelius, in Kaestli, *Eschatologie*, p. 24.
[87] Otto, *Kingdom of God*, pp. 108-112.
[88] Easton, *Luke*, p. 249.
[89] Kummel, "Luke 16:16," pp. 409-410.

running of every risk and the making of every sacrifice to obtain one's share in it. To enter into it now, men must agonize (13:24), even to the extent of breaking familial ties, taking up their crosses, and giving up everything (9:59-62; 14:25-33).[90]

3. A Fourth-Century Solution

One way to solve the problem of 16:16c ("and every man entereth violently into it") is to omit it, as did the original version of Codex Sinaiticus (fourth century), the manuscript G (tenth century), and a few others. Even though the witness of the original hand of Sinaiticus is powerful, this omission is not noted by the *Expositor's Greek Testament* nor the *International Critical Commentary* nor Metzger's *Textual Commentary*. A copyist probably omitted 16:16c as "doubtless too difficult."[91] It seems altogether likely, then, that 16:16c was a part of the original text.

4. The Pharisees Speak

A more likely solution has been proposed by F. W. Danker,[92] which we may summarize as follows:

> At Luke 16:16 Jesus quotes the criticism of Pharisees who claim that Jesus has lowered the standards of the kingdom: the kingdom has been proclaimed and popularized, with the result that not only the righteous but everyone, including sinners, forces his way in.
>
> The Pharisees had been murmuring about Jesus' receiving sinners and eating with them (15:1-2). The three parables of forgiveness in chap. 15 give the impression that the kingdom is a gift with no strings attached. But then follows the story of the ingenious factor (16:1-13) out of which emerges the decisive demand, "You cannot serve two masters" (16:13). Man's entry into the kingdom demands devotion to God.
>
> The sayings in 16:17-18 are Jesus' answer to the Pharisees. The kingdom does not prejudice morality. On the contrary, it guarantees it to a degree not approximated by the Pharisees. 16:17 makes it clear that every precept of the law is safeguarded. The Pharisees' exaggerated "everyone" (*pas*) of 16:16 is answered by Jesus' "everyone" (*pas*) of 16:18. "Everyone, including Pharisees, is subject to God's moral demands." The parable of Dives and Lazarus (16:19-31) is about one of those included in the Pharisees' sarcastic "everyone," Lazarus. But whereas the outcasts in Israel recognize the Messiah in their midst and so do justice to Moses and the prophets, the Pharisees who make their boast in the law reject him who is the fulfilment of the law.

Danker's theory that 16:16 expresses the Pharisees' view rather than Jesus' does a certain justice to the linguistic, theological, and contextual puzzles involved in 16:16. But the surprising thing is not noted by Danker, namely, if 16:16 is a logion spoken by the Pharisees in opposition to Jesus, then the kingdom in 16:16 is a future entity, for so it was to the Pharisees:

---

[90]Gilmour, *Luke*, p. 288; Godet, *Luke*, II, 172-173; Ladd, *Presence*, pp. 123, 164, 203; Manson, *Sayings of Jesus*, p. 426; Montefiore, *Gospels*, II, 534; Plummer, *Luke*, p. 389; Schrenk,"*Biadzomai*," p. 613; Stuhlmueller, *Lukan Reading Guide*, p. 114; *Luke*, p. 149.

[91]Easton, *Luke*, p. 248.

[92]Danker, "Luke 16:16," pp. 231-243.

Blessed is he that shall eat bread in the kingdom of God (Luke 14:15).

And being asked by the Pharisees, when the kingdom of God cometh, ... (Luke 17:20).

5. Pressed by Persuasive Preaching

Since *biadzetai* is either middle or passive in form, it is grammatically possible to construe it as passive:[93]

> Everyone is being pressed (urged, constrained) into the kingdom of God by persuasive preaching of the good news of the kingdom.

This translation is also linguistically sound, for *biadzō* does at times refer to gentle persuasion. Jacob urges or presses (*biadzō*) Esau to accept a gift (Gen 33:11). Manoah urges (*biadzō*) an angel to stay (Judg 13:15) (similarly Judg 19:7).

The idea of compulsion by persuasion also fits the whole evangelistic enterprise of Luke-Acts. Luke repeatedly expresses such constraint in connection with the kingdom. Jesus told the multitudes near Capernaum that he "must preach the good tidings of the kingdom of God to the other cites also" (Luke 4:43). Jesus and the twelve "went about through cities and villages, preaching and bringing the good tidings of the kingdom of God" (8:1). Then Jesus sent the twelve forth on a mission "to preach the kingdom of God" (9:2). He welcomed the crowds at Bethsaida and "spake to them of the kingdom of God" (9:11). He commanded a would-be disciple to go "publish abroad the kingdom of God" (9:60). Men and women of Samaria were baptized, having been convinced by Philip's "preaching good tidings concerning the kingdom of God" (Acts 8:12). At Ephesus Paul spoke boldly in the synagogue, "reasoning and persuading as to the things concerning the kingdom of God" (19:8; so also 20:25). To the Jews in Rome Paul, "from morning till night," "explained and gave to them his message about the Kingdom of God," and "he tried to convince them about Jesus" (28:23, TEV) (similarly 28:30-31).

The concept that men are constrained by persuasion to enter into the kingdom is thus an oft-repeated motif of Luke-Acts. Acts 9:22 does not mention the kingdom, but it illustrates the kind of pressure into the kingdom Luke has in mind: "Saul's preaching became even more powerful, and his proofs that Jesus was the Messiah were so strong that the Jews who lived in Damascus could not answer him" (TEV).

This theme of compelling men by persuasion to enter into the kingdom is clearly expressed in the parable of the great supper (Luke 14:15-24). In Luke 14:23, which is peculiar to Luke, the master says to the servant:

> Go out into the highways and hedges, and constrain (*anangkadzō*) them [by persuasion] to come in [to the kingdom], that my house may be filled.

---

[93] As is done by Hilgenfeld (according to Godet, *Luke*, II, 172-173); Wellhausen, *Lucas*, p. 88; Easton, *Luke*, p. 248; and Bartsch, *Wachet*, pp. 46, 82-83. Unfortunately each of these commentators gives little if any explanation of his translation. Schrenk, "*Biadzomai*," p. 612, followed by Kümmel, "Luke 16:16," p. 408, grants that the passive is philologically possible along the lines of Luke 14:23, but finds this view artificial and unsupported by Greek parallels. Our study seeks to show, on the contrary, that the passive makes good sense for Luke.

Here Luke does not refer to constraint by physical force, for such could hardly have been exercised by a single servant.[94] Rather he has in mind the gentle persuasion befitting oriental courtesy which would be used to overcome the modesty and reluctance which these poor people would naturally feel at accepting the invitation of a great lord.[95] *Anangkadzō* here, like *biadzō* in Gen 33:11 and Judg 13:15, is thus used of genteel restraint. And this is the ruling idea of Luke 16:16 and of the evangelistic efforts throughout Luke-Acts: Just as people are being taken by the hand and gently constrained to come to a banquet, so too people are being pressed by persuasive preaching of the good news of the kingdom to enter into it.

Another parallel between 16:16 and 14:23 is found in the limited universality of the kingdom implied in each passage. The "every one" of 16:16 is undoubtedly hyperbolic, for many according to Luke-Acts are not accepting the invitation. Some translations bring out the correct meaning by rendering *pas* as "every sort of person" (NWT) or "all classes" (Weymouth).[96] Likewise in the parable and in Luke-Acts as a whole "every sort of person" is being compelled to come into the kingdom. It is in this sense that 16:16 and 14:23 are universalistic.

If 16:16 and 14:23 are parallel in respect to the width of the kingdom and the type of force used to compel all sorts of men to enter that kingdom, then it is likely that these verses are also parallel in their view of the kingdom as present or future. There is no question about the futurity of the kingdom in 14:23. Jesus' dinner companions are Pharisees, who think of the kingdom as a future reality: "And being asked by one of the Pharisees, when the kingdom of God cometh, .. (17:20). At this particular meal one of those sitting at table comments: "Blessed is he that shall eat bread in the kingdom of God" (14:15). And the parable concludes: "For I say unto you, that none of those men that were bidden shall taste of my supper" (14:24). It may be of some significance too that Luke 16:16 is in a context concerned with Pharisees (16:14-15). The parallelism between 16:16 and 14:23 would then indicate that the kingdom in 16:16 is also a coming event. Thus 16:16 would read:

> All sorts of people are being compelled by persuasion now to accept the good news of the kingdom of God so that they may enter the kingdom when it comes.

6. Agonizing into the Kingdom

If one is not satisfied with the prevailing understanding of 16:16 as realized eschatology, yet does not want to omit 16:16c, nor attribute it to the Pharisees, nor render it with the passive voice, there is yet another possible interpretation: one may regard 16:16c as parallel with 13:24:

> Strive (*agōnidzomai*) to enter in by the narrow door: for many, I say unto you, shall seek to enter in, and shall not be able.

The "many" of 13:24 is comparable to the hyperbolic "all" of 16:16, which, as we have previously remarked, means "every sort of person" (NWT) or "all

---

[94] *Anangkadzō* appears in Matt 14:22//Mark 6:45; Luke 14:23; Acts 26:11; 28:19; 2 Cor 12:11; Gal 2:3,14; 6:12. Only in Acts 26:11 does it mean physical force: Paul tortured God's people, forcing them (*anangkadzō*) to blaspheme.

[95] Vincent, *Word Studies*, I, 381; Jeremias, *Parables*, p. 177.

[96] Another hyperbolic "all" is found in Luke 3:21.

classes" (Weymouth).

The verbs *biadzō* (exercise force, suffer violence, enter by force, act with gusto, effort, strength)(16:16) and *agōnidzomai* (struggle, fight, do one's best, compete)[97](13:24) are similar in meaning, as is reflected in the various translations:

Luke 13:24

Strain every nerve to force your way in (Weymouth).
You must struggle on to get in (Williams).
Fight your way in (R. Knox) (Chap. VIII.E.8).
You must do your utmost to get in (Phillips).

These translations are saying that "the entrance is narrow, and it is a case of struggling through rather than strolling in."[98]

Luke 16:16

All classes have been forcing their way into it (Weymouth).
Everyman entereth violently into it (ASV).
Anyone presses in (Moffatt).
Everyone has been crowding into it (Goodspeed).
Everyone is storming his way into it (Rieu).
They come crowding in (Norlie).

It would seem probable that two statements so alike in thought would also share the same concept of the kingdom, that is, futuristic, as in 13:24, whose context is concerned with future salvation (13:23), the messianic banquet in the future kingdom (13:28-29), and the coming kingdom symbolized by the fully-grown mustard tree and the fully-leavened loaf (13:18-21) (Chap. VII.E). 16:16 is also located in a futuristic context. The point of the parable of the ingenious factor (16:1-13) is "Act now, for the judgment is near. Make to yourselves friends by means of almsgiving, so that when this world comes to an end they may receive you into the eternal tents of the new age" (Chap. III.F). The passing away of heaven and earth (16:17) has apocalyptic overtones, and the story of Dives and Lazarus (16:19-31) pictures the intermediate state preceding the resurrection and the kingdom (Chap. III.B).

The possibility that the kingdom of 16:16 is futuristic is enhanced if we translate *eis* (to, into, toward) as "toward": "Every sort of person is pressing forward toward it" (NWT). The kingdom is not here yet but men are moving toward the impending reality.[99] BAG[100] lists four instances in Luke-Acts where *eis* means "toward": Jesus raised his eyes "toward his disciples" (Luke 6:20) and "looked up toward heaven" (9:16). The women bowed down their faces "toward the ground" (24:5), and Paul "looked up toward Ananias" (Acts 22:13). There seems to be no lexical reason, then, why Luke did not mean *eis* as "toward" in 16:16c. To translate *eis* here as "toward" strengthens the parallelism between

---

[97]The kindred noun *agōnia* is used in Luke 22:44 of Jesus' struggle in Gethsemane.

[98]Manson, *Sayings of Jesus*, p. 417.

[99]The NWT translators, however, regard the kingdom in 16:16 as present. "Here we see that Jesus is referring to the kingdom as being in the present into which or toward which Jews like the disciples were pressing to become part of along with Christ Jesus" (letter, 28 April 1976, from Watchtower Bible and Tract Society of New York, Inc).

[100]BAG, p. 227.

16:16 and 13:24: As in 13:24 men are striving to enter into the kingdom when it comes, so also in 16:16 men are pressing forward toward the approaching kingdom.

If we read 16:16 together with 13:24 we shall not only avoid the error of finding realized eschatology in 16:16 but we shall also keep from exaggerating the universalism of 16:16 ("everyone has been crowding into it") and the attendant lowering of the moral requirements of the kingdom, even to the point of antinomianism ("anyone presses in"). At 13:24 Jesus admonishes men to "strain every nerve to force their way into the kingdom through the narrow gate." Later at 16:16 he can report that "they come crowding in." But 13:24 reminds us that since the gate is narrow multitudes will endeavor to find a way in but will not succeed, like masses of war refugees crowding the last plane out.

Chap. 16 itself also checks the seeming antinomian and absolutely universalistic implications of 16:16c. Dives is straining every nerve to enter the kingdom, but he began too late (16:26). Dives is one of the "sons of this age" (16:8), as are other lovers of money (16:14), Pharisees (16:15), and those who live in adultery (16:18). On the other hand, only the "sons of light" (16:8), such as Lazarus (16:19-31) and those who use wisely transitory goods (16:1-13), will succeed in pressing their way through the narrow door of the coming kingdom.

Far from being antinomian, the gospel of the coming kingdom is such that even the smallest hook on a Hebrew letter of the law will last until the old heaven and earth pass away (16:17). The law of divorce, by way of example, is much more stringent now (16:18) than under Moses, who permitted divorce for a wide variety of reasons (Deut 24:1). Even the resurrection of Jesus does not end the usefulness of Moses and the prophets in their role of leading men to the kingdom (16:27-31)(cf. Gal. 3:24). This very permanence of the law (16:17-18, 29-31) leads to the rejection of the Pharisees (16:14-15, 19-31), whose boast was in the law. "What is exalted among men" (16:15), such as the Pharisees, or Dives, is an "abomination in the sight of God" (16:15), as illustrated by Dives in Hades (16:19-31). And if one needs further proof that the good news of the kingdom is not destroying morality, he need only remember that it is better to be cast into the sea with a millstone round his neck than to cause a disciple to sin (17:12). Seen in this light, 16:16 is not antinomian and absolutely universalistic, nor is 16:14-18 an awkward bridge between two parables or a rag-bag collection of sayings.

We may also note that the throngs of all sorts and conditions of men who are trying to crowd their way into the kingdom will not all be able to enter not only because of the narrow door of high morality but also because entrance into the kingdom is through "many tribulations" (Acts 14:22). Many who have received the word with joy will in time of tribulation fall away (Luke 8:13) rather than agonize into the kingdom.

7. Conclusion

Although the prevailing interpretation of Luke 16:16c as present eschatology cannot be completely disproved, we have presented four alternative solutions, any one of which may be correct. The manuscripts which omit 16:16c could have preserved the original reading. Possibly the Pharisees, who assumed that the kingdom is a futuristic reality (14:15; 17:20b), are expressing their criticism of Jesus' popularization of the kingdom. Too little attention, however, has been given to the possibility that *biadzetai* should be translated in the passive voice, a translation which would make 16:16c parallel in thought to 14:23. Or if *biadzetai* is middle voice then 16:16c is likely parallel with 13:24. When these dimensions of *biadzetai* are given full consideration we can see that there is no necessity to ascribe to Luke a realized view of the kingdom at 16:16c in contradiction to our findings elsewhere in Luke-Acts. Expressed positively, it is quite probable that at 16:16c Luke thought of the kingdom as futuristic as in 13:24 ("... many, .. shall seek to enter in, ..."), 14:15 ("Blessed is he that shall eat bread in the kingdom of God"), 14:23 ("Constrain them to come in"), and 17:20b ("And being asked by the Pharisees, when the kingdom of God cometh, ..").

G. "Look, Here It Is!" (Luke 17:20-21)

1. Introduction

The little exchange in Luke 17:20-21 between Jesus and the Pharisees has occasioned many interpretations.[101] Some have found the meaning too uncertain to be used for further argument.[102] Others regard Jesus' answer to the Pharisees as a riddle which can be understood only by those whose faith enables them to connect the kingdom of God with Jesus the Messiah.[103] But though the majority of commentators have been more or less baffled by this saying, at least one can declare that this "pithy logion" is "precise and immediately clear in a way surpassed by no other saying of Jesus." Its point is "obvious and absolutely unmistakable," "unequivocally intelligible."[104] But regardless of the degree of clarity of the pericope, it is probably true to observe that "it is possible to study how each expositor in the last analysis is guided by his dogmatic presuppositions."[105] We shall endeavor to add a degree of clarity and objectivity to the exposition by examining three problems of translation (Sections 3, 4, 5) and five major interpretations of our passage (Sections 6-10).

2. The Text

For easy reference it is convenient to subdivide the verses of Luke 17:20-24:

20a. And being asked by the Pharisees,

20b. when the kingdom of God cometh,

20c. he answered them and said,

20d. The kingdom of God cometh not with observation:

21a. neither shall they say, Lo, here! or There!

---

[101]For the history of interpretation see Noack, *Luke 17:20-24*, and Sneed, *Kingdom's Coming*, pp. 6-41, who reviews and updates Noack. Grässer, *Delay*, p. 194, links 17:20-21 to Luke's denial of the imminent expectation. Luke says it is impossible to ask about the time of the kingdom's arrival, since this time lies in the distant future.

[102]Weinel, *Biblische Theologie des Neuen Testaments*, 1911, p. 52, cited by Easton, "Luke 17:20-21," p. 280.

[103]Mussner, "Luke 17:20b-21," p. 110.

[104]Otto, *Kingdom of God*, p. 131.

[105]Flender, *Luke*, p. 150.

21b. for lo, the kingdom of God is within you [margin: in the midst of you].

22a. And he said unto the disciples,

22b. The days will come, when ye shall desire to see one of the days of the Son of man,

22c. and ye shall not see it.

23a. And they shall say to you, Lo, there! Lo, here!

23b. go not away, nor follow after them:

24a. for as the lightning, when it shineth out of the one part under the heaven, shineth unto the other part under heaven;

24b. so shall the Son of man be in his day.

3. "With Observation"

The first problem of translation is found in v 20d, *meta paratēreseōs*, which ASV translates "with observation." The noun *paratērēsis* is found only here in the NT. In classical Greek it is used of observation of the stars, that is, observation of the future by certain signs.[106] The related verb, *paratēreō*, appears in Mark 3:2; Luke 6:7; 14:1; 20:20; Acts 9:24; and Gal 4:10. In Luke-Acts it is used of scribes, Pharisees, and Jews watching Jesus and Paul as closely and maliciously as a cat a mouse. We look briefly at four possible meanings of *paratērēsis*.

a) Predictability.--This understanding of *meta paratēreseōs* is reflected in RSV, "The kingdom of God is not coming with signs to be observed" (17:20d). The verse is negating chronological calculation of the time of the end, the belief that by observation of the movement of heavenly bodies, woes, wars, family strife, social collapse, natural disasters, and the breakup of the cosmic order one can predict the moment the kingdom will appear. This negation of predictability is thus opposed to the method of apocalyptic.

b) Visibility.--"The Kingdom of God does not come in such a way as to be seen" (17:20d) (TEV). As this translation has it, the kingdom is invisible in its coming. The verse negates visibility and externality. The kingdom does not come "with outward show" (KJV margin; Luther). It comes "unwatched by men's eyes" (R. Knox). It "does not admit of observation" (Jerusalem Bible). It is not coming "visibly" (Goodspeed).

If, however, 17:22-37 is a commentary upon 17:20-21 then this negation of visibility collides with 17:22-37, where the coming of the kingdom is pictured as an objective, cosmic event visible to all, not a subjective, invisible end. On the other hand, it is possible that Luke has made an intentional contrast between the kingdom as invisibly present (17:20-21) and as objectively future (17:22-37). But the marked parallelism between 17:21a and 17:23a suggests that Luke intended 17:20-21 and 17:22-37 to interpret each other:

> 21a. neither shall they say, Lo, here! or There!
> 23a. And they shall say to you, Lo, there! Lo, here! (Chap. VII.G.6.g).

Whether a) negation of predictability, or b) negation of visibility is correct can be determined less by linguistic considerations than by the context. Whether negation of signs means negation of all signs, both those preliminary to the

---

[106]*BAG*, p. 628.

coming of the kingdom and those accompanying the coming, or only the negation of accompanying signs must also be determined largely by the context. Since Luke features preliminary signs in his apocalypse of chap. 21, especially 21:29-31, it would seem that Luke 17:20d means for Luke that the kingdom comes without accompanying signs.

c) *Passover Eschatology*.--According to this interpretation,[107] *paratērēsis* is not concerned with apocalyptic calculation based upon observation of heavenly signs or signs of the time but is a technical term connected with the Hebraic calendar and the passover festival. Its background is found in Exod 12:42: "It [the night of the passover and exodus] is a night of watching unto Yahweh for bringing them out from the land of Egypt." In the Jewish passover eschatology, Israel's end-time redemption, like that from Egypt, will be on passover night, the night of watching or observation. Luke recognized that this fixing of a date on the calendar for the final redemption was just as contrary to the spirit of Jesus as the esoteric apocalyptic calculation of the day and hour which Luke also opposed (Acts 1:7). Thus Luke's polemic is directed against the Pharisees (Luke 17:20a), who were the chief advocates of this passover expectation. However, the primitive Christian *Naherwartung* was not uninfluenced by this passover eschatology, which became a passover-parousia-expectation, dating the parousia on the night of the passover, the fourteenth of Nisan. Luke 17:20d would thus dissociate the coming of the kingdom from this date.

Strobel's view has been rejected by Conzelmann and Rüstow on the grounds that Luke did not know the passover haggada or ritual, as his passion narrative reveals. Rüstow nevertheless feels that Strobel's interpretation would hold for Jesus and the Pharisees, who did know the passover haggada. Rüstow, contrary to Strobel, would not limit Luke 17:20d to passover eschatology but would include in it a disavowal of every kind of calculation.[108]

d)*Legality*.--It is possible that the Peshitta (=general) translation of the NT into Syriac may read at Luke 17:20d, "the kingdom of God does not come with observation of the law,"[109] a statement with which Luke would probably agree, even if he did not have it in mind at 17:20d. Some support for this interpretation is found in the fact that Josephus, *Antiquities* 8.96, mentions the observation (*paratērēsis*) of legal prescriptions.

4. "Is"

The problem here is the force of the present tense "is" (*estin*) in 17:21b: "The kingdom of God *is* within you." It could be a strict present, emphasizing the time of speaking: "The kingdom exists already." This meaning would fit those interpretations of 17:21b which regard the kingdom as a present reality.

Or "is" could be a futuristic or apocalyptic present, which speaks of a future reality as if it were already present. Such a present is found in 17:20b, where the

---

[107] A.Strobel,"Passa-Erwartung," pp. 157-183. Strobel was preceded by A. Merx, *Die vier kanonischen Evangelien*, II, 2, 1905, 345 (cited by Strobel, "Passa-Erwartung," pp. 133-134).

[108] Rüstow, "Luke 17:20-21," pp. 200-201. Sneed, *Kingdom's Coming*, pp. 51-54, 65-67, also offers a critique of Strobel's thesis.

[109] See Noack, *Luke 17:20-24*, pp. 5-6, and Sneed, "Luke 17:21," p. 374, who stresses the correspondence between Luke 17:20-21 and Rom 14:17.

Pharisees ask "when the kingdom of God cometh," that is, when it will come. Also in v 20d "cometh" means "will come." This rendition of "is" would harmonize with the futuristic views of the kingdom in 17:2b.

Once more the problem must be solved on other than grammatical bases. "As far as the form [*estin*] is concerned there is no way of settling the question."[110]

5. "Within"

The central problem of translation which we face in Luke 17:20-21 is that of *entos*. Does it mean "within," "among," or something else? In Appendix A we shall deal thoroughly with the evidence. Now we simply state in advance our conclusion: *entos* has four meanings which are applicable to Luke 17:21b: within the interior of, in the midst of, within the power of, and a group within a group. We turn to a presentation and critique of the various interpretations of 17:21b based upon these four relevant meanings of *entos*.

6. "Within You"

According to this view, which was held by all but one or two interpreters of the ancient and medieval church[111] and is still supported by many moderns,[112] the kingdom of God is within you=within your hearts. The kingdom is an inner, mystical, spiritual presence and principle, an interior disposition, a psychological reality, the inner condition of the souls of the faithful. Wherever a heart is properly inclined toward God, there is the kingdom of God, a kingdom which, therefore, is not something outward or material or local, somewhere externally visible, but is an unseen spiritual presence which regenerates the hearts of men. Hence it is impossible to localize the kingdom by pointing to it and saying, "Look, here it is!" or, "There it is!" The time and the place of the kingdom are not only unknown to men but the kingdom is nothing which appears at a definite moment at a definite time. It is neither the church nor a reign which follows a cosmic catastrophe. It is the rule of God in the hearts of men.

Although this understanding has been "sanctioned by a tradition of exegesis almost unbroken until modern times,"[113] there are real difficulties with it. a) We shall note in Appendix A in our discussion of the meaning of *entos* that though "within you" is linguistically possible the parallels are not close enough in

---

[110]Easton, "Luke 17:20-21," p. 277.

[111]See Noack, *Luke 17:20-24*, p. 15. These include Oxyrhynchus Papyrus 654 (see Noack, *Luke 17:20-24*, pp. 4-5; Rüstow, "Luke 17:20-21," pp. 221-223), Syriac Peshitta, Latin versions, Gospel according to Thomas, Hippolytus, Gregory of Nyssa, Chrysostom, Origen, Athanasius, Ambrose, Jerome, Bede, Luther, and KJV.

[112]Creed, *Luke*, p. 219; Dodd, *Parables*, pp. 62-63; Godet, *Luke*, II, 193-194; Harnack (cited by Noack, *Luke 17:20-24*, p. 36); Plummer, *Luke*, p. 406 (as a possibility); Sneed, "Luke 17:21," pp. 380-382; Stuhlmueller, *Luke*, p. 150; TEV; Wellhausen, *Lucas*, p. 95. Streeter, *Four Gospels*, p. 290, accepts "within you" as the correct meaning, and conjectures that Matthew omitted this saying from Q because it "suggested a view of the Kingdom which Matthew, who more than any other evangelist emphasises the objective catastrophic side of the Apocalyptic hope, believed to be incorrect."

[113]Roberts, "Kingdom of Heaven," p. 1. Roberts himself regards the objections both to "within you" and "among you" as "insuperable."

structure and thought to be compelling. If Jesus and/or Luke had desired to say "the kingdom is in your hearts" they could have done so very easily, as is shown by such passages as these, which use "in" (*en*) rather than *entos*:

> The word is very near thee, in thy mouth and in thy heart (*en tē kardia sou*) (Deut 30:14)(LXX) (so also Rom 10:8-9). Mischief is in their hearts (*en tais kardiais autōn*) (Ps 27:3=28:3) (LXX).

b) In Luke's context the kingdom on this view is said to be within the Pharisees (17:21b). But these are the very persons in whose hearts the kingdom "pre-eminently was not."[114] The kingdom as a condition of the soul could not be ascribed less to anyone than to the Pharisees, who, by their fully inappropriate question prove how far they are from such a condition of the soul.[115] Such an answer by Jesus would have left him or Luke open to the retort, "Why then are you in open opposition to us?"[116]

Whether or not the Pharisees were the addressees of the original statement is not our concern here, for to Luke they are the hearers. This fact weakens somewhat the force of the argument just presented, for according to Luke the Pharisees are not so evil as often thought. When Jesus heals the paralytic, the Pharisees glorified God and were filled with awe (Luke 5:17,21,26). Three times Jesus dines in homes of Pharisees (7:36; 11:37; 14:1). Some Pharisees warn Jesus that Herod wants to kill him (13:31). Gamaliel advises the Sanhedrin to leave the apostles alone (Acts 5:34). Some of the disciples are Pharisees (Acts 15:5). Paul lives as a Pharisee (Acts 23:6; 26:5). Pharisees on the Sanhedrin defend Paul against the Sadducees (Acts 23:6-9). When Luke is writing in this vein he might conceivably think of the kingdom as being in the hearts of Pharisees.

On the other hand, the Pharisees, by refusing to be baptized by John, reject the purpose of God (Luke 7:30). Inside of them (*to esōthen humōn*) the Pharisees are full of extortion and wickedness (11:39). They neglect justice and love of God (11:42). They are like unmarked graves (11:44), and their leaven is hypocrisy (12:1). They are lovers of money instead of servers of God (16:14). An unjustified Pharisee is a type of the damned (18:9-14). These verses together, if not 11:39 by itself, would seem to exclude Luke's thinking of the kingdom as being within the Pharisees.

Yet Luke also may have a doctrine of the natural goodness of man. The heart is good and honest before the word of God makes it so (Luke 8:15). "In every nation he feareth him, and worketh righteousness, is acceptable to him" (Acts 10:35), such as Cornelius (10:2,4,22,30-32), Julius (27:3), and the barbarians (28:2). It is here that we can see some justification for Gregory of Nyssa's variant of the view that the kingdom is "within you." According to Gregory, the kingdom is the image of God which God places in every man at birth. Man should cleanse himself from evil in order that the beauty concealed in the soul may appear. This beauty can be overgrown by the cares and pleasures of life, but if one will kindle the light of the word and seek it out, one will find it. God's kingdom is thus the

---

[114]Easton, "Luke 17:20-21," p. 278.

[115]Rüstow, "Luke 17:20-21," p. 208.

[116]Manson, *Sayings of Jesus*, p. 304.

goodness of God which God has placed within man.[117] Luke would perhaps agree with Gregory's doctrine of man and we cannot absolutely exclude the possibility that Luke at 17:20-21 was thinking of the kingdom as this God-given goodness and beauty of the soul.

Luke too may have taken the "you" of 17:21b impersonally. It is "a stereotyped phrase employed whenever anything is said about the coming kingdom."[118] But when all relevant factors are considered it seems more likely that if Luke had meant to say that the kingdom is somehow present in men's hearts he would not have said "within you" but "within the heart," "within men's hearts," or "within men" (Chap. VII.G.6.a).[119]

c) The kingdom as a spiritual state is contrary to the objective, realistic, cosmic conception of the kingdom in Luke-Acts and elsewhere in the synoptics, where it is presented as the new age which will succeed this age, and perhaps is breaking in on this age. This "abstract idea of a wholly spiritual and moral presence of the Kingdom in the hearts of men is ... foreign to the Gospel, and it may be said to the whole Bible."[120] An inner condition of the soul "may qualify for admission to the Kingdom, but it is not itself the Kingdom."[121] Elsewhere in the gospels "it is man that enters into the Kingdom, not the Kingdom into man."[122] "The whole language of the kingdom of heaven being within men, rather than of men being within the kingdom, is modern."[123]

Why, then, has this spiritualistic view of the kingdom persisted into the present?

> It is natural that the modern commentator who likes to pare off from Jesus' teaching as much of the miraculous, or 'Jewish,' or political, or 'material' element as he can, and to read into or out of it as much spiritual, universalist, and permanent teaching as possible, is often keen to adopt and justify this interpretation.... It suits modern spiritual teaching so well. And how constantly are we told that here is the essence of the teaching of Jesus about the Kingdom![124]

d) Nor does this concept of the kingdom as a psychological reality fit the future tense, "shall they say" (17:21a), which naturally refers to a future event rather than to a present condition: "When the kingdom comes in the future, then people will not say, 'Lo, here!' or 'There!'" If the kingdom is in the heart, then v 21a should read something like one of the following:

> Nor shall anyone ever be able to say, "Lo, here!" or "There!"[125]

---

[117]Gregory of Nyssa, "On Virginity," xii; "On the Beatitudes," i; Plummer, *Luke*, p. 406; Noack, *Luke 17:20-24, p. 11.*

[118]*Otto, Kingdom of God*, p. 135.

[119]Cf. Easton, "Luke 17:20-21," p. 279.

[120]Loisy, cited by Montefiore, *Gospels*, II, 549; likewise Rüstow, "Luke 17:20-21," p. 208; Gilmour, *Luke*, p. 300; Bundy, *Gospels*, p. 388.

[121]Creed, *Luke*, p. 219.

[122]Manson, *Sayings of Jesus*, pp. 595-597, cited with approval by Roberts, "Kingdom of Heaven," p. 2.

[123]Trench, quoted by Vincent, *Word Studies*, I, 401.

[124]Montefiore, *Gospels*, II, 547.

[125]Haupt, cited by Easton, "Luke 17:20-21," p. 278.

it cannot now be said, "Lo, here!" or "There!"[126]

From now on no one will be saying, "Lo, here!" or "There!"

e) Luke 17:20b ("when the kingdom of God cometh"), 17:20d ("The kingdom of God cometh not with observation"), and 17:21a ("neither shall they say, Lo, here! or There!") all suppose the kingdom to be a future reality. Hence it seems unlikely that Jesus and/or Luke is correcting the tense of the Pharisees but rather he is rebuking their reliance on observation of accompanying signs. There is no "emphatic change of time from future to present."[127]

f) Nor does this psychological view of the kingdom explain why those of v 21a will be silent and will not say "Here!" or "There!", whereas they will, according to v 23a, speak out with "There!" and "Here!" It is possible, however, that Luke does not mean to imply a future moment of silence. He may mean, "Neither will they say" (with any reason).[128] That is, they will say, "Lo, here!", but it will be a groundless statement.

g) Neither does this view of an internalized kingdom go well with the lightning flashes and fire and brimstone of the end events described in 17:22-30. It could be held that vv 22-30 are by way of contrast to vv 20-21, but Luke by the parallelism between v 21a and v 23a, each followed by "for" (*gar*)(vv 21b, 24a) indicates that he intends vv 22-30 to be an explication of vv 20-21 (Chap. VII.G.3.b).

Yet in spite of these weighty objections, we cannot completely rule out the possibility that "Luke believed that Jesus set the spiritual presence of the Kingdom in men's hearts in antithesis to the expectation of its appearance 'here' or 'there'. But even if this be so, the eschatological conception is by no means superseded in the mind of the evangelist, or eliminated from his Gospel."[129] But in view of all the evidence we have about Luke's eschatology I am convinced that we would be correct in saying that it is highly improbable that Luke understood 21:21b in a spiritualized sense.

7. "In Your Midst" Now

a) Luke and "In Your Midst."--The prevailing view today is that *entos humoñ* in Luke 17:21b means "in your midst." That this view is linguistically possible is shown in Appendix A. But a weighty objection to the translation of *entos humōn* in 17:21b as "in the midst of you" is the fact that whenever Luke elsewhere means "in the midst of" he does not use *entos* but *en mesō*:

> Luke 2:46: Jesus sitting in the midst of (*en mesō*) the teachers.
>
> Luke 8:7: Other seed fell amidst of (*en mesō*) the thorns.
>
> Luke 10:3: As lambs in the midst of (*en mesō*) wolves.
>
> Luke 21:21: Let them that are in the midst of (*en mesō*) her depart.
>
> Luke 22:27: I am in the midst of you (*en mesō humōn*) as he that serveth.

---

[126] Montefiore, *Gospels*, II, 548.

[127] Cadbury, "Eschatology," p. 315.

[128] Plummer, *Luke*, p. 406.

[129] Creed, *Luke*, p. 219.

Luke 22:55: A fire in the midst of (*en mesō*) the court.

Luke 24:36: He himself stood in the midst of (*en mesō*) them.

Acts 1:15: Peter stood up in the midst of (*en mesō*) the brethren.

Acts 2:22: Signs which God did by him in the midst of you (*en mesō humōn*).

Acts 17:22: Paul stood in the midst of (*en mesō*) the Areopagus.

Acts 27:21: Paul stood forth in the midst of (*en mesō*) them.

Luke 22:27 and Acts 2:22 are deserving of special notice, for they contain precisely the form Luke would be expected to use were he to say "the kingdom is in the midst of you" (*en mesō humōn*). Rüstow contends that in view of Luke's uniform usage of *en mesō* for "in the midst of" we may confidently say that Luke must have written *en mesō* if he had meant "in the midst of you."[130] It is true that Luke's usage of *en mesō* does establish a certain probability that if he were forming 17:21b himself he would use *en mesō*. But to say that he must have done so is going too far, for Luke may simply have taken over a statement from the tradition which he, out of respect for his source, did not change.[131] Moreover, Luke may have seen no need to substitute *en mesō* for *entos*, for, as we shall see in Appendix A, *entos* can mean "in the midst of," and there is at least one instance (Exod 34:9) where Symmachus and Theodotion use *en mesō* where Aquila uses *entos*, which suggests that Luke would have had no hesitation in reading *entos* as "in the midst of." But even if one decides that *entos humōn* does mean "in your midst," one must still choose among various interpretations of Luke 17:21b, which we shall now evaluate.

b) The Church.--Some have understood the saying in 17:21b to mean that the kingdom is God's reign in your midst as the salvation brought by Christ and realized in the church.[132] This view however runs afoul of the fact that for Luke the kingdom is not the church (Chap. V.C.5; VII.E.2.b).

c) Society.--Others have taken "the kingdom in your midst" as imminent in society which will be transformed gradually into an ideal social order on earth. But to strip the kingdom of its eschatological features and reduce it to something present and growing in the world would be a modern view which we cannot conceive in Luke (Chap. VII.E.2.a).[133]

d) Jesus and Disciples.--Many think "the kingdom in your midst" is the kingdom present in the midst of men, especially in Jesus' own person and works and those of his disciples. At least in its first dawning the kingdom has descended with power and broken into the world. Satan has fallen (Luke 10:18). Demons are cast out (11:20). The righteousness, peace, and joy of the kingdom (Rom 14:17) are present now as the first fruits of final salvation in the coming eschatological order. The presence of the kingdom "among you" eliminates apocalyptic methods of observation (chronological calculation) and local determinations ("Lo, here!"). All talk of "Here" or "There" is foolish, for the kingdom of God is not

---

[130] Rüstow, "Luke 17:20-21," p. 213.

[131] Easton, "Luke 17:20-21," p. 277; Mussner, "Luke 17:20b-21," p. 109.

[132] Loisy, *L'Evangile selon Luc*, 1924, pp. 428-431, cited by Montefiore, *Gospels*, II, 549, and by Noack, *Luke 17:20-24*, p. 31.

[133] Cf. Otto, *Kingdom of God*, p. 137.

related to place or space but is something dynamic.[134]

To its credit, this view does fit the present tense "is" (*estin*) in Luke 17:21b: the kingdom *is* present. But if Luke here were using the strict present tense he would be expected to put "is" in an emphatic, early position in the sentence to make it plain that there is a marked change from the Pharisees' futuristic conception of the kingdom. But instead of that Luke has placed "is" in the most unemphatic position possible as the last word in the sentence. Luke reads, "The kingdom of God in the midst of you is." To make obvious a shift from future to present he would probably have written, "The kingdom of God *is* in the midst of you," or even "*Is* the kingdom of God in the midst of you." "Is" as the first word in the sentence is found in Deut 30:14: "Is the word very near thee . . . and in thy heart." Moreover, if "is" were used in the strict present tense, it would imply that the kingdom is present already: it already exists. But "already" is not in the text.[135]

The view that the kingdom is present in the midst of Jesus and disciples, like other present views, has difficulty with the future tense of v 21a ("neither shall they say"), which presupposes the kingdom is still in the future. Nor does it eliminate the clash between the silence of v 21a and the speaking out of v 23a. Further, the kingdom "in your midst" would also be localized and thus would not exclude "Here!" and "There!"[136]

8. "In Your Midst" in the Future

It is possible to translate *entos humōn* as "in your midst" and posit a future rather than a present realization of the kingdom. There are at least four varieties of this futuristic interpretation.

a) An Apocalyptic "Is."--Some intepreters render "is" as "shall be": "The kingdom cometh not so that it can be predicted by observation of signs. Neither shall they say, 'Lo, here!' or 'There!' for, lo, the kingdom of God shall be in your midst. When it comes its appearance will be unmistakable, for it will be visible to all."[137] We have seen in Section 4 that this apocalyptic use of "is" is justified both grammatically and in terms of the futuristic context of vv 20b ("when the kingdom cometh") and 20d ("the kingdom of God cometh not with observation"). The future tense of various verbs appears in vv 21a; 22b,c; 23a; 24b; 26; 30; 31; 33; 34; 35; 36; and 37.

> All the sayings in Luke 17:20-18:8 have to do with the coming of the Kingdom of God and the Son of man, and with the responses men will or should make in the interim and at the time the Kingdom and Son of man are revealed. Throughout all this section it is clear that these decisive events are to take place in the future.[138]

---

[134]Ellis, *Luke*, pp. 155, 210-211; Moore, *Parousia*, p. 196; Otto, *Kingdom of God*, pp. 131-137; Plummer, *Luke*, p. 406; Schlatter, *Das Evangelium des Lukas,* 1931 (cited by Noack, *Luke 17:20-24*, pp. 33-34).

[135]On these points see Godet, *Luke*, II, 194; Easton, "Luke 17:20-21," p. 280. Some grammarians, however, would question Godet and Easton on the emphatic position. Green, *Handbook*, p. 350, states: "Generally speaking, the emphatic positions are at the beginning and the end of a clause, especially the former." Plummer, *Luke*, p. 415, comments on Luke 18:8: "*en tachei* [speedily] is placed last with emphasis."

[136]Dodd, *Parables*, pp. 62-63.

[137]Easton, "Luke 17:20-21," pp. 275-283; *Luke*, pp. 261-263.

[138]Hiers, *Kingdom of God*, p. 28.

Moreover, says Easton, on this futuristic interpretation the unemphatic position of "is" at the very end of the Greek sentence (17:21b) is "exactly what would be needed now."[139] Again, if 17:23-24 is a variant of 17:20-21,[140] it would seem that since the former is futuristic the latter must be also. But the "great advantage" of this view is that "it brings vss. 20-21 into close connection with what follows, so that vss. 22-37 are simply an expansion of vss. 20-21."[141]

The chief objection to this view is that simply to say that the kingdom of God when it comes will be among you would be "a pure superfluity, for that the kingdom was to be among them some day the questioners themselves knew. They are asking when it would come."[142]

b) Apocalyptic Suddenness.--To retain the advantages of a futuristic interpretation while avoiding a superfluous statement about the coming of the kingdom, many commentators interpolate the word "suddenly" into the text:

> The kingdom of God is suddenly among you. It is idle for men to say, "Lo, here is a sign," or "Lo, there is a sign," for the kingdom of God will arrive among you with utmost suddenness. As a flash of lightning, behold, it is here and there, everywhere at once. The kingdom will arrive with such dramatic suddenness that you will have neither time nor occasion to observe its coming. The kingdom does not come in such a way you can make a program of its coming. There will be no premonitory signs and portents which may be observed so you can say, "Look at this or that; it cannot be far away now." On the contrary, it comes suddenly and unexpectedly. God's reign comes not so that it can be calculated; and none can say, "Lo here or there!" For lo, God's reign is all at once in your midst![143]

The grand difficulty with this view is stated forcefully:

> In order to salvage a false theory, resort is made to supplying certain words, e.g., 'suddenly,' 'unexpectedly.' . . . It is a peculiar method of interpretation, which interpolates rather than explains. The word put in parenthesis would then be the real point of the discourse, and on it alone everything would depend. Christ would then have forgotten to express the real point of his discourse. What he really wanted to say he would not have said, and what he actually said he would not have wanted to say.[144]

This objection may apply if one is seeking to ascertain the meaning of 17:21b for Jesus. But when it comes to Luke's meaning we are justified in adding words suggested by the context to bring out Luke's thought. We have already noted that Luke probably handed down the statement as he received it (Chap. VII.G.7.a). He did so thinking that the meaning within the context of the fire and brimstone apocalypse (17:20-18:8) would be abundantly clear. The figure of lightning (17:24) would suggest both suddenness and universality, thereby justifying the addition of words like "suddenly," "unexpectedly," and "everywhere." That day will come suddenly upon you as a snare (Luke 21:34).

---

[139]Easton, "Luke 17:20-21," p. 280. But see note #135.

[140]Bultmann, *Synoptic Tradition*, p. 122.

[141]Easton, "Luke 17:20-21," p. 280.

[142]Otto, *Kingdom of God*, p. 135; Rüstow, "Luke 17:20-21," p. 212.

[143]From Bultmann, *Theology*, I, 6; *Synoptic Tradition*, pp. 121-122; Manson, *Sayings of Jesus*, p. 304; and Montefiore, *Gospels*, II, 549.

[144]Otto, *Kingdom of God*, p. 135.

c) *Apocalyptic Universality.*--Another futuristic view involving the translation "in your midst" supplies the word "everywhere." We have just observed that the interpolation of such suitable words is justifiable on the basis of the apocalyptic context. "Everywhere" also makes a good contrast to "Here" and "There." This understanding runs as follows:

> The kingdom of God will be everywhere visibly and dramatically in your midst. When the kingdom comes, the bystanders will not say, "Lo here or there!", for the kingdom will not be invisible but universally and unmistakably visible. No accompanying sign will be needed to identify it nor guide you to find it somewhere. But in the meantime false teachers will say, "Lo, here!" or "There!" Ignore them, for the coming of the kingdom and Son of Man will be universally and unmistakably visible, just as evident as lightning.[145]

The chief advantage of this view is its elimination of the clash between vv 21a and 23a:

> In both instances Jesus is saying exactly the same thing about the Kingdom of God or the Son of man. In the earlier saying the point is that the Kingdom will not come with an accompanying sign, i.e., in such a way that it will be necessary to look for some way of verifying it in case of doubt. The latter saying warns that in the coming days, before the Kingdom of God has come and while the disciples are passionately longing (*epithumēsete*) for the coming days of the Son of man, some will claim to have found him (the Son of man) or it (the Kingdom of God); but the disciples must not be misled, for the arrival of the Kingdom of God and Son of man will be so destructive as to be self-evident and self-authenticating. There will be no doubt about it.[146]

The distinction between "accompanying signs" (signs which accompany the coming of the kingdom) and "preliminary signs" (signs which precede the coming of the kingdom) also avoids a conflict with the signs--preliminary signs--in Luke 21:7-11,25-28 and other passages. This interpretation also fits the preceding pericope, the healing of the ten lepers (17:11-19). The healing of lepers is comparable to the resurrection of the dead and is understood as a preliminary sign of the coming kingdom, about which the Pharisees then ask (17:20).[147]

> The advantages of this view may be summarized as follows: All who read 17:20-21 to mean that Jesus and/or Luke meant the Kingdom was somehow present do not explain who "they" are, why they will not say "Lo, here!" or "There!", or why the appearance of the Kingdom of God "in your midst" will account for (*gar*) this future moment of silence.[148]

As we have already seen (Chap. VII.G.6.f), however, Luke may not mean to imply a future moment of silence but rather that their exclamations will be groundless.

d)*An Apocalyptic Announcement.*--A novel opinion has it that the kingdom of God is a future, supernatural reality which will not come secretly (*paratērēsis*) but visibly and suddenly, nor will they say, "Here it is!" or, "There it is!", for they will say, "The kingdom of God is in the midst of you."

"Is" is taken as an apocalyptic present referring to the future advent of the

---

[145]From Hiers, "'Lo, here!'", pp. 379-384; *Kingdom of God*, pp. 22-29.

[146]Hiers, *Kingdom of God*, p. 27.

[147]Cf. Grundmann, *Lukas*, p. 338.

[148]Hiers, "Delay," p. 154.

kingdom. This effect is achieved by adding the words "they will say." Thus, according to this view, two misunderstandings are avoided: an imperceptible coming, and the localization of the kingdom within the limits of our world.[149] On the other hand, the addition of the words "they will say" appears rather forced, and it seems superfluous to make an apocalyptic announcement, when the kingdom arrives, that the kingdom, which comes openly, is in the midst of you.

9. "Within Your Power"

A futuristic interpretation which has roots in some of the church fathers[150] has been revived independently by the German sociologist Alexander Rüstow, whose view we may summarize as follows:[151]

> The kingdom of God is within your sphere of influence or action, within your power to appropriate it, or at your disposal. It is senseless to look anxiously for the parousia, to calculate in advance the moment of its coming, or to want to determine the place where it will come, for behold, the kingdom of God is in your hand, and it is your responsibility to prove yourself worthy of it, so that you may be received into it when it comes. To fulfill the conditions of entry you must repent, for the kingdom of God is at hand, that is, it is near, but not yet here. That, and that alone, can and must you do; that, and that alone, is the proper attitude in view of the nearness of the kingdom. Preparation is everything. "But seek ye first his kingdom, and his righteousness" (Matt 6:33). Your questions about time and place are not only unanswerable but the very asking demonstrates not only an incorrect conception of this event but also a completely false attitude toward it. "He who calculates the end has no share in eternal life" (Rabbi Jose).

As we shall see in Appendix A, there is linguistic support for rendering *entos humōn* as "within your power."[152] Another advantage not noted by Rüstow is that his stress on seeking the coming kingdom fits well with the emphasis of Luke 13:24 and 16:16 upon struggling to get into the approaching kingdom (Chap. VII.F.6).

10. The Kingdom Group

As noted in Appendix A, *entos* may at times be used to picture one group within

---

[149]J. Héring, *Le Royaume de Dieu et sa venue*, 1937, pp. 43-44 (cited by Noack, *Luke 17:20-24*, p. 37). Héring follows A. Meyer's Aramaic reconstruction in taking "not with observation" as "not in secret," and *entos humōn* as "in the midst of you" (see Noack, *Luke 17:20-24*, p. 7).

[150]Tertullian, "Against Marcion," 4.35; Cyril of Alexandria, *Explanatio in Lucae evangelium*, in Migne, Patrologia graeca, 72: "Do not ask the times, but strive rather to attain the Kingdom, for it is 'within you.' That is, to take it lies among your choices and within your power" (from Cadbury, "Kingdom of God," p. 172).

[151]Rüstow, "Luke 17:20-21," pp. 197-224, especially pp. 216-217.

[152]The idea of the kingdom's being in one's own power is stressed in various ways by the following: Ernst Issel and Otto Schmoller in their essays *Über die Lehre vom Reich Gottes im Neuen Testament* (Leiden: Brill, 1891)(cited by Noack, *Luke 17:20-24*, p. 28, and by Rüstow, "Luke 17:20-21," pp. 220-221); Roberts, "Kingdom of Heaven," pp. 1-8; *Confraternity New Testament*, 1956, p. 162; Cadbury, "Kingdom of God," pp. 172-173; Mussner, "Luke 17:20b-21," pp. 107-111; Danker, *Luke*, p. 181. Danker and Mussner take the kingdom in 17:21b as present, Roberts as conditionally present.

another group. Andrew Sledd makes the unusual suggestion that "in Luke also we have a case of a group within a group: the kingdom-group (whether the kingdom be apocalyptically conceived or not) within the you-group to which Jesus' words were addressed."[153] We would attempt here to develop further Sledd's provocative proposal. Throughout Luke-Acts there is a division between the kingdom group and the anti-kingdom group. Some examples:

Passage	Kingdom Group	Anti-Kingdom Group
Luke 7:29-30	Those baptized by John	Those not baptized by John[154]
Luke 8:9-10	Disciples who know the mysteries of the kingdom	The rest
Luke 9:26-27	Those who will see the kingdom	Those who are ashamed of the Son of Man
Luke 10:3	Lambs	Wolves
Luke 12:30,32	Flock	Nations of the world
Luke 12:41-48	Faithful servants	Unfaithful servants
Luke 13:28-29; 14:15-24	Those at the messianic banquet	Those excluded from the banquet
Luke 19:11-27	Good servants	Enemies of the Lord
Luke 19:37-40	Those who welcome Jesus	Those who reject Jesus
Luke 21:1-4	Sacrificial widow	Greedy rich
Luke 21:12-19	Persecuted disciples	Persecutors
Luke 22:47-53	Jesus and the disciples	Priests and elders
Acts 2:1-13	Recipients of the Spirit	Scoffers
Acts 4:1-31	Primitive Community	Sanhedrin
Acts 5:1-11	Primitive Community	Ananias and Sapphira
Acts 9:20-22	Disciples in Damascus	Jews in Damascus
Acts 13:14-52	Congregation in Antioch	Jealous Jews
Acts 16:11-40	Paul and Silas	Owners of Demoniac Girl

If the *entos humōn* of Luke 17:21b indicates the kingdom group within the anti-kingdom group, we may paraphrase 17:20-24 as follows:

---

[153]Sledd, "Luke 17:21," p. 237.

[154]Conzelmann, *Theology*, p. 21, remarks on Luke 3:21 and 7:29: "All the people are baptized, but their leaders without exception refuse to be baptized. In this way Luke creates a peculiar variant of the idea of the people of God within Israel. We have therefore right at the beginning two distinct groups (in Luke's view, of course, actual historical groups) forming the background to the ministry of Jesus."

From this moment on false teachers will be saying erroneously, "Lo, here!" or "There!" They will be saying that without reason, for the kingdom group is present now within the anti-kingdom group=the you-group, the Pharisees' group. The kingdom group which will enter the kingdom when it comes is now in your midst. The kingdom itself is not yet here but the people of the kingdom are among you Pharisees. In the difficult days ahead when you of the kingdom group would be happy to see only one of the days of the Son of Man do not be led astray by those false teachers who will still be saying about the approaching kingdom, "Lo, there!" of "Lo, here!" For the Son-of-Man-kingdom event will be as suddenly and universally visible as a flash of lightning.

There are a number of advantages to this view. It fits both the present and future aspects of 17:20-37: the kingdom group is present but the kingdom itself is future. This rendition of *entos humōn* is confirmed not only by secular sources but also by Scripture (Lam 1:3)(Appendix A). It fits Luke's continual stress on the tension between the kingdom and anti-kingdom groups (also Chap. VIII.E.10). It explains why Luke does not use *en mesō humōn* (Acts 2:22; 22:27) (Chap. VII.G.7.a), that is, he wants to keep the group-within-group idea expressed by *entos humōn*. This view also eliminates the strange silence of 17:21, and explains the future tense, "they will say," for men will be saying, "Lo, here!" but without reason (Chap. VII.G.6.f), for now the insiders know that the kingdom group is in the midst of the anti-kingdom group.

11. Conclusion

At Luke 17:20-21 we again have found that probability favors a futuristic interpretation of the kingdom. The kingdom will be suddenly and universally among you. Or the kingdom is now within your sphere of action so that you may prove yourself worthy to be received into it when it comes. Or the kingdom group which will enter the approaching kingdom is in your midst. In view of these cogent alternatives there is no need to think of the kingdom as being in the hearts of men or as somehow present in the church, society, or Jesus and his disciples.

We have now completed our exegesis of the six key verses which are commonly understood to mean that for Luke the kingdom is present in this age. In each instance this consensus lacks probative force. Rather we have discovered that linguistic and contextual considerations make it highly probable that Luke thinks of the kingdom as entirely futuristic. Perhaps this is what Luke is trying to tell us at Luke 21:31, where he alone says, "the Kingdom of God is about to come" (TEV).

In Chaps. IV, V, and VI we have seen that Luke-Acts is one in respect to the imminence of the kingdom. Chap. VII suggests that both volumes agree as to the futurity of the kingdom. Hence our study indicates that Luke-Acts is a unity so far as the kingdom as an imminent, futuristic entity is concerned.

Appendix A: The Meaning of *Entos*

We shall list the occurrences of *entos* and then set forth the various renditions which have been proposed.

1. The Occurrences of *Entos*

In the literature on Luke 17:20-21 some forty instances of *entos* are cited:

a) *New Testament.*--Matt 23:26; Luke 17:21.

b) *Classical Writings.*--Homer, *Iliad* 12.374; Herodotus, *Persian Wars* 1.119.6; 7.47.2; 7.100.3; Thucydides, *Peloponnesian War* 6.67.1; 7.5.3; Euripides, *Heracles Mad* 991; Zenophon, *Anabasis* 1.103; *Cyropaedia* 1.4.23; *Hellenica* 2.3.19; Plato, *Laws* 789A.

c) *Septuagint.*--Job 18:19 (Codex Alexandrinus); Ps 38:4 (39:3) (LXX; Symmachus); 102:1 (103:1); 108:22 (109:22); Cant 3:10; Sir 19:26; Isa 16:11 (LXX; Symmachus); 1 Macc 4:48.

d) *Second-Century Greek Versions (Aquila).*--Exod 17:7; 34:9; Job 2:8; Ezek 28:16 (Aquila; Symmachus).

e) *Second-Century Greek Versions (Symmachus).*--Ps 38:4 (39:3)(LXX; Symmachus); 48:12 (49:11); 65:11 (66:11); 72:21 (73:21); 87:6 (88:5); 140:5 (141:5); Isa 16:11 (LXX; Symmachus); Jer 31:20 (38:20); Lam 1:3; Ezek 1:16; 3:24; 28:16 (Aquila; Symmachus); Mic 5:5 (5:6); 6:14; Hab 3:2.

f) *Second-Century Versions (Theodotion).*--Dan 10:16.

g) *Papyri.*--*Oxyrhynchus* 724; 728.15; 729 (c. A.D. 150); 1274.13 (2d-3d century A.D.); 2342.1.7-8 (A.D. 102); *Fayum* 7052.21-22 (2d-3d century A.D.); *Ross.-Georg.* 3.1.8-9 (A.D. 270).

2. The Meanings of *Entos*

One of the stumbling-blocks in the way of a correct interpretation of Luke 21:21b is the fact that writers have generally not distinguished carefully among the various meanings of *entos*. Too often it has been temporarily forgotton that "within" in English has three meanings, not all of which fit Luke 21:21b. Hence not all instances where *entos* may be rendered as "within" are necessarily evidence that Luke 17:21b should be construed as "within your hearts." It should be noted that some examples appear below more than once, since one meaning does not necessarily exhaust *entos* in a particular context.

a) *"Within the Interior Of."*--Here we look at passages where *entos* appears in the sense of "within," as in the inner or interior part of; inside of; not without; inside the body, heart, or mind. Plato, *Laws* 789A, refers to infants who are being nourished within their mothers (*tois entos tōn autōn meterōn trephomenois*). Ezek 1:16 (Symmachus) describes a wheel within a wheel (*entos tou trochou*). Ps 72:21 (73:21) (Symmachus), like Luke 17:21b, uses *entos* before a genitive plural, "within the reins" (*entos tōn nephrōn*). The Psalmist declares, "My heart was warmed within me" (*hē kardia mou entos mou*) (38:4)(39:3)(LXX; Symmachus), and "my heart is troubled within me" (*entos mou*) (108:22) (109:22)(LXX).

Ezekiel admonishes, "Go and shut thyself up within thy house" (*entos tou oikou sou*) (3:24) (Symmachus). Occasionally *entos* may mean "within a house" even when the word "house" (*oikos*) is not expressed.[155] Thus Job 18:19

---

[155] This view is advocated by Riesenfeld, "Luke 17:21," cols. 11-12, and Wikgren, "Luke 17:21," cols. 27-28. It is supported by Kümmel, *Promise*, p 35, but criticized by Rüstow, "Luke 17:20-21," pp. 214-215, as complicated and ambiguous.

(Codex Alexandrinus of LXX) reads that others shall live securely "in his house" (*entos autou*). Judea's persecutors found her "within the dwelling of her oppressors" (*entos tōn thlibontōn autēn*) (Lam 1:3)(Symmachus). The Psalmist is like one set free "in the house of the dead" (*entos nekrōn eleutheros*) (87:6)(88:5)(Symmachus). Papyrus Oxyrhynchus 2342.1.7-8 tells of a woman who has a supply of wine "in her house" (*entos hautēs*). An army doctor asks that his jacket be sent to him that he may find it "in my house" (entos mou) when returning (Papyrus *Ross.-Georg.* 3.1.8-9).

These examples show that *entos* may be used in the sense of "within" suitable to Luke 17:21b, "inside of." Yet none of these references speaks of anything being within the heart. The usages in Plato and Ps 72:21(73:21) are of special interest, for there *entos* is followed by the plural. In Ps 38:4 (39:3) and 108:22(109:22) *entos* is used with a singular pronoun, and though the heart is inside the Psalmist nothing is said to be inside the heart. Thus there are no close parallels to Luke 17:21b in the sense of "the kingdom of God is within you" (=*in your he*arts). As we have seen (Chap. VII.G.6.a), "in your hearts" is expressed with "in" (*en*) rather than with *entos*.

b) *"Within the Limits Of."*--"Within" may also mean in the limits, range, or compass of a specified distance, time, or quantity; not further in length than, as within five miles; not longer in time than, as within an hour; not exceeding in quantity, as within one's income. In this sense Homer, *Iliad* 12.374, tells of men going along "within [the circuit] of the wall" (*teicheos entos iontes*). He of course does not mean that the men were going inside the wall as through a secret chamber. Mic 5:5 (5:6)(Symmachus) sees Israel ruling the land of Nimrod "within [the area of] her gates" (*entos pulōn autēs*).

The idea of being within the limits of time is expressed in Hab 3:2 (Symmachus)("within the years") (*entos tōn eniautōn*), in *Oxyrhynchus* Papyri 724 and 729 ("within the time") (*entos tou chronou*), and *Oxyrhynchus* Papyrus 728.15 ("within the period before Epeiph 10th" = July 4th) (*entos 'Epeiph dekates*).

The meaning of *entos* in these passages is impossible for Luke 17:21b.

c) *"Within the Power Of."*--"Within" also means inside the limits, reach, scope, or influence of, as within my power.[156] Thus the Psalmist (140:5)(141:5)(Symmachus) speaks of being "within the sphere of their wickedness" (*entos tōn kakiōn autōn*). A woman has a supply of wine "in her possession" or "in her hands" (*entos hautēs*) (Papyrus *Oxyrhynchus* 2342.1.7-8). Papyri *Oxyrhynchus* 1274.13 and *Fayum* 7052.21-22 speak of being within jurisdiction of the law (*entos tou nomou*). An army doctor asks, "Send me the woolen jacket so that I may have it in my hands" (=at my disposal, in my sphere)(*entos mou*) (Papyrus *Ross.-Georg.* 3.1.8-9). The Greeks rescued Cyrus' concubine and others who were "in their control" (*entos autōn*) (Xenophon, *Anabasis* 1.10.3). One is "within range of an arrow" (*entos toxeumatos*) (Xenophon, *Cyropaedia* 1.4.23; Euripides, *Heracles Mad* 991). A person may be

---

[156]*Entos* as "within" in this sense is stressed by Roberts, "Kingdom of Heaven," pp. 5-6, and Rüstow, "Luke 17:20-21," pp. 214-216. It is rejected by Kümmel, *Promise*, p. 35, but Cadbury, "Kingdom of God," p. 172, thinks "it may be safely said that in the papyri we have plain cases where the preposition [*entos*] means 'in reach of.'"

beyond his "own sphere of control" (=out of control)(*entos emeŏutou*) (Herodotus, *Persian Wars* 1.119.6; 7.47.2).

d) *"The Inside(s)."--Entos* with the singular article *to* or the plural article *ta* means the inside(s) of something:

> Ps 48:12(49:11)(Symmachus): the things which are inside of their houses (*ta entos tōn oikiōn autōn*).
>
> Ps 102:1 (103:1)(LXX): all the things which are inside me (*panta ta entos mou*).
>
> Isa 16:11(LXX)(Symmachus): the things inside of me (=my entrails)(*ta entos mou*).
>
> Jer 31:20 (38:20)(Symmachus): the things inside me (*ta entos mou*).
>
> Ezek 28:16 (Symmachus)(Aquila): the things inside thee (*ta entos sou*).
>
> Dan 10:16 (Theodotion): the things within me (=my vitals)(*ta entos mou*).
>
> Mic 6:14 (Symmachus): the things inside thee (*ta entos sou*).
>
> Sir 19:26 (LXX): the things inside him (*ta entos autou*).
>
> 1 Macc 4:48 (LXX): the things inside the house (=the interior of the temple)(*ta entos tou oikou*).
>
> Matt 23:26: that which is inside of the cup (*to entos tou potēriou*).

These instances are also of no aid in determining the meaning of Luke 17:21b.

e) *"Between."--*Occasionally *entos* simply means "between," that is, in the space which separates two entities. Herodotus, *Persian Wars* 7.100.3, reports that "the king sailed along in the open space between the prows of the ships and the shore" (*ho de entos tōn prōreōn kai tou aigialou*), the ships being lined up side by side facing the shore. Thucydides, *Peloponnesian Wars* 7.5.3, tells of a commander who confined the ranks of his troops too much between the walls (*entos lian tōn teichōn*), a mistake which rendered useless their cavalry and javelin-men. This sense is also inapplicable to Luke 17:21b.

f) *"Among."--Entos* also means among, in the midst of, that is, mixed or mingled with or surrounded by something. Thucydides, *Peloponnesian War* 6.67.1, tells that the baggage-bearers were placed in the midst of the reserve (*entos toutōn tōn epitaktōn*). Xenophon, *Anabasis* 1.10.3, reports that the Greeks rescued Cyrus' concubine and others who were "in their midst" (*entos autōn*). Xenophon, *Hellenica* 2.3.19, summarizes Theramenes' arguments against the appointment of only 3,000 men to share in the government, as if there could be neither excellent men outside them nor rascals among them (*entos toutōn*). In Aquila's version the Israelites inquire, "Is the Lord among us?" (*entos hēmōn*) (Exod 17:7), and Moses prays to the Lord, "Let the Lord go in the midst of us" (*entos hēmōn*) (Exod 34:9). Here Symmachus and Theodotion read "in the midst of us" (*en mesō hēmōn*), a parallelism which suggests that *entos hēmōn=en mesō hēmōn*. Aquila has Job sitting in the midst of the ash-heap (*entos tēs spodou*) (Job 2:8). The Lord tries his people by bringing them into the midst of tribulation (*entos poliorkias*) (Ps 65:11)(66:11)(Symmachus).

The Psalmist is free among the dead (*entos nekrōn*)(Ps 87:6)(88:5)(Symmachus). He is also in the midst of their evils (*entos tōn kakiōn autōn*) (Ps 140:5)(141:5)(Symmachus). Judea's persecutors find her in the midst of those troubling her (*entos tōn thilbontōn autēn*) (Lam 1:3)(Symmachus).

g)"*A Group within a Group.*--[157] Thucydides, *Peloponnesian War* 6.67.1, reports that the porters are within the reserves (*entos toutōn tōn epitaktōn*), not meaning that the porters are in the hearts of the fighting men but that the porter group is within the reserve group. Xenophon, *Anabasis* 1.10.3, does not describe anything within an individual but rather means that the group of those whom the Greeks saved from their enemies is within (*entos autōn*) the group of rescuing troops. Nor at *Hellenica* 2.3.19 does Xenophon say "within their hearts," but he does mean the group of scoundrels is within the group of 3,000 (*entos toutōn*). Symmachus (Lam 1:3) pictures the Judean group within the oppressor group.

3. Conclusions

Since these forty plus usages of *entos* extend over a period of more than a millennium, they should be used only with caution as clues to understanding the meaning of *entos humōn* in Luke 17:21b.

There is no parallel which says "the kingdom of God is *entos humōn*," nor does any parallel locate anything within the heart (*entos tēs kardias*).

Manson's dictum[158] that the "natural way to translate *entos* is by 'within' or 'in'" is refuted by the evidence set forth here which shows that *entos* has seven well-attested meanings.

Plummer's claim[159] that the meaning "among you," "in your midst," lacks confirmation in Scripture needs to be modified in light of the seven examples from Symmachus and Aquila given above in Section f.

Roberts' statement[160] that to his knowledge only Symmachus (Lam 1:3; Ps 87:6; 140:5) uses *entos* in a sense approaching "in the midst of" needs to be qualified in view of the passages quoted in Section f. The same applies to Allen's conclusion[161] that if *entos humōn* in Luke 17:21b "be rendered 'in your midst,' rather than 'in your hearts,' this rendering is a violation of the known usage of the word *entos.*"

Four of the above meanings of *entos* may justifiably be used in interpreting Luke 17:21b: a) within the interior of; c) within the power of; f) among; g) a group within a group. Since each of these meanings of *entos* undeniably exists, the linguistic evidence alone is not decisive in interpreting *entos* in Luke 17:21b. The other three meanings of *entos* (b, d, e) are not applicable to 17:21b, which means that almost one half of our forty odd uses of *entos* are ruled out of consideration.

---

[157]Sledd, "Luke 17:21," pp. 235-237, is to my knowledge the only commentator to bring out this meaning.

[158]Manson, *Sayings of Jesus*, p. 303.

[159]Plummer, *Luke*, p. 406.

[160]Roberts, "Kingdom of Heaven," p. 4.

[161]Allen, "Luke 17:21," p. 426.

Chapter VIII
"Fire Upon the Earth" (Luke 12:49): A Holy War?

A. Literary Analysis of Luke 12:49-56

Now we come to our last major pericope and parallels:

Matthew	Mark	Luke
	(10:38 But Jesus said unto them, Ye know not what ye ask. Are ye able to drink the cup that I drink? or to be baptized with the baptism that I am baptized with? 39 And they said unto him, We are able. And Jesus said unto them, The cup that I drink ye shall drink; and with the baptism that I am baptized withal shall ye be baptized.)	12:49 I came to cast fire upon the earth; and what do I desire, if it is already kindled? (margin how would I that it were already kindled?).¹ 50 But I have a baptism to be baptized with; and how am I straitened till it be accomplished!
10:34 Think not that I came to send peace on the earth: I came not to send peace, but a sword. 35 For I came to set a man at variance against his father, and the daughter against her mother, and the daugther in law against her mother in law: and a	(cf. Matt 10:21; Mark 13:12; Luke 21:16).	51 Think ye that I came to give peace in the earth? I tell you, Nay; but rather division: 52 for there shall be from henceforth five in one house divided, three against two, and two against three. 53 They shall be divided, father against son, and son

---
¹On the translation of 12:49b see Graystone, "Fire," p. 135 ("And how I wish it were already kindled!"), and Ward, "Luke 12:49," pp. 92-93 ("And what am I to wish, if it is already kindled?").

man's foes shall be they of his own household.	against father; mother against daughter, and daughter against her mother; mother in law against her daughter in law, and daughter in law against her mother in law.
16:2 But he answered and said unto them, When it is evening, ye say, It will be fair weather: for the heaven is red. 3 And in the morning, It will be foul weather today: for the heaven is red and lowering. Ye know how to discern the face of the heaven; but ye cannot discern the signs of the times.	54 And he said to the multitudes also, When ye see a cloud rising in the west, straightway ye say, There cometh a shower; and so it cometh to pass. 55 And when ye see a south wind blowing, ye say, There will be a scorching heat; and it cometh to pass. 56 Ye hypocrites, ye know how to interpret the face of the earth and the heaven; but how is it that ye know not how to interpret this time?

The parallels show that Luke 12:49-50 is found only in Luke, though there is a partial parallel in Mark 10:38 where Jesus asks James and John whether they are able to be baptized with the baptism with which he is baptized. Hence some commentators trace Luke 12:49-50 to Luke's special material. Others, however, find that 12:49-50 stems from Q, which in turn is based upon Aramaic tradition.[2]

Luke 12:51-53, with parallels in Matt 10:34-35 (in Matthew's charge to the twelve), is from Q, as is Luke 12:54-56//Matt 16:2-3(Matt 16:1-4=request for a sign from heaven). This difference of context in Matthew and Luke suggests that these sayings were originally independent. Wellhausen regards Luke 12:49-53 as disparate sayings which Luke has placed together because of some kind of association of ideas.[3] Luke 12:49-50 may have been joined to 12:51-53 by Luke or the pre-Lukan tradition because of the catchword connection "I came" of 12:49 and 12:51. But regardless of the original setting of the sayings in 12:49-56 they are now part of Luke's "fire upon the earth apocalypse" (12:1-13:35), much of which is discourse material, especially 12:22-59.

B. Attempts at De-Apocalypticizing Luke 12:49-56

The fact that Luke 12:49-50 is incorporated into a Lukan apocalypse would lead one to think that Luke understood 12:49-50 in an apocalyptic sense. The Distant Expectation School has attempted, however, to prove that Luke has

---

[2] For example, Wolf, *Luke 12:49-50*, pp. 141, 166, 193.

[3] Wellhausen, *Lucas*, pp. 69-70.

historicized 12:49-56, that is, placed it in the context of his alleged three-fold salvation history in the period of the church.[4] It is pointed out that Luke 12:52 ("there shall be from henceforth five in one house divided,..."), unlike Matt 10:35 ("For I came to set a man at variance against his father,..."), contains the phrase "from henceforth" (*apo tou nun*). The same phrase appears in Luke 22:69: "But from henceforth shall the Son of man be seated at the right hand of the power of God." Thus, it is held, Luke 22:69, in contrast to Mark 14:62, points to a lasting situation, the period of Christ's elevation, the period of the church (Chap. VI.G.2). A similar change occurs at Luke 12:52. The phrase "from henceforth" makes the apocalyptic interpretation impossible by historicizing the statement, so that it does not refer to the eschatological strife preceding the end of the age but simply to the conflicts raging during the era of the church, the *ecclesia pressa*.

In reply to the position of the *Fernerwartungsschule*, we would note that we have already dealt with the problem of "from henceforth" at Luke 22:69 and found that Luke has not de-eschatologized that saying (Chap. VI.G.3). Luke uses the same phrase, "from henceforth," at 22:18: "I shall not drink from henceforth of the fruit of the vine, until the kingdom of God shall come." We have also examined this verse and found it to contain the imminent expectation (Chap. V.J). The "from henceforth" does not at all imply a period of indefinite length before the kingdom comes (see also Chap. V.H.1.b). Thus it seems unlikely that Luke at 12:52 intends his "from henceforth" to de-apocalypticize this unit.

The Distant Expectation School also sees Luke's anti-apocalyptic hand at work in Luke 12:54-56. In Matt 16:3 Jesus says: "Ye cannot discern the signs of the times." Luke 12:56 however reads: "How is it that ye know not how to interpret this time?" Luke, it is claimed, thus means that to interpret the present time is not to discern the signs of the imminent end but to recognize its decisive character without being led astray by the delay of the parousia.

When we come shortly (Section E.4) to our discusson of Luke 12:54-56 we shall try to show, contrary to the Distant Expectation School, that Luke's words ("to interpret the present time") can be understood most naturally in the apocalyptic sense. Montefiore has caught the meaning of the Lukan passage:

> The unbelieving Jews know how to interpret the signs of the coming weather: they wilfully refuse to interpret aright this present season. The time which they do not know how to ... assess rightly is the time which is shortly to culminate and end in the last Judgment, the time which demands the repentance and the belief which will soon be possible no more.[5]

Thus the attempt to fit Luke 12:49-56 into a supposedly non-eschatological Lukan framework is not successful. As Kaestli recognizes, the Distant Expectation School must exercise caution lest they impose on this passage their conception of Lukan eschatology arrived at on other grounds.[6]

C. Spiritualizing Interpretations of Luke 12:49

Figurative views have continued to be popular since the days of the fathers.

---

[4]Conzelmann, *Theology*, p. 109; Grässer, *Delay*, pp. 190-192; Kaestli, *Eschatologie*, pp. 19-23; G. Klein, "Prüfung," pp. 373-390; Wolf, *Luke 12:49-50*, pp. 106-108.

[5]Montefiore, *Gospels*, II, 497.

[6]Kaestli, *Eschatologie*, p. 23.

Cyril of Alexandria thinks of the fire to be cast by Jesus as the doctrine of Christ to be preached all over the earth by the apostles and their successors: "that sacred and divine power was spread abroad by means of the holy preachers."[7] Some fathers and moderns suppose the fire to be the Holy Spirit as the gift of the Risen One (Luke 3:16; 24:32; Acts 2:3).[8] Others regard the fire as the spiritual excitement produced by Jesus' coming, the burning enthusiasm of a new faith.[9] Yet another possibility is the fire of love, the fervor of charity, which Jesus wishes to enkindle in our hearts.[10] Several recent interpreters advocate the fire of judgment, not of the last judgment, but of judgment during Jesus' earthly activity, the fire-flood of God's judgment in which Jesus will be immersed at death when he vicariously takes upon himself God's judgment upon men.[11]

Against these spiritualizing interpretations is the fact that the forceful, realistic word "cast" (*ballō*) is inappropriate to them.[12] Strictly speaking, "to cast fire" means "to throw a firebrand,"[13] a meaning which strongly suggests a literal fire. Moreover, a spiritualization of the fire hardly fits Luke's general tendency toward materialization (Luke 3:22; 24:39; Acts 1:9-11), nor the reference to objective fire in Luke 17:24, 29-30. And Luke himself at Acts 1:5 ("ye shall be baptized with the Holy Spirit") does not connect the gift of the Spirit at Pentecost with John's prediction of a baptism with fire (Luke 3:16) but simply with John's saying about baptism in the Holy Spirit (Mark 1:8). Nor do these spiritualizations fit the Lukan context of family strife, signs, and judgment of Luke 12:51-59. Neither do they all agree with the order of events as set forth by Luke (Section E.1).

D. Sociological Interpretations of Luke 12:49

In view of these objections to spiritualizing interpretations, others have offered what we call sociological interpretations. Luke 12:49 in its present context seems to refer to the fire of discord and strife which arises as men align themselves for or against the Messiah (12:51-53).[14] Tertullian writes: "Wherefore he meaneth the fire of turmoil and upheaval--he who refused to give peace."[15]

Against this view is the lack of any OT background for such a usage of "fire." The nearest instance would be Prov 26:20-21: "As coals are to hot embers, and wood to fire, so is a contentious man to inflame strife." But there is hardly any analogy between a gossipy troublemaker fanning the flames of arguments and strife, on the one hand, and the Messiah creating eschatological division within

---

[7]Cyril, *Commentary on Luke*, II, 94, quoted by Graystone, "Fire," p. 137.

[8]Grundmann, *Lukas*, p. 270; Ellis, *Luke*, p. 182.

[9]Godet, *Luke*, II, 112-114; Bruce, *Gospels*, p. 562.

[10]Graystone, "Fire," pp. 138-141.

[11]Delling, "Baptism," pp. 102-112; Wolf, *Luke 12:49-50*, pp. 217-222, 255-256, though Wolf does not regard Jesus' death in 12:49-50 as vicarious. Delling and Wolf are concerned with the original meaning of 12:49-50, not with the Lukan meaning.

[12]Creed, *Luke*, p. 178.

[13]Godet, *Luke*, II, 111.

[14]Plummer, *Luke*, p. 334; Creed, *Luke*, p. 178; Gilmour, *Luke*, p. 235; BAG, p. 737; Kaestli, *Eschatologie*, pp. 20-21, thinks of both the division of men and the outpouring of the Spirit.

[15]Tertullian, "Against Marcion," 4.29.

families, on the other.

A novel sociological interpretation is given by J. Weiss:[16] Luke 12:49-53 must be taken in connection with the sword passage of 22:36: "Whoever does not have a sword must sell his coat and buy one" (TEV). Why buy a sword except to fight? The parallelism between 12:49 and 12:50 shows that Jesus' death is most closely related to this revolt which he will enkindle in Jerusalem. There Jesus will fall in street fighting, according to a tragic necessity, for a prophet must die in Jerusalem (Luke 13:33). Jesus anticipates his death, not with readiness to suffer as the Lamb of God but with human horror (12:50). Otto similarly finds that Jesus thought he would fall in the struggle occasioned by his work.[17]

So far as the ascertaining of Luke's thought is concerned, these sociological views have the merit of taking 12:49-50 in connection with 12:50-53. But such interpretations, however true they may be to Jesus' own thought, do not fit the larger Lukan context, for, as we shall see (Section E.3), for Luke Jesus' baptism precedes rather than follows the strife and turmoil. "The fire and the divisions are all meant to take place subsequently to Jesus' death."[18]

E. Literal Interpretations: End-Time Fires

Having examined and found wanting spiritualizing and sociological interpretations of the fire Jesus is to cast upon the earth, we turn now to literal views.

1. Jesus' Baptism (Luke 12:50)

Before we can proceed to our own interpretation of Luke 12:49 we must answer two questions about 12:50: 1) To what, according to Luke, does the "baptism" refer? 2) Does this baptism, according to Luke, precede or follow the casting of fire to earth?

1) In answer to the first quesiton, it seems clear that for Luke this baptism refers to Jesus' death.[19] In the first place, Luke would have been familiar with the parallel reference in Mark 10:39 to baptism, which Mark relates to Jesus' death, for 10:39 is sandwiched between the passion predictions of Mark 10:33-34 and 10:45, on the journey to Jerusalem and death.[20] Second, Luke has also included Luke 12:50 in his extended account of the journey to Jerusalem and death (9:51-19:44) and has likewise surrounded it with passion pronouncements: 9:22,31,44; 12:50; 13:31-33; 17:25; 18:31-34; (24:7).

2) As for the second question, if for Luke the "baptism" of 12:50 thus refers to Jesus' death, does Jesus' death precede or follow his casting of fire upon the earth? Here again Luke gives us the answer, this time in 17:22-37,[21] where the day of the Son of Man is described as a day of lightning, fire, and brimstone

---

[16] J. Weiss, "Problem," pp. 441, 459 (quoted by Montefiore, *Gospels*, II, 496).

[17] Otto, *Kingdom of God*, p. 360.

[18] Montefiore, *Gospels*, II, 496.

[19] Wolf, *Luke 12:49-50*, p. 233.

[20] Cf. Wolf, *Luke 12:49-50*, pp. 48-49.

[21] Cf. Wolf, *Luke 12:49-50*, pp. 110-111.

(17:24,29-30). "But first must he [the Son of Man] suffer many things and be rejected of this generation"" (17:25). As Luke looks back upon the Son of Man's sufferings he reminds us that passion or baptism of death is the precondition of the fiery day of the Son of Man.

2. A Fiery Parousia (Luke 12:49)

But what does Luke mean by 12:49, "I came to cast fire upon the earth"? We have already seen the inadequacy of spiritualizing and sociological views. Since the casting of fire comes after Jesus' death, we must search for any clues as to the nature of such a post-resurrection event. We have just noted that Luke expects Jesus' death to be followed by the parousia when the Son of Man will appear with a brightness comparable to lightning (17:24), as prefigured by the transfiguration, when "his raiment became white and dazzling" (9:29). Only Luke tells us precisely "how it will be on the day the Son of Man is revealed" (17:30)(TEV), namely, a day like the day that Lot went out from Sodom when "it rained fire and brimstone from heaven, and destroyed them all" (17:29)(ASV). Luke 12:49 interpreted in light of 17:24, 29-30 would thus mean that Jesus, having experienced the baptism of death, returns as the Son of Man who casts fire upon the earth, the fire of judgment as real and as deadly as the fire and brimstone which the Lord rained out of heaven upon Sodom and Gomorrah (Gen 19:24; Luke 17:29).[22]

The concept of a parousia in the fire of judgment is by no means unique to Luke. OT prophets speak of such an awesome coming of the Lord. He "will come with fire, and his chariots shall be like the whirlwind; to render his anger with fierceness, and his rebuke with flames of fire." The Lord will execute judgment "by fire," and "by sword, upon all flesh" (Isa 66:15-16). He will "send a fire on Magog" (Ezek 39:6). Malachi asks, "Who can abide the day of his coming?" He is "like a refiner's fire" (3:2). The day "burneth as a furnace; and all the proud, and all that work wickedness, shall be a stubble; and the day that cometh shall burn them up" (4:1).

Similar passages are found in the apocryphal and pseudepigraphical books. At the last judgment "shafts of lightning shall fly with true aim, and from the clouds, as from a well drawn bow, shall they leap to the mark" (of the wicked)(Wis 5:21). The Psalmist assures the rightous man that "the flames of fire and the wrath against the unrighteous shall not touch him, when it goeth forth from the face of the Lord against sinners, to destroy all the substance of sinners" (Pss. Sol. 15:6-7).

A most graphic picture of the fiery parousia of the Son of Man is contained in 4 Ezra 13:3-11. This vision is of special significance for our purposes, as it may date from before A.D. 70:[23]

> 3 . . . that man [Son of Man] flew with the clouds of heaven; and wherever he turned his face to look, everything under his gaze trembled, 4 and whenever his voice issued from his mouth, all who heard his voice melted as the wax melts when it feels the fire . . . .9 And behold, when he saw the onrush of the

---

[22]Fuller, *Mission*, p. 62, holds that Jesus at Luke 12:49 means "the fire of the eschatological judgement, the negative aspect of the coming of the Kingdom (cf. Mark 9:49)."

[23]*APOT*, II, 552.

approaching multitude, ... 10 ... he sent forth from his mouth as it were a stream of fire, and from his lips a flaming breath, and from his tongue he shot forth a storm of sparks. 11 All these were mingled together, the stream of fire and the flaming breath and the great storm, and fell on the onrushing multitude..., and burned them all up, so that suddenly nothing was seen of the innumerable multitude but only the dust of ashes and the smell of smoke.

In the NT, Paul predicts that Jesus will return in a similar way "at the revelation of the Lord Jesus from heaven with the angels of his power in flaming fire, 8 rendering vengeance to them that know not God" (2 Thess 1:7-8), when "that Day's fire will reveal every man's work" (1 Cor 3:13).

Another parallel to Luke 12:49 may be found in Mark 9:29, "For every one shall be salted with fire." This enigmatic saying could be a reference to the final fire of judgment and tribulation cast down by the Son of Man. Loisy takes it as referring to "the final crisis of the world, the universal conflagration, in which the wicked would perish, which the just would pass through purified and unharmed."[24]

Luke 12:49 also has affinities with several passages in the Apocalpse of John:

> And the angel taketh the censer; and he filled it with the fire of the altar, and cast it upon the earth (*ebalen eis tēn gēn*): and there followed thunders, and voices, and lightnings, and an earthquake (8:5) . . ..And the first [angel] sounded, and there followed hail and fire, mingled with blood, and they were cast upon the earth (*eblēthē eis tēn gēn*): and the third part of the earth was burnt up, and the third part of the trees was burnt up, and all green grass was burnt up (8:7). And the second angel sounded, and as it were a great mountain burning with fire was cast into the sea (*eblēthē eis tēn thalassan*)(8:8). . . .And the fourth [angel] poured out his bowl upon the sun; and it was given unto it to scorch men with fire, and the men were scorched with great heat (16:8-9). . . . And fire came down out of heaven, and devoured them [the nations] (20:9) (cf. 13:13).

These verses, as indicated by the Greek words in parentheses, use similar terminology as Luke 12:49 to describe casting the fires of judgment and tribulation upon the earth: the verb *ballō* (cast) and the phrase "on the earth." Luke of course could have known of such conceptions without having known the Apocalypse of John itself. Luke may think of the returning Son of Man as casting fire upon the earth like the angels of the Apocalypse. This is only one of many instances where the Apocalypse is helpful in interpreting Luke's thought (Chap. I.B; Chap. V.D.2; G.4; I.4.g; Chap. VI. C.1; F.3; G.4; Chap. VII.C.2.c; Chap. VIII.E.2).

These examples from the OT, apocrypha, pseudepigrapha, and NT show that in Luke's time the idea of a fiery parousia in judgment was current and that such a conception in Luke 12:49; 17:24,29-30 is altogether possible for Luke.

3. Family Strife (Luke 12:51-53)

Returning to the Lukan context of 12:49 we observe that Luke 12:49-50 is followed by a description of apocalyptic family strife, with division between father and mother, on the one hand, and daughter, son, and son's wife, on the other (12:51-53). What is the chronological relationship of the strife to the other events of 12:49-53?

In the synoptic apocalypse Luke refers to this division within families (21:16) as one of the events preceding the parousia of the Son of Man (21:27). Thus in

---

[24]Loisy quoted by Montefiore, *Gospels*, I, 224. See Note #22 on Mark 9:49.

12:49-53 the family strife of 12:51-53 would precede the fiery parousia (12:49). In other words, for Luke the division within families is not the fire of v 49, but is a separate part of the apocalyptic program preceding the fire. We have already observed that in the OT seldom if ever does fire symbolize division. The order of events in Luke 12:49-53, then, is this: 1)Jesus' death (12:50); 2)family strife (12:51-53); and 3)parousia in fire (12:49).

This distinction of events as well as order of events is confirmed by Ezek 38:17-23:

> 17 Thus saith the Lord Yahweh:...18 And it shall come to pass in that day,...that my wrath shall come up into my nostrils. 19 For in my jealousy and in the fire of my wrath have I spoken, Surely in that day there shall be a great shaking in the land of Israel; 20...,and all the men that are upon the face of the earth, shall shake at my presence, and the mountains shall be thrown down,...21...: every man's sword shall be against his brother. 22 And with pestilence and with blood will I enter into judgment with him; and I will rain upon him, and upon his hordes, and upon the many peoples that are with him, an overflowing shower, and great hailstones, fire, and brimstone.

In this passage, as we are also proposing for Luke, the fiery day of the Lord is preceded by familial strife. Since we have already noted how Ezekiel 38-39 shapes Luke's whole apocalyptic program (Chap. VI.F.5.a), additional similarities should not be surprising. Yet another likeness is found in the phrase, "the men that are upon the face of the earth" (Luke 21:35; Acts 17:26; Ezek 38:19) (Chap. V.I.4.c).

The same juxtaposition of fire and dissension within families occurs also in 1 Enoch 100-102:

> 100:2 For a man shall not withhold his hand from slaying his sons and his sons' sons...7 Woe to you, Sinners, ... Ye who afflict the righteous and burn them with fire: ...9... In blazing flames burning worse than fire shall ye burn...102:1 In those days when He hath brought a grievous fire upon you, Whither will ye flee, ...?

Luke in 12:49-53 varies from the chronological order of events suggested by Luke 21, Ezekiel 38, and 1 Enoch 100-102, that is, Luke 12:49-53 mentions the fiery parousia (12:49) before the familial strife (12:51-53). This variation from chronological order may be attributed to the possibility that 12:49-50 was already united with 12:51-53 in the pre-Lukan tradition and Luke simply took it over unchanged. Or it may be because Luke wishes to stress the fiery parousia by mentioning it first (12:49). Even within v 49 "fire" is the first word in the sentence: "*Fire* I came to cast upon the earth."

4. The Face of the Earth (Luke 12:54-56)

This unit continues the apocalyptic motifs begun in 12:49: the fiery parousia (12:49-50); family strife (12:51-53) and interpreting the time (12:54-56). Another link between these three units, a linguistic link, occurs in the references to the earth in each unit: "fire upon the earth" (12:49); "peace in the earth" (12:51), and "the face of the earth" (12:56). Yet a third connection is one that is seldom if ever noticed, that between the "fire" of 12:49 and the "scorching heat" of 12:55. Neither of these terms is found in the Matthean and Markan parallels. As the south wind withers vegetation, so too will the fire cast upon the earth by the Son of Man scorch men with fire, as at Rev 16:8-9. Hence if anyone is to interpret the present time correctly (Luke 12:56), he must perceive that just as the south wind is a precursor of scorching heat (12:55), so too this scorching heat points ahead to the fire with which the Son of Man will scorch the earth (12:49). The right interpreter of the time will know that Jesus' baptism of death (12:50) will bring in the time of familial terror (12:51-53) prophesied of old (Ezek 38:17-23; Mal 7:6; 1 Enoch 100-102), which in turn prepares the way for the fiery revelation of the Son of Man (12:49; 17:24, 29-30) and the appearance of the kingdom (9:26-27; 17:20-30; 21:27-31). Now it is plain why Jesus wishes the fire were already kindled. He so desires "because it must needs be so before the kingdom of God can come."[25] Luke's Jesus is hardly "the gentle Master."[26] This fact has already become obvious at Luke 12:46 ("he will hew him to pieces") and 19:27 ("bring my enemies here and hew them down"). Therefore when Jesus rebukes James and John for wanting to call down fire from heaven to consume the inhospitable Samaritans (9:54-55) he does so not out of gentleness but because the time is not yet come for him to cast the consuming fire upon the earth.

The probability of our proposed connection between "fire" (12:49) and "scorching heat" (12:58) is increased by a comparison with Ps 11:6: "On the wicked will he rain coals of fire and brimstone; a scorching wind shall be the portion of their cup" (RSV). Jesus' casting of fire upon the earth (Luke 12:49) as interpreted above is parallel with Ps 11:6a: "On the wicked will he rain coals of fire and brimstone." And there is a striking connection between the wind and scorching heat of Luke 12:55 and Ps 11:6b: "A scorching wind shall be the portion of their cup." God, says the Psalmist, will punish the wicked with a raging blast of searing wind, accompanied by a devastating fire like a deadly volcanic flame.

A similar juxtaposition of fire and wind is found in Isa 29:6, "You will be visited by the Lord of hosts...with whirlwind and tempest, and the flame of a devouring fire" (RSV). Isa 66:15-16 pictures the Lord coming "with fire, and his chariots shall be like the whirlwind." Thus there is precedent in Ps 11:6 and Isa 29:6; 66:15-16 for linking the fire and wind of Luke 12:49, 55. Incidentally, the many connections of thought and language within 12:49-56 forbid our regarding this pericope as a collection of unrelated sayings, though they originally may have been independent of one another (Chap. VIII.A).

5. Confirmation of a Fiery Parousia by Other Passages in Luke-Acts

a) Luke 3:16.--John the Baptist declares that the greater one who is coming will "baptize you in the Holy Spirit and in fire" (Luke 3:16). John here may have been speaking of the eschatological river of fire described in a Qumran hymn (1QH 3.28 ff.).[27] In its Lukan context, Luke 3:16 is often taken to refer to the gift of the Spirit and the tongues like fire at Pentecost (Acts 2:3).[28] That Luke however does not regard this prophecy as exhausted at Pentecost is indicated by Acts 1:5, where Luke connects Pentecost with baptism in the Spirit (Mark 1:8) but not with baptism in fire (Chap. VIII.C). Thus the pentecostal experience is at most a partial fulfilment of Luke 3:16. The completed baptism in fire remains for a later time.

---

[25] Creed, *Luke*, p. 178.
[26] So named by Graystone, "Fire," p. 137.
[27] Brownlee, "John the Baptist," p. 42.
[28] Godet, *Luke*, I, 180.

Hence we may regard John's prediction of this baptism in fire as referring primarily to the fire which Jesus will cast upon the earth when he appears as Son of Man (Luke 12:49). The "unquenchable fire" which John mentions (Luke 3:17) would then be the fire of hell (=Gehenna=fiery lake) (cf. Isa 66:24) rather than the fire of judgment and tribulation which Jesus is to cast upon earth.

b) *Acts 2:19*.--In his pentecostal address Peter (Acts 2:19) quotes from the prophet Joel (2:30): "And I will show wonders in the heaven above, and signs on the earth beneath; blood, and fire, and vapor of smoke." A connection between this quotation and Luke 12:49-56 is shown by the similar reference to signs in the heaven and on the earth in Luke 12:56 and Acts 2:19, especially since Matt 16:3 (//Luke 12:56) mentions only the heaven. This change by Luke in his Q material indicates that he definitely had the prophecy from Joel in mind while editing Luke 12:49-56.

Moreover, there is a certain parallelism in language and thought between Luke 12:49 ("I came to cast fire upon the earth") and Acts 2:19 ("I will show... signs on the earth") (literally, "I will give signs on the earth"; cf. Luke 12:51: "to give peace in the earth").

In view of these considerations we may be justifed in regarding the fire of Luke 12:49 as being the fire of Acts 2:19, that is, Jesus will cast this fire upon the earth at his second coming, thereby fulfilling not only Luke 12:49 but also Joel 2:30. Jesus' parousia would then be regarded as a sign both at Luke 11:30 and Acts 2:19 (Chap. V.E.4).

We have identified the baptism in fire (Luke 3:16) with the fire Jesus casts (12:49), which in turn is the fire of Acts 2:19. Hence the fire of Luke 3:16 is also that of Acts 2:19. This latter identification then means that the baptism of the Spirit referred to by John (Luke 3:16) would be the outpouring of the Spirit of Acts 2:17 and 2:3-4. Thus the baptism in Spirit and fire of Luke 3:16 would find but a partial fulfilment at Acts 2:3-4 but a complete fulfilment in Acts 2:17 (outpouring of the Spirit) and 2:19 (fire). Acts 2:17 is fulfilled in the eschatological gift of the Spirit at Pentecost, and 2:19 is to be fulfilled by the parousia in the fire of judgment and tribulation. The baptism in the Holy Spirit and fire (Luke 3:16), the casting of fire upon the earth (Luke 12:49), the outpouring of the Spirit (Acts 2:17), and fire (2:19) are, therefore, all eschatological phenomena.

6. The Cosmic Conflagration (Luke 12:49)

Up to this point in our interpretation of Luke 12:49 we have had occasion to consider the fires of judgment-tribulation and Gehenna. Now we look at another kind of end-time fire, the cosmic conflagration. "The idea that the world would be destroyed by fire appears among the Romans as a Stoic doctrine. Probably it was derived from Heraclitus. Among the Jews it was possibly suggested by Oriental influences."[29] Seneca, a Stoic, writes:

> Know that nothing will abide when it is now placed, that time will lay all things low and take all things with it...It [time] will cover with floods the face of the inhabited world, and, deluging the earth, will kill every living creature, and in huge conflagration it will scorch and burn all mortal things. And when the time shall

---

[29] *APOT*, II, 380.

come for the world to be blotted out in order that it may begin life anew, these things will destroy themselves by their own power, and stars will clash with stars, and all the fiery matter of the world that now shines in orderly array will blaze up in a common conflagration.[30]

In the OT there is no clear-cut instance of a world-consuming fire,[31] and only one clear usage in the NT:[32]

> But the day of the Lord will come as a thief; in the which the heavens shall pass away with a great noise, and the elements shall be dissolved with fervent heat, and the earth and the works that are therein shall be burned up... 12 [Ye] looking for and earnestly desiring the coming of the day of God, by reason of which the heavens being on fire shall be dissolved, and the elements shall melt with fervent heat (2 Pet 3:10, 12).

Other apocalyptists, such as the authors of the Sibylline Oracles, also held that the world was to be burned up by fire:

> And then shall a great river of flaming fire flow from heaven and consume all places, the earth and the great ocean and the grey sea, lakes and rivers and fountains, and merciless Hades and the pole of heaven: but the lights of heaven shall melt together in one and into a void (desolate) shape (?). For the stars shall all fall from heaven into the sea (?), and all souls of men shall gnash their teeth as they burn in the river of brimstone and the rush of fire in the blazing plain, and ashes shall cover all things. And then shall all the elements of the world be laid waste, air, earth, sea, light, poles, days and nights, and no more shall the multitudes of birds fly in the air nor swimming creatures any more swim the sea; no ship shall sail with its cargo over the waves; no straight-going oxen shall plough the tilled land; there shall be no more sound of swift winds, but he shall fuse all things together into one, and purge them clean (Sibylline Oracles, Book 2, 197-212)(second to third century A.D.)(from *ANT*, p. 522).... then the mightiest kingdom of the immortal king over men shall appear [cf. Luke 19:11]... Three with piteous fate shall bring ruin on Rome, and all its people shall perish in their own dwellings, whensoever a cataract of fire shall flow from heaven [cf. Luke 12:49] ... For come it [day of the Lord] will, whenever the odour of brimstone pervades all mankind... But at whatsoever time the threatened vengeance of the Almighty God draws near, and fiery energy comes through the swelling surge to earth and burns up Beliar and the overweening men, even all who have put their trust in him, ... then the elements of the world one and all shall be widowed, what time God ... shall roll up the heaven as a book is rolled, and then shall flow a ceaseless cataract of raging fire, and shall burn up land and sea, and the firmament of heaven and the stars and creation itself it shall cast into one molten mass and clean dissolve (Sibylline Oracles, Book 3, 46-87)(mid-second century B. C.)(in *APOT*, II, 379-380).
> But when faith in godliness shall perish from men, ... then be sure that God is no more of tender mercy but gnashing His teeth in wrath and destroying at once the whole race of men by means of a mighty conflagration ... But if with evil mind ye obey me not, but delighting in ungodliness ye receive all these words with ill-affected ears, then fire shall come upon the whole world, and a mighty sign with sword and trumpet at the rising of the sun. The whole world shall hear a rumbling and a mighty roar. And he shall burn the whole earth, and consume the whole race of men, and all the cities and rivers and the sea. He shall burn everything

---

[30] Seneca, *De Consolatione ad Marciam* 26.6.

[31] Lang, "Fire," p. 936.

[32] Mayer, "Weltenbrand," Sp. 1032. Cf. Loisy on Mark 9:49, Note #24.

out, and there shall be sooty dust. But when at last everything shall have been reduced to dust and ashes and God shall quench the giant fire, even as he kindled [cf. Luke 12:49] it, then God Himself shall fashion again the bones and ashes of men, and shall raise up mortals once more as they were before (Sibylline Oracles, Book 4, 152-182)(c. A.D. 80) (in *APOT*, II, 396).

Qumran also expected a world conflagration:

> When the rivers of Belial burst their high banks -- rivers that are like fire devouring all that draw their waters, rivers whose runnels destroy green tree and dry tree alike, rivers that are like fire which sweeps with flaming sparks devouring all that drink their waters --a fire which consumes all foundations of clay, every solid bedrock; when the foundations of the mountains become a raging blaze, when granite roots are turned to streams of pitch, when the flame devours down to the great abyss, when the floods of Belial burst forth unto hell itself; when the depths of the abyss are in turmoil, . . . and the world's foundations rock and reel (1QH 3:19-36) (Book of Hymns) (first century B.C.?)(in *DSS*, pp. 139-140).

And from the Apocalypse of Peter:

And this shall come at the day of judgment upon them that have fallen away from faith in God and have committed sin: Floods (cataracts) of fire shall be let loose; and darkness and obscurity shall come up and clothe and veil the whole world; and the waters shall be changed and turned into coals of fire, and all that is in them shall burn, and the sea shall become fire. Under the heaven shall be a sharp fire that cannot be quenched, and floweth to fulfil the judgment of wrath. And the stars shall fly in pieces by flames of fire, as if they had not been created, and the powers (firmaments) of the heaven shall pass away for lack of water and shall be as though they had not been...And so soon as the whole creation dissolveth, the men that are in the east shall flee unto the west,...And in all places shall the wrath of a fearful fire overtake them; and an unquenchable flame driving them shall bring them unto the judgement of wrath, unto the stream of unquenchable fire that floweth, flaming with fire,...Then shall he command them to enter into the river of fire while the works of every one of them shall stand before them...As for the elect that have done good, they shall come unto me and not see death by the devouring fire. But...their [the unrighteous] chastisement is the fire, and the angels bring forward their sins and prepare for them a place where in they shall be punished for ever (mid-second century A.D.) (in *ANT*, pp. 513-514).

In this passage the fires of the cosmic conflagration, judgment, and of eternal punishment flow together.

These six passages from the second century B.C. through the second century A. D. suggest that Luke would have been familiar with the idea of an all-consuming fire and had this fire in mind as he edited Luke 12:49-56. But it is not necessary for Luke to have distinguished sharply among the various types of end-time fires, any more than for the Apocalypse of Peter to have done so. The flame of judgment and tribulation with which the Son of Man would scorch the earth would ignite a fire strong enough to melt the elements with fervent heat and burn up the earth and the works therein and then coalesce with the everlasting fires of Gehenna. In light of these parallels, we may paraphrase Luke 12:49 as follows:

> I came to cast a ceaseless cataract of raging fire upon the earth (cf. Sibylline Oracles 3.84).
> I came to cast upon earth a stream of unquenchable fire that floweth, flaming with fire (cf. Apocalypse of Peter).

Jeremias[33] takes Luke 12:49 to mean that the parousia will bring the flood of fire which will destroy the sinful cosmos, as in the days of Sodom and Gomorrah (Luke 17:28-30). The deluge of water is also at hand (Luke 17:26-27). The parallelism between 12:49 and 12:50 also couples the deluge of fire with that of water. Jesus is the Bringer-in of the new age, but the way to the new creation lies through the deluge of fire and water. Thus the world and not Jesus, according to Jeremias, is the object of the baptism of water in 12:50. Jeremias declares that the destruction of the world by fire is a conception which runs throughout the NT. Yet he cites only 1 Cor 3:13-15 and 2 Pet 3:7-10.

In favor of Jeremias' idea of a double deluge of fire and water (Luke 12:49-50; 17:26-30) we may recall that the scorching heat of 12:55 prefigures the scorching fire cast by the returning Jesus (12:49). The thunderstorm of 12:54 would then point to the final flood of water (12:50). But we should note that Jeremias is concerned with Jesus' thought at 12:49-50. It is of course possible that Jesus may have referred to a cosmic baptism of suffering and destruction, as Jeremias contends. But in its Lukan context we have seen that the baptism of 12:50 must refer at least primarily to Jesus' death.

Conzelmann[34] also is against spiritualizing the fire in 12:49 and regards this fire as the cosmic conflagration, but does not cite evidence in favor of this view.

7. The Flaming Flame (Luke 23:31)

Luke 23:31 is an obscure verse which deserves more attention in studies of Luke's eschatology, especially in connection with Luke 12:49, than it has received. Echoes of the cosmic conflagration may be heard in the mysterious proverb of Luke 23:31:

> For if they do these things in the green tree, what shall be done in the dry?

This dark saying has naturally given rise to numerous interpretations:

---

[33] Jeremias, *Weltvollender*, pp. 11, 70; *Parables*, pp. 163-164; *Theology*, p. 127.
[34] Conzelmann, *Theology*, p. 109.

> If I must suffer this, how much more this guilty nation![35]

> If the Romans have dealt thus with the innocent Jesus, how hardly will they deal with those who are guilty?[36]

> The fire of judgment will pass on from the green wood to the dry, that is, Jesus' suffering will be the prelude to the collective suffering of the tribulation.[37]

> The saying refers symbolically to the fires of judgment to come upon the Jewish people (dry wood) and Jesus (green wood) in his death.[38]

But in view of the fact that this proverb is within a little apocalypse (23:27-31)(Chap. I.C.7), and in light of Luke's predilection for fire, may we not understand it as follows?

> If Jerusalem (the green tree), which is called the Holy City, be destroyed by fire by its enemies (cf. Luke 19:39-44; 21:20-24), how much more will the wicked pagan world (dry tree) be utterly devoured by the flames of the cosmic conflagration kindled by the Son of Man?

It is true that 23:31 does not explicitly mention "fire." But that fire may be included in the reference to trees is suggested by Luke 3:9: "Every tree therefore that bringeth not forth good fruit is hewn down, and cast into the fire." Another passage pointing in the same direction is Ezek 20:45-48:

> And the word of Yahweh came unto me, saying 46 Son of man, set thy face toward the south, and drop thy word toward the south, and prophesy against the forest of the field in the South: 47 and say to the forest of the South, Hear the word of Yahweh: Thus saith the Yahweh God, Behold I will kindle (*anaptō*) a fire in thee, and it shall devour every green tree in thee, and every dry tree: the flaming flame shall not be quenched, and all faces from the south to the north shall be burnt thereby. 48 And all flesh shall see that I, Yahweh, have kindled (*ekkaiō*) it; it shall not be quenched.

According to Ezekiel, the fire kindled by Yahweh devours every green and dry tree. It is not unlikely that Luke, if not Jesus, understood the saying of Luke 23:31 to mean the fire to be kindled by Jesus as Son of Man.

That Luke had Ezek 20:45-48 in mind is indicated not only by the parallels with Luke 23:31 and by the strong influence which Ezekiel exerted upon Luke's eschatological program (Chap. VI.F.5.a; VIII.E.3) but also by the parallels between Ezek 20:45-48 and Luke 12:49-56. In Ezek 20:45-48 there is reference to Ezekiel as Son of Man (though simply in the sense of "mortal man"), to the South, and to kindling a fire, an unquenchable one. The same verb (*anaptō*) for "kindle" is used in Ezek 20:47 (=21:3, LXX) as in Luke 12:49. Likewise in Luke 12:49-56, Jesus is thought of as Son of Man (in the apocalyptic sense), and there are references to the south (wind) and to kindling a fire. If our interpretation is correct, this kindling of fire means that Jesus as the Son of Man will kindle the judgment-tribulation fire which cannot be quenched but which will ignite the cosmic conflagration and continue to burn forever as the unquenchable fire of Gehenna.

---

[35] Easton, *Luke*, p. 346.

[36] Franklin, *Christ the Lord*, p. 90, who finds scarcely any influence of Isa 10:16-19 and Ezek 20:47 upon Luke 23:31.

[37] Jeremias, *Theology*, p. 284.

[38] Delling, "Baptism," p. 110.

222

The likelihood that Luke 23:31 alludes to the world conflagration is increased by the similar reference in Qumran's Book of Hymns (1QH)(*DSS*, pp. 131, 139):

> The flash of their spears is like fire devouring timber (2.26).--rivers that are like fire devouring all that draw their waters, rivers whose runnels destroy green tree and dry tree alike, . . . (3.19-36).

Our study of Luke 12:49 against the background of various passages leads to this conclusion: At Acts 7:55-56 (Chap. IV.G.8; Chap. VI.G.4) Jesus is standing, ready to return in fiery judgment, about to fulfil his wish to throw a firebrand upon the earth:

> I came to set the earth on fire, and how I wish it were already kindled! (Luke 12:49)(TEV).

8. Luke's Holy War of the Last Days

But are not these descriptions of literal end-time fires reminiscent of a "holy war"? Yet does not the very idea of war clash with the message of the gospels in general and of Luke-Acts in particular?

> Blessed are the peacemakers (Matt 5:9).
> Resist not him that is evil (Matt 5:39).
> For all they that take the sword shall perish with the sword (Matt 26:52).

Amazingly, not one of these pacifistic verses appears in Luke-Acts. Luke in fact is rather partial toward centurions (Luke 7:1-10; 23:47; Acts 10:1-8,22,31). Luke of course begins his gospel with "a multitude of the heavenly host praising God, and saying, Glory to God in the highest, And on earth peace among men in whom he is well pleased" (2:13-14). But here "peace" (*shalom*) probably means "salvation," and "men in whom he is well pleased" indicates those persons who are the objects of God's favor, that is, the "elect."[39] "Peace to the men he favors" (Goodspeed). The verse thus means "salvation to the elect."

We recall also Luke 12:51: "Think ye that I am come to give peace in the earth? I tell you, Nay; but rather division." We have observed too (Chap. VIII.E.4) that Jesus' refusal to call down fire upon the Samaritans is a matter of timing rather than a manifestation of the gentleness of Luke's Jesus. When we consider these data the way would seem to be open to broach the idea of Luke's "holy war."

A "holy war" as practiced in Israel (Deuteronomy 20), especially during the conquest of Canaan, was a war declared, led, and won by "Yahweh, a man of war" (Exod 15:3). A chief aspect of a holy war is expressed by the term *cherem* (Josh 6:17-18), which is translated as "doomed" or "devoted" or "accursed" things. *Cherem* means something forbidden to common use, set apart for the deity, devoted to destruction as a holocaust to Yahweh. Thus the spoils of war, including people and livestock, were to be *cherem*, devoted to deity. Precious objects, such as silver and gold, gained in conquest could be set apart in the sacred tent as the exclusive possession of Yahweh. But since towns and peoples could not be so set apart or dedicated to the deity, they were to be destroyed in order not to be capable of further opposition to Yahweh. Israel regarded the Canaanites as *cherem*, devoted to Yahweh, and therefore to be destroyed.

---

[39]Cf. J. Weiss, in Bruce, *Gospels*, p. 473; Vogt, "Peace," pp. 114-117.

The practice of the holy war largely faded away after the days of Samuel, who championed it rigorously against Saul, who disregarded it (1 Samuel 15). But during the second century B.C. the rules of the holy war were followed by the Jewish Maccabees in their revolt against Syria and accepted by the Jews who lived in the Qumran community by the Dead Sea, as set forth in the scroll entitled "The War between the Children of Light and the Children of Darkness" (1QM). A holy war at the end of days became a feature of apocalypticism.

Of special interest to us is the appearance of the idea of the eschatological holy war in Ezekiel 38-39. Here the final conflict is declared, led, and won by the Lord, to whom the enemy are *cherem*. The forces of Israel play only a passive role:

> And it shall come to pass in that day, when Gog shall come against the land of Israel, saith the Yahweh God, that my wrath shall come up into my nostrils. 19 For in my jealousy and in the fire of my wrath have I spoken, Surely in that day there shall be a great shaking in the land of Israel; 20 so that the fishes of the sea, and the birds of the heavens, and the beasts of the field, and all creeping things that creep upon the earth, and all the men that are upon the face of the earth, shall shake at my presence, and the mountains shall be thrown down, and the steep places shall fall, and every wall shall fall to the ground. 21 And I will call for a sword against him unto all my mountains, saith the Lord Yahweh: every man's sword shall be against his brother. 22 And with pestilence and with blood will I enter into judgment with him; and I will rain upon him, and upon his hordes, and upon the many peoples that are with him, an overflowing shower, and great hailstones, fire and brimstone... 39:3 and I will smite thy bow out of thy left hand, and will cause thine arrows to fall out of thy right hand. 4 Thou shalt fall upon the mountains of Israel, thou, and thy hordes, and the peoples that are with thee....6 And I will send a fire on Magog, and on them that dwell securely in the isles; and they shall know that I am Yahweh.

Since the incipient apocalypse of Ezekiel 38-39 exercises such a formative influence upon Luke's eschatological program (Chaps. VI.F.5.a; VIII.E.2.3.7), it would appear altogether likely that Luke is also influenced by Ezekiel's concept of the holy war of the last days. This suggestion is confirmed by the appearance in Luke-Acts of several motifs of the final war of Ezekiel 38-39.

The motif of fire is prominent in Ezekiel's holy war. The Lord speaks in the fire of his wrath (38:19). He rains fire and brimstone upon Gog and all his hordes (38:22), and sends fire upon Magog and on them that dwell securely in the isles (39:6). Similarly in Luke fire plays a key role in the last conflict. Messiah is to baptize in fire (Luke 3:16). He kindles the final conflagration (12:49) of scorching heat (12:55). He rains fire and brimstone from heaven (17:29-30). Flames will devour the world (23:31). Fire will be one of the wonders of the day of the Lord (Acts 2:19)(Chap. VIII.E.5.b).

For Ezekiel and Luke supernatural forces produce chaotic masses of water. A great shaking will cause the fishes of the sea to shake (Ezek 38:19-20). Nations will be in perplexity for the roaring of the sea and the billows, for in this battle against the power of chaos the powers of the heavens will be shaken (Luke 21:25-26).

Ezekiel and Luke regard the Lord's enemies as *cherem*, devoted to the deity for destruction by fire and sword. Gog and all those with him will fall upon the mountains of Israel (Ezek 39:4). It will take Israel seven months to bury them

(39:12), and birds and beasts will feast upon the flesh of warriors, princes, and horses (39:17-20). Also in Luke the Lord's enemies are to be cut asunder (12:46), slain (19:27), and fall by the edge of the sword (21:24).

Both Ezekiel and Luke feature the sword of the end-time battle, to which the godless will fall. The Lord calls for a sword against Gog and every man's sword will be against his brother (Ezek 38:21). The people of Jerusalem will fall by the sword (Luke 21:24). The returning Son of Man will cut his enemies in two (12:46) or to pieces (19:27), as Samuel did Agag in the holy war against the Amalekites (1 Sam 15:33). In preparation for the final battle the Lord calls for a sword: "He that hath none, let him sell his cloak, and buy a sword. . . . And they said, Lord, behold, here are two swords. And he said unto them, It is enough" (Luke 22:36,38). Two swords are enough, for in a holy war there is absolute trust in the power of God to win the victory. "How could two swords be enough unless God or His angels were also going to intervene?"[40] We are reminded of the sword of the triumphant Christ in Rev 1:16; 2:12,16; 19:15,21 and of the supreme confidence of Judas Maccabeus when confronted by overwhelming forces during a holy war:

> It is easy for many to be hemmed in by few, for in the sight of Heaven there is no difference between saving by many or by few. It is not on the size of the army that victory in battle depends, but strength comes from Heaven. . ..He himself will crush them before us; as for you do not be afraid of them (1 Macc 3:18-19, 22).

For Luke, the holy war to defeat the kingdom of Satan began with Jesus' power struggle with Satan and his forces in the temptations (Luke 4:1-13), and was continued through the exorcisms of Jesus and his disciples (Luke 9:1; 10:17-19; 11:14-23; Acts 10:38; 16:18; 19:12), as well as through the missionary proclamation that men should turn "from the power of Satan unto God" (Acts 26:18). The Spirit rushed (Acts 2:2) upon the disciples, empowering them for the holy war, even as it rushed (Judg 14:19, American) upon the judges (Judg 3:10; 6:34; 11:29; 13:25; 14:6,19), Saul (1 Sam 10:6,10; 11:6), and David (1 Sam 16:13), to make their hands prevail mightily (Judg 3:10). At the crucifixion Jesus was handed over to the power of darkness (Luke 22:53), and darkness ensued over the whole land while the sun's light failed (Luke 23:44-45). The victory of the resurrection over the dark forces of Satan will be consummated in the fiery parousia of the Son of Man (Luke 12:49; 17:29-30), when the sons of this world (Luke 16:8) will be devoted to the deity as *cherem* (Luke 12:46; 19:27; 21:24) and the sons of light (Luke 16:8) will enter into the kingdom.[41] But they will enter only after much tribulation (Acts 14:22) in the holy war against the anti-kingdom group: "Sorrow, like a sharp sword" breaks Mary's heart (Luke 2:35)(TEV); Stephen is stoned (Acts 7:59), and James is killed with the sword (Acts 12:2). The supreme command of the holy war is this: "Fight your way in at the narrow door" (Luke 13:24)(R. Knox). "Every one enters it [the kingdom of God] violently" (Luke 16:16)(RSV) through the holy war. The preaching of the good news of the kingdom (16:16) is, as we have just noted, an aspect of the holy war (on 13:24 and 16:16 see Chap. VII.F.6).

Luke then, pictures Jesus, not as a political Zealot seeking to foment a revolt

---

[40] Hiers, *Historical Jesus,* p. 104.

[41] *Cf.* Betz, "Krieg," pp. 116-137, though Betz is concerned with Jesus's holy war rather than with Luke's. Betz thinks Luke 16:16 misses the implication for the holy war of Jesus' violent saying in Matt 11:12.

against Rome, but "as an apocalyptic Zealot, proclaiming a final impending War against Belial and all his followers in heaven and on earth, even in the same family."[42]

9. "Greet No One on the Way" (Luke 10:4b)[43]

This half-verse, which is peculiar to Luke, reflects the hostility between the kingdom group and the anti-kingdom group which erupts as these two groups engage in the holy war of the last days. The command to the seventy to greet no one on their journey reflects both the eschatological haste of the mission (Chap. V.D.4) and the whole-hearted devotion to the mission, a single-mindedness characterstic of soldiers in a holy war. This complete dedication required of disciples is spelled out in the preceding pericope, 9:57-62. Like soldiers on the march, disciples have nowhere to lay their heads. They must let the dead bury the dead, and must not look back, once they have put their hands to the plow. "A man would have to leave his father unburied to join his regiment in war."[44] How much more so should he do so now that the final holy war is being waged. In this kind of war the greatest urgency is the preaching of the approaching kingdom (Luke 9:60).

Luke 10:4b, however, connotes not only haste and devotion but also hostility. The immediate context of 10:4b is concerned with stating emphatically the opposition between the world and Jesus' envoys. They will be lambs in the midst of wolves (10:3), who threaten on every side the harbingers of peace. This metaphor implies hostility of the world towards the disciples. Shaking the dust of a town off the feet (Luke 10:11; Acts 13:51) is another image denoting positive hostility on the seventy's part, for this sign means that the missionaries reject the wicked like dust shaken off the feet, thereby indicating that these inhospitable persons have no part in the end-time peace (*shalom*). They are damned like Sodom (Luke 10:12,15) and like Satan himself (10:18). For as the necessary correlative to the nearness of the kingdom of God (10:9) is the nearness of the judgment (10:18): the former is acted out in the greeting of peace, the latter in the refusal to greet. Saluting no one on the road is an image of the radical hostility between the missioners and the many to whom they will announce their peace in vain, that is, the enmity between the kingdom of God (Luke 10:9) and the kingdom of Satan (10:18). Men would deliberately reject the missioners and the missioners would reject men. The sons of the kingdom the missioners greeted with "peace"; to the wolves they could say no "*shalom*," for the world of salvation (*shalom*) and the world of evil are at radical variance.

Similar opposition to the world is expressed by the Psalmist: To the wicked "passers by will not say, 'The Lord's blessing on you'" (129:8). And 1 Enoch

---

[42]Black, "Violent Word," p. 118; Black's study, however, is oriented less toward Luke 12:49 than toward Matt 10:34. His statement quoted here is in reference to the sword of Matt 10:34.

[43]Adapted from O'Hagan, "Greet No One," but I attempt to relate his findings to the holy war, which he does not do.

[44]Montefiore, *Gospels*, II, 133.

states eleven times that the wicked will have no peace (e.g., 103:8). "Peace" (*shalom*) is the greeting to be given or withheld by the seventy (Luke 10:5-6).

Such hostility toward a hostile environment is also expressed by Paul, who delivered an incestuous man over to Satan (1 Cor 5:5), and by Matt 18:17, "Let him [who refuses to hear the church] be unto thee as the Gentile and the publican" (that is, give him no greeting in the way). Ignatius of Antioch reminds one of Luke 10:4b when he writes: "Such men you must avoid as you would avoid wild beasts" (Ephesians 7). Still more explicit is Didache 15:3, saying that when anyone offends with regard to charity "let nobody speak to him."

An attitude of enmity was adopted by the church particularly toward men who opposed the work of missionaries. 2 Tim 4:14-15 exhorts Timothy to avoid Alexander, who did Paul much evil. In Gal 1:9 Paul admonishes: "If anyone preaches a gospel to you, contrary to that which we preached to you, let him be accursed" (*anathema*)(*cherem*) (Section 8). Let those who thwart the missionaries be unmasked and opposed for what they are, members of the hostile unregenerate order. How much more so false teachers: "If anyone come to you and does not bear this teaching, do not receive him into your house, and do not greet him" (2 John 10).

With this missionary material in mind we may return to Luke 10:4b. As Luke's seventy walk along the roads of Israel they express their hostility toward the inimical world of evil by refusing to salute anyone on the way, whether of Satan or not. As they go in haste they are not concerned to know which few if any of the passers by are sons of light. But when they seek lodging (10:5-6) they will discover who are the sons of peace. The missioners will allow their greeting of peace to abide upon those who are hospitable, but will take back their salutation from those who show themselves to be sons of this world. Thus the mission of the seventy, and the world mission it symbolizes, is one phase of the end-time holy war between the forces of evil and those of Christ. Perhaps Luke's involvement in this final struggle explains his omission of Matt 5:47: "And if ye salute your brethren only, what do ye more than others? do not even the Gentiles the same?" The hostility of the holy war is also reflected in the italicized words of the Lukan version of Matt 10:37//Luke 14:26: "If any man cometh unto me, and *hateth* not his own father, and mother, and wife, and children, and brethren, and sisters, yea, *and his own life also*, he cannot be my disciple."

10. Luke's Switch to Action

In a holy war human activity plays a more (conquest of Canaan) or less (Ezekiel's war against Gog) important role. In Luke's holy war we have noted the activity of Jesus and the disciples in exorcisms and preaching. Can we say more about man's part, especially that of Luke, in this final conflict? Fortunately for our purposes a German sociologist, Wilhelm Mühlmann, has made an instructive study of the transition from inaction to action among apocalyptic groups from ancient to modern times.[45] He has found that although according to apocalyptic belief God himself will bring in the new age, situations do arise when such believers, for whom expectation is everything, may turn to action, even violent,

---

[45] Mühlmann, *Chiliasmus*, especially pp. 273-277, 315-353. Our summary of Mühlmann continues until otherwise indicated.

revolutionary action, or to a holy war. The switch to action may occur when the prophet links his prophecies to specific demands: The Savior and Paradise will come when you behave in a certain way. Conversely, the prophet may rationalize by saying the prophecies did not occur because his followers did not behave properly, or lacked faith, or tolerated too many doubters among them. And when men lose patience they may act to bring in the coming salvation. Man is a much too active being to endure in the long run a purely passive waiting. The prophecy may be turned into action when the group seeks to fulfil the prophecy according to the motto: "We must use the short span of time so that the prophecies will be fulfilled in our day."

Interestingly enough, if the parousia does not occur, men do not necessarily fold their hands and do nothing, nor is the prophet inevitably discredited. The prophet may in fact seek to outdo himself by making broader, more colorful predictions. The failure of the prophecy may even be a spur to action, as in the case of the "Seekers" (dubbed "Flying Saucer Clubs" by outsiders). This small, exclusive group believed the end of the world was at hand. They only would be saved by human-like beings from another world, who were supposed to land in flying saucers at a definite place at a definite time to pick up the believers and thus to rescue them from the cosmic catastrophe. The event did not occur, even though it had been postponed several times. Surprisingly, these disappointments did not destroy the group. Instead it became an organized sect. The fact that the prophecies were unfulfilled was answered with a "nevertheless." The emotional vacuum was filled with increased propagandistic and organizational activity, which indeed was successful, for more proselytes were made than ever. Precisely because the prophecies were not fulfilled there arose a greater urgency among the propagandists to convince more and more people that their belief, "in spite of," was correct. The principle was that if all people on earth would believe the same thing, then no more questions could arise about the soundness of their belief.

If the paradise does not come of itself, people finally seek to anticipate it. Such anticipation can take several forms:

a) One seeks to identify with the role of the masters. Natives wear European clothing. Peasants appear as bourgeois and bourgeois as nobility. Here belongs the motif of the "heavenly banquet," which the prophet celebrates with his followers as they anticipate the role of their masters. Natives sit down at European tables in their best clothes.

b) Ethical rigorism results when believers feel they must improve themselves to experience the new condition of salvation and to be received into the kingdom of God. Since believers feel they are unworthy to enter the kingdom they must promptly repent and be changed. The result may be teetotalism, pacifism, or perfectionism.

c) Cessation of work is characteristic of some apocalyptic movements. "Be not anxious about tomorrow, nor for food and clothing" (Matt 6:33). Stoppage of work was Jesus' demand of the fisherman who were to let their nets lie to become "fishers of men" (Matt 4:18-22; Mark 1:16-20; Luke 5:10-11). He who leaves a house will receive it back a hundred fold. He who ceases to cultivate his own acre will be sent out by God into God's harvest (Matt 9:37; Luke 10:2). The faithful are to forsake all work and practice "non-cooperation." Some, such as the

Qumranites, flee to the desert to await in purity the breaking-in of the kingdom, prepared to wage the eschatological holy war against unbelievers. In the Wilsnaker movement of 1475 peasants left their fields and women hearth and home to join processions through the land in expectation of the approaching end.

d) Eschatological action may include the destruction of the means of production. The Papuans of New Guinea, members of the Cargo movement, at the command of their prophets laid waste their gardens, killed their swine, destroyed houses, and the vessels, masks, and other paraphernalia of the old religion, all in the expectation of receving many fold that which they had given up as evidence of their strong faith. What is now destroyed will be replaced by more and better in the new order (Matt 19:27-30; Mark 10:28-31; Luke 18:29-30). Here two motives are at work: the hope of many-fold reward and the tabula-rasa idea of making a clean sweep for the appearance of the Redeemer.

e) Authority may be questioned, an action which may range from questioning whether one should pay taxes to the governing power to an actual tax-strike, as in the case of the Koréri movement of the Papuans, who in anticipation of the end proclaimed they would pay no more taxes.

Mühlmann makes it plain that we must recognize the revolutionary character of eschatology and the easy transition from adventism to activism. The tendency to revolt came into the world through Jewish-Christian apocalyptic, especially through the books of Enoch, Daniel, and Revelation, which, ever newly interpreted, are still effective in adventist-activist movements. This apocalypticism may be termed a "proletariat eschatology," in that over and over it has appealed to the proletariat of the world. It also involves a polarization between the we group (the elect, the elite of the new age, though the proletariat of this age) and the you group (the non-elect, the elite of this age who will be the non-elite of the new age). This elite consciousness is reflected in the contrast between the true Israel, the new people of God (we group) and the nations or Gentiles (you group). This proletariat eschatology includes the principle of the inverted world (compensatory megalomania), in which those who are now oppressed will reign in the new age over their present oppressors. Social positions will be inverted but not destroyed, for the elevation of us (the we group) and the putting down of them (the you group). Those who are miserable now will be judges in the good time to come. In the kingdom the black people of this age will be white and the white will be black.

The psychological reverse side of the motto, "Destroy everything," is the subjective inability to accept the present order. This attitude can lead to self-destruction as a means of forcing the end. In Russia in the seventeenth century the old believers opposed the western reforms of Peter the Great and branded him as anti-Christian. After 1666 there spread abroad the expectation of the destruction of the world. The end of the age was to occur in 1669, but was postponed again and again. Finally the adventist mood shifted to an activist one: the old believers sought to bring the end to pass by self-cremation. Such took place in large numbers, especially between 1670 and 1690. Not seldom these sectarians reported their intention to destroy the world in order to save themselves in this way from the Antichrist. From 1666-1690 more than 20,000 people are supposed to have burned themselves to death. During the eighteenth and nineteenth centuries the number decreased.[46]

One of the most striking of all social phenomena is that of the prophets who at one moment preach love rather than force but in the next moment issue a summons to force, to the final use of force which will bring the conditions which will abolish the use of force. The we group sees the you group as sinners of Satan's army who must be destroyed in a holy war. When the hour of revenge comes, the imitation of Christ refers not to his grace but to his wrath. The Taborites murdered men, women, and children, appealing to the cry at midnght of Matt 25:6.

So much for our summary of Mühlmann. Mühlmann of course does not work out the implications of his studies for Luke's eschatology. But by seeking to apply to Luke the results of Mühlmann's sociolgoical analysis of adventist, apocalyptic, and chiliastic movements we may perhaps better understand Luke's dialectic between expectation and action. It becomes clear that Luke as an apocalyptist did not necessarily have to sit idly by awaiting the *eschaton*. A delayed *eschaton* may, as we have seen, lead to action of various kinds. Such is the case with Luke, whose actions are much in accord with those of the apocalyptists described by Mühlmann. In general we may say that Luke seeks to transform the prophecies into action according to the principle, "One must use the short time before the end so as to insure the fulfilment of the prophecies." Such a Lukan program of action is as follows:

a) Luke acted by postponing the date of the parousia. We have dealt with this aspect of Luke's program in Chap. VI, where we noted the adjustments Luke made in line with his situation in Period C.

b) Luke did not retrench in respect to his eschatological expectations but broadened them to make the program even more attractive than before. As we have pointed out (Chap. VI.F.5), he makes more of the restoration of Israel to be followed by the restoration of all things than any other NT writer.

c) Luke stresses organizational activity, such as the choice of a successor to Judas (Acts 1:12-26), communal living (2:42-47; 4:32-5:1), appointment of the seven helpers (6:1-7), the appointment of elders in the churches (14:23), the council of Jerusalem (15:1-35), and the distribution of the apostolic decree (16:4).

d) Luke exhorts to endless praying for the end (Chap. V.G; Chap. V.I.4.c; Chap. VIII.E.11), an activity appropriate to an imminent expectation. Prayer is a weapon in Luke's arsenal for the holy war. It is profitable to compare a prayer before a battle in the Maccabees' holy war with a prayer of the Jerusalem church:

1 Macc 4:30-33	Acts 4:24-30
30 When he [Judas] saw that the army was strong, he prayed, saying, Blessed art thou, O Savior of Israel, who didst crush the attack of the mighty warrior by the	24 And they, when they heard it [order not to speak in Jesus' name], lifted up their voice to God with one accord, and said, O Lord, thou didst make the heaven and

---

[46] We are reminded of 1 Cor 13:3, "If I give my body to be burned, . . ." Is Paul alluding to persons who were trying to force the end? Cf. Tacho and sons, Stephen's death, and Luke 11:49-51 (Chap. VI.G.4).

hand of thy servant David, and didst give the camp of the Philistines into the hands of Jonathan, the son of Saul, and of the man who carried his armor, 31 So do thou hem in this army by the hand of thy people Israel, and let them be ashamed of their troops and their cavalry. 32 Fill them with cowardice; melt the boldness of their strength; let them tremble in their destruction. 33 Strike them down with the sword of those who love thee, and let all who know thy name praise thee with hymns.

the earth and the sea, and all that in them is: 25 who by the Holy Spirit, by the mouth of our father David thy servant, didst say, Why did the Gentiles rage, And the peoples imagine vain things? 26 The kings of the earth set themselves in array, And the rulers were gathered together, Against the Lord, and against his Anointed: 27 for of a truth in this city against thy holy Servant Jesus, whom thou didst anoint, both Herod and Pontius Pilate, with the Gentiles and the peoples of Israel, were gathered together, 28 to do whatsoever thy hand and thy counsel foreordained to come to pass. 29 And now, Lord, look upon their threatenings: and grant unto thy servants to speak thy word with all boldness, 30 while thou stretchest forth thy hand to heal; and that signs and wonders may be done through the name of thy holy Servant Jesus.

Each prayer arises out of a situation in which the kingdom group is threatened by the anti-kingdom group. Each prayer expresses confidence that God, who has acted mightily in the past, especially through David, can deliver his people against overwhelming odds. Each appeals for boldness in the conflict; implores God to act against his enemies; and asks for divine empowerment to use effectively its weapon in the holy war: the Maccabees, the sword; the church, missionary preaching (=to speak thy word) and wonders. The Maccabees pray for the destruction of their enemies, the church for the conversion of theirs (though the ultimate fate of most of the church's foes will be eternal destruction by the sword of the Son of Man--Luke 12:46; 19:27). A similar prayer of Qumran's holy war is 1QM 10.1-12.18 (*DSS*, pp. 293-297).

e) Luke encourages his community to anticipate their roles as lords and judges in the messianic banquet (Luke 12:37; 13:28-30; 22:29-30). Luke's is a proletarian eschatology with a special appeal to the poor, oppressed, and dispossessed. Luke with his "poverty piety" takes up only those beatitudes concerned with the poor, hungry, weeping, and persecuted (Luke 6:20-23). He adds, in line with his concept of the inverted world, woes upon the rich and comfortable in this age who will suffer a reversal of fortune in the new age (6:24-26), like Dives and Lazarus (16:16-31). Mary sings with a compensatory vision of grandeur: "He hath scattered the proud in the imagination of their heart. He hath put down princes from their thrones, And hath exalted them of low degree. The hungry hath he filled with good things; And the rich he hath sent empty away" (1:51-53).

We have already discovered that Luke makes a strong dichotomy between the we group (the kingdom group) and the you group (the anti-kingdom group)(Chap. VII.G.10). Luke's elite consciousness is seen especially in 17:21b, "The kingdom group (the elite group) is in the midst of the anti-kingdom group (the you group)." Already the kingdom group is "turning the world upside down" (Acts 17:6), a foreshadowing of the complete inversion to come with final victory.

f) Luke admonishes his people to repent and live ethical lives so as to be fit for the coming age of righteousness. The few who will be saved must agonize to enter in through the narrow door of high morality (Luke 13:24; 16:16). They are to be merciful as the Father is merciful (Luke 6:36), to love their enemies (6:35), and to give to every one that asks (6:30). Yet they do not reject the sword (22:35-38).[47] At 18:8b Luke apparently adopts the position that the blame for the delay lies with Christians themselves in their "lack of faith . . . and of that joyousness and constancy in prayer which spring from it."[48]

g) Luke advocates an "eschatological renunciation of property" in preparation for the holy war and impending kingdom. Disciples are to sell their possessions and give alms (12:33; 18:22), and at least some of them are to live communally (Acts 2:42-47; 4:32-5:11). Some disciples cease work, leave all, and follow Jesus to catch men (Luke 5:10-11, 28). Even women forsake hearth and home to proceed through the land in expectation of the end (Luke 8:1-3; 23:27,55; 24:10). Like the ravens, disciples are to sow not, neither reap (12:24). Like lilies they are not to toil nor to spin (12:27), but, like Jesus, live off the bounty of others (8:1-3; 9:1-6; 10:1-8). "Instead [of the things of this life] seek his kingdom, and these things shall be yours as well" (12:31)(RSV). It is worthy of note that Luke's command is absolute, whereas Matthew makes a concession to material things: "But seek *first* his kingdom . . ." (Matt 6:33)(RSV). Those who have left all to follow Jesus will "receive manifold more in this time, and in the world to come eternal life" (18:28-30). But those who refuse to leave their fields, oxen, and wives infuriate the householder, for they not only lack faith in the eschatological program and its doctrine of manifold reward but they also being entangled in wordly pursuits fail in that single-minded devotion to God which is required of recruits to the holy forces (cf. Deut 20:5-8; 24:5, where those burdened with domestic concerns are released from service) (Luke 14:17-21; cf. Acts 5:1-11).

Only Luke records the parable of the king preparing for war (Luke 14:31-32). Luke takes the parable not only as "a warning to count the cost of discipleship" but also as "a summons to disciples to renounce all their possessions" (14:33): "None of you can be my disciple unless he gives up everything he has" (TEV). This latter point is Luke's, for the parable itself has "no apparent reference to the theme of renunciation (vss 26-27) but Luke attempts to impose it."[49] Is not Luke imposing this point on the parable because he wishes to take advantage of a good opportunity to advocate to his contemporaries the eschatological renunciation of family (14:26) and of property (14:33) as a part of his holy war? Even if Luke did not have in mind the concept of holy war at this point, we may certainly conclude that "it is in the context of the need for the utmost urgency in the extremes of an eschatological situation that Luke's attitude toward riches and

---

[47]On the tension between love and hostility see O'Hagan, "Greet No One," pp. 82-83.

[48]Montefiore, *Gospels*, II, 554-555; Grässer, *Delay*, pp. 37-38; Schneider, *Parusiegleichnisse*, p. 78.

[49]Gilmour, *Luke*, p. 262.

poverty is best interpreted."⁵⁰

h) Luke approves the destruction of the paraphernalia of the old religions, as evidence of a turn from Satan to the power of God (Acts 26:18). At Ephesus "not a few of them that practiced magical arts brought their books together and burned them in the sight of all; and they counted the price of them, and found it fifty thousand pieces of silver" (Acts 19:19)($50,000---TEV). Possibly these books were regarded as "doomed things" (*cherem*) and therefore destroyed as part of the holy war against evil spirits (cf. Joshua 7:22-26).

Now that we have applied Mühlmann's analysis of apocalyptic movements to Luke-Acts, we can see that Luke, confronted by delay of the parousia, has reacted remarkably like apocalyptists of all ages. This fact is one more weighty objection to the contention of the Distant Expectation School that Luke acted out of apocalyptic character by solving the problem of the delay once and for all by shifting the end to the remote future. That, it seems, is not the way apocalyptists, ancient or modern, behave. If Luke made a switch, it was from passivity to activity, not from *Naherwartung* to *Fernerwartung*.

11. Luke's Ultimate Weapon

Luke, as we have seen, adopted a many-faceted program of action in preparation for the coming kingdom. But how can Luke most effectively implement his strategy for the holy war? Luke decides that the best way to advocate all of these actions (Section 10.a-h) is by writing. And if the results of our long study are correct, Luke does not write as a detached historian serenely surveying the non-eschatological past and confidently looking forward to a lengthy period of church history during which the church marches on from victory to victory. Rather, Luke writes out of a specific eschatological situation, out of the midst of the final holy war. Many battles lie ahead, more than had been expected during Periods A and B, but the Son of Man is standing, ready to return (Acts 7:55-56).

It is at this stage of the eschatological process that Luke takes his pen in hand. Like modern apocalyptists confronted with the problem of the delay (Chap. VIII.E.10), Luke presses the propagandistic activity of the preachers of the kingdom (Chap. I.E). The good news of the kingdom is being preached as a key phase of the holy war and all sorts of people are being constrained to enter into the kingdom (Luke 14:23; 16:16). More converts are being made than ever (Acts 2:47; 4:4; 5:14; 6:1,7; 9:31; 11:21,24; 12:24; 13:49; 16:5; 19:10,20). In accord with the principle of using the time before the end to help fulfil the prophecies, Luke gives the explicit command, "Trade with these till I come" (Luke 19:13) = "Make disciples through missionary activity" (Chap. VI.D.3).

But if the end is imminent, why does Luke bother to write at all? The Distant Expectation School finds the very existence of Luke-Acts incompatible with the imminent expectation, for historians write for future generations: "The earliest Christian congregations, which expected the imminent end of the world, had no

---

⁵⁰Franklin, *Christ the Lord*, p. 151. Franklin makes a careful study of Luke's attitude toward riches and poverty. "Hate" as a condition of discipleship, required only at Luke 14:26, may reflect the hostility of a holy war.

interest in leaving behind to posterity reports on their origin and development."⁵¹ But our contention is that it was precisely because of his imminent hope that Luke penned his two volumes. He has made it plain that the world mission is an eschatological necessity and as such is as much a part of the end-time program as wars and woes (Chap. VI.H.2.b). The end cannot come before the gospel has been preached "to the remotest parts of the earth" (Acts 1:8)(Weymouth). Therefore Luke wanted to promote the Pauline mission in particular and the world mission as a whole, for the proclamation of "repentance and remisison of sins... unto all nations" (Luke 24:47) was one of the preconditions of the imminent end. The Son of Man could not return in fiery glory (Luke 12:49) until that mission had been completed.⁵²

Luke and his people, who were praying endlessly for the end (Luke 18:1-8), desired nothing more than the coming of the kingdom (Chap. I.D). Impelled by this eager desire for the new order, Luke writes to expedite the world mission and thereby to help fulfill the eschatological program. The Gentile mission was well on the way toward completion with Paul's arrival in Rome: "...the Good News... has been proclaimed in the whole creation under Heaven..." (Col 1:23)(Weymouth). Were Paul to preach longer in Rome, where "all meet from every quarter" (Irenaeus), or in Spain (Rom 15:24; 1 Clem 5:7), or elsewhere (Pastoral Epistles), and were others to continue their labors (Acts 11:20; 1 Clem. 42:3-4), they would need all the encouragement and support possible from the churches to give all men everywhere opportunity to repent (Acts 17:30). As his part in this evangelistic effort Luke writes to insure that the world mission will be completed during the "times of the Gentiles" (Luke 21:24) to prepare the way for the "consolation of Israel" (Luke 2:25) and the "restoration of all things" (Acts 3:21).

Luke knew that his two-volume work was an eschatological phenomenon and an integral part of the scheme of messianic progress, helping to accomplish speedily all parts of this program. Far from being paralyzed by his imminent expectation, Luke, like Paul and other missioners who were laboring for the accomplishment of all things, was rather stimulated by it to fulfil his eschatological role. "Luke was trying a little 'mission' of his own to aid in fulfilling the conditions of 'Period C' by turning loose on the literary world a magnificent piece of religious propaganda."⁵³

Luke thus writes for the purpose of effecting the imminent end. He aims to push the end-time program ahead, to keep it moving with all deliberate speed toward completion at the predestined time. He writes to give the world mission a new impetus now that the goal is in sight. It may even be that Luke had hopes of bringing about the day of the Lord ahead of schedule. He reports Peter as saying: "Repent ye therefore, and turn again, that your sins may be blotted out, that so there may come seasons of refreshing from the presence of the Lord" (Acts

---

⁵¹Vielhauer, "Paulinism," p. 47.

⁵²Although I assume that Luke wrote while Paul was still alive, my main point that Luke was promoting the Gentile mission as a pre-condition of the end is also consistent with datings of Luke-Acts later in the first century (Chap. V.D.5). See "Rackham Reconsidered."

⁵³Letter of 5 February 1975 from D. J. Selby.

3:19). Peter implies that repentance would speed the coming of the end. Rabbis also taught that if all Israel would repent for one single day redemption through Messiah would come.[54] 2 Pet 3:12 admonishes readers not only to look for but to hasten the coming of the day of God: "Do your best to make it come soon" (TEV). Another rabbinical saying has it that "if thou keepest this precept thou hastenest the day of Messiah."[55] At least in some quarters human participation in preparing for, if not hastening, the eschaton was called for.

Luke may have thought the period of waiting could be shortened by prayer:

> Thy kingdom come (Luke 11:2).
> They ought always to pray (for the end)(18:1).
> Every moment pray that you may be fully strengthened to escape from all these coming evils (21:36)(Weymouth).

It has even been suggested that Luke commanded prayer to cause the coming of the ardently expected day.[56] Certainly if Luke did not think of his literary efforts and prayers as causing the parousia to come more quickly he at least intended to do his best to help fulfil those conditions without which it could not come and without which those prayers could not be answered.

The International Congress on World Evangelization, which met in Lausanne, Switzerland, in July 1974, had as its goal "to arouse all believers to a new obedience to Christ in world evangelism which will prepare the way for our Lord's triumphant return," and to gain "a new vision for evangelizing the world in this generation."[57] That was precisely Luke's eschatological purpose--twenty centuries ago!

Luke however does not allow his role as an apocalyptic activist to diminish his pastoral concern, a concern which we have had occasion to notice from time to time (see Chap. V.C.9). Luke was troubled by over-heated apocalyptists who expected too much of the eschatological program too fast (Chap. VI.D.3). For their benefit he included the passages of delay discussed in Chap. VI (Luke 9:23; 11:3; 19:11-27; 21:7-13; 21:24; 22:69; Acts 1:6-8), thereby assuring them that the great original apocalyptic truths of Period A were still basically valid in Period C. The apocalyptic agenda, correctly understood, however, contains many items, each one of which must come to pass before the end.

Luke also was mindful of those who were doubting the parousia, especially since some of the brethren were dying before the day of the Lord (Chap. VI.D.5). To shore up those of little faith Luke gives parables of confidence (mustard seed and leaven)(13:18-21) and stresses the imminent expectation in the passages handled in Chaps. IV and V (Acts 10:42; 17:30-31; 24:15,25; Luke 3:7,9; 9:26-27; 10:9,11; 11:30; 12:35-48; 18:1-8; 21:32; 21:34-36; 22:18). In spite of appearances, all is not lost. Suffering and tribulation are part of the final holy war. Only through much tribulation can anyone enter into the kingdom (Acts 14:22).

---

[54] Rackham, *Acts*, p. 53.

[55] Quoted by Vincent, *Word Studies*, I, 707.

[56] Bartsch, *Wachet*, p. 118. "Perhaps their prayers will bring the *parousia*" (Cadbury, *MLA*, p. 296). In Rev 8:3-5 the same censer is used to lay the prayers upon the altar and to cast fire upon the earth from that altar, for these prayers are the means of accomplishing the destruction of evil men and an evil world.

[57] Olson, "In Our Generation," p. 3.

Yet God will vindicate his needy people speedily; their endless prayers for the end will be answered (Luke 18:1-8).

Luke wants Theophilus and all of his readers to "know the full truth of all those matters which [they] have been taught" (Luke 1:4)(TEV), including such eschatological truths as these: Jesus is the Consummator of the world, the Bringer-in of the new age; the end comes speedily but not immediately (Luke 18:8; 19:11; 21:9); Israel's national hope will be fulfilled in the last days; the Gentiles will have opportunity to hear the good news; the world mission to the ends of the earth must be completed before the day of the Son of Man, who thereupon will return to hurl the firebrand of the cosmic conflagration upon the earth (Luke 12:49). If Theophilus will only interpret aright the time he will perceive that the world deluges of fire and water are on the way (Luke 12:51-56; 17:26-30).

"But the Son of Man when he comes won't find faith on earth, will he?" Those of little faith answer at once, "No, he won't." But Luke, with invincible courage, replies "Yes, he will find a persistence in faith answering to the widow's. The light of faith may flicker but it will not fail." To spread such faith Luke writes to expedite the mission "to all nations" (Luke 24:47), and in so doing he hammers out his ultimate weapon in the holy war against the kingdom of Satan, the Acts of the Apostles and a Gospel, "the most beautiful book ever written" (Renan).

Bibliography

(Shortened forms of titles are used in the footnotes)

Aalen, S. "St. Luke's Gospel and the Last Chapters of 1 Enoch," *NTS*, 13 (1966-1967), 1-13 (="Enoch").

Albright, W.F., and Mann, C.S. *Matthew.* "The Anchor Bible." Garden City: Doubleday, 1971 (=*Matthew*).

Allen, P.M.S. "Luke 17:21," *ET*, 49 (1937-1938), 476-477; 50 (1938-1939), 233-235 (="Luke 17:21").

Allen, Willoughby C. *A Critical and Exegetical Commentary on the Gospel according to S Matthew.* "The International Critical Commentary." New York: Charles Scribner's Sons, 1907 (=*Matthew*).

Bacon, Benjamin W. "The Autobiography of Jesus," *AJT*, 2 (1898), 527-560 (="Autobiography of Jesus").

Baer, Heinrich von. *Der Heilige Geist in den Lukasschriften.* "Beiträge zur Wissenschaft vom Alten und Neuen Testament," 3. Folge, 3. Heft. Stuttgart: W. Kohlhammer, 1926 (=Der Heilige Geist).

Bagster. *The Septuagint Version of the Old Testament and Apocrypha, with an English Translation. Grand Rapids: Zondervan (Bagster), 196* (=Bagster).

Baillie, John. *The Belief in Progress.* New York: Charles Scribner's Sons, 1951 (=*Progress*).

Baird, William. "The Gospel according to Luke," *The Interpreter's One-Volume Commentary on the Bible*, ed. C.M. Laymon. Nashville: Abingdon Press, 1971, pp. 672-706 (=*Luke*).

Barclay, William. *The Gospel of Luke.* "The Daily Study Bible." Philadelphia: Westminster Press, 1953 (=*Luke*).

Barrett, C. K. "Stephen and the Son of Man," in W. Eltester and F. H. Kettler (eds.), *Apophoreta: Festschrift für Ernst Haenchen.* Berlin: Alfred Töpelmann, 1964, pp. 32-38 (="Son of Man").

Bartsch, Hans-Werner. "Early Christian Eschatology in the Synoptic Gospels," NTS, 11 (1965), 387-397 (="Eschatology").

Bartsch, Hans-Werner. *Wachet aber zu jeder Zeit! Entwurf einer Auslegung des Lukasevangeliums.* Hamburg-Bergstedt: Herbert Reich, Evangelischer Verlag GMBH, 1963 (=*Wachet*).

Berkey, R.F. "Realized Eschatology," *JBL*, 82 (1963), 177-187 (="Realized Eschatology").

Betz, O. "Jesu Heiliger Krieg," *NovT*, 2 (1957-1958), 116-137 (="Krieg").

Biederwolf, William E. *The Second Coming Bible.* Grand Rapids: Baker Book House, 1972 (=*Second Coming Bible*).

Black, Matthew. "Uncomfortable Words. III. The Violent Word," *ET*, 81 (1970), 115-118 (="Violent Word").

Borgen, Peder. "Von Paulus zu Lukas," *ST*, 20 (1966), 140-157 (="Paulus").

Brown, Francis; Driver S.R.; and Briggs, Charles A. *A Hebrew and English Lexicon of the Old Testament.* Oxford: At the Clarendon Press, 1907 (=Brown-Driver-Briggs).

Browning, W. R. F. *The Gospel according to Saint Luke.* 3d ed. "Torch Bible Commentaries." London: SCM, 1974 (=*Luke*).

Brownlee, W. H. "John the Baptist in the New Light of Ancient Scrolls," in Krister Stendahl (ed.), *The Scrolls and the New Testament.* New York: Harpher & Brothers, 1957, pp. 33-53 (="John the Baptist").

Bruce, Alexander B. *The Synoptic Gospels.* "The Expositor's Greek Testament." Grand Rapids: Eerdmans, 1956 (=*Gospels*).

Bruce, F.F. "Is the Paul of Acts the Real Paul?" *Bulletin of the John Rylands University Library of Manchester*, 58 (1976), 282-305 (="The Real Paul").

Bultmann, Rudolf. *Existence and Faith,* ed. S. M. Ogden. New York: Meridan, 1960 (=*Existence and Faith*).

Bultmann, Rudolf. *History of the Synoptic Tradition.* E. T., John Marsh. New York: Harper and Row, 1963 (=*Synoptic Tradition*).

Bultmann, Rudolf. *Theology of the New Testament.* 2 vols. E.T., Kendrick Grobel. New York: Charles Scribner's Sons, 1955 (=*Theology*).

Bundy, Walter C. *Jesus and the First Three Gospels.* Cambridge: Harvard University Press, 1955 (=*Gospels*).

Cadbury, Henry J. *Acts.* See Lake, Kirsopp.

Cadbury, Henry J. "Acts and Eschatology," in W. D. Davies and D. Daube (eds.), *The Background of the New Testament and Its Eschatology, in Honour of Charles Harold Dodd.* Cambridge: At the University Press, 1964, pp. 300-321 (="Acts and Eschatology").

Cadbury, Henry J. "The Kingdom of God and Ourselves," *The Christian Century*, 67 (1950), 172-173 (="Kingdom of God").

Cadbury, Henry J. *The Making of Luke-Acts.* London: S.P.C.K., 1968 (=*MLA*).

Cadbury, Henry J. "Note 30. Names for Christians and Christianity in Acts," *Beginnings of Christianity,* 1/5, pp. 375-392 (="Names").

Campbell, J.Y. "'The kingdom of God has come,'" *ET*, 48 (1936-1937), 91-94 (="Kingdom").

Carpenter, J. Estlin. *The First Three Gospels.* 4th ed. London: Philip Green, 1906 (=*Gospels*).

Charles, R. H. *Eschatology: The Doctrine of a Future Life in Israel, Judaism and Christianity.* New York: Schocken Books, 1899 (1913)(1963)(=*Eschatology*).

Clark, Kenneth W. "'Realized Eschatology,'" *JBL*, 59 (1940), 367-383 (="Realized Eschatology").

Clarke, W. K. L. "Studies in Texts: Luke 10:18," *Theology*, 7 (1923), 101-104 (="Luke 10:18").

Collins, Adela Y. "The Political Perspective of the Revelation to John," *JBL*, 96 (1977), 241-256 (="Political Perspective").

Conzelmann, Hans. *Die Aposteigeschichte.* "Handbuch zum Neuen Testament," 7. Tübingen: J.C.B. Mohr, 1963 (=*Apostelgeschichte*).

Conzelmann, Hans. *The Theology of St. Luke.* E. T., Geoffrey Buswell. New York: Harper and Row, 1960 (=*Theology*).

Craig, Clarence T. "Realized Eschatology," *JBL*, 56 (1937), 17-26 (="Realized Eschatology").

Craig, Clarence T. "The Teaching of Jesus," *IB*, 7 (1951), pp. 145-154 (="Teaching of Jesus").

Cranfield, C. E. B. "The Parable of the Unjust Judge and the Eschatology of Luke-Acts," *SJT*, 16 (1963), 297-301 (="Unjust Judge").

Creed, John Martin. *The Gospel according to St. Luke.* London: Macmillan, 1930 (1953) (=*Luke*).

Cullmann, O. "Le caractère eschatologique du devoir missionnaire et de la conscience apostolique de S. Paul. Étude sur le katechon (-ōn) de 2 Thess. 2:6-7," *RHPR*, 16 (1936), 210-245 (="Missionary Task").

Danker, Frederick W. *Jesus and the New Age According to St. Luke: A Commentary on the Third Gospel.* St. Louis: Clayton Publishing House, 1972 (=*Luke*).

Danker, Frederick W. "Luke 16:16--An Opposition Logion," *JBL*, 77 (1958), 231-243 (="Luke 16:16").

Delling, Gerhard. *"Baptisma baptisthēnai,"* *NovT*, 2 (1957-1958), 92-115 (=*"Baptisma"*).

Dibelius, Franz. "Zwei Worte Jesu" (Matt 5:19; 11:11), *ZNW*, 11 (1910), 188-192 (="Worte").

Dodd, C.H. *The Apostolic Preaching and Its Developments.* New York: Harper and Row, 1936 (1964) (=*Apostolic Preaching*).

Dodd, C. H. "The Kingdom of God Has Come," *ET*, 48 (1936-1937), 138-142 (="Kingdom of God").

Dodd, C. H. *The Parables of the Kingdom.* Revised ed. New York: Charles Scribner's Sons, 1961 (=*Parables*).

Dupont, Jacques. "L'après-mort dans l'oeuvre de Luc," *RTL*, (1973), 3-21 (="Mort").

Dupont, Jacques. "Les paraboles du sénevé et du levain," *NRT*, 89 (1967), 897-913 (="Paraboles").

Easton, Burton Scott. "The Development of Apostolic Christology," *ATR*, 1 (1918-1919), 148-163, 371-382 (="Christology").

Easton, Burton Scott. *The Gospel according to St. Luke. A Critical and Exegetical Commentary.* New York: Charles Scribner's Sons, 1926 (=*Luke*).

Easton, Burton Scott. "Lk. 17:20-21. An Exegetical Study," *AJT*, 16 (1912), 275-283 (="Luke 17:20-21").

Easton, Burton Scott. "The Purpose of Acts," in F. C. Grant (ed.), *Early Christianity: The Purpose of Acts and Other Papers*. London: S.P.C.K., 1955 (="Purpose of Acts").

Edwards, Richard A. *The Sign of Jonah in the Theology of the Evangelists and Q*. "Studies in Biblical Theology," 2d Series, 18. Naperville: Alec R. Allenson Inc., 1971 (=*Sign of Jonah*).

Einheitsübersetzung der Heiligen Schrift: Das Neue Testament. Stuttgart: Katholische Bibelanstalt, 1972 (=*Einheitsübersetzung*).

Elliott, J.K. "Did the Lord's Prayer Originate with John the Baptist?" *TZ*, 29 (1973), 215 (="Lord's Prayer").

Ellis, E. Earle. *Eschatology in Luke*. "Facet Books. Biblical Series," 30. Philadelphia: Fortress Press, 1972 = "Die Funktion der Eschatologie im Lukasevangelium," *ZTK*, 66 (1969-1970), 387-402 (=*Eschatology*).

Ellis, E. Earle. *The Gospel of Luke*. "The Century Bible." New Edition. London: Nelson, 1967 (=*Luke*).

Ellis, E. Earle. "Present and Future Eschatology in Luke," *NTS*, 12 (1965-1966), 27-41 (="Present and Future").

Evans, Howard Heber. *St. Paul the Author of the Acts of the Apostles and of the Third Gospel*. 2 vols. London: Wyman and Sons, 1884-1886 (=*Paul*).

Findlay, J. A. "Luke," *The Abingdon Bible Commentary*, ed. F. C. Eiselen, E. Lewis, and D. G. Downey. Nashville: Abingdon-Cokesbury Press, 1929, pp. 1022-1059 (=*Luke*).

Fitzer, Gottfried. "Phthanō," *TDNT*, 9, 88-92 (="Phthanō").

Flender, Helmut. *St. Luke: Theologian of Redemptive History*. E. T., Reginald H. and Ilse Fuller. Philadelphia: Fortress Press, 1967 (=*Luke*).

Flückiger, Felix. "Luk. 21:20-24 und die Zerstörung Jerusalems," *TZ*, 28 (1972), 385-390 (="Luke 21:20-24").

Francis, Fred. O. "Eschatology and History in Luke-Acts," *JAAR*, 37 (1969), 49-63 (="Eschatology").

Franklin, Eric. "The Ascension and the Eschatology of Luke-Acts," *SJT*, 23 (1970), 191-200 (="Ascension").

Franklin, Eric. *Christ the Lord: A Study in the Purpose and Theology of Luke-Acts*. Philadelphia: Westminster Press, 1975 (=*Christ the Lord*).

Fuller, Reginald H. *The Mission and Achievement of Jesus*. "Studies in Biblical Theology," First Series, 12. London: SCM Press, Ltd, 1954 (=*Mission*).

Gilmour, S. MacLean. "The Gospel According to St. Luke," *IB*, 8 (1952), 1-434 (=*Luke*).

Godet, F. *A Commentary on the Gospel of St. Luke*. 2 vols. E.T., E. W. Shalders and M. D. Cusin. 5th ed. "Clark's Foreign Theological Library." Edinburgh: T. & T. Clark, 1870 (1957) (=*Luke*).

Goodspeed, Edgar J. *Paul*. Nashville: Abingdon Press, 1947 (=*Paul*).

Gordon, R. P. "James 5:11," *JTS*, 26 (1975), 91-95 (="James 5:11").

Grässer, Erich. *Das Problem der Parusieverzögerung in den synoptischen Evangelien und in der Apostelgeschichte*. "Beihefte zur Zeitschrift für die neutestamentliche Wissenschaft," 22. Berlin: Alfred Töpelmann, 1957; 2. Auflage 1960 (=*Delay*).

Graystone, G. "'I Have Come to Cast Fire on the Earth...,'" *Scr*, 4 (1950), 135-141 (="Fire").

Green, Samuel G. *Handbook to the Grammar of the Greek Testament*. Revised by S. Walter Green. New York: Fleming H. Revell Company, n.d. (=*Handbook*).

Grelot, Pierre. "'Aujourd'hui tu seras avec moi dans le Paradis,'" *RB*, 74 (1967), 194-214 (="Luke 23:43").

Grensted, L. W. "The Use of Enoch in St. Luke 16:19-31," *ET*, 26 (1914-1915), 333-334 (="Enoch").

Griffiths, J. Gwyn. *"Entos humōn* (Luke 17:21)," *ET*, 63 (1951-1952), 30-31 (=*"Entos humōn"*).

Grobel, Kendrick. "'He That Cometh after Me,'" *JBL*, 60 (1941), 397-401 (="He That Cometh after Me").

Grundmann, Walter. *"Dei," TDNT*, 2, 21-25 (=*"Dei"*).

Grundmann, Walter. *Das Evangelium nach Lukas*. 2. Auflage. "Theologischer Handkommentar zum Neuen Testament." Berlin: Evangelische Verlagsanstalt, 1963 (=*Lukas*).

Haenchen, Ernst. *Die Apostelgeschichte*. 13. Auflage. Göttingen: Vandenhoeck & Ruprecht, 1961 (=*Apostelgeschichte*).

Harnack, Adolf. *The Date of the Acts and of the Synoptic Gospels*. E.T., J.R. Wilkinson. "Crown Theological Library," 33. New York: G. P. Putnam's Sons, 1911 (=*Date of Acts*).

Harrison, P. N. *Paulines and Pastorals*. London: Villiers, 1964 (=*Pastorals*).

Hawkins, John C. *Horae Synopticae: Contributions to the Study of the Synoptic Problem*. 2d ed. Grand Rapids: Baker Book House, 1899 (1909) (1968) (=*Horae Synopticae*).

Hiers, Richard H. "Friends By Unrighteous Mammon: The Eschatological Proletariat (Luke 16:9)," *JAAR*, 38 (1970), 30-36 (="Friends").

Hiers, Richard H. *The Historical Jesus and the Kingdom of God*. "University of Florida Humanities Monograph," 38. Gainesville: University of Florida Press, 1973 (=*Historical Jesus*).

Hiers, Richard H. *The Kingdom of God in the Synoptic Tradition*. "University of Florida Humanities Monograph," 33. Gainesville: University of Florida Press, 1970 (=*Kingdom of God*).

Hiers, Richard H. "The Problem of the Delay of the Parousia in Luke-Acts," *NTS*, 20 (1974), 145-155 (="Delay").

Hiers, Richard H. "Why Will They Not Say, 'Lo, here!' or 'There!'"? *JAAR*, 35 (1967), 379-384 (=""Lo, here!'").

Higgins, A. J. B. *Jesus and the Son of Man*. Philadelphia: Fortress Press, 1965 (=*Son of Man*).

Howard, Wilbert F. "The Gospel according to St. John," *IB*, 8 (1952), 435-811 (=*John*).

Jeremias, Joachim. "Gehenna," *TDNT*, 1, 657-658 (="Gehenna").

Jeremias, Joachim. "Hades," *TDNT*, 1, 146-149 (="Hades").

Jeremias, Joachim. "Ionas," *TDNT*, 3, 406-410 (="Ionas").

Jeremias, Joachim. *Jesus als Weltvollender*. "Beiträge zur Förderung christlicher Theologie," 33. Band, 4. Heft. Gütersloh: C. Bertelsmann, 1930 (=*Weltvollender*).

Jeremias, Joachim. *Jesus' Promise to the Nations*. "Studies in Biblical Theology," 24. London: SCM Press, 1967 (=*Promise*).

Jeremias, Joachim. *The Lord's Prayer*. E.T., John Reumann. "Facet Books-- Biblical Series," 8. Philadelphia: Fortress Press, 1964 (=*Lord's Prayer*).

Jeremias, Joachim. *New Testament Theology: The Proclamation of Jesus*. E.T., John Bowden. New York: Charles Scribner's Sons, 1971 (=*Theology*).

Jeremias, Joachim. *The Parables of Jesus*. E.T., S.H. Hooke. Revised ed. New York: Charles Scribner's Sons, 1963 (=*Parables*).

Jeremias, Joachim. *"Paradeisos," TDNT*, 5, 769-771 (="Paradise").

Kaestli, Jean-Daniel. *L'Eschatologie dans l'oeuvre de Luc. Ses caracteristiques et sa place dans le développement du Christianisme primitiv*. "Nouvelle série théologique," 22. Geneva: Labor et Fides, 1969 (=*Eschatologie*).

Keck, Fridolin. *Die öffentliche Abschiedsrede Jesu in Lk 20:45-21:36*. Inauguraldissertation, Universität Freiburg im Breisgau, 1973 (="Farewell Address").

Klein, G. "Die Prüfung der Zeit (Lk 12, 54-56)," *ZTK*, 61 (1964), 373-390 (="Prüfung").

Kohler, K. "The Testament of Job. An Essene Midrash on the Book of Job reëdited and translated with introductory and exegetical notes [by Rev. Dr. K. Kohler]," in George Alexander Kohut (ed.), *Semitic Studies in Memory of Rev. Dr. Alexander Kohut*. Berlin: S. Calvary & Co., 1897, pp. 264-338 (="Job").

Kümmel, Werner G. *Introduction to the New Testament*. E.T., A.J. Mattill, Jr. 14th ed. Nashville: Abingdon Press, 1966 (=*Introduction*).

Kümmel, Werner G. "Lukas 16:16 im Zusammenhang der heilsgeschichtlichen Theologie der Lukasschriften," in Georg Braumann (ed.), *Das Lukas-Evangelium*. "Wege der Forschung," 280. Darmstadt: Wissenschaftliche Buchgesellschaft, 1974, pp. 398-415 (="Luke 16:16").

Kümmel, Werner G. *Promise and Fulfilment: The Eschatological Message of Jesus*. E.T., Dorothea M. Barton. 2d ed. "Studies in Biblical Theology," 23. London: SCM, 1961 (=*Promise*).

Kümmel, Werner G. *The Theology of the New Testament.* E.T., John E. Steely. Nashville: Abingdon Press, 1973 (=*Theology*).

Ladd, George Eldon. *The Presence of the Future: The Eschatology of Biblical Realism.* Grand Rapids: Eerdmans, 1974 (=*Presence*).

Lake, Kirsopp, and Cadbury, Henry J. *The Acts of the Apostles. Beginnings of Christianity,* 1/4. Grand Rapids: Baker Book House, 1933 (1965) (=*Acts*).

Lang, F. *"Pur,"* TDNT, 6, 928-948 (=*"Fire"*).

Lange, J.P. *Das Evangelium nach Matthäus.* Bielefeld: Velhagen und Klasing, 1861 (=*Matthäus*).

Leaney, A.R.C. *A Commentary on the Gospel according to St. Luke.* 2d ed. "Black's New Testament Commentaries." London: Adam and Charles Black, 1966 (=*Luke*).

Lenski, R.C.H. *The Interpretation of the Acts of the Apostles.* Minneapolis: Augsburg, 1934 (1961) (=*Acts*).

Lewis, F. Warburton. "'I beheld Satan fall as lightning from heaven' (Luke 10:18)," *ET,* 25 (1913-1914), 232-233 ("Luke 10:18").

Liddell, Henry George, and Scott, Robert. *(Abridged Greek-English) Lexicon.* Oxford: Clarendon Press, 1966 (=*Abridged Lexicon*).

Liddell, Henry George, and Scott, Robert. *A Greek-English Lexicon.* Revised H. S. Jones. Oxford: Clarendon, 1968 (=*Unabridged Lexicon*).

Lock, Walter. *A Critical and Exegetical Commentary on the Pastoral Epistles.* "The International Critical Commentary." New York: Charles Scribner's Sons, 1924 (=*Pastoral Epistles*).

Lohmeyer, Ernst. *The Lord's Prayer.* E.T., John Bowden. London: Collins, 1965 (=*Lord's Prayer*).

Lövestam, Evald. *Spiritual Wakefulness in the New Testament.* E.T., W.F. Salisbury. "Lunds Universitets Årsskrift," N.F. Avd. 1. Bd. 55 Nr. 3. Lund: C. W. K. Gleerup, 1963 (=*Wakefulness*).

Macgregor, G.H.C. "The Acts of the Apostles," *IB,* 9 (1954), 1-352 (=*Acts*).

McKenzie, John L. "The Gospel according to Matthew," *The Jerome Biblical Commentary,* ed. R.E. Brown, J.A. Fitzmyer, and R.E. Murphy. Englewood Cliffs: Prentice-Hall, 1968, 2, 62-114 (=*Matthew*).

Maisch, Ingrid. "Die Botschaft Jesu von der Gotterherrschaft," *GKR,* pp. 27-41 (="Botschaft").

Manson, T.W. "The Sayings of Jesus," in H.D.A. Major, T.W. Manson, and C.J. Wright, *The Mission and Message of Jesus.* New York: E.P. Dutton and Co., Inc., 1938, pp. 301-639 (=*Sayings of Jesus*).

Martin, H.V. "The Messianic Age," *ET,* 52 (1940-1941), 270-275 (="Messianic Age").

Marxsen, W. *Der Evangelist Markus.* 2. Auflage. Göttingen: Vandenhoeck & Ruprecht, 1959 (=*Markus*).

Mattill, A.J., Jr. "The Date and Purpose of Luke-Acts: Rackham Reconsidered," *CBQ*, 40 (1978), 335-350 (="Rackham Reconsidered").

Mattill, A.J., Jr. "The Good Samaritan and the Purpose of Luke-Acts: Halévy Reconsidered," *Encounter*, 33 (1972), 359-376 (="Halévy Reconsidered").

Mattill, A.J., Jr. "The Jesus-Paul Parallels and the Purpose of Luke-Acts: H. H. Evans Reconsidered," *NovT*, 17 (1975), 15-46 (="Evans Reconsidered").

Mattill, A.J., Jr. "*Naherwartung, Fernerwartung,* and the Purpose of Luke-Acts: Weymouth Reconsidered," *CBQ*, 34 (1972), 276-293 (="Weymouth Reconsidered").

Mattill, A. J., Jr. "The Purpose of Acts: Schneckenburger Reconsidered," in W. W. Gasque and R. P. Martin (eds.), *Apostolic History and the Gospel: Biblical and Historical Essays presented to F. F. Bruce.* Exeter: Paternoster Press, 1970, pp. 108-122 (="Schneckenburger Reconsidered").

Mattill, A. J., Jr. and Mattill, Mary Bedford. *A Classified Bibliography of Literature on the Acts of the Apostles.* "New Testament Tools and Studies," 7. Leiden: E. J. Brill, 1966 (=*NTTS*, 7).

Mayer, R. "Weltenbrand," *Lexikon für Theologie und Kirche*, 2. Auflage, Band 10, Sp. 1032 (="Weltenbrand").

Metzger, Bruce M. *Index to Periodical Literature on Christ and the Gospels.* "New Testament Tools and Studies," 6. Leiden: E. J. Brill, 1966 (=*NTTS*, 6).

Metzger, Bruce M. *A Textual Commentary on the Greek New Testament.* New York: United Bible Societies, 1971 (=*Textual Commentary*).

Meyer, H. A. W. *Critical and Exegetical Handbook to the Acts of the Apostles.* E. T., P. J. Gloag and W. P. Dickson. 4th ed. New York: Funk and Wagnalls, 1883 (=*Acts*).

Michel, Hans-Joachim. "Heilsgegenwart und Zukunft bei Lukas," *GKR*, pp. 101-115 (="Lukas").

Minear, Paul S. "Luke's Use of the Birth Stories," in L. E. Keck and J. L. Martin (eds.), *Studies in Luke-Acts . . . in Honor of Paul Schubert.* Nashville: Abingdon Press, 1966, pp. 111-130 (="Birth Stories").

Montefiore, C. G. *The Synoptic Gospels.* 2 vols. 2d ed. New York: Ktav Publishing House, 1927 (1968) (=*Gospels*).

Moore, A. L. *The Parousia in the New Testament.* "Supplements to Novum Testamentum," 13. Leiden: E. J. Brill, 1966 (=*Parousia*).

Moscato, Mary. "A Critique of Jervell's *Luke and the People of God*," in George MacRae (ed.), *Society of Biblical Literature 1975 Seminary Papers.* Missoula: Scholars Press, 1975, Vol. 2, 161-168 (="Critique of Jervell").

Mühlmann, Wilhelm E. *Chiliasmus und Nativismus.* "Studien zur Soziologie der Revolution," 1. Band. Berlin: Dietrich Reimer Verlag, 1961 (=*Chiliasmus*).

Munck, Johannes. *The Acts of the Apostles.* Revised by W. F. Albright and C. S. Mann. "The Anchor Bible." Garden City: Doubleday, 1967 (=*Acts*).

Munck, Johannes. *Paul and the Salvation of Mankind.* E.T., Frank Clarke. Richmond: John Knox Press, 1959 (=*Paul*).

Mussner, Franz. "Die Idee der APOKATASTASIS in der Apostelgeschichte," in H. Gross and F. Mussner (eds.), *Lex Tua Veritas, Festschrift für H. Junker*. Trier: Paulinus Verlag, 1961, pp. 293-306 (="Acts 3:21").

Mussner, Franz. "1Q Hodajoth und das Gleichnis vom Senfkorn (Mk 4:30-32 Par.)," *BZ*, 4 (1960), 128-130 (="Senfkorn").

Mussner, Franz. "'Wann kommt das Reich Gottes?'" (Lk 17:20b-21), *BZ*, 6 (1962), 107-111 (="Luke 17:20b-21").

Noack, Bent. *Das Gottesreich bei Lukas: Eine Studie zu Luk. 17, 20-24*. "Symbolae Biblicae Upsalienses," 10. Uppsala: C. W. K. Gleerup, 1948 (=*Luke 17:20-24*).

Nösgen, Friedrich. *Commentar über die Apostelgeschichte des Lukas*. Leipzig: Dörffling und Francke, 1882 (=*Apostelgeschichte*).

Nunn, H. P. V. *A Short Syntax of New Testament Greek*. Cambridge: University Press, 1963 (=*Syntax*).

Nützel, Johannes M. "Zur Eschatologie des Markusevangeliums," *GKR*, pp. 79-90 (="Eschatologie").

Oberlinner, Lorenz. "Die Stellung der 'Terminworte' in der eschatologischen Verkündigung des Neuen Testaments," *GKR*, pp. 51-66 (="Terminworte").

O'Hagen, Angelo. "'Greet No One on the Way' (Lk 10, 4b)," *Studii Biblici Franciscani Liber Annuus* (Jerusalem), 16 (1965-1966), 69-84 (="Greet No One").

Oliver, H. H. "The Lucan Birth Stories and the Purpose of Luke-Acts," *NTS*, 10 (1964), 202-226 (="Birth Stories").

Olson, Warwick. "In Our Generation," *Sunday Digest*, 14 July 1974, pp. 1-3 (= "In Our Generation").

Otto, Rudolph. *The Kingdom of God and the Son of Man*. E.T., F. V. Filson and B. L. Woolf. Revised ed. London: Lutterworth Press, 1938 (=*Kingdom of God*).

Owen, H. P. "Stephen's Vision in Acts 7:55-56," *NTS*, 1 (1955), 224-226 (="Stephens's Vision").

Perrin, Norman. *The Kingdom of God in the Teaching of Jesus*. "New Testament Library." Philadelphia: Westminster Press, 1963 (=*Kingdom of God*).

Pickering, John. *A Comprehensive Lexicon of the Greek Language*. Boston: Sanborn, Carter, Bazin, and Co., 1857 (=*Lexicon*).

Plummer, Alfred. *A Critical and Exegetical Commentary on the Gospel according to S. Luke*. 5th ed. "The International Critical Commentary." Edinburgh: T. & T. Clark, 1922 (1975) (=*Luke*).

Rackham, Richard B. *The Acts of the Apostles*. Grand Rapids: Baker Book House, 1901 (1964) (=*Acts*).

Reicke, Bo. *The Gospel of Luke*. E.T., Ross Mackenzie. Richmond: John Knox Press, 1964 (=*Luke*).

Riesenfeld, Harald. "*Emboleuein--Entos*," *Nuntius Sodalicii Neotestamentici Upsaliensis*, 2 (1949), cols. 11-12 (="Luke 17:21").

Rist, Martin. *Daniel and Revelation*. Nashville: Abingdon-Cokesbury Press, 1947 (=*Daniel and Revelation*).

Rist, Martin. "The Revelation of St. John the Divine," *IB*, 12 (1957), 345-551 (=*Revelation*).

Roberts, Colin H. "The Kingdom of Heaven (Lk. 17:21)," *HTR*, 41 (1948), 1-8 (="Kingdom of Heaven").

Robinson, William C., Jr. *Der Weg des Herrn: Studien zur Geschichte und Eschatologie im Lukas-Evangelium. Ein Gespräch mit Hans Conzelmann.* "Theologische Forschung," 36. Hamburg-Bergstedt: Evangelischer Verlag, 1964 (=*Weg*).

Rüstow, Alexander. "*Entos humōn estin*: Zur Deutung von Lukas 17:20-21," *ZNW*, 51 (1960), 197-224 (="Luke 17:20-21").

Schneckenburger, Matthias. *Ueber den Zweck der Apostelgeschichte*. Bern: Chr. Fischer, 1841 (= *Apostelgeschichte*).

Schneider, Gerhard. *Parusiegleichnisse im Lukas-Evangelium*. "Stuttgarter Bibelstudien," 74. Stuttgart: Katholisches Bibelwerk, 1975 (=*Parusiegleichnisse*).

Schrenk, Gottlob. "*Biadzomai*," *TDNT*, 1, 609-614 (="*Biadzomai*").

Schubert, Paul. "The Structure and Significance of Luke 24," in W. Eltester (ed.), *Neutestamentliche Studien für Rudolf Bultmann*. Beihefte zur *ZNW*, 21 (1954), 165-186 (="Luke 24").

Schweitzer, Albert. *The Mystery of the Kingdom of God*. E.T., Walter Lowrie. New York: Schocken Books, 1901 (1964) (=*Mystery*).

Schweitzer, Albert. *The Mysticism of Paul the Apostle*. E.T., W. Montgomery. New York: Henry Holt, 1931 (=*Mysticism of Paul*).

Schweitzer, Albert. *Out of My Life and Thought*. "A Mentor Book." New York: The New American Library, 1933 (1953) (=*My Life*).

Schweitzer, Albert. *The Quest of the Historical Jesus*. E.T., W. Montgomery. 3d ed. London: Adam & Charles Black, 1906 (1956) (=*Quest*).

Selby, Donald J. "Changing Ideas in New Testament Eschatology," *HTR*, 50 (1957), 21-36 (="Changing Ideas").

Selby, Donald J. *Introduction to the New Testament*. New York: Macmillan, 1971 (=*Introduction*).

Shinn, Roger L. *Christianity and the Problem of History*. New York: Charles Scribner's Sons, 1953 (=*History*).

Sledd, Andrew. "The Interpretation of Luke 17:21," *ET*, 50 (1938-1939), 235-237 (="Luke 17:21").

Smith, Robert H. "The Eschatology of Acts and Contemporary Exegesis," *CTM*, 29 (1958), 641-663 (="Eschatology").

Smith, Robert H. "History and Eschatology in Luke-Acts," *CTM*, 29 (1958), 881-901 (="History and Eschatology").

Sneed, Richard. *The Kingdom's Coming (Luke 17:20-21)*. "Catholic University Studies in Sacred Theology," 133. Ann Arbor: University Microfilms, 1962 (=*Kingdom's Coming*).

Sneed, Richard. "'The Kingdom of God is Within You,'" *CBQ*, 24 (1962), 363-382 (="Luke 17:21").

Songer, Harold S. "Luke's Portrayal of the Origins of Jesus," *RevExp*, 64 (1967), 453-463 (="Origins of Jesus").

Spitta, Friedrich. "Der Satan als Blitz," *ZNW*, 9 (1908), 160-163 (="Blitz").

Stählin, Gustav. "Das Bild der Witwe," *JAC*, 17 (1974), 5-20 (="Witwe").

Standen, A. O. "The Parable of Dives and Lazarus, and Enoch 22," *ET*, 33 (1921-1922), 523 (="Enoch 22").

Stevens, George B. "Is There a Self-Consistent New Testament Eschatology?" *AJT*, 6 (1902), 666-684 (="Eschatology").

Stratton, Charles. "Pressure for the Kingdom," *Int*, 8 (1954), 414-421 (="Pressure").

Streeter, B. H. *The Four Gospels: A Study of Origins*. New York: Macmillan, 1925 (=*Four Gospels*).

Streeter, B. H. "Was the Baptist's Preaching Apocalyptic?" *JTS*, 14 (1912-1913), 549-552 (="The Baptist's Preaching").

Strobel, August. "Die Passa-Erwartung als urchristliches Problem in Lc 17,20f.," *ZNW*, 49 (1958), 157-196; 51 (1960), 133-134 (="Passa-Erwartung").

Stuhlmueller, Carroll. "The Gospel according to Luke," *The Jerome Biblical Commentary*, ed. R. E. Brown, J. A. Fitzmeyer, and R. E. Murphy. Englewood Cliffs: Prentice-Hall, 1968, 2, 115-164 (=*Luke*).

Stuhlmueller, Carroll. *The Gospel of St. Luke*. 2d ed. "New Testament Reading Guide," 3. Collegeville, Minnesota: Liturgical Press, 1964 (=*Lukan Reading Guide*).

Talbert, Charles H. "The Redaction Critical Quest for Luke the Theologian," in D. G. Buttrick (ed.), *Jesus and Man's Hope*, 1. "A Perspective Book." Pittsburgh: Pittsburgh Theological Seminary, 1970, 171-222 (="Redaction").

Tatum, W. Barnes. "The Epoch of Israel: Luke I-II and the Theological Plan of Luke-Acts," *NTS*, 13 (1966-1967), 184-195 (="Epoch of Israel").

Thompson, James W. "The Gentile Mission As an Eschatological Necessity," *RQ*, 14 (1971), 18-27 (="Gentile Mission").

Thomson, Charles, and Muses, C. A. *The Septuagint Bible*. E.T., Charles Thomson and C. A. Muses. Indian Hills, Colorado: The Falcon's Wing Press, 1954 (=Thomson-Muses).

Thomson, P. "Luke 10:18," *ET*, 19 (1907-1908), 191 (="Luke 10:18").

Throckmorton, Burton H., Jr. (ed.). *Gospel Parallels: A Synopsis of the First Three Gospels*. 3d ed. Nashville: Thomas Nelson, 1967 (=*Gospel Parallels*).

Vaughan, Curtis (ed.). *The New Testament from 26 Translations*. Grand Rapids: Zondervan, 1967 (=*26 Translations*).

Vincent, Marvin R. *Word Studies in the New Testament.* 4 vols. New York: Charles Scribner's Sons, 1911 (=*Word Studies*).

Vogt, Ernest. "'Peace Among Men of God's Good Pleasure' Lk. 2:14," in Krister Stendahl (ed.), *The Scrolls and the New Testament.* New York: Harper & Brothers, 1957, pp. 114-117 (="Peace").

Völkel, Martin. "Zur Deutung des 'Reiches Gottes' bei Lukas," *ZNW*, 65 (1974), 57-70 (="Reich Gottes").

Walvoord, John F. "The Times of the Gentiles," *BS*, 125 (497, 1968), 3-9 (="Times of the Gentiles").

Ward, Ronald A. "St. Luke 12:49," *ET*, 63 (1951-1952), 92-93 (="Luke 12:49").

Webster, Charles A. "St. Luke 10:18," *ET*, 57 (1945-1946), 52 (="Luke 10:18").

Weiss, Johannes. *Earliest Christianity.* E.T. ed. F. C. Grant. 2 vols. New York: Harper and Brothers, 1937 (1959)(=*Earliest Christianity*).

Weiss, Johannes. *Jesus' Proclamation of the Kingdom of God.* E. T., R. H. Hiers and D. L. Holland. "Lives of Jesus Series." Philadelphia: Fortress Press, 1892 (1971) (=*Kingdom of God*).

Weiss, Johannes. "Das Problem der Entstehung des Christentums," *ARW*, 16 (1913), 423-515 (="Problem").

Weiss, Johannes. "Die Verteidigung Jesu gegen den Vorwurf des Bündnisses mit Beelzebul," *TSK*, 63 (1890), 555-569 (="Luke 11:14-26").

Wellhausen, J. *Das Evangelium Lucae.* Berlin: Druck und Verlag von Georg Reimer, 1904 (=*Lucas*).

Weymouth, Richard F. *The New Testament in Modern Speech*, ed. Ernest Hampden-Cook. 3d ed. Boston: Pilgrim Press, 1909 (=Weymouth).

Wikgren, Allen. "*Entos*," *Nuntius Sodalicii Neotestamentici Upsaliensis*, 4 (1950), cols. 27-28 (="Luke 17:21").

Wilson, S. G. "Lukan Eschatology," *NTS*, 16 (1969-1970), 330-347 (="Lukan Eschatology").

Wink, Walter. *John the Baptist in the Gospel Tradition.* "Society for New Testament Studies Monograph Series," 7. Cambridge: At the University Press, 1968 (=John the Baptist).

Wolf, Peter. *Liegt in den Logien von der 'Todestaufe' (Mk 10,38f., Lk 12,49f.) eine Spur des Todesverständnisses Jesu vor?* Inaugural-Dissertation, Universität Freiburg im Breisgau, 1973 (=*Luke 12:49-50*).